Abolitions as a
Global Experience

Abolitions as a Global Experience

Edited by
Hideaki Suzuki

NUS PRESS
SINGAPORE

Published by:

NUS Press
National University of Singapore
AS3-01-02, 3 Arts Link
Singapore 117569

Fax: (65) 6774-0652
E-mail: nusbooks@nus.edu.sg
Website: http://nuspress.nus.edu.sg

ISBN: 978-9971-69-860-7 (Paper)

National Library Board, Singapore Cataloguing-in-Publication Data

Abolitions as a global experience/edited by Hideaki Suzuki. – Singapore:
NUS Press, [2016]
pages cm
Includes bibliographic references and index.
ISBN: 978-9971-69-860-7 (paperback)

1. Antislavery movements – History. 2. Slavery – History. I. Suzuki,
Hideaki, editor.

HT993
306.362 — dc23   OCN911167665

Cover: "Slaves cutting the sugar cane in Antigua", Plate IV from *Ten Views
in the Island of Antigua, in which are represented the process of sugar making,
and the employment of the negroes...From drawings made by W. Clark, etc.*
(London: Thomas Clay, 1823). © The British Library Board

Printed by: Mainland Press Pte Ltd

Contents

List of Figures

List of Tables

CHAPTER 1

Abolitions as a Global Experience: An Introduction

Hideaki Suzuki

Introduction

This collection of articles examines issues relating to abolitions as a globally shared experience. It is a by-product of a five-year project on world history entitled "Eurasia in the Modern Period: Towards a New World History".[1] I would like to express my gratitude here to the project members, particularly the principal investigator, Professor Masashi Haneda, as well as to those who kindly shared their insights at our workshops, seminars and session.[2]

It would be appropriate to explain this project, that is, the context within which this collection originated. If we are to understand our globalizing world, we need histories that cover the entire globe. Increasingly, globalization requires each of us to deal with various "others". Given that history creates and supports our identity, different identities can trigger conflict and prevent us from effectively challenging various issues, for example environmental issues, which require global cooperation. If each of us can be said to have a multi-layered identity, what is required today is a new layer—that of so-called "earthmen" and "earthwomen". Such considerations call for a new paradigm of history, which our project sets out to develop. This project discussed the potential for describing a world history that goes beyond a mere combination of geographically divided histories, such as national history or regional history.[3] It instead sought alternative perspectives and methods to capture the history of the globe.[4] Several topics were identified, some focusing on piracy, one on second-hand clothes and another on slavery. Though initially we were certain that slavery had a huge potential to meet our needs, we had no firm conviction about the direction we would take; it was rather experimental. After several workshops and seminars, we eventually set our focus on abolition, because it reflected global dynamics and has a long chronology, running right up to the present.

Several methodological insights are discussed in the following section. The significance of the issues relating to abolitions as a globally shared experience is examined in terms of its spatial and temporal extent. Finally, each article is briefly introduced.

Global Experience and World History

As a phenomenon, from the late 18th century onwards slavery and its related institutions were gradually abolished by several European countries and their colonies; in the following century, abolition spread more rapidly and extensively within, and even beyond, those spheres. Furthermore, since the late 19th century, and particularly in the first half of the 20th century, the abolition of slavery was on the agenda of various international bodies, including, for instance, the League of Nations, 44 of whose members ratified the 1926 Slavery Convention.[5] Regardless of whether people in different societies were conscious or unaware of sharing the same or similar experience, they did. Within a period of roughly 150 years, slavery and many similar institutions were statutorily abolished throughout the world. If we assume that these institutions formed an important feature of each society over a long period, the significance of this change should not be underestimated. This series of statutory abolitions can be regarded as a globally shared experience; this is the starting point of the present volume.

The institutions abolished were by no means a tangential feature of each society; as the Ethiopian emperor Haile Selassie noted in his autobiography, "the institution of slavery was deeply rooted in tradition".[6] This was the case not only in his empire, but also in many other societies. Those who were bonded in these institutions contributed hugely to each society. They provided a labour force, prestige and much else to their masters and their host society. Plantations could produce almost nothing without slave labour; many masters would have lost their dignity without their slaves. Even though the slave population was not especially evident in the metropolises of the empires of Britain, France and Spain, public life in these cities was closely tied to slavery through the profits and products produced by those slaves: cotton, sugar, palm oil and spices such as pepper—such consumer staples were produced mainly by slaves. It is hard to deny the role of slave-based production in the emergence of industrialization and the global economy.[7] In addition, as is often emphasized, in many societies around the Indian Ocean as well as in Africa, slaves were deeply embedded in close-knit social relationships.[8] An important characteristic of slavery in Africa and the Indian Ocean World was assimilation. Slaves were not completely excluded from their host society. Instead, they were encouraged to integrate through marriage, acquisition of languages and adoption of local customs.[9] Why then did people decide to abolish slavery and similar institutions, even if just *de jure*? In other words, why, in those cases where slaves produced enormous profits for their masters, did that slave-based society end such a profitable institution? Why, if slavery was closely integrated into other social systems, did they repudiate it? Indeed, we could even ask what abolition constituted. This is the initial question posed by this volume. It is also a question posed within the framework of each society. It considers, too, a much broader framework: given that abolition was part of a globally and synchronically shared experience, we need to extend our scope globally.

One methodological key that has proved fruitful in addressing this question in global history is the combination of comparison and connection.[10] Even though slavery studies are fairly advanced, there are few comparative studies of abolition. As William Mulligan has noted, while the existing literature has been keen to compare slavery in different societies, slavery has been the subject of much more comparative research than its abolition.[11] This is largely owing to paradigmatic issues. As he points out, abolitionists concentrated on the national or imperial framework.[12] Slavery could be statutorily abolished only by a political authority, and within the limit of its sphere of jurisdiction. While Mulligan's point is about people of the past, another point that should be made here is that the paradigm relates to people today who interpret and locate historical phenomena within certain frameworks. Many instances of abolition are indeed firmly embedded within the national history paradigm, and debates on these cases of abolition tend to concentrate on this paradigm. The Japanese case of the *Yūjo* Release Act was part of the Meiji Restoration;[13] similarly, the anti-slavery policy of the Ottoman Empire can be placed in the context of the Tanzimat reform movement;[14] and the abolition of Thaat was one element of the reforms implemented by Thailand's Chakri dynasty.[15] These reforms tend to be placed within the context of each individual nation's historiography and are often linked closely with the modernization of each national historical context.

Nonetheless, abolition and anti-slavery policies were not pursued in isolation. Returning to the three examples given above, in the Japanese case the British lawyer's interpretation of the institution of *yūjo* as slavery led to pressure on the Meiji government to push forward with the abolition of yūjo, as Yuriko Yokoyama points out in Chapter 8. As for the anti-slavery policy of the Ottoman Empire, British pressure is clearly the key to understanding this phenomenon.[16] As regards Thaat, international flows of human beings propelled abolition forward; more precisely, cheap immigrant labour from China proved more efficient than this *corvée*-like system. Furthermore, the Chakri dynasty wanted to put an end to what it regarded as unfair, unilateral treaty provisions, and abolishing Thaat, which foreign powers regarded as tantamount to slavery, was one measure demanded by European countries in return for agreeing to revise those provisions.[17] Here, we need to consider the element of connection. The relationship between comparison and connection lays bare the tension between the local and global contexts. As the following section notes, while it is hard to completely ignore global elements such as the influence of British abolitionists, it is equally hard to ignore each local context. The local context here includes not only those causes that emerged locally, but also those global elements that were transformed differently in different local contexts. Of course, the degree of connection varied. The dilemma of bush administrators between metropolitan idealism and the actual conditions of colonies in West Africa described in Chapter 9 by Martin A. Klein is a vivid example. In West Africa, metropolitan idealism could only be realized in the context of colonization. A perspective that links such varied instances of abolition enhances our understanding of each individual act of abolition, creating a much broader context that will ultimately enrich our understanding of abolition even in regional or national contexts.

Ours is not the first attempt to place abolition within a global historical context. Klein advocated a global history of emancipation more than 20 years ago,[18] and several other excellent studies have already appeared. However, with a few exceptions, they deal almost exclusively with the Atlantic World.[19] David Brion Davis, for example, has studied "the influence of the American Quakers on the British abolitionists, the influence of the British abolitionists on America, and of American abolitionists on Brazilian reformers".[20] However, in terms of geographical sphere, the horizon of this global experience extends far beyond this statement. As the articles in this volume show, abolition was a global phenomenon.

Another connection we emphasize in this volume is the temporal one. The question of abolition is not limited to a certain time period; it instead invites researchers to extend their view towards the post-abolition period, and even towards today. Given that what slaves formerly provided was important to society, we need to examine the impact on each society of the loss of slavery, and how that loss was resolved. We do not ignore the fact that abolition could not physically emancipate the people bonded within the institution that had been *de jure* abolished; indeed, abolition triggered the emergence of new institutions, such as indentured labour, which bound other people. As studies on modern slavery have revealed,[21] millions of people continue to live in circumstances almost identical to those once experienced by slaves. This fact provides a perspective for viewing abolition as a trans-historical phenomenon, which extends up to the present. Furthermore, abolition emerges as a political issue from time to time, from place to place. While in 2007 the bicentenary of the abolition of the slave trade in the British Empire was being celebrated in the UK and in many Commonwealth states, the issue of reparations has still not been settled. Contemporary debates concerning abolition recall our initial question: what were these abolitions? To place the issue of abolition in a global context, we need not only to compare case studies of different societies but also to compare dialogues between the past and the present and the local and the global within each case study.

Before introducing the individual articles comprising this volume, the next two sections explore further this globally shared experience in terms of its spatial and temporal extent.

Spatial Extent

As has been mentioned, scholars have debated the background to abolition in each society. The literature on societies in the Atlantic World reveals two major lines of argument as to why slavery was statutorily abolished in those societies. One is economic. Since the work of Eric Williams,[22] it has been one of the most debated points in abolition studies. Williams' main argument can be summarized as follows: slavery was an economic phenomenon. The slave economy of the British West Indies caused or largely contributed to the industrial revolution in Britain. After the independence of the United States, the slave economy lost its significance to Britain, even in terms of profitability. And the abolition of slavery and the slave trade in the British West Indies was driven not by humanitarianism or by philanthropism, but by economic motives.[23] This materialistic interpretation provoked major debates that eventually contributed to the further development of studies on slavery and abolition.[24] Williams' main legacy is the economic perspective within the framework of abolition. Scholars subsequently explored the interrelationship between abolitionism and the capitalist economy.[25] The most effective objections to Williams' interpretation can be found in a series of works by Seymour Drescher, who claimed that the decline of the British West Indies' economy originated not with US independence but with the abolition of the slave trade.[26] Furthermore, he re-evaluated the abolitionist campaign, stressing the importance of popular movements against slavery.[27] This moral and ideological focus forms the second major line of argument in the literature.[28]

On the other hand, once we turn our sight to abolition beyond the Atlantic World, another, largely political and diplomatic, motive vividly emerges. As Davis has written, "the question of abolishing slavery was ultimately a question of power".[29] The cases of abolition by the Meiji government, the Chakri dynasty and the Ottoman Empire are good examples. It is not difficult to identify political motives for these reforms. And we can safely add Ethiopia to this list.[30] Haile Selassie, Emperor of Ethiopia at the time, was more or less forced to abolish slavery and the slave trade in order to prevent an invasion by the European powers that surrounded his country: Britain, France and Italy. The abolition of slavery and the slave trade was adduced as proof that Ethiopia was a "civilized" country. In order to protect his empire from any possible invasion utilizing the existence of slavery and the slave trade as a pretext, he needed to take steps to abolish them.

In short, in most cases these three factors—economic, moral and ideological—and political and diplomatic, were the main contributors to making abolition possible. However, the degree to which these factors were influential varied from case to case, and even the nature of these factors was vague. To understand abolition as a globally shared experience, we need to examine the degree of variation in and the precise nature of each of these factors.

To consider abolition in a global context, while we need to examine the similarities behind each case of abolition, we also need to look at what connected them. In many cases, abolition was a result of a combination of local and global factors. Tracing the path of such global factors is one way to locate abolition in a global context. However, global factors were not uniform in the abolition experience. Instead, they were transformed differently in different contexts. Here, we will consider British abolitionism as a case study.

Needless to say, the abolitionist campaign played an important role in British abolition. Furthermore, British abolitionist activities influenced many other cases. However, though the influence of the abolitionist campaign was indeed an important element in furthering abolitions as a globally shared experience, we need to evaluate this element carefully. Abolition has conventionally been narrated as a success of the humanitarian movement. For example, Howard Temperley has stated that the abolition of slavery "is arguably the greatest humanitarian achievement of all time".[31] The chronology of abolition seems to confirm this statement. Starting with the British abolition movement, backed by a large body of public opinion and encouraged by Enlightenment and Quaker activists, abolitionism spread throughout the world. However, this interpretation is neither entirely right nor entirely wrong. Assuming that abolition started in Europe and subsequently became a global phenomenon, we can claim that there were strong links between abolition and the humanitarian movement. However, a detailed analysis of various cases of abolition around the globe reveals to what extent other intentions, shrouded in the cloak of humanitarianism, or at least different intentions operating alongside humanitarian intentions, played a role. The solo emphasis on humanitarian efforts in the abolition of slavery might therefore be misplaced. Humanitarian motives might have been an element enabling abolition in many cases, but not in all. Apart from discovering the different logic behind abolition, we also need to examine how abolitionism, in its different varieties and to different degrees, affected cases of abolition different in terms of time and space. After their success in getting Britain's parliament to pass the Slave Trade Act in 1807, abolitionists succeeded in ensuring the abolition of slavery itself within the empire. They also supported abolition movements in other European countries, which naturally extended to their colonies overseas.[32] Simultaneously, the British government pressured other governments, including those of non-European countries, to abolish the slave trade. In the western Indian Ocean, the first treaty to limit the slave trade was concluded in 1822 with Sultan Sa'id b. Sultan, and various similar treaties were subsequently concluded between Britain and indigenous polities. These treaties having been concluded, Britain engaged, from the mid-19th century onwards, in a naval campaign to enforce them.

Interpretations of Britain's motives for launching this naval campaign vary; we can, however, hardly deny that there was an element of imperial design, as Behnaz A. Mirzai claims in Chapter 5. Furthermore, the naval campaign included another element, largely attributed to naval officers on the spot. The reality of naval suppression was rather harsh, as one American trader wrote, complaining that the naval campaign was "raising the devil with the trading Dows on the coast and will ruin trade if they keep on".[33] For example, between 1867 and 1869, 77 cases were judged at the Prize Court in Zanzibar. They included 49 cases (63.6 per cent) in which the "slavers" had no slaves on board when they were captured.[34] Underlying this zeal was the desire among naval officers and crews to seize prizes, as one Royal Navy captain admitted in his memoirs: "many captains have gone to extremes when prize-money has been the sole motive, and captured every dhow with even a shadow of a slave on board, thus doing as much damage as good".[35] The reality of maritime patrols against slave trafficking in the western Indian Ocean was a conjuncture of abolitionists' motives, territorial control of the seas of the British Empire and a personal desire for prize money on the part of British naval officers.[36] In this context, abolitionism worked partly, being effective only when combined with other elements. Another example is the Ethiopian case mentioned earlier. The campaign against Ethiopian slavery and the slave trade by anti-slavery groups such as the Anti-Slavery and Aborigines Protection Society triggered international criticism of Ethiopia. In order to eradicate slavery, Ethiopia accepted interference in its domestic affairs by the League of Nations.[37] In this case, abolitionist endeavours coincided with the geopolitical goals of the major powers.

Temporal Extent

As well as extending our perspective spatially, we need to extend it temporally. Abolition tends to be understood as something monumental; that is, the focus is on a particular event on a particular date. In Chapter 10, Alessandro Stanziani explores the foundational conditions on which abolition of Russian serfdom stood. We need to extend our scope to include not only the process leading towards abolition but also its aftermath. How many of the slaves freed actually obtained freedom to the degree the abolitionists originally intended? Further, we cannot ignore the phenomenon whereby others, such as indentured labourers, simply replaced those who had obtained their "freedom". As debates on "modern slavery" claim, phenomena that in the past would have constituted slavery are with us even today. We cannot deny the frequent instances during the long 19th century of slavery being abolished, but at the same time, we are compelled to admit that abolition did not really put an end to slavery nor to its institutions; new forms of exploitation emerged which are not always clearly distinct from those that were abolished. In addition, as Isabel Tanaka-Van Daalen mentions in Chapter 4, we can claim that the Cultivation System in the Dutch East Indies that was introduced around the 1830s eventually financed compensation to the slave-owners in the Caribbean. In order to examine abolition as a globally shared experience, we have to face its diverse aftermath.

In most cases, statutory abolition did not bring effective emancipation to the enslaved. In many cases they were unable to escape their bonded condition, largely because providing freedom was not the main aim of those who abolished slavery. The case of a yūjo called Kashiku, which Yokoyama relates, is nothing less than tragic, and demonstrates how the emancipation of yūjo was something of a whitewash. These acts of emancipation were designed to benefit not yūjo but the Meiji government. Klein vividly describes the continuity of pre- and post-abolition relationships. As Sue Peabody points out in Chapter 2, even in post-1794 emancipation Haiti, the authorities sought to bind labourers to plantations in order to maintain exports. The relationship established by slavery was ostensibly terminated but in reality it continued to exist. Reference could also be made to a recent study by Douglas A. Blackmon, which shows that more than a few imprisoned Black Americans were impressed as forced labour in the US after the Civil War, a phenomenon he describes as "slavery by another name".[38]

Another point we cannot ignore is that of replacement. In her PhD dissertation, Mirzai shows how, in the case of Iran, the geographical sourcing of slaves transitioned in response to international circumstances. The Treaty of Turkmenchay ended slave imports from Central Asia, but this led to an increase in demand for African slaves. However, once both the Royal Navy and Indian Navy intensified patrols to halt the import of African slaves to the Persian Gulf, making it difficult to import slaves from East Africa, Baluchistan emerged as a new slave ground.[39] The Baluchi accounted for more than a quarter of the bonded labourers who sought refuge with British representatives in the Persian Gulf between 1908 and 1950.[40] While replacing one source of slaves by another might have been a local phenomenon, a more geographically widespread phenomenon was triggered by the introduction of alternative institutions. In many societies, indentured labour replaced slave labour. As Dharma Kumar has stated, one effect of abolition was increased reliance on other forms of bondage.[41] In particular, labour from India and China, and to a lesser extent from Japan and Italy, was exported to societies across the oceans, when additional labour needs could no longer be met by slaves. According to David Northrup, within 90 years of Britain abolishing slavery over 2 million people, nearly two-thirds of whom were from India, became indentured labourers.[42] For example, Mauritius, where a large number of slaves left their plantations after abolition, saw a complete transformation of the labour force from African slave labour to Indian indentured labour within ten years of slavery being abolished there. The nature of the two systems needs to be distinguished, and the term "new system of slavery"[43] coined by Hugh Tinker is not a proper one to describe the indentured labour system. Having said that, there was a physical continuity between the two systems, with Indian indentured labour replacing African slaves in Mauritius. As Ei Murakami shows in Chapter 6, in the eyes of British staff at the consulate in China the status of coolies was scarcely any different from that of slaves, and they therefore made a great effort to control the export of coolies. The post-abolition experience of the newly bonded was not much different from that of their predecessors, not just in terms of their role on the plantation but also in terms of the circumstances of their recruitment and of how they were trafficked.[44]

The third point I make in this section concerns the legacy of abolition today. As Klein shows, former slaves continued to struggle with the stigma of slavery. The legacy of abolition today is limited not only at an individual level but also at the mass level. Even though statutory abolition did not bring an end to systems of exploitation, once abolition had been declared it became a historical objective not only for those closely tied to what was abolished but also for the general public. As Peabody points out, along with the 1848 decree abolishing slavery, France's provisional republic decreed that the abolition of slavery be commemorated annually. As this French commemoration suggests, such official memorialization contains a political intent. Several news items relating to the bicentenary of Britain's abolition of the slave trade show how abolition has been memorialized in different ways and in different places, and scholars such as Kwame Nimako and Glenn Willemsen have pointed out that "while official events are largely led by whites, the religious commemorations are largely led by blacks".[45] Such variety of memorialization creates tension. Among the most recent news items on this issue is the fact that Caribbean nations are going to sue Britain, France and the Netherlands for reparations.[46] The issue of commemoration and apologies has become highly visible in the past 20 years.[47] How abolition has been memorialized and in what context such memories appear are aspects that have not yet been fully examined. In Chapter 3, Kumie Inose addresses the issue of memory and celebration in Britain. In order to consider abolition as a globally shared experience, we need to include these diversified memories, which are quite capable of creating tension even today.

Structure of the Present Volume

The volume shows the complex dynamics of abolition, in which local and global contexts as well as the past and the present were entangled. Each separate abolition was a result of the *mélanger* of local and global causes. Global factors were supported by local factors and vice versa, resulting in abolitions as a globally shared experience. Such interaction is an indispensable feature in considering global history, as the recent volume edited by Anthony G. Hopkins that deals with interactions between the universal and the local shows.[48] The local/global dichotomy is a feature not only of our topic but also of our practice as historians. Historians generally specialize in a particular period and geography. They have been trained to contribute to the literature while developing a firm foothold in a certain time and space. One negative aspect of such specialization is "fortification", that is, they tend to limit their scope to a narrow time and space and to be unconcerned about matters outside their "fort". However, history considered on a global scale eschews such an approach, without, of course, denying the merits of specialization. Various approaches to the issue of abolition have been cultivated in the historiography. The mere addition of local histories cannot constitute the global history that we are looking for nor does it deny that the key to approaching global history can be found in well-cultivated local historiographies. The wide variety of ways in which to explore a single globally shared experience is one of the most important points we wish to demonstrate in this volume.

Chapter 2 by Sue Peabody, that follows this Introduction, is titled "France's Two Emancipations in Comparative Context" and looks at the French abolition of slavery. France had quite an interesting history in the context of abolition, abolishing slavery on no fewer than three occasions. The first was in 1794, during the French Revolution. It was abolished again, in 1848, by the Second Republic after the restoration of slavery in France's colonies under Napoleon. The third occasion on which slavery was abolished was in French West Africa at the turn of the 19th century. The article deals with the first two cases of abolition, while Martin A. Klein, in Chapter 9, focuses on the third. Peabody first traces the progress of studies on French abolition. She reviews previous studies of abolition in France and notes that they tend to deal with each case of emancipation separately, being limited largely to the context of French national history. She, however, shows how the first and second abolitions were characterized by continuity, and provides a comparative perspective on abolition in Britain and the US. The first abolition, in 1794, was prompted by direct military action on the part of slaves themselves, in what is generally called the Haiti Revolution, while the second, in 1848, was

the product of liberal reformers in Paris. She connects the two abolitions through the anti-slavery movement, which comprised only the
social elite, in contrast to its British counterpart, which successfully
involved the masses too. In her comparative analysis, Peabody examines similarities and dissimilarities, connection and disconnection,
and metropolitan idealism and the colonial realities of French abolitions, as well as comparing the Haiti Revolution with other acts of
abolition, and in doing so placing the French experience in a global
context. As for metropolitan idealism and colonial realities, additional details concerning the French West African case can be found
in Chapter 9. The final part of this article deals with memory and
emancipation. Here Peabody explores the temporal extent of emancipation, while comparing the French and British cases, the latter being
the focus of the next article.

Chapter 3 by Kumie Inose, titled "What was Remembered and
What was Forgotten in Britain in the Bicentenary of the Abolition
of the Slave Trade?" demonstrates the connection between past and
present through a study of the issue of abolition in Britain. Inose asks
who abolished the slave trade and slavery. A unique feature of this
article is that she asks this question while comparing the commemorations during the 2007 bicentenary of Britain's abolition of the slave
trade with previous commemorations, such as the centennial celebrations in 1907. Her focus is not abolition per se, but historicized
abolition. The centennial commemorations were characterized by a
discourse that justified colonialism and imperialism and which praised
William Wilberforce and his evangelical friends as "saints". However,
as Inose points out, the bicentennial celebrations in 2007 were characterized by a divergent discourse, one that placed the spotlight on
the agency of Africans and women. Simultaneously, she provides an
example of dramatic change in local perceptions of the slave trade.
Inose connects this transition to the issue of identity in Britain. In
other words, she finds parallels between the transition of British
society and attitudes towards the slave trade and its abolition. She
regards immigration from the former British colonies as an important factor in that transition. Here, she connects the issue of abolition
not only to the historical experience of the slave trade and slavery,
but also to the historical experience of colonialism.

Chapter 4, "Dutch Attitudes towards Slavery and the Tardy Road
to Abolition: The Case of Deshima", by Isabel Tanaka-Van Daalen,
deals with the issue of abolition with a different approach from the

previous two articles. That is, she questions why the Dutch took so long time for abolition in its sphere. Tanaka-Van Daalen explores how slavery occupied an essential part of the daily life of officers serving with the Dutch East India Company (VOC). After looking at trends of both academic and public interest on slavery and slave trade issue in the Netherlands, which is comparable with the French and British cases in the previous articles, Tanaka-Van Daalen focuses on the situation under the VOC, particularly in Deshima, the trading post of this company in Japan. While Deshima is unfamiliar to the field of slavery and slave trade studies so far, she points out that because of the VOC's firm network as well as the fluidity of its employees over the network, there could be found uniformity, to a large extent, in the lifestyle and outlook in VOC establishments. Another point she stresses on, in her focus on Deshima, is a richness of Japanese sources that provide a perspective other than that of the masters or the slaves. Relying largely on *dagregisters* (official daily records by the heads of the trading post) and Japanese travelogues while combining a wide range of other sources as well as secondary literature, she brings the shape of slaves in Deshima into relief and, furthermore, provides an answer to the question she posed at the beginning.

Behnaz A. Mirzai in Chapter 5, "The Persian Gulf and Britain: The Suppression of the African Slave Trade", shows clearly how Britain's attempts to abolish the slave trade in the Persian Gulf were part of its imperial designs in this region. As the Persian Gulf was, and still is, a strategically important communications route linking India and Britain, control over this water was essential for this purpose. Furthermore, what the British attempted to suppress was not the slave trade in its entirety but only the trade in African slaves. It was a major step for Britain to intervene in maritime communication in this region and in the western Indian Ocean, and an officer of the Indian Navy engaged in the anti-slave trade campaign in this region admitted that "the slaves that may be on board constitute but a minimum part of the cargo in the vessel [...]".[49] Therefore, complete abolition of the slave trade was not an aspect of the framework of British control, nor was the abolition of slavery. Treaties with local polities were concluded which included admitting the right of search and on-board inspection by British naval officers. Naval patrols guaranteed by these treaties contributed to ensuring the abolition of the African slave trade. The decline in African slave exports to the Persian Gulf prevented many Africans from being slaves in remote places, and, in this context, the campaign to abolish the African slave trade deserved praise. However, we need to also look at contemporaneous events elsewhere. For example, Baluchistan emerged as a new slave ground and the slave trade continued in association with another "illegal" trade, that of armaments. The campaign to abolish slavery did not initially tackle that issue, and this aspect of the slave trade continued until the mid-20th century.

Chapter 6, "The End of the Coolie Trade in Southern China: Focus on the Treaty Port of Amoy" by Ei Murakami, deals with the end of coolie trade in Amoy, a treaty port in southern China. Murakami's detailed descriptions of this trade allow us to identify structural similarities with the trade in slaves elsewhere, such as in Zanzibar in the 1850s. There were unmistakable similarities between indentured labour and plantation slave labour not only in terms of functional continuity but also in terms of recruitment. Furthermore, Murakami provides a detailed structural analysis of the suppression of the coolie trade, identifying the different motives of the various groups campaigning for suppression. Those groups were distinct but united in the aim of suppressing the coolie trade. For instance, while British officials wanted to ensure that British subjects observed the treaty, local Qing officials were more concerned with stabilizing the area under their jurisdiction. The coolie trade was not the sole cause of instability in the region under their jurisdiction, but officials nonetheless regarded it as offering a good opportunity to request the assistance of British officials. The suppression of the coolie trade was a chemistry of different motives among different groups. The influence of British abolitionists was certainly one ingredient, but we cannot overestimate its role. The significance of Murakami's article is in how it identifies the motives and strategies of Qing officials in utilizing the suppression of the coolie trade for their own goals. Qing officials used Western institutions and manpower to secure their control over the region for which they had responsibility. As he concludes, "those foreign countries and citizens ultimately became agents of the Qing government". We cannot ignore such a side story in the globally shared experience.

Amitava Chowdhury in Chapter 7, "Freedom Across the Water: British Emancipation of Slavery and Maritime Marronage in the Danish West Indies", starts with a quote from a petition to the Danish monarch, King Christian VIII, written by a former slave. This former slave called William Gilbert, escaped from the Danish West

Indies to Boston, where he settled at the time of writing. He aspired to visit his birthplace, St Croix. The problem was that there was no guarantee that his freedom would be recognized in his birthplace. The geographical border between freedom and its opposite for certain individuals certainly existed at that time. Relating to such a border, we may be reminded of stories of the so-called "Underground Railroad", a network to support slaves in the US to escape to free states as well as to Canada, during the antebellum period. In these stories, Detroit was called "Midnight" while one of the ex-slavery settlements in Windsor, Ontario, Canada was "Dawn" because once slaves reached "Dawn" from "Midnight", they could live freely under the protection of British law.[50] Crossing the border between freedom and bondage was fragile, especially for those who crossed it from bondage to freedom. Chowdhury's focus in this article is on free soil policy. Combining this political as well as legal topic with *marronage* as physical behaviour, this article describes a dynamic picture of marronage in the Caribbean world during the period when abolition was becoming a common experience in this region. During such a transition period, the fragility of geographical border between freedom and slavery emerged vividly due to the uneven nature of interpretation and practice of abolition of slavery, and the emancipation of slaves including free soil policy. Chowdhury shows that a number of slaves who fled the Danish Virgin Islands were denied freedom in the British Caribbean at the request of the islands' Danish governors and administrators; a number of them were deported to the Danish Virgin Islands. He examines how the laws, made in a metropolitan context, were interpreted in colonial and diplomatic contexts. The distinction between metropolitan idealism and colonial realities, evidence of which this article provides, is also confirmed in other articles such as Chapter 9.

Yuriko Yokoyama in Chapter 8, "The *Yūjo* Release Act as an Emancipation of Slaves in the Mid-19th-Century", offers a multidimensional interpretation of the Yūjo Release Act in Japan, demonstrating its impact by means of a detailed observation of particular *chou* (community) in the Edo period. Yūjo is not a familiar subject in the field of slavery and abolition; Yokoyama's detailed description of not only yūjo—or licensed prostitutes—but also the system and powers surrounding them would therefore be helpful to those who are interested in this field. We can identify external influences on the Yūjo Release Act because it was accelerated largely by disputes at the International Court between Japan and Peru regarding an incident involving the *Maria Luz*, which stopped at Yokohama en route to Peru with hundreds of Chinese coolies on board. During court proceedings, Japanese officials were confronted with the fact that, according to international law, Japan was engaged in domestic slavery. Behind the claim that the system of yūjo was similar to slavery, Yokoyama highlights a sort of distorted influence by the movement to abolish prostitution in Britain, which appeared as a countermovement opposing the rise of capitalism. Simultaneously, there was a significant domestic factor in the form of the Meiji government. Yokoyama points out that as regards the Meiji government, which aimed at the direct control of citizens, the dissolution of middle-level groups in between government and citizens, such as the chou, which held privileges granted by the Tokugawa shogunate, had a major significance, and certain chou, to whom a monopoly on prostitution had been granted, were determined to resist any reforms. Furthermore, the story of one particular yūjo called Kashiku, which Yokoyama relates, provides another level of perspective. While this tragedy shows how unconcerned the Meiji government was regarding individual yūjo, it also displays how the yūjo gained agency owing to multiple factors. An understanding of the Yūjo Release Act therefore requires us to analyse the conjuncture of many struggles at several levels.

In Chapter 9, "The End of Slavery in French West Africa", Martin A. Klein begins by tracing three different acts of emancipation by French colonial regimes in the region. Owing to a strategic necessity to push on with territorial expansion, they needed, on some occasions, to cover a shortage of soldiers with slaves; at other occasions they needed to win over local chiefs, which required colonial officers to respect and protect local traditions. This meant that, to a certain extent, they had to protect and even access slavery. However, as Klein clearly demonstrates, once territorial expansion had been sufficiently achieved a policy of abolition was applied more strictly. Here, we see the reality of the relationship between colonialism and abolition. Colonialism did not bring about abolition straightaway. For France's colonial regimes, abolition was nothing more than a tool to enforce their rule. However, at the same time we have to admit that, for colonial officers, especially "bush administrators", it was a dilemma between metropolitan idealism and colonial reality, which

Klein describes vividly. Another significant feature of this article is Klein's careful exploration of the agency of slaves, who took advantage of the opportunities provided by the inconsistency of colonial policy on abolition in the vast territory of French West Africa. Some moved to the motherland or what they imagined to be their motherland; others, who remained, struggled to create a new relationship with their masters. However, again drawing on this agency of slaves, the French established liberty villages where the freedom of former female and child slaves could be protected while the males went off to seek out their original homeland. The concept of the liberty village originated not with an awareness of human rights on the part of the colonists, but as a means to control former slave labour. Even after slavery had ended, forced labour continued in French West Africa until 1946. Furthermore, drawing on his own fieldwork, Klein demonstrates the resilience of slaves and former slaves in the continuity of their relationship with current and former masters. His observation reminds us that, even though slavery might have become invisible and different after abolition, the ties between manumitted slaves and their former masters could not be severed completely.

The final article in this volume, Chapter 10, "The Abolition of Serfdom in Russia", is by Alessandro Stanziani. The subject of the article has been guarded by several "myths": economic retardation due to serfdom in the pre-abolition period, overestimation of the abolition in 1861 and the role of the tsar in this event, and so on. With his review of the existing literature, it is clear that Stanziani's approach is different from those which created the "myth" mentioned above. What he tries to do in this article is to reconsider the abolition of serfdom in a long-term process of social and economic evolution. His argument, based on rich data, successfully refutes or at least revises these "myths". In the Russian context, capitalism and coercion are compatible. Stanziani carefully deals with court cases in order to dig out contributions from "below" to the reform. In addition, he examines several attempts to reform serfdom since the late 18th century. Political elements (its stability, the interests of the state and some of the nobility), contest between "real" nobles and quasi-nobles, economic efficiency, paternalistic criticism of serfdom and a desire on the part of the peasants to protect their own rights pushed along reform. As a result, three-quarters of the Russian peasantry were no longer coerced labour by the time serfdom was abolished in 1861. Stanziani captures a series of reforms over a century and a half and views them as part of a process to change forms of power and hierarchy, a process that spanned the late 18th century up until the eve of World War I, when ownership of inhabited estates was opened up to newly emerging social classes such as urban residents and merchants. Peasants, too, purchased land and became connected to the market. Overall, claims Stanziani, the growth in Russian agriculture, trade and industry as well as living standards was much higher than is conventionally acknowledged, equivalent indeed to the growth seen in major Western countries. Furthermore, as he shows, this growth continued during the post-abolition period. He provides a key to reconsidering conventionally understood dichotomies between feudalism and capitalism, bonded and free labour, pre-abolition and post-abolition. Borders were much more vague than they are conventionally understood to have been.

We can begin by reading any of the nine articles. Each article examines abolition in a different region or country with a variety of focuses, such as politics, diplomacy, economy and so on. This proves that there is no single best focus to understand abolition as a globally shared experience. The effectiveness of each method will be proved in each article. Each deals with a different region or country, but together all of them view and analyse each abolition as a part of this global experience, and show connections, similarities and relation to other abolitions. Article by article, this globally shared experience takes shape.

Notes

1. The project ran from Apr. 2009–Mar. 2014 and was financially supported by the Japan Society for the Promotion of Science. The principal investigator was Masashi Haneda, University of Tokyo. At the stage of compiling this volume, lectures, seminars and workshops organized by the Japan Society for the Promotion of Science Core-to-Core Program "Global History Collaborative" (2014–) inspired the editor. I would like to thank the members of this programme.

2. Three workshops, two seminars and one session were organized. The first workshop, "On 'Slaves' in Eurasia from the 17th to the 19th Century" (15 May 2010 at the University of Tokyo), included the following papers: "Introduction" (Yoko Matsui), "On 'Slaves' in Eurasia from the 17th to the 19th Century" (Masashi Hirosue), "'Slaves' and the Slave Trade in India: On Shipment" (Ikuko Wada) and "Slavery and the Slave Trade in the Western Indian Ocean: A Review" (Hideaki Suzuki).

Tomoko Morikawa, Ryuto Shimada and Takeshi Fushimi provided comments.

The Atlantic Slave Trade Seminar with Stephan D. Behrendt (23 Oct. 2010, University of Tokyo) included the following: "Introduction" (Yoko Matsui), "Historians and Scholarship on the Transatlantic Slave Trade", "The Transatlantic Slave Trade and World History" and "Merchants, Mariners and Transatlantic Networks of Trade: Britain and Old Calabar (Nigeria) in the 18th Century" (all by Stephan D. Behrendt). Hideaki Suzuki commented.

The second workshop, "Slaves and Host Society" (29 May 2010, University of Tokyo), included the following contributions: "Introduction" (Hideaki Suzuki), "Slaves on the 19th-century East African Coast: Reading *Destsuri za Waswahili*" (Hideaki Suzuki), "Subordinates and East India Companies' 'Slaves' in 18th-Century India" (Ikuko Wada) and "Daily Lives of the Dutch and their Slaves: Case Studies of Batavia and Deshima" (Isabel Tanaka-Van Daalen). Comments by Kumie Inose and Ryuto Shimada followed.

On 11 Dec. 2011, James Warren gave a seminar at Gakushuin Women's University titled "'Broken Birds: An Epic Longing': An Outdoor Theatrical Production inspired by My Book *Ah Ku and Karayuki-san: Prostitution in Singapore, 1870–1940*".

The third workshop was held on 24 Jan. 2012 at the University of Tokyo and included the following papers: "Prostitution Release Act in Meiji 5 and Yūjo" (Yuriko Yokoyama), "Indians in Indentured Servitude in the Indian Ocean: Its Historical Position and Significance" (Kohei Wakimura) and "1870 in *Cultuurstelsel*: Perspective and Method for the Study of 19th-Century Java" (Atsuko Ohashi).

The "Abolition of Slavery as a Global Experience" session of the international conference on "Sugar and Slavery: Towards A New World History" (18–19 Nov. 2012, University of Tokyo) included the following contributions: "Introduction" (Hideaki Suzuki), "What is Remembered and What is Forgotten in the Bicentenary of the Abolition of Slave Trade in Britain" (Kumie Inose), "French Emancipation in Comparative Context" (Sue Peabody), "The Path Leading to Abolition in the Dutch East Indies" (Isabel Tanaka-Van Daalen), "The Yūjo Release Act and the Emancipation of Slaves in the Mid-19th Century" (Yuriko Yokoyama), "The 1848 Abolitionist Farman in Iran" (Behnaz A. Mirzai), "Abolition and its Aftermath in Madagascar" (Gwyn Campbell), "The End of Slavery in French West Africa" (Martin A. Klein), "The End of the Coolie Trade in Southern China" (Ei Murakami) and "Abolitions: Local Dynamics in Global Perspectives, 18th to Early 20th Centuries" (Alessandro Stanziani). Comments were provided by Jun'ichi Himeno and Kohei Wakimura.

3. Masashi Haneda, *Atarashii Sekaishi he: Chikyū shimin no tameno kousou* [Towards a New World History: A Conception of Global Citizenship] (Tokyo: Iwanami Shoten, 2012).

4. See the website for this project: http://haneda.ioc.u-tokyo.ac.jp/english/eurasia/ (accessed 27 Dec. 2013).

5. For a useful chronological chart, see Paul Lovejoy, *Transformations in Slavery: A History of Slavery in Africa*, 2nd ed. (Cambridge: Cambridge University Press, 2000), pp. 290–4. For international conventions on the abolition of slavery, see Kevin Bales, *Understanding Global Slavery: A Reader* (Berkeley and Los Angeles, CA: University of California Press, 2005), pp. 41–53.

6. Haile Selassie, *My Life and Ethiopia's Progress*, vol. 2, ed. Harold Marcus et al. (East Lansing, MI: Michigan State University, 1994), p. 175.

7. Dale W. Tomich, *Through the Prism of Slavery: Labor, Capital, and World Economy* (Lanham: Rowman and Littlefield, 2004), p. 115; J.R. McNeill and W.H. McNeill, *The Human Web: A Bird's-Eye View of World History* (New York and London: W.W. Norton, 2003), pp. 252–3.

8. See Martin A. Klein, "The Emancipation of Slaves in the Indian Ocean", in *Abolition and its Aftermath in the Indian Ocean Africa and Asia*, ed. Gwyn Campbell (London and New York: Routledge, 2005), pp. 198–9.

9. Gwyn Campbell, "Introduction: Slavery and Other Forms of Unfree Labour in the Indian Ocean World", in *Structure of Slavery in Indian Ocean Africa and Asia*, ed. Gwyn Campbell (London: Frank Cass, 2004), pp. vii–xxxii and "Slave Trades and The Indian Ocean World", in *India in Africa, Africa in India: Indian Ocean Cosmopolitanisms*, ed. John C. Hawley (Bloomington, IN: Indiana University Press, 2008), pp. 20–1, 34–5; Paul Lovejoy, *Transformations in Slavery: A History of Slavery in Africa*, 3rd ed. (Cambridge: Cambridge University Press, 2011), pp. 169–72; Igor Kopytoff and Suzanne Miers, "African 'Slavery' as an Institution of Marginality", in *Slavery in Africa: Historical and Anthropological Perspectives*, ed. Suzanne Miers and Igor Kopytoff (Madison, WI: University of Wisconsin Press, 1977), pp. 3–81; James H. Vaughan, "Mafakur: A Limbic Institution of the Margi (Nigeria)", in *Slavery in Africa*, ed. Miers and Kopytoff, pp. 85–102.

10. Patrick O'Brien, "Historiographical Traditions and Modern Imperatives for the Restoration of Global History", *Journal of Global History* 1, 1 (2006): 4–7.

11. William Mulligan, "Introduction: The Global Reach of Abolitionism in the Nineteenth Century", in *A Global History of Anti-Slavery Politics in the Nineteenth Century*, ed. William Mulligan and Maurice Bric (Basingstoke: Palgrave Macmillan, 2013), p. 3.

12. Ibid., pp. 2–3.

13. See Chapter 8 by Yuriko Yokoyama in this volume.

14. Y. Hakan Erdem, *Slavery in the Ottoman Empire and Its Demise, 1800–1909* (Oxford: St Martin's Press, 1996).

15. David Feeny, "The Demise of Corvee and Slavery in Thailand, 1782–1913", in *Breaking the Chains: Slavery, Bondage, and Emancipation in Modern Africa and Asia*, ed. Martin A. Klein (Madison, WI: University of Wisconsin Press, 1993).

16. Erdem, *Slavery in the Ottoman Empire*, pp. 67–124.

17. Feeny, "The Demise of Corvee".

18. Martin A. Klein, "Introduction: Modern European Expansion and Traditional Servitude in Africa and Asia", in *Breaking the Chains*, ed. Klein, p. 27.

19. Mulligan and Bric, eds., *A Global History*; Seymour Drescher, *Abolition: A History of Slavery and Antislavery* (Cambridge: Cambridge University Press, 2009); Klein, ed., *Breaking the Chains*; Derek R. Peterson, ed., *Abolitionism and Imperialism in Britain, Africa, and the Atlantic* (Athens, OH: Ohio University Press, 2010); Howard Temperley, ed., *After Slavery: Emancipation and its Discontents* (London: Frank Cass, 2000), p. 1.

20. David Brion Davis, "Looking at Slavery from Broader Perspectives", *American Historical Review* 105, 2 (2000): 452–66.

21. See Kevin Bales, *Disposable People: New Slavery in the Global Economy* (Berkeley, CA: University of California Press, 1999).

22. Eric Williams, *Capitalism and Slavery* (Chapel Hill, NC: University of North Carolina Press, 1944).

23. See Barbara Lewis Solow and Stanley L. Engerman, "British Capitalism and Caribbean Slavery: The Legacy of Eric Williams: An Introduction", in *British Capitalism and Caribbean Slavery: The Legacy of Eric Williams*, ed. Barbara L. Solow and Stanley L. Engerman (Cambridge: Cambridge University Press, 1987), p. 1.

24. See Solow and Engerman, eds., *British Capitalism*.

25. Gwyn Campbell, "Introduction: Abolition and its Aftermath in the Indian Ocean World", in *Abolition and its Aftermath*, ed. Campbell, p. 2; Paul Lovejoy, *Transformations in Slavery: A History of Slavery in Africa*, 1st ed. (Cambridge: Cambridge University Press, 1983), p. 246; Klein, "Introduction", in *Breaking the Chains*, ed. Klein, pp. 18–9.

26. Seymour Drescher, *Econocide: British Slavery in the Era of Abolition* (Pittsburgh, PA: University of Pittsburgh Press, 1977).

27. Seymour Drescher, "Capitalism and Abolition: Values and Forces in Britain, 1783–1814", in *Liverpool, the African Slave Trade, and Abolition: Essays to Illustrate Current Knowledge and Research*, ed. R. Anstey and

P.E.H. Hair (Liverpool: Historic Society of Lancashire and Cheshire, 1976), pp. 167–95.

28. Christopher Leslie Brown, *Moral Capital: Foundations of British Abolitionism* (Chapel Hill, NC: University of North Carolina Press, 2006); John R. Oldfield, *Popular Politics and British Anti-Slavery: The Mobilisation of Public Opinion against the Slave Trade, 1787–1807* (Manchester: Manchester University Press, 1995).

29. David Brion Davis, *The Problem of Slavery in the Age of Revolution, 1770–1823* (Ithaca, NY: Cornell University Press, 1975), p. 49.

30. Antoinette Iadarola, "Ethiopia's Admission into the League of Nations: An Assessment of Motives", *The International Journal of African Historical Studies* 8, 4 (1975): 601–22; Jean Allain, "Slavery and the League of Nations: Ethiopia as a Civilised Nation", *Journal of the History of International Law* 8 (2006): 213–44; Sterling Joseph Coleman Jr, "Gradual Abolition or Immediate Abolition of Slavery? The Political, Social and Economic Quandary of Emperor Haile Selassie I", *Slavery and Abolition: A Journal of Slave and Post-Slave Studies* 29, 1 (2008): 65–82.

31. Howard Temperley, "Introduction", in *After Slavery*, ed. Temperley, p. 1.

32. See Chapter 2 by Sue Peabody in this volume.

33. Philips Library, Peabody and Essex Museum, Salem, MA, USA, MH201/ Box 3 [F.R. Webb to E.D. Ropes, Zanzibar, 13 Apr. 1869].

34. Zanzibar National Archives, Zanzibar, Tanzania, AA7/2-3.

35. W. Cope Devereux, *A Cruise in the "Gorgon;" or, Eighteen Months on H.M.S. "Gorgon", Engaged in the Suppression of the Slave Trade on the East Coast of Africa. Including a Trip up the Zambesi with Dr. Livingstone* (London: Bell and Daldy, 1869), p. 343.

36. Erik Gilbert, *Dhows and the Colonial Economy in Zanzibar, 1860–1970* (Oxford: James Currey, 2004); Hideaki Suzuki, "Indo-you nishi-kaiiki ni okeru 'doreisen' gari: 19 seiki dorei koueki haizetsu katsudou no ichidanmen" ["Slaver" Hunting in the Western Indian Ocean: An Aspect of the 19th-century British Campaign against Slave Trade], *Afurika Kenkyū* 79 (2011): 13–25.

37. Coleman, "Gradual Abolition", pp. 74–6; Iadarola, "Ethiopia's Admission", pp. 608–11; Allain, "Slavery and the League of Nations", pp. 219–23.

38. Douglas A. Blackmon, *Slavery By Another Name: The Re-Enslavement of Black Americans from the Civil War to World War II* (New York: Doubleday, 2008).

39. Behnaz A. Mirzai, "Slavery, the Abolition of the Slave Trade, and the Emancipation of Slaves in Iran (1828–1928)", unpublished PhD dissertation (Canada: York University, 2004).

40. Hideaki Suzuki, "Baluchi Experiences under Slavery and the Slave Trade of the Gulf of Oman and the Persian Gulf, 1921–1950", *The Journal of the Middle East and Africa* 4, 2 (2013): 205–23.

41. Dharma Kumar, "Colonialism, Bondage, and Caste in British India", in *Breaking the Chains*, ed. Klein, pp. 112–30.

42. David Northrup, *Indentured Labor in the Age of Imperialism 1834–1922* (Cambridge: Cambridge University Press, 1995), pp. 156–61.

43. Hugh Tinker, *A New System of Slavery: The Export of Indian Labour Overseas, 1830–1920* (Oxford: Oxford University Press, 1974).

44. To these cases we can add so-called "reversion" of Europe, namely forced labour under the Nazi regime and the Soviet Union. For a detailed analysis in the context of slavery, see Drescher, *Abolition*, pp. 415–55. As regards "reversion", see Davis, *The Problem of Slavery*, p. 336.

45. Kwame Nimako and Glenn Willemsen, *The Dutch Atlantic: Slavery, Abolition and Emancipation* (London: Pluto Press, 2011), p. 181.

46. See "Slavery Compensation: Caribbean Nations Propose Mau Mau Model", *Guardian*, 26 July 2013 (www.theguardian.com/world/2013/jul/26/caribbean-countries-slavery-compensation-claim, accessed 5 Jan. 2014); "Caribbean Nations to Seek Reparations, Putting Price on Damage of Slavery", *New York Times*, 20 Oct. 2013 (www.nytimes.com/2013/10/21/world/americas/caribbean-nations-to-seek-reparations-putting-price-on-damage-of-slavery.html, accessed 5 Jan. 2014).

47. Nimako and Willemsen, *The Dutch Atlantic*, p. 181.

48. Anthony G. Hopkins, ed., *Global History: Interactions between the Universal and the Local* (Basingstoke and New York: Palgrave Macmillan, 2006).

49. Oriental and India Office Collection, British Library, London, UK, IOR/R/15/1/171/23 [Report on the Slave Trade in the Persian Gulf extending from 1 Jan. 1852 to 30 June 1858 compiled by H. Disbrowe].

50. For the Underground Railroad, see Jacqueline L. Tobin, *From Midnight to Dawn: The Last Tracks of the Underground Railroad* (New York: Knopf Doubleday, 2007).

CHAPTER 2

France's Two Emancipations in Comparative Context

Sue Peabody

Introduction

France officially abolished slavery thrice: first in 1794, during the French Revolution; then, following the Napoleonic restoration of slavery in France's colonies in 1802 by decree, again as one of the first acts by the Second Republic in 1848; and finally, as Martin A. Klein discusses in Chapter 9 in this volume, at the turn of the 19th–20th centuries in colonial West Africa. For the purposes of this analysis, I will confine myself to the first two abolitions, which affected France's plantation colonies in the Americas and the Indian Ocean. For many years France celebrated only its second abolition, that of 1848, preferring not to remember the abolition of 1794, since it was also an occasion of France's military defeat in Saint-Domingue (Haiti) and today is viewed as a forerunner of 20th-century anti-colonial resistance movements. In recent times, French historiography of general emancipation has been driven, to a certain degree, by the commemoration of anniversaries. A flood of studies appeared in 1948 (centenary of the 1848 abolition),[1] 1994 (bicentennial of the 1794 abolition),[2] 1998 (sesquicentennial of 1848),[3] 2004 (bicentennial of Haitian independence)[4] and even 2002 (bicentennial of Napoleon's restoration of slavery in 1802).[5] Efforts to recognize these milestones of French liberty were not, however, without controversy; several scholars (notably Michel-Rolph Troulliot, Yves Bénot and Marcel

Dorigny), pushed against a prevailing "amnesia" about France's historical relationship with slavery to bring to light a history that many contemporaries would sooner forget.[6] By the end of the first decade of the 21st century, however, it was no longer accurate to refer to the "silencing" of Haiti's past, at least for its foundation as a nation without slavery.[7]

In this article I will review the particular history of France's two emancipations in 1794 and 1848, and then step back with a wider lens and look at the different processes by which various European empires effected the abolition of slavery to place France's emancipations in a more widely comparative perspective. Although both of France's abolitions occurred during revolutions effecting new republican governments in Paris, the first was prompted by direct military action of the slaves themselves while the second was a long-considered product of liberal reformers in Paris. The first emancipation emerged within the events now recognized as the Haitian Revolution, a seminal event in modern world history, and had powerful repercussions for independence and citizenship struggles throughout the Atlantic World. The progressive characteristics of the 1848 emancipation were soon overshadowed by reactionary responses; it would be almost a century before full citizenship was formally granted to the descendants of former slaves. Even so, the lingering inequalities rooted in colonial slavery and exacerbated by global capitalism prevent the full realization of equality for many blacks in France today.

France's Two Emancipations: 1794 and 1848

For the most part, historians of French anti-slavery tend to focus on either 1794 or 1848, with very little scholarship tracing the two events in the continuity of French history.[8] Likewise, until recently, most historical scholarship on France's two emancipations has been confined within French national history, with little comparison across European imperial regimes or more broadly; this collection seeks to address this gap.

Even before the French Revolution (1789–99) began, a handful of French liberals—many of them elites of noble or wealthy bourgeois status—had started organizing for the amelioration of slavery, abolition of the slave trade and eventual abolition of slavery itself. In a speech given at its inaugural meeting in Paris on 19 February 1788, the founding members of the Gironde credited the American Quakers and the British anti-slavery movement with inspiring French liberals to challenge the colonial slavery system.[9] The president of this society, Jacques Pierre Brissot, and other founding members (such as Condorcet and Abbé Grégoire) would go on to play important roles in the moderate, liberal Girondist faction of the French Revolution. They lobbied successfully for equal civil rights for free people of colour, but eventually found themselves suppressed by Robespierre's Jacobin radicals during the Reign of Terror (1793–94).

The events surrounding the French abolition of 1794 have been narrated by some very talented historians, beginning with C.L.R. James.[10] More recently, especially since the bicentennial celebrations of the French and Haitian Revolutions, there has been an explosion of historical study on the Haitian Revolution and its relationship with the Paris emancipation decree, and its impact on the wider world.[11] One of the key tensions in interpreting France's first emancipation of 1794 is the degree to which it can be seen as the result of French Enlightenment and republican thought or the result of collective action of self-liberation on the part of the slaves.[12] There can be no doubt that the slave revolt of 1791, framed in Haitian memory as arising from the Bois Caïman ceremony, was planned and executed by African and Creole slaves who were attuned to rumours of freedom circulating throughout the Atlantic World and aware of the vulnerability of the planter class, due to tensions between patriots and royalists in France and in the colonies.[13] However, while free people of colour saw the French Revolution as an opportunity to press for equal civil and political rights, the slaves who revolted in Saint-Domingue did not see abolition of slavery or the establishment of a republic without slavery as their immediate goals. John Thornton's very interesting work on the rebels' ideology suggests that they operated within a monarchical framework at the outset, whereby their grievances for unjust treatment might be petitioned to a king, whether the king of France or the "King of Congo".[14]

Jeremy Popkin's detailed study of France's first emancipation argues for a highly contingent sense of causality. For Popkin, everything boils down to the events of one day: 20 June 1793. This was the day that extreme tensions between Saint-Domingue's white planter elite and free men of colour erupted in bloody violence in the streets of Cap-Français, the capital city. Sonthonax and Polverel, the republican commissioners, had already alienated many of Saint-Domingue's elite planters by seeking alliances with free men of colour, courting their leadership to put down the slave revolt. General Galbaud, the newly appointed governor of the colony who had family ties to the island's white planter elite, had recently arrived in the harbour with hundreds, if not thousands, of sailors who resented the mulattos and the republican commissioners. On 20 June, Galbaud and his murderous sailors landed at the docks and began a 24-hour street fight to capture the city, all the way up to the Government House, where the commissioners were defended by just a handful of officers of colour. It was Jean-Baptiste "Mars" Belley who led the counterattack that secured the commissioners' safety overnight.[15] The following day, the commissioners issued their first emancipation decree, offering freedom to those slaves who would fight on behalf of the republic.

Over the months that followed, the republican commissioners would extend this offer, first to soldiers' wives and children, if they married in a civil ceremony conducted by republican authorities. Then, in desperation, they declared general emancipations in the northern, western and southern provinces of Saint-Domingue, which were engulfed in extended warfare between the revolting slaves, the French, the Spanish and the British armies.[16] At the end, slavery was officially abolished wherever republican French occupation was in effect, though navigating real conditions and relationships was complicated for slaves and free people of colour throughout the colony.[17] It was only when a delegation headed by Belley, a mulatto and a white Frenchman, brought the news of the commissioners' emancipation decrees to the National Convention in Paris that the 1794 decree proclaimed general emancipation universally throughout the French empire. This was facilitated, no doubt, by the radical ideology of liberty, equality and fraternity then dominant in Paris, and the linguistic equivalence whereby the very name of "France" is synonymous with freedom.[18] French legislators expected that this decree would be implemented in all French colonies, according to local conditions.

However, despite the intended universal reach of the 1794 French emancipation decree, its application fell short of its framers' enthusiasm. Martinique remained under British occupation during the war and emancipation was never effected there.[19] Guadeloupe and Guyana effected emancipation, but in ways that will anticipate many post-emancipation regimes later in the 19th century.[20] Colonial authorities used force to require the "new citizens" to continue to work on the same plantations, theoretically for wages and limited hours but with severe restrictions of civil rights, such as mobility. The colonial governments employed vagrancy laws to arrest, imprison or otherwise penalize those who refused to work. Colonists in Île de France successfully repelled the evolutionary delegates who came to pronounce the emancipation declaration in the Indian Ocean, and it was never put into effect there or in Réunion.[21]

The restoration of pre-revolutionary slavery was high on Napoleon's agenda when he came to power.[22] When Napoleon sent troops to restore slavery to Guadeloupe and Saint-Domingue in 1802 his agents met with armed resistance but it was only in Saint-Domingue, where a yellow-fever epidemic aided the "new citizens" in destroying the French army, that the restoration of slavery was successfully resisted, resulting in the declaration of Haitian independence on 1 January 1804. In Guadeloupe, the followers of Louis Delgrès, rather than submit to re-enslavement, committed mass suicide with their leader.[23]

The French and Haitian revolutions yielded contradictory effects on anti-slavery in the wider Atlantic World. On the one hand, leaders of some slave revolts took Haiti as their inspiration; likewise, the Latin American independence leader, Simón Bolivar, in his campaign to liberate colonies from Spain, received inspiration, protection and resources from Haitian president Alexandre Pétion.[24] On the other hand, anti-slavery activists in England and the United States found it difficult to generate support for general emancipation initiatives in the 1790s, as their publics feared that the abolition would unleash the violence witnessed in Saint-Domingue and Paris.[25] Although the twin revolutions impeded support for general emancipation, the threat of slave revolts stimulated support for banning the Atlantic slave trade. In 1807, the US and Britain banned the importation of slaves from Africa.[26] Following Napoleon's defeat in 1814 (and again in 1815), Britain began to pressure France, Spain and Portugal to abolish their slave trades through treaties, resulting in King Louis XVIII's bans of the slave trade of 8 January 1817 and 15 April 1818. However, the French government was not truly committed to the slave-trade ban and enforced it half-heartedly. (In contrast, British ships did intercede and capture French and other foreign slaving ships, especially in the Indian Ocean.[27])

With the restoration of the French monarchy following Napoleon's defeat, the beginnings of a French anti-slavery lobby re-emerged, also prodded by British anti-slavery activists and a few lone voices in France such as the Abbé Grégoire, Madame de Staël and Chateaubriand. Zachary Macaulay made trips to Paris and Grégoire maintained correspondence with his counterparts in London, but progress was slow over the next three decades as colonial interests worked to delay and undermine anti-slavery initiatives.[28] Drawing its membership from elite Protestant and Catholic liberal circles, the Société de la morale Chrétienne (1821–30), a voluntary society with humanitarian and anti-slavery sentiments and aims, included the future king Louis-Philippe (1830–48) and advanced a broadly humanitarian agenda, including several anti-slavery initiatives (to improve the condition of slaves, enforce the slave trade ban and bring about emancipation gradually) that coexisted alongside philanthropy, education and social reform. The British and Foreign Anti-slavery Society, founded in 1834, was organized primarily from London, but developed extensive ties with both the elite members of the Société française pour l'abolition de l'esclavage (French Society for the Abolition of Slavery, SFAE) and, later, independent anti-slavery agents like Cyrille Bissette and Victor Schoelcher.[29]

The July Revolution of 1830 ushered in a more liberal constitutional monarchy, and for a moment, it seemed that the anti-slavery lobby was making progress for slaves and free people of colour. Led by Victor, Duc de Broglie, the SFAE was able to push forward a series of legislative reforms in the early 1830s, adding significant penalties to enforce the slave-trade ban, stimulating manumission, recognizing civil and political rights for free people of colour (though voting was restricted to those capable of paying an expensive tax), banning the branding and mutilation of slaves and ordering a new slave census, a necessary preliminary step to abolishing slavery. At the same time, however, the July Monarchy reorganized the political structure of the colonies to allow (wealthy) colonists to elect local colonial councils with legislative powers and review royal colonial legislation, as well as electing non-voting delegates to the Chamber of Deputies in Paris. When the Duc de Broglie was appointed Prime Minister in 1835, however, he bowed to pressure from Duperré, Minister and Secretary of State of the navy and colonies, to slow down any initiatives leading towards general emancipation.[30] François Mauguin and Charles Dupin, who already served as voting deputies for their districts in metropolitan France, were elected by the planter elite to represent their interests in Paris, in the 1830s. Together with elected slave-holding delegates from Guiana, Guadeloupe, Martinique and Bourbon, this colonial lobby, with a substantial budget for propaganda (it founded and purchased several newspapers to distribute its views widely in the metropole), would prove extremely effective in countering the mild and ultimately ineffective efforts of the SFAE to build momentum for emancipation.[31]

In the 1830s, Bissette, exiled from Martinique in 1824 for promoting civil rights for men of colour, began publishing pamphlets and journals, becoming an urgent voice for immediate abolition in Paris.[32] Schoelcher, the son of a porcelain factory owner, began to lobby for amelioration and then abolition of slavery after the ascendance of the July Monarchy in 1830.[33] Just as Schoelcher emerged as an anti-slavery activist in the early 1840s, the older legislative anti-slavery momentum stalled, as a result of tensions escalated between Britain and France over the "right of search" controversy (1841–42).[34] Sadly, Bissette and Schoelcher became rivals rather than allies, with Bissette, who received extensive support from the British anti-slavery society, becoming increasingly marginalized from French governmental reforms.

The French anti-slavery movement had, until this point, been conducted primarily by elite legal and political figures with ties to the government in Paris. Indeed, France's labour movement had only begun to organize itself in the late 1830s and the members' primary initial focus concerned gaining political representation for France's working class. Therefore, it was not until 1844 that French labour began to imitate the populist anti-slavery petition drives that had proven so effective in England in the first third of the 19th century.[35]

In January, Parisian and provincial printers circulated France's first anti-slavery petition beyond the narrow, gradualist Parisian elite, calling for immediate emancipation; this ultimately garnered 8,832 signatures. While falling far short of the British precedent (1.5 million signatures in 1833), a second petition drive in 1846–47 garnered 12,395 signatures.[36] Immediately following the legislative reception of the first workers' petition, the colonial minister Mackau introduced a series of bills into the Chamber of Peers in 1844, which was passed in the 1845 session. The Mackau laws, as they became known, further clarified the government's legislative relationship between the metropole and the colonies, introduced ameliorative measures for the maintenance and conditions of slaves and encouraged gradual emancipation through *rachat* (self-purchase) and *pécule* (independent savings by slaves). French and British abolitionists viewed the Mackau laws as a delaying tactic, designed to slow down progress towards full emancipation.[37]

In February 1848, a popular revolt expelled the French monarchy and replaced it with a provisional republican government that included at its helm several noted abolitionists, including Schoelcher. In less than two months, the provisional government adopted Schoelcher's Act for General Emancipation (27 April 1848), which proclaimed that slavery would be abolished within two months of its promulgation in the colonies, and then passed a constellation of legislation regulating the aftermath of emancipation. Key amongst these provisions was the accordance of full political and civil rights for former slaves.[38] Slaves in Martinique, hearing rumours of the coming emancipation, demonstrated in the streets, hastening the official declaration of emancipation there. The law of 30 April 1849 provided for the indemnification of slaveholders for their loss of property, at rates that varied by colony and did not approach market value for the slaves.[39]

In plantation colonies of the Antilles and the Mascarenes, the newly liberated left the plantations in large numbers, often migrating up the mountains where they established small independent dwellings and gardens. As in 1794, colonial governments issued decrees trying to coerce the workers to return to the plantations. Schoelcher's emancipation plan accepted the need to compensate masters but in the end, they only received one-third of the value of each slave in cash and one-third in credit. Although the law recognized full political rights for male slaves, equivalent to those enjoyed by men in France, subsequent elections saw intimidation and violence aimed at former slaves. Nevertheless, some courageously participated in the elections of 1848, 1849 and 1850, especially in Guadeloupe and Martinique, where both Bissette and Schoelcher ran for as colonial representatives to the national legislature.[40] In France's African colonies, Algeria and Senegal, where indigenous societies relied on Old World slavery systems and slaves were viewed as extensions of domestic households, French colonial administrators tried not to antagonize local elites, to the point of discouraging slaves who might try to claim the privilege of Free Soil in areas under French sovereignty, such as Gorée and St Louis.[41]

French Emancipation in Comparison

A number of historians have begun to consider one or both of France's two abolitions of slavery within a broader, Atlantic frame.

David Brion Davis, an early pioneer of anti-slavery thought and action, presented the emergence of anti-slavery activism in the late 17th century as a problem of intellectual history: whence came the idea, so contrary to millennia of human history, that slavery was wrong?[42] Robin Blackburn has argued that the pivot points of abolition in each Atlantic imperial regime—British, French, Spanish and Portuguese— arose within a political crisis for the ruling class, whether during the American and French revolutions, the Latin American wars of independence or the economic woes of Britain in the decade leading up to the 1833 Emancipation Act.[43] In 2000, several collections argued that too many studies of slavery and abolition stopped with the congratulatory telos of abolition, and urged historians to consider the real conditions for former slaves in the societies formed after emancipation.[44] A document textbook, designed for classroom use, allows students to consider the ways that the four dominant Atlantic imperial regimes regulated slavery and achieved abolition.[45] In 2009, Seymour Drescher capped decades of research on anti-slavery as a transnational phenomenon with a wide-ranging and exceptionally well-integrated synthesis, which traces the emergence of an idea that enslavement was wrong from the 16th through the 20th centuries, and places Atlantic anti-slavery within a global context.[46] Several aspects of France's experiences of emancipation emerge as distinctive in these works.

First is the radical nature of the Haitian Revolution, which must be seen as the primary cause of the first abolition of 1794. Slaves in Saint-Domingue, the majority of whom were born in West or Central Africa and experienced the horrors of enslavement and the transatlantic slave trade first-hand, took advantage of the fractures within France's colonial elite to press for their own liberation. Likewise, Creole slaves (that is, those born in the colony) and free people of colour claimed the rhetoric emerging from the Enlightenment and republican vanguard in France to press for equal rights. Beginning with Toussaint Louverture's 1801 constitution, the abolition of slavery became foundational in all subsequent Haitian constitutions.[47] What is perhaps less well recognized is the degree to which the aftermath of the 1794 emancipation also catalysed the regulation of former slaves in each of the colonies where slavery was nominally abolished: Saint-Domingue, Guadeloupe and Guyana. The directives issued by French colonial authorities, from Toussaint Louverture to Victor Hughes, sought to bind labourers to plantations where they had served as slaves and to maintain plantation production for export, offering nominal cash rewards when profits from their labour were realized while penalizing vagabondage. Conditions for agricultural workers after emancipation were therefore not remarkably different from the reality of slavery.

The 1794 abolition cannot be understood apart from its immediate context of revolt and warfare, whereby emancipation and citizenship became inextricably linked with manhood and soldiering. As with American slaves who had been offered their freedom for fighting on the side of the British in 1775, the French republican commissioners' earliest emancipation decrees in Saint-Domingue (in 1793) offered freedom in exchange for soldiering. Subsequent independence movements in Latin America and Lincoln's Emancipation Proclamation were predicated on attracting the loyalty of slaves to one side of an armed conflict.[48]

The Haitian Revolution impacted the rest of the Atlantic World in ways that both accelerated and confounded emancipation elsewhere. The 1794 emancipation stirred leaders in the Spanish colonies to consider the injustice of slavery and racial inequality, especially where the enslavement of Africans was a relatively minor part of the local economy. The wars of independence in Chile, Columbia and Mexico were soon followed by the abolition of slavery in the 1820s; Venezuela, Ecuador and Peru waited until the 1850s to effect emancipation acts. Cuba and Brazil, highly dependent on African slave labour, were the last American nations to abolish slavery in the 1880s. However, Haiti's independence also stimulated fear in the planter class, prompting reactionary oppression and undermining support for abolition in the US, Britain and France's remaining colonies in the first decades of the 19th century.[49]

French anti-slavery, with its limited coterie of liberal elites, stands in marked contrast to anti-slavery activism of the same period in the United Kingdom and the US, which was predicated on stimulating public opinion. The Anglophone anti-slavery movement was characterized by the organization of public meetings, publication of pamphlets and slave biographies, and coordination of petition campaigns designed to influence electoral politics. French anti-slavery was a far more tepid, pragmatic enterprise, conducted for the most part by elite insiders, with little attempt to stir up the masses. The differences in these anti-slavery campaigns reflected both the charged

morality of its proponents (in the US and Britain, activists were propelled by Protestant convictions of the morality of their crusade) and
the more robust democratic nature of their governments—popular
opinion mattered to politicians in the US and Britain but was mis-
trusted or ignored by France's successive regimes until the Revolution
of 1848 (since only wealthy male property owners could vote).[50]

In both 1794 and 1848, France rejected another tested system
of emancipation which was deployed throughout the Atlantic World:
gradual emancipation through Free Womb Laws. Free Womb laws
emancipated children born to enslaved mothers after a particular
date but these children owed years of service to their masters up to
adulthood (stipulated as a particular age between 18 and 30). Free
Womb emancipations addressed three of the concerns of bourgeois
reformers: (a) masters' costs of raising a child from infancy to ado-
lescence were "compensated" by the labour that they performed until
the age of liberation; (b) children received training in a particular
trade or industry, thereby preparing them to sustain themselves in
the wage labour market; and (c) emancipation occurred gradually,
over a generation, not suddenly, with all of the problems anticipated
in immediate abolition. The "Free Womb" model was first adopted in
Pennsylvania in 1780, although it was not called by this name until
the Spanish American and Brazilian emancipation acts of the 19th
century. However, the gradual nature of these laws meant that slavery
lingered in most of the societies, so that a second set of laws was
necessary to finally eradicate slavery in those polities.[51]

France's 1848 emancipation recalled the radical roots of the first
abolition in its granting of full, immediate political rights to former
slaves. However, in colonies such as Réunion, where the democratic
tradition was already very weak, the local planter elite effectively dis-
couraged participation, and these provisions were soon swept away
by the reactionary Second Empire established by Louis-Napoleon
in 1851.

As with the British Empire, France's expanding colonization of
Africa and Asia in the second half of the 19th century provoked a
dilemma between the European celebration of liberty and the realities
of colonial rule in lands where various forms of slavery bound the
social order. The contradictions between metropolitan abolitionism
and indigenous slavery and the tenuousness of European rule meant
that, as dictated by pragmatism, administrators alternately accommodated local practices or deployed abolitionism against rival leaders.

Drescher argues that, with the exception of the "mighty experiment" of 1833—which sought to fully compensate masters for their loss in property through indenture and high taxes on colonial products— subsequent British emancipation policy in India and Africa was founded upon "delegalization", whereby slavery was abolished within a specific jurisdiction but enforcement of abolition was left to the slaves themselves who challenged their masters before courts or commissions individually.[52] French authorities followed a similar pattern in French West Africa and the Sudan in the late 19th and early 20th centuries.[53] In the slaveries of many Old World societies in Africa and Asia, slaves may have preferred their relationships of dependency with their masters to emancipation, especially if "freedom" meant social ostracism, unemployment or even famine.[54]

Memory and Emancipation

From the moment of general emancipation to the present, the French government has sought to harness the symbolic meanings of general emancipation. Alongside the abolition decree of 27 April 1848, the provisional republic decreed that the abolition of slavery should be celebrated annually. A *"fête de travail"*, presided over by the highest officers of the colonial government, would select and reward a worker, "(man or woman) who is the most distinguished by his good conduct", with either a cash award of 200 francs or a plot of arable land.[55]

Today, France wrestles with the memory of its colonial past, including its role in the slave trade and plantation slavery. Over the past two decades, two key anniversaries of France's emancipations have been celebrated in the context of a postcolonial France: the bicentennial of 1794 in 1994 and the sesquicentennial of 1848 in 1998. On 21 May 2001, France decreed the black slave trade and slavery as a "crime against humanity". In February 2005, however, the French legislature passed a law requiring all public schoolteachers and textbooks to "acknowledge and recognize in particular the positive role of the French presence abroad". Though generated by conservatives seeking to restore the reputation of French colonial and military rule in Algeria, the implications for France's slaveholding colonies are significant, particularly when the universal educational curriculum did not even require the teaching of the history of slavery. The 2005 law was repealed the following year and in 2006, France declared 10 May as the "national day of memory for slave trade, slavery and their abolition". On 25 March 2012, after years of pressure by local activists, the Memorial of the Abolition of Slavery opened along the riverfront in Nantes, France's slave-trading capital in the 18th century.[56] Other ongoing efforts seek to provide textbooks and teacher training for secondary schools to make the legacies of slavery and abolition relevant to young people in the metropole and the former colonies, now full departments (states) of France.

Kumie Inose, in Chapter 3 of this volume, deals with the British commemoration of abolition and offers a useful point of comparison between French and British public recollection of these events for audiences of the early 21st century. As in Britain, French commemoration reflects a tension between competing memories. On the one hand, there is a discourse that represents general emancipation as a benevolent act bestowed by the French state upon "uncivilized" and dependent colonial slaves, a carryover from imperial attitudes from the 19th and early 20th centuries.[57] This view reinforces the positive view of the French state and, as in Britain, helps unite a national identity of "Frenchness" ("francité") among disparate people.[58] A competing discourse rejects the idea that emancipation originated primarily in French thought and action but derived from the struggle of the slaves themselves, especially in the Haitian Revolution, a clear analogy for anti-colonial struggles of the 20th century. Such a view draws important links between slave resistance and emancipation[59] and seeks to validate modern struggles for human rights by oppressed peoples across national boundaries, as well as the legacies of inequality and dependence that persist in the overseas departments today.

In sum, the French Revolution, like the American Revolution, celebrated the abstract value of "liberty", to which it added "equality" and "fraternity" as essential ideological cornerstones to French republicanism. Colonial slavery mocked the universalism premised in each of these ideals. Leaders emerging from the ranks of the slaves and free people of colour in the French colonies embraced this revolutionary rhetoric as justification for their struggles, leading not only to the founding of Haiti but to other independence struggles in Latin America. In the wake of all emancipations, all former slave societies faced questions about the civil and political rights of former slaves as well as the economic challenges of restoring the productivity that had made the colonies so valuable to their imperial centres and the local ruling classes. However, French conservative powers' reaction to each emancipation was strong and brutal. After a brief experiment with full political rights for former slaves in 1848, France quickly reversed these policies, deploying vagrancy laws and other regulations to try to control their labour, all while importing new indentured labour from other parts of the world. France's "old colonies"—Martinique, Guadeloupe, Réunion, Guyana and the four communes of Senegal— did not receive the status of "department", with equal citizenship rights, until 1946, the same year that French women gained the right to vote. Today the struggle for equality, and a clear-eyed recognition of the past, continues in a postcolonial France.[60]

Notes

1. Patricia Motylewski cites several examples: *La Société française pour l'abolition de l'esclavage, 1834–1850* [The French Society for the Abolition of Slavery, 1834–1850] (Paris: L'Harmattan, 1998), p. 31.

2. Nelly Schmidt, *Victor Schœlcher et l'abolition de l'esclavage* [Victor Schoelcher and the Abolition of Slavery] (Paris: Fayard, 1994); Marcel Dorigny, ed., *Les abolitions de l'esclavage: de L.F. Sonthonax à V. Schœlcher, 1793, 1794, 1848, Actes du colloque international tenu à l'Université de Paris VIII les 3, 4 et 5 février 1994)* [The Abolitions of Slavery: From L.F. Sonthonax to V. Schoelcher, 1793, 1794, 1848, Proceedings from the International Colloquium Held at the University of Paris VIII, 3, 4, and 5 February 1994] (Saint-Dénis, France: Presses universitaires de Vincennes; Paris: UNESCO, 1995.

3. Motylewski, *La Société française pour l'abolition de l'esclavage* (op cit.); Claude Wanquet, *La France et la première abolition de l'esclavage, 1794–1802: le cas des colonies orientales, Ile de France (Maurice) et la Réunion* [France and the First Abolition of Slavery, 1794–1802: The Case of the Eastern Colonies, Île de France (Mauritius) and Réunion] (Paris: Éditions Karthala, 1998); Oruno D. Lara, *De l'oubli à l'histoire: Espace et identité caraïbes* [From the Forgotten to History: Caribbean Space and Identity] (Paris: Éditions Maisonneuve et Larose, 1998); David Rigoulet-Roze, "A propos d'une commémoration: L'Abolition de l'esclavage en 1848" [Concerning a Commemoration: The Abolition of Slavery in 1848], *L'Homme: Revue française d'anthropologie* 145 (1998): 127–36; Fabien Federnini, *L'Abolition de l'esclavage en 1848: Une Lecture de Victor Schœlcher* [The Abolition of Slavery in 1848: A Lecture of Victor Schoelcher] (Paris: L'Harmattan, 1998); Motylewski, *La Société française pour l'abolition de l'esclavage*; Gilbert Pago, *Les femmes et la liquidation du système esclavagiste à la Martinique 1848–1852* [Women and the Liquidation of the Slave System in Martinique 1848–1852] (Paris: Ibis Rouge, 1998); Christine Chivallon, *Espace et identité à la*

Martinique: Paysannerie des mornes et reconquête collective, 1840–1960 [Space and Identity in Martinique: Peasantry of the Hills and Collective Reconquest, 1840–1860] (Paris: C.N.R.S. Editions, 1998); Marcel Dorigny and Bernard Gainot, *La Société des Amis des Noirs, 1788–1799: Contribution à l'histoire des abolitions de l'esclavage* [The Society of the Friends of the Blacks, 1788–1799: Contribution to the History of the Abolitions of Slavery] (Paris: UNESCO, 1998).

4. Laurent Dubois, *Avengers of the New World: The Story of the Haitian Revolution* (Cambridge, MA: Belknap Press, 2004a) and *A Colony of Citizens: Revolution & Slave Emancipation in the French Caribbean, 1787–1804* (Chapel Hill, NC: University of North Carolina Press, 2004b); Frédéric Régent, *Esclavage, métissage, liberté: la révolution française en Guadeloupe, 1789–1802* [Slavery, Hybridity, Freedom: The French Revolution in Guadeloupe, 1789–1802] (Paris: B. Grasset, 2004); Claude Moïse, ed., *Dictionnaire historique de la Révolution haïtienne (1789–1804)* [Historical Dictionary of the Haitian Revolution, 1789–1804] (Montréal: Éditions Images/Cidihca, 2003); Jacques de Cauna, ed., *Toussaint Louverture et l'indépendance d'Haïti* [Toussaint Louverture and Haitian Independence] (Paris: Éditions Karthala, 2004); Olivier Pétré-Grenouilleau, "Introduction" and "Abolitionnisme et nationalisme: le douloureux positionnement des abolitionnistes français" [Abolitionism and Nationalism: The Distressing Positioning of the French Abolitionists] in *Abolitionnisme et société (France, Suisse, Portugal, XVIIIᵉ–XIXᵉ siècles), Actes d'un colloque tenu à Lorient en 2004* [Abolitionism and Society (France, Switzerland, Portugal, 18th–19th Centuries), Proceedings of a Colloquium Held in Lorient in 2004], ed. Olivier Pétré-Grenouilleau (Paris: Éditions Karthala, 2005); Yves Bénot, *La Révolution française et la fin des colonies, 1789–1794: postface inédite* [The French Revolution and the End of the Colonies, 1789–1794: A New Postface] (Paris: La Découverte, 2004).

5. Yves Bénot and Marcel Dorigny, *Rétablissement de l'esclavage dans les colonies françaises, 1802: ruptures et continuités de la politique coloniale française, 1800–1830: aux origines d'Haïti, Actes du colloque international tenu à l'Université de Paris VIII les 20, 21 et 22 juin 2002* [Re-establishment of Slavery in the French Colonies, 1802: Ruptures and Continuities of French Colonial Policy, 1800–1830: From the Origins to Haiti, Proceedings of the International Colloquium held at the University of Paris VIII, 20, 21 and 22 June 2002] (Paris: Maisonneuve et Larose, 2003).

6. Michel-Rolph Trouillot, *Silencing the Past: Power and the Production of History* (Boston, MA: Beacon Press, 1995); Bénot, *La Révolution française*, esp. Chapter 10; Dorigny, *Les abolitions de l'esclavage*, p. 7. See also Hubert Gerbeau, *Les Esclaves Noirs: Pour une Histoire du Silence*

[The Black Slaves: Toward a History of Silence] (Paris: André Balland, 1970).

7. Alyssa Goldstein Sepinwall, *Haitian History: New Perspectives* (New York: Routledge, 2013).

8. Dorigny is exceptional in his treatment of the two abolitions within one synthetic perspective: Dorigny, ed., *Les abolitions de l'esclavage* and *Anti-esclavagisme, abolitionnisme et abolitions: débats et controverses en France de la fin du XVIIIe siècle aux années 1840* [The Abolitions of Slavery and Anti-Slavery, Abolitionism and Abolitions: Debates and Controversies in France, from the End of the 18th Century to the 1840s] (Quebec: Presses de l'Université Laval, 2008).

9. Anonymous, "Discours sur la nécessité d'établir à Paris une Société pour concourir, avec celle de Londres, à l'abolition de la traite & de l'esclavage des Nègres. Prononcé le 19 Février 1788, dans un Société de quelques amis, à la prière du Comité de Londres" [Speech on the Necessity to Establish in Paris a Society to Contribute, with that of London, to the Abolition of the (Slave) Trade and of Negro Slavery. Given on 19 February 1788, in a Society of Some Friends, at the Behest of the Committee from London], Paris, s.d. 1788, in *La Révolution française et l'abolition de l'esclavage* [The French Revolution and the Abolition of Slavery], 12 vols (Paris: EDHIS, 1968), 6, 1, p. 1.

10. C.L.R. James, *The Black Jacobins* (New York: Dial Press, 1938). This was still assigned as the essential account of the Haitian Revolution when I was in graduate school in the 1980s.

11. Some of the most important recent scholarship, in addition to that already cited, includes: David Patrick Geggus, *Slavery, War, and Revolution: The British Occupation of Saint Domingue, 1793–1798* (Oxford: Clarendon Press, 1982); Carolyn E. Fick, *The Making of Haiti: The Saint Domingue Revolution from Below* (Knoxville, TN: University of Tennessee Press, 1990); David P. Geggus, *Haitian Revolutionary Studies* (Bloomington, IN: Indiana University Press, 2002); Dubois, *Avengers of the New World*; Jeremy D. Popkin, *You Are All Free: The Haitian Revolution and the Abolition of Slavery* (Cambridge: Cambridge University Press, 2010); Malick W. Ghachem, *The Old Regime and the Haitian Revolution* (Cambridge: Cambridge University Press, 2012); Rebecca J. Scott and Jean M. Hébrard, *Freedom Papers: An Atlantic Odyssey in the Age of Emancipation* (Cambridge, MA: Harvard University Press, 2012).

12. Yves Bénot acknowledges that the slave revolt in Saint-Domingue is the unquestionable origin of the Parisian decree but he offers extensive analysis of the threads of metropolitan thought on colonial slavery, especially in the revolutionary press, to restore the debates over slavery into the conventional narrative of the Revolution. Bénot, *Révolution française et la fin des colonies*, pp. 7–9.

13. In Aug. 1791, dozens of slaves planning a revolt gathered secretly at Bois Caïman where they pledged to support each other, using rituals drawn from African spiritual traditions; today Haitians celebrate this as the origins of their nation, much like the signing of the Declaration of Independence in the US. For a careful analysis of the written records of the Bois Caïman ceremony, today remembered as Haiti's foundational congress, see David P. Geggus, "The Bois Caïman Ceremony", *Haitian Revolutionary Studies* (op cit.), pp. 81–92.

14. John K. Thornton, "'I Am the Subject of the King of Congo': African Political Ideology and the Haitian Revolution", *Journal of World History* 4, 2 (Fall, 1993): 181–214.

15. Popkin, *You Are All Free*, pp. 202–45.

16. Robert Stein, "The Abolition of Slavery in the North, West, and South of Saint Domingue", *The Americas* 41, 3 (Jan. 1985): 47–55; Dubois, *Avengers*, pp. 154–66.

17. Geggus, *Slavery, War, and Revolution*, pp. 290–331, Fick, *Making of Haiti*, pp. 118–82; Scott and Hébrard, *Freedom Papers*, pp. 20–64.

18. Popkin, *You Are All Free*, pp. 327–74.

19. Abel A. Louis, *Les libres de couleur en Martinique. tome 2, Quand révolution et retour à l'ancien régime riment avec ségrégation, 1789–1802* [The Free People of Color in Martinique, vol. 2, When the Revolution and the Return to the Old Regime Coincided with Segregation, 1789–1802] (Paris: Harmattan, 2012).

20. Dubois, *A Colony of Citizens*, pp. 192–213; Régent, *Esclavage, métissage, liberté*, pp. 272–88, 333–54, 368–98; Jacques Adélaïde Merlande, *La Caraïbe et la Guyane au temps de la Révolution et de l'Empire* [The Caribbean and Guiana during the Revolution and the Empire] (Paris: Karthala, 1992), pp. 185–201; Yves Bénot, *La Guyane sous la Révolution française, ou, L'impasse de la révolution pacifique* [Guiana during the French Revolution, or the Dead End of the Peaceful Revolution] (Kourou: Ibis Rouge, 1997), esp. pp. 186–90.

21. Claude Wanquet, *La France et la première abolition de l'esclavage, 1794–1802: le cas des colonies orientales, Ile de France (Maurice) et la Réunion* [France and the First Abolition of Slavery, 1794–1802: The Case of the Eastern Colonies, Ile de France (Mauritius) and Réunion] (Paris: Éditions Karthala, 1998), pp. 279–309. See also Uttama Bissondoyal, ed., *L'Île de France et la Révolution française, Actes de colloque Mahatma Gandhi Institute, 4–8 Aug. 1989)* [Île de France and the French Revolution, Proceedings of the Colloquium of the Mahatma Gandhi Institute, 4–8 Aug. 1989] (Mauritius: Mahatma Gandhi Institute Press, 1990); Claude Wanquet and Benoît Julien, *Révolution française et océan Indien: Prémisse, paroxysmes, héritages et déviances* [French Revolution and the

Indian Ocean: Premise, Climaxes, Legacies and Deviations] (St Denis: Université de la Réunion; Paris: L'Harmattan, 1996).

22. Yves Bénot, *La Démence Coloniale sous Napoléon* [Colonial Madness under Napoleon] (Paris: La Découverte, 1992, rpr. 2006); Bénot and Dorigny, ed., *Rétablissement de l'esclavage dans les colonies françaises.*

23. Dubois, *Colony of Citizens*, esp. pp. 317–22, 354–64, 381–400, 423–31 and Régent, *Esclavage, Métissage, Liberté*, esp. pp. 410–20; see also Josette Fallope, *Esclaves et citoyens: Les Noirs à la Guadeloupe au XIXe siècle dans les processus de résistance et d'intégration (1802–1910)* [Slaves and Citizens: Blacks in Nineteenth-Century Guadeloupe in the Processes of Resistance and Integration (1802–1910)] (Basse-Terre, Guadeloupe: Société d'Histoire de la Guadeloupe, 1992), pp. 48–50. Louis Delgrès' heroic stand against Napoleon's re-imposition of slavery in 1802 has remained important to the shared memory of Guadeloupeans, from the 19th-century historical novel *Le Commandant Delgrès* by Gustave Aimard (Paris, 1876) to the popular historical retelling by Germain Saint-Ruf, *L'épopée Delgrès: la Guadeloupe sous la Révolution française (1789–1802)* [The Delgrès Epic: Guadeloupe during the French Revolution (1789–1802)] (Paris: Éditions Librairie de l'Étoile, 1965; 2nd ed., Paris: Editions L'Harmattan, 1977). On the efforts of Guadeloupeans to advance the memory of Delgrès, who led the resistance against Napoleon's re-imposition of slavery on the free people of the colony, see Laurent Dubois, "Haunting Delgrès", *Radical History Review* 78 (Fall, 2000): 166–77.

24. Eugene Genovese, *From Rebellion to Revolution: Afro-American Slave Revolts in the Making of the Modern World* (Baton Rouge: Louisiana State University Press, 1979), pp. 95–6; Ada Ferrer, "Speaking of Haiti: Slavery, Revolution, and Freedom in Cuban Slave Testimony", in *The World of the Haitian Revolution*, ed. David Patrick Geggus and Norman Fiering (Bloomington, IN: Indiana University Press, 2009), pp. 223–47; João José Reis and Flávio dos Santos Gomes, "Repercussions of the Haitian Revolution in Brazil, 1791–1850", in *The World of the Haitian Revolution*, ed. David Patrick Geggus and Norman Fiering, (Bloomington, IN: Indiana University Press, 2009), pp. 284–313; Robin Blackburn, *The Overthrow of Colonial Slavery, 1776–1848* (London: Verso, 1988), pp. 342–63; Doris Lorraine Garraway, *Tree of Liberty: Culture Legacies of the Haitian Revolution in the Atlantic World* (Charlottesville, VA: University Press of Virginia, 2008).

25. Alfred N. Hunt, *Haiti's Influence on Antebellum America: Slumbering Volcano in the Caribbean* (Baton Rouge, LA: Louisiana State University Press, 1988); Ashli White, *Encountering Revolution: Haiti and the Making of the Early Republic* (Baltimore, MD: Johns Hopkins University Press, 2010).

26. Article 1, Section 9, Clause 1 of the US Constitution (1787) prohibited the federal government from banning the transoceanic slave trade until 1808 (a concession to the pro-slavery South) but by 1807 most states had banned the trade, believing that African slaves were more likely to revolt. The US Act Prohibiting Importation of Slaves (*2 Stat. 426*, 2 Mar. 1807) preceded the British Slave Trade Act (*47 Geo III Sess. 1 c. 36*, 25 Mar. 1807) by only three weeks; British legislators anticipated the American ban and moved to pass the laws in tandem.

27. Serge Daget, *La Répression de la Traite des Noirs au XIXe Siècle: L'Action des Croisières Françaises sur les Côtes Occidentales de l'Afrique (1817–1850)* [The Suppression of the Slave Trade in the Nineteenth Century: The Activities of the French Fleet on the Eastern Coast of Africa (1817–1850)] (Paris: Éditions Karthala, 1997), pp. 36–55; Olivier Pétré-Grenouilleau, *Les Traites négrières: Essai d'histoire globale* [The African Slave Trades: Essay in Global History] (Paris: NRF-Gallimard, 2004), pp. 271–3.

28. The two most important synthetic studies of 19th-century French anti-slavery are: Lawrence C. Jennings, *French Anti-slavery: The Movement for the Abolition of Slavery in France, 1802–1848* (Cambridge and New York: Cambridge University Press, 2000) (henceforth, *FA*) and Nelly Schmidt, *Abolitionnistes de l'esclavage et réformateurs des colonies, 1820–1851: Analyse et documents* [Abolitionists of Slavery and Reformers of the Colonies, 1820–1851: Analysis and Documents] (Paris: Éditions Karthala, 2000) (henceforth, *AERC*). Jennings offers a chronological study of the French anti-slavery lobby and evolving policy of the French government, while Schmidt's 1,200-page compendium is organized thematically and includes hundreds of pages of transcribed documents from the period.

29. Lawrence C. Jennings, *French Reaction to British Slave Emancipation* (Baton Rouge, LA: Louisiana State University Press, 1988), esp. pp. 96–106, 178–93; Schmidt, *AERC*, p. 83.

30. The baron Victor Guy Duperré had a long military career, from the Revolution through Napoleon and the Restoration, serving in combat in the Antilles and the Mascarenes. Jean-Philippe Zanco, *Dictionnaire des Ministres de la Marine, 1689–1958* [Dictionary of the Ministers of the Navy], Kronos 58 (Paris: SPM, 2011), pp. 263–6.

31. Jennings, *FA*, pp. 30–6, 67–71.

32. Schmidt, *AERC*, pp. 229–66; Stella Pâme, *Cyrille Bissette: Un martyr de la liberté* [Cyrille Bissette: A Martyr for Liberty] (Fort de France: Désormeaux, 1999); Lawrence C. Jennings, "Cyrille Bisette: Radical Black French Abolitionist", *French History* 9, 1 (1995): 48–66; Schmidt, *AERC*, pp. 254–63, and documents, pp. 665–83, 743–84; Chris Bongie,

"*'C'est du papier ou de l'Histoire en marche?*' [Is it [Mere] Paper or is it History in Motion?]: The Revolutionary Compromises of a Martiniquan Homme de Couleur, Cyrille-Charles-Auguste Bissette", *Nineteenth-Century Contexts* 23, 4 (2002): 439–74.

33. Schmidt, *Victor Schœlcher et l'abolition de l'esclavage*; her orientation to the Schœlcher corpus and its archival situations (pp. 319–49) is invaluable. See also Victor Schœlcher, *La correspondance de Victor Schœlcher* [The Correspondence of Victor Schœlcher], ed. Nelly Schmidt (Paris: Maisonneuve et Larose, 1995); Anne Girollet, *Victor Schœlcher abolitionniste et républicain* [Victor Schoelcher, Abolitionist and Republican] (Paris: Éditions Karthala, 1999).

34. Jennings, *FA*, pp. 170–2, 192.

35. David Brion Davis, *Inhuman Bondage: The Rise and Fall of Slavery in the New World* (New York and Oxford: Oxford University Press, 2006), pp. 236–8; Seymour Drescher, *Abolition: A History of Slavery and Antislavery* (Cambridge: Cambridge University Press, 2009), pp. 205–41, *Capitalism and Antislavery: British Mobilization in Comparative Perspective* (New York and Oxford: Oxford University Press, 1987) and "British Way, French Way: Opinion Building and Revolution in the Second French Slave Emancipation", *American Historical Review* 96 (1991): 725–34; Jennings, *FA*, pp. 197–8; Schmidt, *AERC*, pp. 283–95.

36. Jennings, *FA*, pp. 239–40. Schmidt reproduces the text of these petitions in *AERC*, pp. 845–72.

37. Jennings, *FA*, pp. 204–28; Schmidt, *AERC*, pp. 128–37.

38. Schmidt, *AERC*, pp. 319–86; Schmidt, *Victor Schœlcher et l'abolition de l'esclavage*, pp. 101–48; Jennings, *FA*, pp. 273–84. The text of the decree, consisting of nine articles, can be found in Schmidt, *AERC*, pp. 979–81. One set of laws addressed the living and working conditions for former slaves: new colonial institutions would be established to care for aged, disabled and orphan slaves; new compulsory and tuition-free primary schools would be established to educate the children of the newly freed; a new tribunal system, based upon term-appointed juries, would hear labour and civil disputes, and punish those who resisted the new labour regime. Though slavery was abolished, labour was compulsory and wage-based; all vagabonds would be subject to arrest and required to join "national work-teams [*ateliers nationaux*]". A second group of laws prepared to address colonial debt: each colony would establish savings' banks and new detailed regulations sought to manage mortgages, foreclosure and seizure of assets. Taxes were levied on distilled liquor and wines. A third set of laws concerned the political rights of colonists and former slaves now that universal male suffrage had been declared for France: all adult males "of French nationality" were

eligible to elect representatives to the National Assembly; colonial councils were abolished; and freedom of the press was declared for the colonies. Schmidt, *AERC*, pp. 331–7; texts of these decrees can be found in ibid., pp. 981–1003.

39. Algerian slaveholders were exempted from the government's indemnization plan. Jennings, *FA*, p. 282; Schmidt, *AERC*, pp. 323–7; Alain Buffon, "L'Indemnisation des planteurs après l'abolition de l'esclavage" [The Planters' Compensation after the Abolition of Slavery], *Bulletin de la Société d'histoire de la Guadeloupe* (1986): 67–8; M.A.I. Fischer-Blanchet, "Les travaux de la commission de l'indemnité coloniale en 1848" [The Efforts of the Commission of Colonial Compensation in 1848], *Espaces caraïbes* (1983): 37–56; Laurent Blériot, "La loi d'indemnisation des colons du 30 avril 1849, aspects juridiques" [The Law for the Compensation of Colonists of 30 April 1849, Juridical Aspects], *Revue historique des Mascareignes* 2, 2 (2000): 147–65.

40. Oruno D. Lara, *La liberté assassinée. Guadeloupe, Guyane, Martinique, La Réunion, 1848–1856* [Freedom Murdered: Guadeloupe, Guiana, Martinique, Réunion, 1848–1856] (Paris: L'Harmattan, 2005). See also Nelly Schmidt, *La France a-t-elle aboli l'esclavage? Guadeloupe, Martinique, Guyane, 1830–1935* [Did France Abolish Slavery? Guadeloupe, Martinique, Guyana, 1830–1935] (Paris: Perrin, 2009); Jennings, *FA*, pp. 282–3. For the aftermath of emancipation in specific colonies, see Christine Chivallon, *Espace et identité à la Martinique*; Pago, *Les Femmes et la liquidation du système esclavagiste*; Fallope, *Esclaves et citoyens* (Guadaloupe), pp. 346–93; Sudel Fuma, *L'abolition de l'esclavage à La Réunion: Histoire d'un insertion des 62,000 affranchis de 1848 dans la société réunionnaise* [The Abolition of Slavery in Réunion: History of an Insertion of 62,000 Freedmen into Reunionais Society] (Saint-André, La Réunion: G.R.A.H.TER and Ocean Éditions, 1998); see also Françoise Pitou and Claude Wanquet, *Les affranchis et les engagés à la Réunion (1848–1870)* [Freedmen and the Indentured in Reunion (1848–1870)] (N.p., 1989); Yvan Combeau, *La Réunion républicaine: l'avènement de la IIe et de la IIIe République 1848/1870* [Republican Réunion: The Arrival of the Second and the Third Republic, 1848/1870] (Le Port, La Réunion: Les Deux mondes, 1996); Edmond Maestri, *Esclavage Et Abolitions Dans L'Océan Indien: 1723–1860, Actes Du Colloque De Saint-Denis de La Réunion, 4–8 Décembre 1998* [Slavery and Abolitions in the Indian Ocean: 1723–1860, Proceedings of the Colloquium of Saint-Denis of Réunion, 4–8 Dec. 1998] (Paris: l'Harmattan, 2002); Gérard Thélier and Pierre Aliber, *Le grand livre de l'esclavage: des résistances et de l'abolition* [The Big Book of Slavery: Of Resistances and Abolition] (Réunion: Orphie, 2000).

41. Martin A. Klein, *Slavery and Colonial Rule in French West Africa* (New York: Cambridge University Press, 1998), pp. 19–26. See also Roger Pasquier, "A propos de l'émancipation des esclaves au Sénégal en 1848" [Concerning the Emancipation of Slaves in Senegal in 1848], *Revue française d'histoire d'outre-mer* 54 (1967): 188–208; François Renault, "L'Abolition de l'esclavage au Sénégal: L'Attitude de l'Administration française (1848–1905)" [The Abolition of Slavery in Senegal: The Attitude of the French Administration (1848–1905)], *Revue française d'histoire d'outre-mer* 58 (1971): 5–81; Trevor Getz, *Slavery and Reform in West Africa: Toward Emancipation in Nineteenth-Century Senegal and the Gold Coast* (Athens: Ohio University Press, 2004); Mamadou Badji, "L'abolition de l'esclavage au Sénégal: entre plasticité du droit colonial et respect de l'Etat de droit" [The Abolition of Slavery in Senegal: Between the Elasticity of Colonial Law and Respect for the State of Law], *Droit et Cultures* 52 (2006): 239–74; and Benjamin Claude Brower, "Rethinking Abolition in Algeria: Slavery and the 'Indigenous Question'", *Cahiers d'Études Africaines* 195, 3 (2009): 805–28.

42. David Brion Davis, *The Problem of Slavery in Western Culture* (Ithaca, NY: Cornell University Press, 1966); *The Problem of Slavery in the Age of Revolution, 1770–1823* (Ithaca and London: Cornell University Press, 1975). His most recent synthesis, *Inhuman Bondage: The Rise and Fall of Slavery in the New World* (New York and Oxford: Oxford University Press, 2006), situates slavery and emancipation in the US within the wider contexts of Atlantic and world slavery.

43. In addition to Blackburn, *Overthrow of Colonial Slavery* (op. cit.), see his *The Making of New World Slavery: From the Baroque to the Modern, 1492–1800* (London: Verso, 1997) and *The American Crucible: Slavery, Emancipation and Human Rights* (London: Verso, 2011). This last shows how new conceptions of human rights, framed by the Haitian Revolution, permeated subsequent Atlantic and world political struggles.

44. Frederick Cooper, Thomas C. Holt and Rebecca J. Scott, *Beyond Slavery: Explorations of Race, Labor, and Citizenship in Postemancipation Societies* (Chapel Hill, NC: University of North Carolina Press, 2000); Howard Temperley, ed., *After Slavery: Emancipation and its Discontents* (London: Frank Cass, 2000).

45. Keila Grinberg and Sue Peabody, eds., *Slavery, Freedom and the Law in the Atlantic World* (New York: Bedford/St Martin's, 2007).

46. Seymour Drescher, *Abolition: A History of Slavery and Antislavery* (New York and Cambridge: Cambridge University Press, 2009). Drescher's earlier works were also influential. *Econocide: British Slavery in the Era of Abolition*, published in 1977 (2nd ed., Chapel Hill, NC: University of North Carolina Press, 2010), challenged Eric William's contention that slavery was unprofitable to Britain at the time that it was abolished.

Capitalism and Antislavery: British Mobilization in Comparative Perspective (New York and Oxford: Oxford University Press, 1987) analysed the role of religion and political movements in the widespread popular mobilization to combat slavery in Britain, contrasting it with France's more elite approach, mostly conducted within government circles. *The Mighty Experiment: Free Labor versus Slavery in British Emancipation* (New York and Oxford: Oxford University Press, 2002) considered the aftermath of Britain's 1833 Emancipation Act, arguing that the compensation programme offered to colonial planters in British colonies could in no way compete with the thriving sugar production of its chief rivals, Brazil and Cuba.

47. Ada Ferrer, "Haiti, Free Soil, and Antislavery in the Revolutionary Atlantic", *The American Historical Review* 117, 1 (2012): 40–66. See also Blackburn, *American Crucible*; Nick Nesbitt, *Universal Emancipation: The Haitian Revolution and the Radical Enlightenment* (Charlottesville: University of Virginia Press, 2008); and Mimi Sheller, *Democracy After Slavery: Black Publics and Peasant Radicalism in Haiti and Jamaica* (Gainesville, FL: University Press of Florida, 2000).

48. Mimi Sheller, "Sword-Bearing Citizens: Militarism and Manhood in Nineteenth-Century Haiti", *Plantation Society in the Americas* 4, 2–3 (1997): 233–78; Benjamin Quarles, *The Negro in the American Revolution* (Chapel Hill, NC: University of North Carolina Press, 1961), pp. 42–50; Silvia R. Frey, *Water from the Rock: Black Resistance in a Revolutionary Age* (Princeton, NJ: Princeton University Press, 1991), pp. 55–6; Christopher Leslie Brown and Philip D. Morgan, ed., *Arming Slaves: From Classical Times to the Modern Age* (New Haven, CT: Yale University Press, 2006); Peter Blanchard, *Under the Flags of Freedom: Slave Soldiers and the Wars of Independence in Spanish South America* (Pittsburgh, PA: University of Pittsburgh Press, 2008).

49. Alyssa Goldstein Sepinwall, "The Spector of Saint-Domingue: American and French Reactions to the Haitian Revolution", in *The World of the Haitian Revolution*, ed. David Patrick Geggus and Norman Fiering (Bloomington, IN: Indiana University Press, 2009), pp. 317–38.

50. Drescher, *Abolition*, pp. 205–66; see also Jennings, *French Reaction* (op. cit.); Christopher Leslie Brown, *Moral Capital: Foundations of British Abolitionism* (Chapel Hill, NC: The University of North Carolina Press, 2006).

51. Gary B. Nash and Jean R. Soderlund, *Freedom by Degrees: Emancipation in Pennsylvania and its Aftermath* (New York and Oxford: Oxford University Press, 1991); George Reid Andrews, *Afro-Latin America, 1800–2000* (New York and Oxford: Oxford University Press, 2004), pp. 64–5; Rebecca J. Scott, *Slave Emancipation in Cuba: The Transition to Free Labor, 1860–1899* (Princeton, NJ: Princeton University Press,

1985; 2nd ed., Pittsburgh, PA: University of Pittsburgh Press, 2000), Chapter 3; Peabody and Grinberg, *Slavery, Freedom and the Law*, pp. 74–7, 121–3, 156–61.

52. Drescher borrows the term "delegalization" from Howard Temperley, "The Delegalisation of Slavery in British India", *Slavery and Abolition: A Journal of Slave and Post-Slave Studies* 21, 2 (2000): 169–87 and Suzanne Miers, "Slavery to Freedom in Sub-Saharan Africa: Expectations and Realities", *Slavery and Abolition: A Journal of Slave and Post-Slave Studies* 21, 2 (2000): 237–64. Drescher's analytical framework emphasizes the historical origins of this process with the Free Soil principle that emerged in northern Europe, especially England and France, but also the Netherlands, in the 16th and 17th centuries. See also *Slavery and Abolition, Special Issue: Free Soil in the Atlantic World* 32, 3 (2011).

53. Martin A. Klein, *Slavery and Colonial Rule in French West Africa* (New York: Cambridge University Press, 1998).

54. Igor Kopytoff and Suzanne Miers, "'African Slavery' as an Institution of Marginality", in *Slavery in Africa: Historical and Anthropological Perspectives*, ed. Suzanne Mieres and Igor Kopytoff (Madison, WI: University of Wisconsin Press, 1977), pp. 3–81.

55. The text of this decree can be found in Schmidt, *AERC*, pp. 991–2.

56. For the most comprehensive study of the recent history of the memory of French emancipation, see Christine Chivallon, *L'esclavage, du souvenir à la mémoire: contribution à une anthropologie de la Caraïbe* [Slavery, from Recollection to Memory] (Paris: Éditions Karthala, 2012). See also Prosper Eve, *Le 20 décembre à la Réunion et sa célébration: du déni à la réhabilitation (1848–1980)* [20 December in Réunion and its Celebration: From Denial to Rehabilitation (1848–1980)] (Paris: L'Harmattan, 2000); Catherine A. Reinhardt, *Claims to Memory: Beyond Slavery and Emancipation in the French Caribbean* (New York: Berghahn Books, 2006); Jacques Adelaide-Merlande, "*La Commission d'abolition de l'esclavage*" [The Abolition of Slavery Commission], *Bulletin de la Société d'histoire de la Guadeloupe* 53–54 (1982): 3–34; Chris Bongie, "A Street Named Bissette: Nostalgia, Memory, and the Cent-Cinquantenaire of the Abolition of Slavery in Martinique (1848–1998)", *South Atlantic Quarterly* 100, 1 (2001): 215–57.

57. Alice Conklin, *A Mission to Civilize: The Republican Idea of Empire in France and West Africa, 1895–1930* (Stanford, CA: Stanford University Press, 1997).

58. Cécile Vidal, ed., *Être et se revendiquer Français dans le monde atlantique: Nation, empire et race (XVIe–mi-XIXe siècle)* [French? The Nation and Debate between the Colonies and the Metropole (16th–19th Centuries)] (Paris: EHESS, 2014).

59. There is a parallel strain in the historiography of emancipation which points to a series of colonial slave revolts in the early 19th century as hastening the emancipation acts in the metropole. See, for example, Gelien Matthews, *Caribbean Slave Revolts and the British Abolitionist Movement* (Baton Rouge, LA: Louisiana University Press, 2004). Interestingly, Matthews completed her PhD at Hull, one of the cities that Kumie Inose highlights in her article in this volume.

60. See, for example, Tricia Danielle Keaton, T. Denean Sharpley-Whiting and Tyler Edward Stovall, ed., *Black France/France Noire: The History and Politics of Blackness* (Durham, NC: Duke University Press, 2012) and Dominic Thomas, *Africa and France: Postcolonial Cultures, Migration, and Racism* (Bloomington, IN: Indiana University Press, 2013).

CHAPTER 3

What was Remembered and What was Forgotten in Britain in the Bicentenary of the Abolition of the Slave Trade?

Kumie Inose

Introduction

Around 2007, special events were held across Britain in commemoration of the abolition of the transatlantic slave trade in 1807. Commemorations had already begun in a countdown to the bicentenary. A growing number of novels, with slavery as their theme, were published, and several films, plays and television dramas, whether fictionalized or documentary, were produced based on these novels.[1] Books with "slave trade" or "slavery" in their title were published, and academic historical journals including *Slavery and Abolition: A Journal of Slave and Post-Slave Studies*, newspapers such as the *Guardian* and the *Independent*, and magazines for lay readers such as the *BBC History Magazine* published special commemorative issues.[2] Not only in Britain, but also among the countries and regions once involved in the transatlantic slave trade, the bicentenary of its abolition by Britain seemed to trigger a dialogue between the past and the present in today's globalized world.[3]

Commemorative exhibitions in public places such as museums, galleries or town halls were everywhere in Britain in 2007. It is perhaps surprising that, besides the three main ports that played such a significant role during the heyday of the slave trade, namely Liverpool, Bristol and London, the museums and galleries of many other cities and towns in the United Kingdom, notably in northern England, were ready to explore the relationship of those cities and towns to the history of the slave trade.[4] These exhibitions were easy to access, open to the public, with admission free in most cases and had their own duration, corresponding to one of the three peaks of the bicentenary. I will say more on this later. With many using the latest computer technology to appeal to visitors, these exhibitions are worth noting to see what is to be remembered and what is to be forgotten in the present as a memory of the abolition of the slave trade 200 years ago. They certainly varied in form and content and had characteristics of their own, but it is not difficult to find some common trends amongst them. In them we can identify cover-ups, manipulation and efforts to rewrite and re-edit the memory of abolition.

This article analyses what was remembered and what was forgotten or invented in the British bicentenary exhibitions,[5] and hopefully, it will identify the broader meaning of abolition in world history.

Emphasis on Slaves' Initiative

Regardless of their theme, exhibitions in museums and galleries mirror the times and global trends. They do not treat academic research with irreverence either. On the contrary, exhibitions in museums and galleries usually reflect some scholarly learning, even in a modified way, because of the involvement of scholars and researchers as editors or supervisors. The exhibitions commemorating the abolition of the slave trade in 1807 were no exception.

During the countdown to the bicentenary, a particular atmosphere was gradually, but more rapidly than before, created to determine how the abolition of the slave trade in 1807 was to be remembered.[6] A decision of the World Conference against Racism (WCAR) organized by UNESCO and held in Durban, South Africa in 2001 strongly influenced the atmosphere surrounding the bicentenary. The WCAR acknowledged slavery and the slave trade, and particularly transatlantic slavery, as a crime against humanity.[7] Since then, the tendency to see slavery and the slave trade in terms of humanity and human rights has increased. The global community has come to connect slavery with contemporary concepts such as racial discrimination, responsibility for colonialism and historical reconciliation or apology. Consequently, in the early 21st century, the abolition of the slave trade in 1807 and the Slavery Abolition Act of 1833 have come to be regarded, more than previously, not as a one-sided story in which benevolent Europeans who regarded themselves as being on a civilizing mission conferred freedom upon benighted slaves, but as an interactive project with the active participation of slaves and former slaves.

We can see this trend clearly in the message of the International Slavery Museum in Liverpool. When it opened on the third floor of the Merseyside Maritime Museum in Albert Dock on 23 August 2007, "the International Day for the Remembrance of the Slave Trade and of its Abolition",[8] a banner in front of the museum proclaimed that "Abolition was not given, but we fought", which urges us to reconsider the abolition movement from a different perspective, through the eyes not of the whites but of the slaves, in a narrative we are not used to. At the entrance to the museum is an information board entitled "An African Story", which describes the conceptual underpinnings of this museum as follows:

> The story of transatlantic slavery is a fundamental and tragic human story that must be told and retold, and never be forgotten. Africa and its peoples are central to this story. This section of the museum explores some threads in the complex weave of Africa's history.[9]

With an emphasis on slaves' initiative in the abolition, the exhibitions at the International Slavery Museum, like many other commemorative exhibitions, asked a fundamental question: who abolished the slave trade, and subsequently slavery?

The situation in 2007 seems very different from that during the centenary of the abolition of the slave trade in 1907 at Wilberforce House in Hull, and it differs much even from the atmosphere in the early 1990s.[10]

Two Narratives of Abolition: Humanitarian and Economic Decline

That question of who abolished the slave trade, and subsequently slavery, was once meaningless because the answer was obvious to anyone in Britain: William Wilberforce was responsible for "An Act for the Abolition of the Slave Trade", which received the Royal Assent on

25 March 1807. A year before the 1907 centenary, for example, when Wilberforce House was opened as a museum in his hometown Hull, it was taken for granted that the abolition was a splendid achievement accomplished by him and his group known as the Clapham Sect or "the saints". In Victorian days, towards the height of Britain's global empire, the dominant image had portrayed the abolition of the slave trade as a philanthropic contribution by the British (that is, the whites) and Britain's Parliament for the sake of the non-white slaves in their colonies. At the same time, British imperial government continued using "anti-slavery" as a political wedge in expanding its rule in Africa, Asia and the Middle East, as we shall see later.[11]

It was an Oxford historian, W.E.H. Lecky, who harnessed anti-slavery sentiment to British morality. In his *History of European Morals from Augustus to Charlemagne* (1869), Lecky insisted that: "The unweary, unostentatious and inglorious crusade of England against slavery may probably be regarded as among the three or four perfectly virtuous pages comprised in the history of nations."[12] Sir Reginald Coupland, another Oxford British colonial historian, confirmed Lecky's phrase in his book, *The British Anti-Slavery Movement* (1933),[13] which was published to celebrate the centenary of the Slavery Abolition Act.

Thus, the abolition of the slave trade and slavery, together with the abolition movement in British society, was taken primarily to be a product of the white Briton's own virtues. Abolition was the act of a humane, benevolent and self-sacrificing British people, especially so for those belonging to the upper and middle classes. This sense of morality transformed a general anti-slavery sentiment since the mid-18th century into an effective, practical anti-slavery movement in the late 18th to early 19th century. This kind of humanitarian narrative may be what the British people had long been used to.[14]

It is well known that Eric Williams rebutted this humanitarian narrative and established a new theory that claimed abolition reflected purely economic concerns. In his *Capitalism and Slavery* (1944), Williams argues that it was not the humanitarian efforts of British citizens such as Wilberforce and Thomas Clarkson but the changing economic circumstances in the Caribbean—decline of sugar production—that led Britain to abolish the slave trade, and later, to enact the Slavery Abolition Act. Williams also points to the inconsistent response of politicians such as William Pitt the Younger, prime minister from 1783–1801 and 1804–06. Pitt the Younger was famous for supporting the abolition of the slave trade, but he suppressed the slave revolt in Santo Domingo in the early 1790s because of Britain's commercial rivalry with France. Williams argued that such actions were hypocritical.[15]

Williams' "decline thesis" has been controversial ever since its publication and has long been criticized, for example by Roger Anstey and Seymour Drescher, since the 1960s.[16] Although Williams' thesis has done much to stimulate the debate on transatlantic slavery and its abolition, it seems to have played no significant role in the commemorative exhibitions in 2007.

On the other hand, a humanitarian narrative was also eclipsed in the bicentenary exhibitions. Though the shadows of imperialism and colonialism have not entirely been cast off and still influence contemporary thinking and attitudes, a completely Eurocentric interpretation of abolition is no longer valid in postcolonial British society. Most bicentenary exhibitions were curated together with local non-white communities and backed by Anti-Slavery International, whose origins lie in the Anti-Slavery Society formed by Thomas Clarkson and other abolitionists in 1839, just after the Slavery Abolition Act had been enacted. These partnerships partly determine what is to be remembered and what is to be forgotten in the context of the early 21st century, as we discuss later in this article.

As British society is becoming more and more postcolonial, some serious corrections are needed in the interpretation of the past as well as in the present situation surrounding former immigrants. In parallel with this, academics have started rereading historical facts and discovering and rediscovering forgotten things and individuals.

David Brion Davis' pioneering study, *The Problem of Slavery in Western Culture* (1966), shows how slavery—which existed throughout the globe for millennia—came to be considered wrong in intellectual and cultural terms by certain individuals in Britain, France and their American colonies. Christopher Leslie Brown's *Moral Capital* goes a step beyond Davis' work to explore why anti-slavery sentiment suddenly developed into practice in the late 1780s and how British people came to regard the slave trade as inhumane, horrid and shameful enough for it to be banned by the Parliament. He argues that the profound change in public anti-slavery sentiment was a response to Britain's defeat in the American War of Independence (1775–83). Anti-slavery forged a common cause between people depressed by the failure of colonial America to reform society and improve morality. Abolition of the slave trade became an important indicator of British national identity, especially in contrast to the perceived corruption of American slaveholders.[17]

During the early 19th century, the idea of anti-slavery was firmly linked to an emergent nationalism, which Victorians were to adopt as a vital sense of moral superiority over other civilizations and which fuelled the expansion of its empire even as the memory of Wilberforce and Clarkson faded.

Anti-slavery and British Diplomacy

In the same year in which the Act for the Abolition of the Slave Trade was enacted (1807), the African Institution was established to monitor observance of this Act.[18] British leadership was forcefully demonstrated by the establishment of a naval base in Freetown, Sierra Leone to keep watch on and intercept slave ships, and to liberate slaves and settle them there.[19] The slave trade under the British flag did decrease through the efforts of the British navy.

The 1807 Act for the Abolition of the Slave Trade was enacted during the Napoleonic Wars, when British interests were seriously threatened. British people in the West Indies, both military and civilian, might have quickly realized the merit of suppressing foreign slave traders lest Britain's ban should shift the slave trade to the ships of other nations.[20] After the declaration of war against France and Britain's subsequent victory over the French, it seemed natural for the British government to negotiate new treaties forcing the defeated nations (France, but also Spain and Portugal) to adopt legislation banning their own imperial transoceanic slave trades. The Congress of Vienna (1814–15) condemned the slave trade as counter to the "principles of humanity and universal morality", though unfortunately this had no practical or immediate effect on furthering moves to ban slavery itself.[21]

The abolition of the slave trade also accorded with transatlantic and colonial affairs. During this period, abolitionists in Britain urged their government to make suppressing the slave trade a focus of diplomacy and treaty-making, establishing, as a result, an anti-slavery international network with Britain at its centre.[22] These treaties created the world's first international human-rights courts, to confiscate ships engaged in the illegal slave trade and to liberate Africans.

The British government thus began to use anti-slavery as a lever in international relations and imperial expansion. The British government promoted the alternative trade, the "legitimate trade", and persuaded African chiefs to substitute this for the slave trade. This promotion of "legitimate trade" enabled the British government to intervene in local matters and extend its imperial rule on the African continent. For instance, the journal of Sir Frederic Forbes, a British naval officer in command of the *Bonetta*, suggested how "legitimate trade" became the raison d'être for expanding British influence on the King of Dahomey in West Africa, whose kingdom had thrived owing to the trade in slaves with European countries. Forbes' activities there ended with the rescue of a local chief's young daughter, a victim of the slave trade who had been captured by Dahomey; in 1850, she was renamed Sara Forbes Bonetta by Captain Forbes. Her subsequent life in England, raised as a goddaughter by Queen Victoria, might have been taken to illustrate the benevolence and humanitarianism of the expanding British Empire.[23]

Ethnicity and Gender as Aspects of Abolitionism

There were, in fact, two stages in Britain's abolition of slavery within the empire: first, the abolition of the slave trade in 1807, and then the abolition of slavery itself in the 1833 Slavery Abolition Act. In one sense, the former was more radical because it opened up the path from anti-slavery ideology or sentiment against slavery to a definite movement for the abolition of slavery.[24] These two were not naturally interwoven.

Ever since the development of an anti-slavery movement in Britain, politicians had thought of abolition as being a gradual process. This was evident in the official name of the most prominent society in this emancipation process: the Society for the Mitigation and *Gradual* Abolition of the State of Slavery throughout the British Dominions [emphasis added].[25] It implied that the organization aimed at improving the working and living conditions of slaves and ensuring the gradual abolition of slavery, with due consideration being given to and compensation paid for the loss incurred by the planters. It was during that period, which extended more than 20 years, that abolitionism became popular to such a degree that we can trace to it the origins of a grassroots movement that continues to exist today.

It was this two-stage process that gave British abolitionism its unique character compared with abolitionism in France, as Sue Peabody points out in Chapter 2 of this volume. It is important to note that, like French emancipation, progress was spurred by a sudden change in public opinion, an abrupt increase in anti-slavery activism in the late 1820s to the early 1830s. It resulted directly from the "democratization" of British society, and the abolition of slavery in 1833 should be seen as one of a series of dramatic and progressive achievements during that period.[26]

It was during this period of social and political turmoil following the 1830 July Revolution in France that cooperation between British and French abolitionists was built and developed, as Peabody notes. British abolitionists, working with those in France, the US and other countries, tried to extend their network for abolition, and as a result, in June 1840 London hosted the first World Anti-Slavery Convention.[27]

Recent research has emphasized that the process of popularizing abolitionism corresponded with the rise of women's rights activism.[28] Ever since the anti-slavery campaign began in British society, women had been taking an active role in efforts to abolish the slave trade, as Clare Midgley has vividly described,[29] by boycotting sugar and signing petitions to Parliament in the early 1790s. In this process, women, especially from middle-class families, fostered political interests and began campaigning for their own neglected rights. After the 1833 Slavery Abolition Act and the reorganization of the Anti-Slavery Society in 1839, British women turned their eyes to the abolition of slavery in the US and developed transatlantic sisterhood in cooperation with American women activists in this field.[30] It is well-known that in the 1840s Harriet Beecher Stowe, author of *Uncle Tom's Cabin*, was invited more than twice to Britain by the women's section of the Anti-Slavery Society in Birmingham and Glasgow respectively.[31]

Birmingham was noted as a centre of the sugar boycott in the 1790s and famous for women's participation in that boycott, as was clearly shown in the bicentenary exhibition at the Birmingham Museum and Art Gallery. It also boasted a special exhibition representing Olaudah Equiano (known as Gustavus Vassa before he changed his name) during the third peak of the bicentenary exhibitions in 2007, as we will find out later. Neither, however, particularly mentions the hardship of slave women, nor the names of particular slave women.[32]

In relation to slave women, who had long been disregarded by the anti-slavery movement, a notable exhibition was the special exhibition in Kenwood House, London: "Slavery and Justice: The Legacies of Lord Mansfield and Dido Elizabeth Belle". Dido was an illegitimate daughter of Sir John Lindsay, a naval officer, and an enslaved African woman named Maria; she lived with Lindsay's uncle, the first Earl of Mansfield, who was famous for his judgement in the case of an escaped slave, known as Somerset's Case (1772). Dido was the subject of a famous painting of 1779 attributed to Johann Zoffany (a German neoclassical painter), with her white cousin, Elizabeth, but her personal history had long been forgotten by the time the painting was moved to Scotland from Kenwood House. Her status had been ambiguous while she was in Lord Mansfield's household, evidenced by the few references to her. Even in the bicentenary exhibition, her life with Lord Mansfield, as well as her life after leaving Kenwood House, was still ambiguous, though this ambiguity inspired plays and films during and after the bicentenary celebrations.[33]

Three Peaks in the Bicentenary Celebrations

In light of the academic discussions and research being conducted, both narratives relating to the cause of abolition, humanitarian and economic, underwent revision. What kind of narrative did the British people get? The three peaks in the commemorations that took place to mark the 1807 ban might tell us something about it.

As already mentioned, there were three peak dates in the bicentenary exhibitions: 25 March, 23 August and throughout October. Each date had its own symbolic exhibition in accordance with the significance of that date: 25 March at the Wilberforce House Museum in Hull; 23 August at the International Slavery Museum in Liverpool; and "Equiano" at Birmingham Museum and Art Gallery for the Black History Month of October (though the duration of each was longer than a single day or month).

On 25 March 1807 the British Parliament passed the Act for the Abolition of the Slave Trade, the campaign for which had been led by William Wilberforce, Member of Parliament for Hull, with the support of the Quakers and of an evangelical group within the Anglican Church called the Clapham Sect.[34] The 2007 exhibition at Wilberforce House in Hull represented the bicentenary in terms of human rights.[35] In 1980, Hull had twinned with Freetown, Sierra Leone, a

British naval base, in order to commemorate the 1807 Act, "to promote friendship and strengthen commercial, educational and cultural links".[36] Thus the Abolition Act was recalled in the city's tradition.

Controversially, the British government celebrated the abolition of the slave trade on 25 March 2007,[37] and Prime Minister Tony Blair gave a memorial speech, carefully avoiding offering any apology for the enslavement of Africans and their descendants and going no further than "express[ing] our deep sorrow and regret". A complete apology would have implied responsibility for the actions by Britain's citizens in perpetrating the slave trade and the enslavement of millions of Africans, and perhaps a recognition of the benefits and privileges that these activities had conferred on modern (white) Britons, a responsibility and a recognition which he perhaps wished to avoid.

Two days later, on 27 March, during a memorial service at Westminster Abbey, Toyin Agbetu, an activist member of Ligali (a pan-African human rights organization based in Britain), suddenly stood up from his seat and stepped forward to a position just 10 feet from where the Queen was sitting, and said to her: "You should be ashamed. We should not be here. This is an insult to us. I want all the Christians who are Africans to walk out of here with me!"[38] Outside the abbey, he told reporters that the ceremony was an insult to black people in Britain because there was no mention of the African slaves who had fought for freedom.[39] The effect of his protest was, however, weakened in the post-9/11 atmosphere and the "war on terrorism". Newspaper headlines framed Agbetu's action as a threat to the Queen's safety, claiming: "if this guy had had a bomb in his bag or a gun in his belt, it would have been a catastrophe".[40] Agbetu's intervention, though controversial, forced the world to realize Britain's complicity in slavery and the slave trade rather than just its role in the abolition process. As a result, during the bicentenary events, even during the first peak, the subject of slaves and former slaves seemed to assume a larger focus than simply Wilberforce.[41]

The bicentenary commemoration reached its second peak on 23 August 2007. UNESCO had earlier declared 23 August to be the "International Day for the Remembrance of the Slave Trade and its Abolition" in commemoration of the slave revolt in Santo Domingo (now Haiti and the Dominican Republic), which ultimately played a crucial role in the British abolition of the transatlantic slave trade as well as in Haiti's independence in 1804.[42]

The opening of the International Slavery Museum in Liverpool on 23 August 2007 was a symbol of the second peak. The city of Liverpool had been Britain's most profitable centre in the days of the transatlantic slave trade just prior to abolition. Although other museums hold temporary or permanent exhibits on slavery and emancipation,[43] this is the only museum in the world that bears the word "slavery" in its name. Throughout this museum, the centrality, or initiative, of Africans and their descendants in the Atlantic World is clearly shown. For example, one panel asks visitors: "What does it mean to be Black British, African American or of African descent in other parts of the world?" It goes on to assert that

> Cultural identity is important to everyone, but can be difficult to define—it is not just about the colour of our skin. It is also about our birthplace, our nationhood, our experiences, our history. Transatlantic slavery has shaped the identity of many people from across the African Diaspora.

Here we find another key concept in the bicentenary exhibitions: the identity of the slaves and their ancestors living in contemporary Britain. Again, the leading actor in the process to ban the slave trade was cast not from among whites but from among non-whites.

The third peak was in Black History Month, in October in Britain. Black History Month, which started in the United States as "Negro History Week" in February 1926, expanded in the 1970s to be reorganized under the name we now know. It is an annual observance in remembrance of key people and events in the history of the African diaspora. Though in February in the case of the US and Canada, the UK celebrates Black History Month in October to coincide with the start of the new school year, and in 2007 it constituted the last peak in the bicentenary exhibitions.[44]

The exhibition "Equiano: Enslavement, Resistance and Abolition" at the Birmingham Museum and Art Gallery was also held at this time. This clearly reveals how exhibitions connected with Black History Month paid more attention to the slaves and their efforts to change the brutal world they had to face daily. Based on Equiano's autobiography, *Interesting Narrative of the Life of Olaudah Equiano, or Gustavus Vassa, the African* (1789), and using the latest technologies of speech recognition, the exhibition represented enslaved Africans, forcibly and violently cut off from their homeland, as the protagonists.

It is interesting that the museum chose to accompany a text explaining Equiano's change of name with a newspaper article by Kwame Kwei-Armah, a British actor and playwright who had changed his name from Ian Roberts at the age of 19 after tracing his ancestors and discovering his African roots in Ghana.[45] Here, we can clearly see the organizers' intention to set "Equiano" in Black History Month.

New Strategy: Reflecting on the Past, Looking to the Future

Every peak in the commemoration had its own meaning. But in linking these three peaks together we can easily imagine a narrative that differs from the humanitarianism or economic narrative we are used to, namely a narrative of the slaves who fought for and achieved the abolition of the slave trade through their own will and power. In this context, it is useful to point out two things that most of the exhibitions in 2007 seemed to have in common.

First, joining the bicentenary celebrations was perceived as an opportunity for the local government to redevelop its city or town, as the motto of the Home Office adequately suggested: "Reflecting on the past, looking to the future".[46] Liverpool is a good example in this regard. Liverpool was registered as a World Heritage Site in 2004 and was named European Capital of Culture in 2008 because of its tangible efforts to face the dark side of its history, in this case its role as the main centre of the transatlantic slave trade in Britain. Earlier, in December 1999, Liverpool City Council made the following public and "unreserved apology" for the city's involvement with the trans-atlantic slave trade:

> On behalf of the city, the City Council expresses its shame and remorse for the city's role in this trade in human misery. The City Council makes an unreserved apology for its involvement in the slave trade and the continual effects of slavery on Liverpool's Black community.[47]

Like Liverpool, many cities and towns other than the three main ports for the slave trade joined the bicentenary events and tried to connect their own past with the slave trade and its abolition. This gave the exhibitions in 2007 huge scope for variety, and these variations force us to consider what the 1807 Act means to the inhabitants, and what its context is. Each city (or town) might have selected "what must be remembered and what must be forgotten" from among a variety of facts surrounding the abolition of the slave trade.

Second, in relation to this, it was emphasized that no one living in Britain at that time could escape being involved in the slave trade. Every aspect of British society, even in the daily life of the common people, everything and everyone in those days was touched by the slave trade: materials made for slave ships; food for the crew and slaves; manufactures such as bullets and commodities in exchange for slaves along the African coast; the iron used to chain the enslaved Africans—all these things were manufactured in Britain by British workers and brought in slave ships. Exhibits showed how items had been produced in various places in the British Isles, and tied the people of all classes to the slave trade. At the exhibition in Birmingham, in connection with the enslavement of Equiano, visitors learn how this industrial city has a relationship with the slave trade. "Evidence suggests that in 1765 alone, around 150,000 guns may have been sent out from Birmingham to be traded for enslaved Africans." And "Many of the guns made in Birmingham and traded in Africa for enslaved Africans were poor, un-proofed weapons, which 'burst in the first hand that fires them', and were described as 'maiming muskets'." The message of most bicentenary exhibitions seemed to be that every citizen in Birmingham, like every British person in any other place, had, and should still have, responsibility for the slave trade.

This reminds us of the graffiti on a famous statue dedicated to a local prominent dignitary, Edward Colston (1636–1721), in Bristol in 1998.[48] Colston was famous, in his day, for philanthropic activities and donating money to the poor, sick and orphaned. In the Victorian Age Bristol's citizens were so proud of him that, in 1895, they erected a statue of him in the heart of the city. More than a hundred years later, however, Colston was condemned as a "slave trader", and these two words were smeared on his statue. What he was condemned for in 1998 was the source of the money he donated. He was a leading member of the London-based Royal African Company, a group with an official monopoly of the slave trade during that period. This issue had not been raised either in Colston's days or when the statue was unveiled. The act of remembering and forgetting was clearly different in between, and a new focal point had emerged by the time of the 2007 bicentenary of the abolition of the slave trade. It is no accident that the BBC television dramatization of *A Respectable Trade*, based on Philippa Gregory's novel, aired in 1998, gave a sense of Bristol at the time of the first abolition bill being defeated in 1787.[49]

Why, in 2007, were Britons willing, or at least ready, to recognize their role in slavery and the slave trade?

Affinity between British Identity and Abolitionism

Two types of response are possible to this question: one by those involved in the bicentenary exhibitions and the other by those who supported them. These two have overlapped to determine the direction taken in commemorations to mark the abolition of the slave trade.

Concerning the former, African and African-Caribbean communities were involved in most of those exhibitions. More than 50 years had passed since the arrival, in June 1948, of the *Empire Windrush*, carrying about 500 immigrants from Jamaica. This event triggered a mass influx of non-white population and marked the beginning of the multiracial and multicultural Britain that we observe today. The time of more than half a century is enough for the West Indian immigrants to have acquired their own voice in British society. The bicentenary of the abolition of the slave trade became an opportunity for these non-whites to represent not only their own African origin but also their efforts to be British citizens.[50] The questions repeatedly asked in most of the exhibitions might well be fundamental and essential to them: "Who abolished the slave trade and who emancipated the slaves?"

Most exhibitions, I suggest, assumed the initiative and identity of slaves as their starting point, to such an extent indeed that the International Slavery Museum adopted the phrase "An African Story". In the commemoration process, we can see how African and African-Caribbean inhabitants took up the initiative of slaves in the abolition movement to reread abolitionism as "An African Story" and tried to rewrite "the British Story" of the abolition of the slave trade. In other words, the descendants of the immigrants with African origins who are now a part of British society have appropriated and remade "the British Story".

In this way, their involvement in the bicentenary of the abolition of the slave trade seems to have strengthened the relationship between abolitionism and national identity in Britain. Opposition to slavery was, and is, by no means incompatible with a sense of British national identity, as Christopher Leslie Brown has insisted in his book *Moral Capital*. Abolitionism remained a key component of national identity, along with parliamentary democracy, even in post-colonial Britain.[51] To be British implied that anti-slavery was, and is, *their* mission, as in Victorian days.

The other group, which played a crucial role in promoting an affinity between national identity and abolitionism, is Anti-Slavery International, an organization that supported most of the commemorations in 2007. It was founded in 1839 following the success in abolishing slavery within the British Empire; subsequently, under the name of the British and Foreign Anti-Slavery Society, it continued to campaign against the practice of slavery in other countries as well as in the UK. It adopted its present name, Anti-Slavery International, in 1990 and unveiled its motto: "Today's fight for tomorrow's freedom". It insists that the abolition movement has not yet completed its work, and that abolition is still its mission.

The motto of Anti-Slavery International was evident in the concluding section of most of the abolition exhibitions held in 2007, which was often titled "Modern Slavery". Modern slavery refers to "bonded labour, early and forced marriage, forced labour, slavery by descent, and human trafficking".[52] These customs and activities have not been solely a Third World phenomenon; they have also characterized Europe.[53]

We must be cautious, however, of what is forgotten when there is a close relationship between national identity and the creed of anti-slavery in Britain today. One thing is that opposition to modern slavery quietly identifies the perpetrators as individual Muslims or Muslim countries, such as Sudan and Iraq, thus justifying British opposition, especially after 9/11. Also, it must be remembered that slavery and the slave trade beyond the Atlantic were almost completely neglected or not fully discussed in the exhibitions held in 2007.[54]

Conclusion: Critical Reading in the Flood of Commemoration

We must not forget that the practice of commemoration is largely political, and thus we need to critically examine the past as well as the way in which the past appears today. By focusing on the successful abolition of the transatlantic slave trade in 1807, these exhibitions elided the ways in which British anti-slavery helped justify the expansion of the British Empire in the late 19th and early 20th centuries. A narrative in which abolitionism was conferred upon slaves by philanthropic white Britons was attractive at the 1907 centenary, that is, at the peak of British imperial power. This connection between anti-slavery and the British Empire has been too complicated to commemorate in a world where Britain continues to intervene through military action in the Muslim world. It forged national discussions and a political culture long after the famous abolitionist campaigns of Wilberforce and Thomas Clarkson had faded into memory. It is this anti-slavery sentiment that shaped racist and imperialist prejudices, new forms of forced labour and the expansion of colonial possessions.

Thus, a critical examination of the 2007 commemoration reveals the ways in which postcolonial anti-racist movements have successfully replaced the self-congratulatory message that permeated celebrations in the British Empire 100 years earlier. During Black History Month, at least, black Britons in 2007 properly received credit for their efforts to abolish the forced migration of African slaves to the New World. However, an unremarked "shadow" to modern anti-slavery in Britain is the way it can reinforce a sense of national superiority and feed into a justification to intervene in the societies of people deemed "enemies" by the British government. We must be vigilant about accepting such "histories" uncritically.

Notes

1. Elizabeth Kowaleski Wallace, *The British Slave Trade and Public Memory* (New York: Columbia University Press, 2006); Cora Kaplan and John Oldfield, eds., *Imagining Transatlantic Slavery* (Houndmills: Palgrave Macmillan, 2010).

2. On the analysis of such special features in the mass media, see Geoffrey Cubitt, "Museums and Slavery in Britain: The Bicentenary of 1807", in *Politics of Memory: Making Slavery Visible in the Public Space*, ed. Ana Lucia Araujo (London and New York: Routledge, 2012), pp. 159–77.

3. In terms of commemorations outside Britain, the "Lest We Forget: The Triumph Over Slavery" project is an outstanding example. The exhibition was originally developed in 2004 by the Schomburg Center for Research in Black Culture in cooperation with UNESCO for the 2004 International Year to Commemorate the Struggle against Slavery and its Abolition. Since 19 May 2007, it has travelled within the UK (the

Swiss Cottage Gallery was the first venue for the exhibition) to mark the bicentenary of the abolition of the transatlantic slave trade. Presented in English, French, Portuguese and Spanish, the exhibition has toured internationally in countries such as the Bahamas, Brazil, Ecuador, Jamaica, Senegal, the United Republic of Tanzania and the US. See http://digital.nypl.org/lwf/english/site/flash.html, accessed 15 Feb. 2015.

4. See the list of websites, "2007 Bicentenary of the Abolition of the Slave Trade Act: Calendar of Events", http://www.100greatblackbritons.com/articles/government_plans_for_2007_abolition_celebrations, accessed 15 Feb. 2015.

5. I visited the following museums, galleries and town halls in 2007–08: Wilberforce House Museum, Hull; "Seeing Slavery", Potteries Museums & Art Gallery, Stoke-on-Trent; opening event of the International Slavery Museum, Liverpool; commemorative service at the Church of Our Lady and Saint Nicholas, Liverpool; "Unfair Trade", York Castle Museum; "Revealing Histories: Remembering Slavery", Manchester Museum (University of Manchester); "Blake, Slavery and the Radical Mind", Tate Britain, London; "Breaking the Chains", British Empire and Commonwealth Museum, Bristol; "Enfield and the Transatlantic Slave Trade", Forty Hall, Enfield; "The British Slave Trade: Abolition, Parliament and People", Houses of Parliament, London; "Inhuman Traffic: The Business of the Slave Trade", British Museum, London; "London, Sugar & Slavery", Museum in Docklands, London; "Remembering Slavery", South Shields Museum and Art Gallery, Newcastle-upon-Tyne; "Equiano", Birmingham Museum and Art Gallery; "Slavery and Justice: The Legacies of Lord Mansfield and Dido Belle", Kenwood House, London; "Bitter Sweet: Legacies of Sugar and Slavery in the Caribbean", Harris Museum & Art Gallery, Preston; and "Bombay Africans, 1850–1910", Royal Geographical Society, London.

6. In the case of the National Maritime Museum, see Douglas Hamilton, "Representing Slavery in British Museums: The Challenges of 2007", in *Imagining Transatlantic Slavery*, ed. Kaplan and Oldfield, pp. 127–44.

7. Maria Miguel Sierra, "The World Conference against Racism and the Role of the European NGOs", *European Journal of Migration and Law* 4, 2 (2002): 249–60.

8. UNESCO proposed that the human tragedy of the slave trade should be remembered as the memory of all peoples, and showed its understanding that the beginning of the uprising on the night of 22–23 Aug. 1791 in Santo Domingo (today Haiti and the Dominican Republic) played a crucial role in the abolition of the transatlantic slave trade. The riots in Santo Domingo induced the Maroon War in Barbados in 1795, the lessons of which the British government learned in order to halt bloodshed. Britain was subsequently to take on a leadership role

in abolishing slavery. For further details on slave resistance see, for instance, Karla Gottlieb, *The Mother of Us All: A History of Queen Nanny, Leader of the Windward Jamaican Maroons* (Trenton, NJ: Africa World Press, 1998); Lomarsh Roopnarine, "Maroon Resistance and Settlement on Danish St. Croix", *Journal of Third World Studies* 27, 2 (2010): 89–108.

9. See also the museum's guidebook.

10. Hamilton points out that "despite this century-long tradition, a widespread museum engagement with issues of slavery and abolition took a great deal longer to develop" ("Representing Slavery in British Museums", p. 127).

11. See Richard Huzzey, *Freedom Burning: Anti-Slavery and Empire in Victorian Britain* (New York: Cornell University Press, 2012); Howard Temperley, ed., *After Slavery: Emancipation and its Discontents* (London and Portland: Frank Cass, 2000).

12. W.E.H. Lecky, *A History of European Morals from Augustus to Charlemagne*, vol. 2, 6th ed. (London: Longmans Green, 1884), p. 153.

13. See also Reginald Coupland, *Wilberforce* (Oxford: Oxford University Press, 1923) and "The Abolition of the Slave Trade", in *The Growth of the New Empire, 1783–1870*, ed. J. Holland Rose et al. (Cambridge: Cambridge University Press, 1940).

14. Christopher Leslie Brown, *Moral Capital: Foundations of British Abolitionism* (Chapel Hill, NC: University of North Carolina Press, 2006).

15. Eric Williams, *Capitalism and Slavery* (Chapel Hill, NC: University of North Carolina Press, 1944), pp. 146–50. Brown points out that in addition to emphasizing the economic perspective, Williams stressed this aspect, too. See Brown, *Moral Capital*, pp. 12–8.

16. Roger Anstey, "Capitalism and Slavery: A Critique", *Economic History Review*, 2nd ser. XXI, 2 (1968): 307–20 and *The Atlantic Slave Trade and British Abolition, 1760–1810* (London: Macmillan, 1975); Seymour Drescher, *Econocide: British Slavery in the Era of Abolition* (2nd ed., Chapel Hill, NC: University of North Carolina Press, 2010); Barbara Lewis Solow and Stanley L. Engerman, eds., *British Capitalism and Caribbean Slavery: The Legacy of Eric Williams* (Cambridge: Cambridge University Press, 1987).

17. Brown was a student of David Brion Davis at Yale. See Brown, *Moral Capital*, p. 41, n. 10.

18. For the 20 years of its existence, the African Institution was an antislavery reform group of crucial importance after the abolition of the slave trade. It strongly influenced Britain's diplomatic relations. Its members included royalty, members of parliament and famous abolitionists such as William Wilberforce, Thomas Clarkson and Zachary Macaulay. See Wayne Ackerson, *The African Institution (1807–1827) and*

the *Antislavery Movement in Great Britain* (Lewiston, NY: E. Mellen Press, 2005).

19. Jenny S. Martinez, *The Slave Trade and the Origin of International Human Rights Law* (Oxford: Oxford University Press, 2012).

20. Keith Hamilton and Patrick Salmon, ed., *Slavery, Diplomacy and Empire: Britain and the Suppression of the Slave Trade, 1807–1975* (Brighton: Sussex Academic Press, 2009), pp. 1–19.

21. On this, see Joel Quirk and David Richardson, "Religion, Urbanisation and Anti-Slavery Mobilisation in Britain, 1878–1833", *European Journal of English Studies* 14, 3 (2010): 264; Mike Kaye, "The Development of the Anti-Slavery Movement after 1807", *Parliamentary History* 26 (2007): 238–9.

22. Farida Shaikh, "Judicial Diplomacy: British Officials and the Mixed Commission Courts", in *Slavery, Diplomacy and Empire*, ed. Hamilton and Salmon, pp. 42–64.

23. Frederic E. Forbes, *Dahomey and the Dahomans: Being the Journals of Two Missions to the King of Dahomey, and Residence at His Capital, in the Years 1849 and 1850*, 2 vols (London: Longman, 1851; rpt. London: Frank Cass, 1966), vol. 2, pp. 206–9. For details of Sara's rescue, see Kumie Inose, "Jo-ou ha 'Teikoku no Haha' dattanoka?" [Was the Queen "A Mother of the Empire"?], in *Queen Victoria: Gender, Monarchy, and Representation*, ed. Shizuko Kawamoto and Masaie Matsumura (Kyoto: Minerva-shobo, 2006), pp. 281–332; Walter Dean Myers, *At Her Majesty's Request: An African Princess in Victorian England* (New York: Scholastic Press, 1999).

24. See Brown, *Moral Capital*, pp. 17–30.

25. The idea of gradual abolition was a response to the perceived failure of the French 1794 experiment, which was associated with slave revolt and the subsequent tyranny against slaveholders by the founders of Haiti.

26. The democratization of British society during this period included: the abolition of the Test and Corporation Acts in 1828 and the passing of the Roman Catholic Relief Act (1829), the Metropolitan Police Act (1829) and, following the general election of 1830, the Reform Act (1832), Factory Act (1833), Slavery Abolition Act (1833), Poor Law Amendment Act (1834) and the Municipal Corporations Act (1835). See, for example, Arthur Burns and Joanna Innes, ed., *Rethinking the Age of Reform: Britain 1780–1850* (Cambridge: Cambridge University Press, 2003).

27. Douglas H. Maynard, "The World's Anti-Slavery Convention of 1840", *The Mississippi Valley Historical Review* 47, 3 (1960): 452–71. In relation to the women's movement, see Kathryn Kish Sklar, "'Women Who Speak for an Entire Nation': American and British Women Compared

at the World Anti-Slavery Convention, London, 1840", *Pacific History Review* 59, 4 (1990): 453–99.

28. The anti-slavery movement was linked to the first international movement for women's rights. See Bonnie S. Anderson, *Joyous Greetings: The First International Women's Movement, 1830–1860* (Oxford: Oxford University Press, 2000).

29. Clare Midgley, *Women Against Slavery: The British Campaigns, 1780–1870* (London: Routledge, 1992).

30. Kathryn Kish Sklar and James Brewer Stewart, *Women's Rights and Transatlantic Antislavery in the Era of Emancipation* (New Haven, CT: Yale University Press, 2007).

31. Midgley, *Women Against Slavery*, pp. 145–9.

32. On slave women see, for example, David Barry Gaspar and Darlene Clark Hine, ed., *More Than Chattel: Black Women and Slavery in the Americas* (Bloomington and Indianapolis: Indiana University Press, 1996).

33. *Let Justice Be Done*, a play by the Mixed Blessings Theatre Group in 2008; *An African Cargo* by Margaret Busby, staged by Nitro (Black Theatre Co-operative) at Greenwich Theatre; *Dido Belle*, a film by Jason Young, in 2006; *Belle* in 2013, a film by Amma Asante.

34. At this point, Wilberforce himself believed that immediate abolition was dangerous and that it would be necessary for the liberated slaves to be educated by Christian missionaries before they could freely join civil society.

35. Hull was the first municipal council in Britain to join the world human rights organization, Amnesty International. It also appointed world leaders such as Desmond Tutu freemen of the city.

36. From the panel accompanying the exhibition.

37. This official event by the British government marked the zenith of abolition commemorations.

38. *Guardian*, 27 Mar. 2007.

39. On his protest, see Toyin Agbetu, "My Protest was Born of Anger, Not Madness", *Guardian*, 3 Apr. 2007; "Protest at Slavery Service", *Independent*, 28 Mar. 2007.

40. *Daily Mail*, 28 Mar. 2007.

41. In relation to this, Marcus Wood's reference to Lola Young's article "The Truth in Chains" in the bicentenary week in the *Guardian* is remarkable. See Lola Young, "The Truth in Chains: Two Centuries after Britain Began to Dismantle the Slave Trade, the Whole Issue is Still Beset by Myths, Half-truths and Ignorance", *Guardian*, 15 Mar. 2007, G2 Section, pp. 17–8; Marcus Wood, "Significant Silence: Where was Slave Agency in the Popular Imagery of 2007?" in *Imagining Transatlantic Slavery*, ed. Kaplan and Oldfield, pp. 162–3.

42. On the influence of the Santo Domingo revolt, see Carolyn E. Fick, "Emancipation in Haiti: From Plantation Labour to Peasant Proprietorship", in *After Slavery*, ed. Temperley, pp. 11–40.

43. Sue Peabody suggested the National Underground Railroad Freedom Center (Cincinnati, Ohio) and the Musée d'histoire de Nantes (France) as such examples.

44. The exhibition "London, Sugar & Slavery" opened at the Museum in Docklands (now the Museum of London Docklands) in 2007 and has since become a permanent exhibition.

45. See *Observer*, 25 Mar. 2007.

46. "The 1807 Act marked an important point in this country's development towards the nation it is today—a critical step into the modern world and into a new, and more just, moral universe." Quoted from the Home Office (UK) website. The site is now preserved by the National Archives online, http://webarchive.nationalarchives.gov.uk/+/www.direct.gov.uk/en/slavery/DG_065859, accessed 15 Feb. 2015.

47. Quoted on the museum's website: http://www.liverpoolmuseums.org.uk/podcasts/transcripts/liverpool_slavery_apology.aspx, accessed 15 Feb. 2015.

48. Kumie Inose, "Dorei wo Kaihou suru Teikoku" [The Empire Emancipating Slaves], *Daiei-Teikoku toiu Keiken* [Experiences of the British Empire] (Tokyo: Kodansha, 2007), pp. 131–48; Wallace, *The British Slave Trade*, pp. 61–3.

49. See Wallace, *The British Slave Trade*, pp. 140–7. See also Tony Forbes' illustration of "Sold Down the River", http://discoveringbristol.org.uk/browse/slavery/sold-down-the-river/, accessed 15 Feb. 2015.

50. On how Africans and African-Caribbeans have struggled to settle down in Britain since the *Empire Windrush*, see Mike Phillips and Trevor Phillips, *Windrush: The Irresistible Rise of Multi-Racial Britain* (London: Harper Collins, 1998).

51. Brown's argument reminds us of the similarity in British society after American independence more than 200 years ago and the postcolonial British society of today. According to a report for the British Department of Justice, there has been, since 1979, a significant decline in the proportion of British citizens who consider their nationality to be primarily British; the number of those who describe themselves as Scottish, Welsh or English has risen (Anthony Heath and Jane Roberts, *British Identity: Its Sources and Possible Implications for Civic Attitudes and Behaviour* (Oxford: Oxford University Press, 2006). It has been argued that the historical process which saw the birth of the British nation and on which British identity was built is important for understanding why British national identity is now less self-evident.

52. See the website of Anti-Slavery International: http://www.antislavery. org/english/, accessed 15 Feb. 2015.

53. The campaign against modern slavery replicates some of the darker elements of British nationalism, while efforts to rescue people from abusive situations are no doubt laudable.

54. One exception was "Bombay Africans", held in Oct. 2007 at the Royal Geographical Society, during the third peak of the bicentenary exhibitions. On this neglect, see Emma Christopher et al., ed., *Many Middle Passages: Forced Migration and the Making of the Modern World* (Berkeley, CA: University of California Press, 2007).

CHAPTER 4

Dutch Attitudes towards Slavery and the Tardy Road to Abolition: The Case of Deshima

Isabel Tanaka-Van Daalen

Regarding the purchase of a number of slaves, this should be done in every way possible, because it would be of great benefit to the Company, for it could not survive without slaves.[1]

Self-interest! Indeed, that is the real, the sole purpose of this reprehensible trade with all that it entails, its opponents will say. True words, because, were it not for gain and advantage, traders would not jeopardize their treasures on such long and perilous voyages; nor would ships' commanders or the other officers and sailors expose their lives not only to the perils of the sea but also to a constant fear of rebellion, and torture their bodies having to be alert and on guard more than usual. But let these opponents tell me this, should this trade be discontinued and no supply of slaves reach our Colonies, what would become of these precious Colonies in just a few years, and let them consequently estimate the resulting state of our country, our commerce and shipping, our citizens in general and of the tradesmen, artists and craftsmen in particular; yea, even that of themselves and their children![2]

Introduction

Only after some initial moral reservations did the Dutch step into the slave trade at the beginning of the 17th century. However, when they acquired colonies of their own, their first scruples faded away and they became major participants in this trade, remaining so until the end of the 18th century. The trade itself was executed by the Dutch East India Company (VOC) as well as by the West India Company (WIC) (from 1730 also by the Middelburg Commercial Company), which were established in respectively 1602 and 1621 and accredited with state power in chartered areas by the States General of the newly founded Dutch Republic. In building and maintaining a maritime and commercial empire—too large to be sustained by its own people—these companies heavily relied on slaves for labour on the plantations and in the urban and domestic spheres in both the Caribbean as well as in Asia right from the start.

At first glance it seems a bit of a paradox that the Dutch, who had fought a hard struggle for independence from Roman Catholic Spain in the course of the Eighty Years War (1566–1648) and who took such pride in the freedom and tolerance of their new republic, could proceed so unquestioningly in the slave trade and the practice of slavery elsewhere. Slaves were thought to be needed for the survival of the overseas territories, as Jan Pietersz Coen, the architect of the VOC empire, stated at various occasions (see quotation above), and economic interests tended to override moral reservations. Dutchmen were hardly directly confronted with slaves in the metropolis, and if they gave the matter any thought at all, they could choose from a wide range of theoretical arguments justifying slavery. This kind of pragmatism and self-interest, coupled with a variety of other typically Dutch circumstances, such as a growing general feeling of unease about its decaying economy and the state of its colonies, were the main obstacles to a swift abolition of the Dutch slave trade and slave emancipation. In the end, it was only under external political, moral pressures and global change that the slave trade was abolished in 1814, while formal emancipation of the slaves dragged on to as late as 1860 in the East and 1863 in the West.

In this article, I will give a general overview of abolitionism in the Netherlands and the Dutch colonies, and then proceed to the attitudes and mindsets of the Dutchmen who took slavery for granted or who chose to ignore its moral implications in their daily lives overseas, notwithstanding exposure from the late 18th century onwards to various abolitionist ideas filtering in from the metropolis. By focusing on how those Dutchmen on the spot perceived their slaves and slavery as an institution, it may be possible to throw extra light on some factors contributing to the long and tardy trajectory towards abolition. This tardiness is one of the most conspicuous features of the Dutch case.

As Dutch historiography on the slave trade and slavery has been mainly concerned with the Atlantic and studies on its counterparts in the Indian Ocean World have not yet caught up, I have opted to direct my attention to the Dutch employees of the Dutch East India Company, and from 1824, of its semi-national successor, the Dutch Trading Company (NHM). Within that area, I want to restrict myself even further to those residing on the trading post of Deshima (1641–1859) in Japan. In spite of the availability of a variety of Dutch and Japanese sources, slavery on Deshima has eluded most scholars up till now. Moreover, although situated at the easternmost part of the Dutch overseas orbit, originally spanning from the Cape Colony, the Middle East, India, Ceylon, the Indonesian Archipelago, Siam, Burma, Indochina, Taiwan (until 1662) to Japan, and despite its small number of personnel, Deshima was firmly imbedded within the VOC and NHM network. Being one of the few posts providing precious metals for the trade within Asia, the Japanese trading post was of much economic importance. In 1619, Batavia, present-day Jakarta, became the centre of VOC administration, jurisdiction and trade; employees, of whom many already had experienced life in Batavia or at other posts in Asia, were all dispatched from that centre to the various posts within the Dutch trading network. For that reason, quite a large uniformity in lifestyle and outlook persisted within the whole area (including the Cape Colony). The character of the VOC establishments ranged from settler colonies, such as those of the Cape and Batavia, to extremely small posts, such as Deshima and Canton, where the VOC employees resided on closely guarded compounds under strict rules imposed by the local authorities. The nature of slavery also depended on local circumstances, but despite these differences, Deshima can serve as a *pars-pro-toto* to illustrate the Dutch outlook towards slavery that was largely responsible for the slow and lukewarm adoption of slave emancipation in these regions.

Historiographical Trends and Commemoration of Dutch Slavery and Its Abolition in the Atlantic

The slow and lukewarm process towards abolition, not a matter of pride in terms of national history, also lies at the root of the half-hearted acknowledgement and interest in the Netherlands in its slave trade and slavery. Only from the 1970s, a few Dutch scholars started to focus on the situation in the colonies in the Caribbean, such as Suriname, the Dutch Antilles, Dutch Guiana as well as the trading posts on the African West Coast, of which El Mina (in present-day Ghana) was the central point from where most of the slaves for the plantations in the Americas were transported. Dutch Brazil and the New Netherland, agglomerated around present-day New York, were only temporarily under Dutch control.[3]

It is estimated that until the abolition of the slave trade in 1814 nearly 550,000 slaves from Africa were "exported" on Dutch ships, of which 460,000 landed alive in the Americas.

With these numbers the Dutch ranked fourth, after Great Britain, Portugal and France, taking a share of approximately 7.5 per cent (at its peak close to 10 per cent) of the total traffic. During the years 1636–48, the Dutch even took the lead when they also carried slaves to their colony in northern Brazil.[4] The slave trade has been one of the pillars of the WIC trade.[5]

The Caribbean descendants of slaves, for whom the slave trade and slavery have become important means for the construction of a Caribbean identity, should be credited for instigating a more general interest in slavery in the Americas.[6] Together with a steadily growing number of academic publications in the 1990s, national debates were provoked, largely initiated by descendants of slaves from Suriname who migrated to the Netherlands around Suriname's independence in 1975. Their call for recognition was part of their integration process into Dutch society. The debates, almost entirely restricted to the slave trade from Africa to the Caribbean and slavery in the Americas, concerned Dutch responsibility for its colonial past (including acknowledgement of the so-called "black pages" of that history); a rethinking of the problems related to migration, integration and racism; and a new assessment of cultural heritage, multiculturalism and national identity.[7] This trend also materialized in several slave monuments,[8] in the establishment in 2002 of the research and educational Institute for the Study of Dutch Slavery and its Legacy, the NiNsee,[9] documentaries on slavery,[10] exhibitions[11] and popular writings.[12] Similar critical debates in Britain as well as in France, likewise stirred by the emergence of expanding multicultural societies and treated by Sue Peabody in Chapter 2 and Kumie Inose in Chapter 3 in this volume, offer many remarkable parallels to the Dutch case.

The contents of a national history canon, presented to the Dutch Minister of Education, Culture and Science in 2007 and integrated in the national school curriculum in 2010, also reflects more awareness of that colonial history: out of 50 "windows", five, including "Slavery, circa 1637–1863: Human Trafficking and Forced Labour in the New World", are directly related to that past.[13] Coinciding with the 150th anniversary of the abolition of slavery in the Caribbean, 2013 sparked further events[14] but also heated public discussions over racist implications of Black Pete, the black servant of Sinterklaas. These discussions have been ongoing for many years, but the fact that this servant or helper of the Dutch Santa Claus, who developed into a black caricature with an obvious Surinamese accent, wearing golden earrings and a page costume, was condemned by the UN-related "Working Group on People of African Descent" as being "a racist stereotype" and called for a ban or radically changed appearance drew emotional, in some cases very nasty, reactions from Black Pete advocates.[15] The recent hard political stances of an openly xenophobic right-wing government (mainly directed at Muslim immigrants, regarded to be unwilling to integrate),[16] certainly do not contribute much to feelings of empathy with people of other colour either.

In 2013, the Dutch government was faced with demands from 14 Caribbean countries suing Britain, Holland and France for slavery reparations, of which the outcome is still unclear.

In spite of its actuality to modern Dutch society, full acknowledgement and objective knowledge are still wanting. The situation in regard to the Indian Ocean World is even worse.

Historiographical Trends and (the Absence of) Commemorations of Dutch Slavery and Abolition in the Indian Ocean World

As late as 2008, it was maintained that the historiography of the Indian Ocean World slavery in general was in an embryonic stage,[17] and in the following year, that the Dutch Indian Ocean slave trade had been the subject of not a single monograph.[18] In comparison to studies in regard to the Caribbean this is certainly a meagre result but this overall picture passes over the efforts of a few, but very prolific, historians, who have focused on these topics in specific regions or cities or who have referred to them in broader contexts, such as urban history and migration.[19] Studies on the Cape Colony[20] are already in an advanced stage, almost a sub-field of its own, while Batavia and the coastal region of Ceylon have been thoroughly studied as well.

One turning point in the recognition of Dutch slave trade and slavery in its Eastern empire lies around 2002, when the founding of the VOC was "celebrated" on a national scale.[21] The self-congratulatory character of this commemoration immediately drew criticism from countries affected by Dutch colonialism, such as Indonesia and South Africa, but also from historians and Caribbean circles inside the Netherlands, pointing out that some of the so-called "shadow sides" related to the VOC, such as the brutal ways in which the VOC had built and maintained its monopolistic empire, and its participation in the slave trade and slavery had been completely ignored.[22] The same critical reactions could be heard in 2006 after Prime Minister Jan Peter Balkenende made a call in Parliament for more "positive thinking" in the same spirit as the VOC mentality of mercantile vigour, decisiveness and guts.[23] Until then, the VOC was viewed in national thinking as an institution to be proud of, in sharp contrast with how the WIC, predominantly associated with the despicable and shameful slave trade, was viewed in the popular mind. That unfortunate remark by a prime minister inspired further awareness of the Dutch slavery past. However, notwithstanding growing knowledge, Dutch slavery in Asia was not mentioned in the history canon and commemorations of its abolition in 1860 have been largely absent. Moreover, slavery has never been a topic of concern among the Dutch, Indo-Dutch or Moluccan migrants from the former Dutch East Indies, who came to the Netherlands after the independence of Indonesia in 1945. Possible slave descendants have not come forward in Indonesia either, which contrasts sharply with South Africa, where genealogical research into slave ancestry has become quite widespread.[24]

Markus Vink was one of the first to point out that the scope of the Dutch slave trade and slavery in Asia equalled or even surpassed that in the Caribbean.[25] He noted three sub-regions in the Indian Ocean from which slaves for the VOC territories were drawn: the

African circuit of East Africa, Madagascar, Mauritius and Réunion; the South Asian circuit of the Indian subcontinent of Malabar, Coromandel and the Bengal/Arakan coast; and the South East Asian circuit of Malaysia, the Indonesian Archipelago, New Guinea and the southern Philippines.[26] Social changes in the "catch" areas due to warfare and famine as well as changing policies of indigenous rulers, could cause fluctuations in "the supply".[27] After 1660, coinciding with the collapse of the sultanate of Goa, the central slaving market of Makassar came within reach and slaves from the Indonesian Archipelago started to outnumber slaves from India. Slaves from the African circuit were mostly transported to Cape Colony, and to a lesser extent to Batavia, intended for hard Company labour and work in the gold mines on Sumatra.[28] Moreover, the value of the VOC trade in slaves, "mainly for Company use", consisted in the 18th century of only 0.5 per cent of all its other "commodities", as estimated by Els Jacobs.[29] The relative economic unimportance of the slave trade within VOC confines, geographical fragmentation of the area and imbalance in the available source material are but a few of the reasons why slavery in the East, let alone its abolition, has received little attention in historiography.[30]

Some Further Traits of Dutch Slavery in the Indian Ocean World

When the Dutch arrived in Asia at the end of the 16th century, slavery and a variety of other forms of bondage and slave trafficking were already firmly in place. All they did was to step in. The VOC has never had a monopoly in the trade of slaves, who were also supplied by private traders and indigenous merchants, but it is certain that the presence of the VOC caused a rise in demand and consequently of slave raiding in the region.[31] After the 1770s slave imports decreased, which was also a reflection of the dwindling importance of Batavia.[32]

Although the VOC owned so-called Company slaves who performed all kinds of unskilled labour, their number was small in comparison to privately owned slaves.[33] Slaves were hardly employed for the production of export crops. One exception formed nutmeg and mace production on the Banda Islands, which were depopulated by the VOC in 1621 in order to establish a monopoly in this product.

The production was supervised by Dutch and mestizo settlers who exploited their allotted lands by using slave labour.[34]

Most of the slaves were employed as domestic servants, unskilled labourers or artisans in the master's shop by Dutchmen who directly or indirectly belonged to the VOC establishment. Women could end up as concubines or quite often as legal wives. In cities such as Batavia and Colombo, slaves made up more than half of the total population.[35] This ratio dropped drastically after part of the Dutch colonies became part of the British Empire in the Napoleonic era (1795–1815) and never picked up after part of the colonies returned to Dutch rule.[36] The fact that a better infrastructure linking Batavia with its indigenous hinterland and a steady increase in population was making free labour increasingly attractive, led to a further decline. By 1860, the slave population in Batavia had dwindled to less than 0.2 per cent of its total population, making slave emancipation almost a matter on paper.[37]

The predominantly urban character, a relatively high proportion of manumissions, the absence of a so-called "middle passage", short-distance migration, a multi-ethnic local population resulting in less clear racial and ethnic distinctions, gender balance and legislation which curtailed the most extreme excesses of maltreatment, have also contributed to a more benign image of slavery in the East, taking the edge off its urgency as a topic.[38]

The Dutch Enigma of Late Abolition

As regards abolitionism in the Netherlands and the Dutch colonies as well as abolition of the Dutch slave trade and slavery, we can draw on a few, however quite detailed, older publications,[39] but it was only in the mid-1990s that these topics came to be viewed in a broader, comparative international context: in *Fifty Years Later: Antislavery, Capitalism and Modernity in the Dutch Orbit*.[40] In this publication, the famous article by Seymour Drescher on Dutch anti-slavery, "The Long Goodbye", was taken as a starting point to address the question of why Dutch abolition has taken so long and did not translate to social mobilization, political action and legislation much earlier, and when it did, largely only in reaction to international pressure.

One of the most plausible answers was given by Angelie Sens who has argued that "the élites' prevailing pessimism in the late

eighteenth century and their obsession with restoring economic pros-
perity" stood in the way of emancipation, despite the emergence of
(rather individual) enlightened ideas about democratic and individual
freedom and equality, and growing doubts over the monopolistic
nature of its semi-national trading companies and the economic
validity of un-free labour.[41]

That these enlightened ideas had so little social impact on the
first half of the next century can also be blamed on historical events,
as Robert Ross has done, pointing out that the French Revolution and
its radical occupation of the Netherlands "imbued the Dutch protestant Dutch élites with an abhorrence of radicalism",[42] which plunged
the Netherlands into a conservative mood, preoccupied by economic
recovery after the restoration of royal rule in 1813.

Other factors said to have led to lukewarm abolitionism in the
19th century included that colonial politics was a royal prerogative
until 1848, when responsibility for colonial affairs was finally transferred to the Parliament by the Constitution. Until then, the suc-
ceeding kings were able to prevent the information flow from the
colonies through censorship and by withholding permission for the
establishment of possible critical societies or a free press in the colonies. Criticism could be a hazard to economic recovery and was therefore deemed to be a-patriotic.[43] As colonial trade directly or indirectly
affected the livelihood of most Dutchmen, this was a powerful argument. Missionary activities in the colonies, another possible source of
direct knowledge about social abuses, were negligible for a long time
as well.

Real distance and the disparity between the colonies and the
metropolis, where slavery as an institution had ended well before the
17th century and the presence of former slaves was low due to the
fact that Dutchmen returning to their country would rather sell their
slaves than having to free them at arrival in the Netherlands according
to the "free soil principle",[44] contributed to a further lack of interest
in slavery at home.

However, recently, new research by Maartje Janse, based on the
discovery of the huge archive of one of the founders of one the first
active anti-slavery societies in the Netherlands, has made it possible
to re-adjust the lukewarm image of abolitionism, at least from the
1840s onwards.[45] Anti-slavery protest, which became one of the first
manifestations of civil protest in Dutch politics, has been more extensive than hitherto thought, and although in numbers it did not

compare with Britain, different groups within Dutch society did rally for its cause.

It was David Brion Davis who called the Dutch case an enigma, but further research from the mid-1990s onward has shown that such attitudes were actually quite common among the smaller European nations and that it was Britain that was the exceptional case.[46] Davis himself had already noted that the ambivalence and disagreement in the metropolis and the overseas territories, which he terms "dualism", seemed to be inherent in slavery itself.[47] What was exceptional, in the case of the Netherlands, was the particularly large gap between what was professed at home and what was practised overseas.

The Road to Abolition

First Period

Dutch abolitionism can be roughly divided into two phases: the period before 1814–18 when the slave trade was abolished, and the period from 1840 until the abolition of slavery in 1860 and 1863. Before 1840, hardly any active abolitionism existed and anti-slavery thoughts of both periods are hardly connected.

Although there were some initial moral reservations prior to Dutch participation, condemning the Spanish and the Portuguese for that "inhuman practice and Godless villainy",[48] these were quickly thrown overboard as soon as the Dutch followed in the footsteps of Portugal and Spain.[49] Pragmatism prevailed over morality, and "Company servants put their mouth where their money was".[50] After all, they could draw from a vast store of justifications from the Bible, the classics and humanist thinking, such as the primacy of spiritual over physical freedom, or the curse of Noah, condemning the descendents of Canaan to live in servility.[51] Other arguments were based on Christian humanitarian reasoning such as saving the slaves from paganism and harsh circumstances at home, or of a presumed inferiority of the slaves.

Anti-slavery discussion by a small number of clergymen, politicians and literary writers in the metropolis during the 17th and 18th century were focused on philosophical arguments and remained mainly theoretical.[52] Rather than calling for an end to slavery itself, anti-slavery thought was directed at the cruelty of the slave traders and planters, and the means to improve the treatment of the slaves. Almost all discussions concerned the Atlantic.

Critical opinion in the overseas empire in the East was almost non-existent until the end of the 18th century, and restricted to the writings of a small number of visitors to Batavia, who commented on the abusive and cruel treatment of the slaves, especially by the Batavian womenfolk, often from slave descent themselves.[53] Critical voices did not find their way into print in Batavia either; the VOC had a long history of censorship and secrecy, leaving no room for independent printing work or the publication of a newspaper.[54] It is telling that the writings of military man, VOC employee and diplomat Dirk van Hogendorp, dubbed the first abolitionist in colonial circles,[55] propagating immediate abolition of the slave trade and gradual abolition of slavery, were almost all published in the Netherlands, and that the staging in the Hague of his play *Kraspoekol*,[56] about a cruel female slave owner in Batavia, was disrupted by loud booing of colonial lobbyists. To him, slavery was one of the manifestations of colonial abuse by its oligarchic rulers, but the times were not ready for his radical proposals for reform. The negative impact of the bloody Haitian Revolt was another motive to abstain from too abrupt emancipation.[57]

Anti-slavery writings by European Enlightenment advocates such as Raynal,[58] and the ideas of the so-called pro-French *Patriotten*, a group of mixed composition, who were all dissatisfied with Dutch weakness, the corrupt rule of the regent elite of the big cities and their lack of political involvement, did circulate at the end of the 18th century in the VOC area, but also failed to result in abolition.[59] How could it be otherwise, when in the metropolis, references to the abolition of the slave trade did not make it into the new Constitution of 1798? National interest took the upper hand as soon as these patriots came into power after the Netherlands came under French rule in 1795.[60] The Dutch economy had fallen into arrear; its overseas trade in Asia, especially in India, was outstripped by Britain after the fourth Anglo-Dutch war (1780–84) and a general feeling of national malaise, whether founded or not, prevailed. By the end of that century, both the WIC (1791) and the VOC (1799) were dissolved and their possessions nationalized. In spite of patriot proclamations of "freedom, equality and brotherhood", emancipation of slaves was regarded as the fatal blow to the, by then, ailing overseas possessions.[61] The quotation by the pro-slavery Barrau at the beginning of this article is but one example of such sentiments.

However, when Britain took over part of the Dutch colonies, this reasoning became all the more theoretical. During the British interregnum (1811–16) under Thomas S.B. Raffles in Batavia, the *Java Government Gazette* was established and used as a vehicle to target all kinds of despicable Dutch practices, such as slavery.[62] Further efforts to abolish the Dutch slave trade and slavery consisted of measures such as a poll tax on slaves and a prohibition on the import of slaves into Batavia (1813).[63] In 1814, King William I in the Netherlands put an end to the trade by royal decree to please the British.[64] When the Netherlands became an independent kingdom in 1815, a renewal of the prohibition on the slave trade was one of the conditions for the restoration of Dutch rule over Batavia in 1816. This prohibition was officially ratified in 1818, when the Dutch Parliment had to consent to joint British control of the illegal slave trade. Although some steps were taken after that date to improve the lot of the slaves and a better registration of the slaves was established to prevent the illegal trade, the Batavian authorities remained quite non-committal in the name of economic interests, in spite of recommendations in 1825 by a special commission advising gradual abolition of slavery.[65] The activities of the Java Humanitarian Association, which had succeeded the Java Benevolent Institution (founded in 1816 by Raffles for the promotion of anti-slavery), were not to much avail either.[66] In the Netherlands, economic recovery and reduction of the national debt took top priority; colonial affairs were handled by the king and ordinary people had to refrain from politics.

Second Period

The abdication of King William I in 1839 finally seemed to herald a new era more susceptive to political change, paving the way for renewed anti-slavery efforts, the awakening of a public opinion and active participation in politics.[67]

The direct impulse towards the second period of Dutch anti-slavery came from abroad again: visits, in 1840, by leading abolitionists of the British and Foreign Anti-Slavery Society and Quakers such as Elizabeth Frey triggered renewed interest and led to the birth of various clubs of so-called "negro friends".[68] These clubs were of diverse composition, counting amongst their members leading Dutchmen of the so-called anti-revolutionary *Réveil* group working towards orthodox Calvinist revival, as well as more liberally inclined persons who finally became a force in Parliament. Their motives were also different: the orthodox Christians found slavery more difficult than before to reconcile with Christian principles but their main aim was Christianization, which seemed easier to accomplish among freedmen.[69] To the liberals, slavery ran against principles of the equality of men and free labour. Moreover, by now it was thought that the ailing American plantations with declining slave population could only benefit economically from emancipation.[70]

However, already in the following year, attempts to establish a united national anti-slavery society fell flat.[71] Influenced by British examples, both groups separately petitioned to the king but clear support was withheld. The orthodox Christians refrained from further action, but the liberals continued their meetings, while in Utrecht a closed "publishers' association" was formed for the publication of a periodical, "Contributions to the Knowledge of the Dutch and Foreign Colonies, especially with Regards to the Emancipation of Slaves", which appeared between 1841 and 1847.[72] The liberals aimed at more openness with regard to colonial affairs, and felt that pure factual information directly obtained from the colonies would lead to better awareness among a broader public willing to voice protests over the abusive system of slavery. What seems to be typically Dutch is that the abolitionists were keen not to antagonize the king and other conservatist forces, expecting more results from a less radical and less emotional approach. For that reason, they also tried to distance themselves as much as possible from too much direct interference by the British abolitionists.[73]

Besides these male societies, several women's groups became active, stressing their non-political character and moral affinity with the female slaves.[74] In 1841, the Rotterdam Ladies Anti-Slavery Committee was the first to send a petition to the king, who appeased the abolitionists with a vague reply in 1842 in which he did not oppose the principle, but postponed concrete measures in the name of colonial interest until an unspecified future time.[75]

A breakthrough came in 1848, when the revolutionary mood in Europe led to liberal parliamental reforms in the Netherlands, as well as to amendments of the Constitution, providing for the rights of free association and a free press. From this moment, colonial affairs became the responsibility of the Secretary of Colonies who needed approval from the Parliament. With this, the issue of slavery came in sight of the metropolis at last. The year 1848 could have been a perfect moment for Dutch emancipation to be realized but it only did so on St Maarten in the Caribbean, after slaves in the French part of the island became free following French abolition that year. The liberals, who had come to power in Parliament in 1848, hesitated to emancipate the slaves, as national finances to pay compensation to the slave-owners were still lacking at that time.[76]

Around the same time anti-slavery feelings reappeared in the Dutch Indies, mainly through the efforts of the liberal-minded protestant minister Wolter R. van Hoëvell, an ardent critic of Dutch colonialism.[77] The periodical *Tijdschrift voor Neêrlandsch Indië*, which he had founded in 1838, became his platform, much to the chagrin of the Batavian authorities. His participation in a protest meeting in May 1848 organized by a wide range of Batavian inhabitants (including Europeans, persons of mixed blood and native Indonesians), in which all kinds of grievances against discriminatory governmental measures were ventilated and which ended in chaos, was used as an excuse to have him resign. This short-lived protest, sometimes called the "Batavian Revolution", was clearly inspired by similar 1848 protests in Europe; calls for a free press could also be heard, but it did not come into effect until 1854.[78] Back in the Netherlands and no longer held to promises to refrain from publication, Hoëvell published a treatise on the immediate emancipation of slavery in the East Indies, regarded to be a morally embarrassing issue.[79] He resumed publication of his *Tijdschrift* in the Netherlands the following year and was elected into Parliament as a liberal member, where he became the "colonial specialist" rallying against slave auctions, slavery and other forms of forced labour in the colonies.[80]

Another breakthrough in the anti-slavery campaign was due to the Dutch translation of *Uncle Tom's Cabin* in 1853, which brought sentimentalism into the debates, appealing to a broader segment of society. Pity and identification with the abused led directly to active moral indignation.[81] The anti-revolutionaries revived the Dutch Society for the Promotion of the Abolition of Slavery, and were able to mobilize the general public through a periodical and the financing of manumissions of individual slaves in Suriname.[82] Women's groups contributed through donations collected from the sales or raffles of handmade articles, and by petitioning.[83] The same year also saw the establishment of youth associations inspired by *Uncle Tom's Cabin*,[84] while a state commission started looking into ways to improve the condition of the slaves. In Parliament, once more ruled by the conservatives, the Secretary of the Colonies was pressed into a statement declaring that abolition of slavery itself was not the problem, but that the issue was the way in which that would be achieved.[85] The publication of another book by Van Hoëvell the following year, in similar emotional style as *Uncle Tom's Cabin* and discussing the deplorabe situation in both the Americas and the East Indies, was meant to speed up the parliamentary process.[86] By that time, the national treasury could draw from the revenues of the very lucrative cultivation system, which mainly depended on the exploitation of lands and compulsory labour of Indonesian peasants. That it still took another ten years was mostly due to political bickering in Parliament about the amount of compensation to the slave-owners, the length of slave apprenticeship (in Suriname) thought to be needed to prepare the slaves for their new life, and to look for a substitutional workforce.[87] The difficulties Britain and France had faced in reviving their colonies after emancipation had made the Dutch politicians all the more cautious.

Abolition was finally proclaimed in 1860 in the East and 1863 in the Atlantic. This made the Netherlands one of the last European countries to emancipate its slaves. It is rather ironical that the compensation to the slave-owners (and not to the freed slaves) in the Caribbean was financed by the surplus of the cultivation system of forced labour in the Dutch East Indies; in the words of Pieter Emmer: "One form of unfree labour was used to abolish another."[88] After emancipation of the slaves in the East Indies, part of their work was taken over by convict labourers who had already outnumbered slaves before that time.[89] Many slaves in the cities remained in their former domestic services, only from then on with free status. The existence of an already multi-ethnic environment seems to have facilitated social integration. In the Caribbean, contract labourers, transported from India and China, were hired to do the slaves' former work.[90] After their apprenticeship the slaves moved to the cities, where colour would become an important factor in determining social mobility.

Several of the typically Dutch circumstances contributing to the slow pace of emancipation, among which self-preservation stands out, have already passed our review. The case of Deshima will now serve as an example to describe how and in what form that typically Dutch outlook translated into daily life at a particular post, providing us with further clues to explain the long absence of abolitionist action. However, the lack of publications on this topic first demands a description of slavery on Deshima.[91]

Slavery on Deshima

Deshima, the Dutch trading post in Japan where the Dutch resided from 1641, was built on an artificial island in Nagasaki and consisted of only a few buildings, warehouses, quarters for cattle, a flagpole, gardens and other greenery, not much bigger than a soccer stadium. It was linked with the city by a well-guarded bridge; access to and from the island was severely restricted.[92]

We are well informed about daily life on Deshima by the *Dagregisters*, the daily records of the heads (*opperhoofden*) of the trading post.[93] These records are, however at the centre of a large corpus of official reports to the governor-general in Batavia and should therefore be handled with caution: events were sometimes put in too advantageous a light.

Once a year, the *opperhoofd* went on court journey to pay his respects to the shogun in Edo (present Tokyo), accompanied by a small party of Dutchmen and a large retinue of Japanese officials, interpreters, carriers and personal servants. Slaves, for whose expenses the opperhoofd would be personally billed, were normally left behind. There have been instances, such as in 1735 and 1792, when the shogun, out of curiosity or to be diverted by their music, explicitly asked for them to be sent, but this did not materialize both times.[94] Slaves with knowledge of Japanese were sometimes taken along by the opperhoofd to check on the Japanese interpreters.[95] In 1641, measures aimed at barring all Roman Catholic influences (including the expulsion of the Spanish and Portuguese traders and missionaries) thought to endanger Japan's political authority, were firmly in place and Japan entered a period of exclusion, in which the remaining foreigners were segregated from the Japanese population as much as possible. From the end of the 17th century, undesirable private trade transactions and smuggle became another concern as well. One of the new regulations to hold the Dutchmen in check was to prohibit Japanese servants from staying overnight, making it imperative to bring personal live-in servants from Batavia.[96] Dutchmen were not allowed to bring their wives or other females to Deshima. This absence of female slaves is one of the main characteristics of slavery on Deshima; specific female services were provided by prostitutes from the city. The opperhoofd had to alternate every year but lower-ranked employees with their slaves were allowed to stay longer, making some of them fluent in the Japanese language and familiar with life on Deshima and with the Japanese in charge, which led to all kinds of illegal practices.

It is difficult to collect numerical facts for the 17th century, but from sporadic references in the Dagregisters, such as when the remaining people were "mustered" by the Japanese after the departure of the Dutch ships, it seems that the slaves on Deshima did not exceed ten persons per year in that period.[97] This number gradually increased in the 18th century, when ownership of slaves also contributed to status. For example, in 1787, the new opperhoofd Frederik van Reede tot de Parkeler, from a noble background, brought 23 slaves with him, all boys aged 15–35.[98] This was an extreme case, as previous research of so-called *monsterrollen* (muster rolls), which have been preserved only for limited periods, shows.[99] On these lists we can find the names, places of origin and ages of crew and passengers of the incoming and outgoing ships, including those of the accompanying slave servants or "*slaave jongens*" (slave boys).[100] Opperhoofden would normally account for 12–20 at the most and lower personnel for 1–8 slaves. There were also employees who came without slaves, presumably for economic reasons. Most of the slaves would be in their teens and 20s, although there were slaves as young as seven or as old as 51. In 1781, eight employees coming to Japan, including the opperhoofd, were accompanied, in all, by 33 slaves.[101] This clearly shows that in the 18th century, the Dutchmen, even adding those who had stayed over on Deshima, were by far outnumbered by their slave servants.[102] During the British interregnum of Batavia, Dutch traffic between Batavia and Deshima came to a complete standstill and judging from the sparse references in the Dagregisters and from the existing muster rolls it seems that in the 19th century, ownership of slaves would never equal its 18th-century level.[103] The accompanying servants on the muster rolls, on an average three persons per incoming ship, were now called *Javaansche bediende*s (Javanese servants) or *inlanders van Java* (natives from

Java), without distinguishing between servants with slave or free status. Dutch ownership of slaves on Deshima seems to have followed the same trends as in Batavia: a steady decrease in number after the abolition of the slave trade and a gradual transition to free labour.

As for the places of origin of the slaves, we are also well informed by the above-mentioned muster rolls: in the 18th century 86 per cent came from the Indonesian Archipelago, including slaves from Sulawesi, Makassar, Bali and Sumbawa, as well as the 13 per cent stated to originate from Batavia; 3 per cent came from South and South East Asia (Siam, Malakka, Keda); 4 per cent from India (Bengal, Malabar, Surat and the Coromandel Coast) and 7 per cent from unknown origin.[104] In the 17th century the only clear references we have are to slaves from Bengal and the Coromandel Coast.[105] Contrary to the Portuguese, who are known to have brought many slaves from Mozambique and Angola before their expulsion from Japan,[106] amply represented on the so-called Namban screens, there is a remarkable absence of Dutch slaves from Africa in the Dagregisters. That does not mean that there were no slaves from Africa on Deshima; they just did not do anything remarkable to be mentioned. We do come across slaves who were called *kaffer* (*caffir*) but they did not necessarily come from Africa,[107] and slaves from Monomotapa (present Zimbabwe) were mentioned by the famous artist Kōkan Shiba, who visited Nagasaki in 1788.[108] In the 19th-century muster rolls we only find servants originating from the Indonesian Archipelago or "resident in Batavia".

Upon leaving Japan, the Dutchmen normally returned to Batavia with their slaves, but auction lists of possessions of Dutchmen deceased on Deshima and other notarial documents[109] show that some of the slaves changed hands on Deshima and could be renamed on that occasion.[110] Slave prices in these documents ranged from 60–230 *rijksdaalders* (for comparison: a gold watch on the same sales list fetched 32 rijksdaalders).[111] It becomes clear, from these sales lists, that slaves were the most expensive of a person's possessions. Hendrik Doeff, who, due to the Napoleonic wars, had to stay on Deshima as opperhoofd from 1803–17, explicitly warned his successor against the practice of taking over slaves from other employees:

An *opperhoofd* in Japan needs four slaves, to be brought from Batavia. Among them, one who knows how to cook, or at least how to warm up the food. It would not be bad either to have one who knows how to tailor. The other two should be house- and manservants. This is enough; do not take more with you. It is a burden. You would do good sending one back every year to Batavia to receive a new one the following year. The boys should not stay long. Never take over in Japan one who has stayed long there, because he is sure to be spoiled (*bedurven*).[112]

This passage also refers to some of the work slaves on Deshima were supposed to do. Gentaku Otsuki, a scholar of Dutch Studies who visited Deshima in 1785, tells us that the slaves, who were called *kurobō* or *kuronbō* (literally "black boys"), "prepare food and run all kinds of other errands. They also do sewing work or the laundry, fetch water, clean the rice and help in the [communal] kitchen."[113] In times of emergency, the Company relied on them for reparation work of the buildings or for extra help during the busy trade season.[114] We also have pictorial evidence for most of these tasks, such as picture scrolls of the Deshima trading post, book illustrations, Nagasaki woodblock prints as souvenirs for Japanese tourists, and even pottery, lacquerware and glasswork.[115]

There is one aspect of slavery on Deshima, called "slave re- sponses" by Nigel Worden, about which we are particularly well informed by the Dagregisters, because these constituted extraordinary events.[116] Some of these cases also feature in the Japanese Judicial Records of Nagasaki.[117] The responses varied from throwing stones or spitting on Japanese outside the compound,[118] incidents of a sexual nature,[119] escaping from the island or hiding in town,[120] to more violent fits of amuck,[121] attacks on Dutchmen and suicides.[122] Involve- ment in all kinds of petty crime and smuggle, often in league with Japanese water carriers or coolies, could also be classed under these responses.[123] Many such incidents resulted in extreme punishment by flogging or by putting the slaves in chains or "in the blocks". Quite a few slaves died while in detention or for no specified reason at all.[124] In principle, criminal cases involving Dutchmen and slaves were handled and punished by the Dutch side or handed over to Batavia when they concerned capital crimes; the only punishment the Japa- nese could mete out was eternal banishment from the country. As Dutch-Roman law did not provide slave legislation because of the absence of slavery in the Netherlands, Roman law was applied to the slaves. Amendments made on the spot to fit the local circumstances in Asia were collected in 1642 in the *Statutes of Batavia*, which had legal force throughout the VOC Empire.[125]

Dutch Attitudes towards Slaves and Slavery

Slaves constituted an essential part of daily life on Deshima but their presence, if acknowledged at all, was taken for granted and never questioned by the Dutchmen themselves. Whenever they rebelled, these "responses" were immediately suppressed. The daily records by the opperhoofd give ample account of how these dealings were glossed over. These Dagregisters also reveal all kinds of Dutch "sentiments", which can be inferred from the manner in which the events and persons are described. Searching for these sentiments is a way of reading the VOC sources "along the archival grain", as Ann Stoler has proposed in her recent book in which she has pointed out a move from the "archive-as-source" to the "archive-as-subject".[126] An extreme matter-of-fact tone when commenting on the death or other mishap of slaves, which strikes us as quite heartless now, or personal condescending comments inserted in the text, can therefore also be taken as indications of certain attitudes. One should not forget, though, that these were sentiments prevailing at the time and that more empathetic or sympathetic expressions in the official reports would certainly have been regarded as odd by the superiors in Batavia, who normally would not have given their slaves much thought either. Generally we only come across slaves in the Dagregisters in cases of death, crime or other exceptional events.

The absence of references to the slaves on Deshima in contemporary Dutch literature on Japan points to a similar indifference. This stands in sharp contrast with the numerous references to the slaves in Japanese travelogues or descriptions of Deshima from the mid-18th century onwards, which are often very compassionate in tone.[127] A description of the slaves' origin, appearance, customs, language, food and their treatment by the Dutch became a fixed component of such literature.

In Japanese pictorial sources, slaves are invariably depicted in a servile position, mostly as barefoot children in Indonesian dress and with headscarves, but these Japanese representations never seem disdainful.

Judging from the Dagregisters alone, contact between the Dutchmen and their slaves seems to have been quite impersonal, and indifference and lack of sympathy the rule. The fact that many of the slaves on Deshima were very young also led to paternalism and condescension. As a result, Dutchmen did not shy away from severe disciplinary action, often meant to set an example as well.

A few references from the Dagregisters may suffice to illustrate these points, but the indifference is also evident from the relative lack of references and detailed personal description. Very often, slaves would be only denoted as "the slave or black boy from so-and-so", who misbehaved or suddenly died.

One such detached report is of 2 March 1744, when the deputy on Deshima was called to inspect the body of a slave, by the name of Connemon from Makassar, who had badly injured himself in an attempt to take his own life. "His entrails were spilling out onto his stomach, covering the wound", but he was still able to make a statement in the presence of a scribe and two employees as witnesses. After the governor was informed, two Japanese officials followed by a retinue came to ask for the cause of the incident. The report abruptly ends with the officials leaving with the statement provided by the deputy, "as, in the meantime, the boy had breathed his last". The next day he was taken away and buried in the cemetery on Mount Inasa.[128] That is all we know about Connemon. The deputy seemed more concerned with producing an official statement than with the well-being of the dying slave.

In 1792 the Shogun asked to be sent one of the black slaves of the opperhoofd out of curiosity, but all the opperhoofd was thinking of was who would pay for the expenses of the trip and of another European who would be needed to accompany the slave to translate the Malay, which the Japanese interpreters did not speak. When the opperhoofd was pressed again he said he would comply, but not without pointing out:

> that the interpreters were finding problems where there were none, for one could not expect a slave to have any knowledge of any matter, thus any answer he would give to the Shogun would be easy to translate as his Dutch is not much worse than that of most interpreters. Moreover, I have such a great esteem for the Shogun and the councilors that I do not think they will condescend to engage in a profound conversation with such a person.[129]

In the end, the dispatch was postponed until further notice because of the Governor's death and two years later it was put off to prevent delays on the court journey: "the curiosity of some lords would only create impediments".[130]

Dutch opperhoofden did not fail either to deploy their slaves in breaking the ice in their relations with other Japanese dignitaries equally fascinated by the slaves' exotic appearances. Whenever they had to entertain high-ranking Japanese guests, slaves were sent for to be marvelled at or to liven up the visits with their music. This inter-cultural effect of the slaves' presence and their contribution to smooth contact between both parties should not be underestimated.[131]

Notwithstanding their contributions and obvious benefit in smoothing out Dutch-Japanese (trade) relations, severe punishment and harsh treatment were the lot of many slaves, a practice not ques-tioned by the Dutchmen at the time but which often left the Japanese, no longer familiar with the institution of slavery, much puzzled.[132] The following description by the physician Kai Hirokawa, who had visited Nagasaki in 1790 and 1795, is a representative example of how the Japanese viewed the Dutch slaves and their Dutch masters:

> The *kurobō* are brought by the Dutch and are treated as their servants from a land called Kaburi [Africa], a large land which lies to the southwest of India. (…). The climate is very hot so their skin is black, and thus we call them *kurobō*. If they stay a few years in our country their skin lightens and becomes no different from the complexion of dark-skinned Japanese. In Kaburi it never snows. When the *kurobō* in Japan see snow for the first time, they are quite surprised. The *kurobō* possess a fine character. They per-form backbreaking and dangerous tasks for their masters without complaint. They work hard, climbing the masts of ships without the least display of fear. The *Kōmōjin* ['Red-Hairs', that is: the Dutch] have brought many of them here. I cannot fathom the ways of the Red-Hairs, who work and lash [their slaves] as if they were beasts and who kill the young and the strong who resist and throw their bodies into the sea.[133]

The end of the last sentence needs some explication, because it refers to the fate of one specific slave, 12-year-old Sjako from Ternate, who had been involved in theft of textiles, in league with Japanese water carriers.[134] Another slave, Augusto, a Buginese, who, according to the interrogation statements, did not know his own age, had witnessed the theft and had been given a piece of cloth to keep quiet. Sjako, threatened by the opperhoofd, that he would be handed over to the Japanese to be tortured, confessed right from the start, and with that condemned himself to be sent to Batavia to undergo the death penalty. Confessions by the watermen were harder to obtain, but the opperhoofd held firm in resisting the handover of Sjako for torture by the Japanese, as according to Dutch law, criminals cannot be tortured after confession. Only after finding contradictions in Sjako's and Augusto's confessions did the opperhoofd agree to "pressure" Sjako for further confession, "the means for which we do not have access to on Deshima for want of the required persons and appliances".[135] The governor declined for lack of precedent and Sjako was locked in the pillory on Deshima with screws put on both legs, "for the holes were too big for his feet".[136] The following year, awaiting his deportation, he died on board the ship and was handed over to the Japanese, "wrapped in a piece of sailcloth filled with sand, to be thrown into the sea".[137]

His was an exceptional case especially hard to understand for incidental Japanese visitors, who on the whole felt sympathy for the slaves and noted their fine character, as Kai Hirokawa had. However, in the same period, we also come across more negative remarks, such as their being considered "extremely dirty"[138] or "principally dumb",[139] characterizations the Japanese visitors may have recorded from the mouths of the Dutchmen or the interpreters. From these references Midori Fujita, Gary P. Leupp and John G. Russell have all noted a gradually declining image of persons of colour, by then all slaves, who were looked down on in the same manner as they were by their Dutch masters.[140]

To the Dutchmen on Deshima, as in Batavia and at the other Asian trading posts, slavery was convenient and justified by all kinds of argumentation, making it all the more difficult to dispose of.

The Case of Gijsbert Hemmij, the Last VOC Opperhoofd on Deshima

If there was one opperhoofd who could have had moral scruples towards slavery, it would have been Gijsbert Hemmij.[141] He was the last head under VOC rule on Deshima, where he resided from 1792 until 1798, when he died on his way back from his second court journey to Edo (held every fourth year from 1792 onwards). Already at the time, rumours surfaced that he was poisoned for secret dealings with the powerful Lord of Satsuma,[142] or for private trade transactions, quite common among VOC personnel in that period. As a matter of fact, in 1784, while heading the trading post in Palembang on Sumatra, he had been accused by the Sultan of private trade in tin and was sent back to Batavia for investigation. Lack of evidence led to his reinstatement and finally to an appointment to Japan. What made him special was his personal background, learning and enlightened outlook, in particular on the legal position of slaves.

Born in 1746 in Cape Town to Otto Lüder Hemmij from Bremen and Elizabeth le Fèbre, he was sent to the Latin school in Hamburg in 1763, where he presented an *oratio* in Latin about the Cape, signed "Gijsbertus Hemmij from Africa". His opinion about the Hottentots, "the ancient inhabitants" of the Cape, is remarkably open-minded and unbiased:

> They are not unintelligent, nor are they complete strangers to religion. They have no knowledge of any written laws, but at the same time their hatred of treachery, adultery, incest and murder proves that natural law is graven in their hearts. In charitable deeds and hospitality to fellow-members and to foreigners they are superior to many Christians. Above all, they are particularly scrupulous in keeping faith and practicing justice.[143]

In 1769 he enrolled in the Law Faculty of Leiden University in the Netherlands, receiving his doctoral degree the following year for his thesis "*De Testimoniis*: The Testimony of the Chinese, Aethiopians and other Pagans", this time signed "a Dutchman from the Cape of Good Hope". At the end of this thesis he also discusses the legal validity of testimonies of Hottentots and the complaints of East Indian slaves against their masters, "which ought to be heard".[144] The tendency of his survey is generally in line with what is proclaimed in the Batavian Statutes, including a typically paternalistic tone:

> However, because slaves are upset by generally trivial causes and complain of their masters with unjust hatred, consequently credence must not immediately be given to their complaints. For unless the signs of cruelty appear manifest and marks, other circumstantial testimony, arguments and suitable witnesses confirm the injury and harm of which they are complaining, (...), the judge will exclude them and having beaten them, send them back to their masters.[145]

In the preface of his thesis Hemmij states that the subject was suggested by his father, who had become Acting Fiscal (prosecutor) at the Cape in 1767 and Deputy Governor in 1773, in which last capacity he had welcomed James Cook "with the greatest civility" on his third-world travel.[146] In earlier days Hemmij had been involved in slaving expeditions to Madagascar. In 1740 he was the official responsible for keeping the log of the *Brack*, dispatched in October to purchase slaves.[147] Gijsbert's mother, on the other hand, was a great-granddaughter of the famous free black Engela from Bengal, who came to the Cape in 1657 and was sold to Jan van Riebeeck, the first VOC commander, which proves that Gijsbert had slave ancestry as well.[148]

In 1772 Gijsbert joined the VOC in which he served in various capacities, including his posting in Palembang and several other functions in Batavia, before coming to Japan. Last but not least, he was a member of the enlightened Batavian Society for Arts and Sciences, founded in 1778, which published several slave-related articles and in 1780 summoned readers to contribute articles on "the best ways to have house service in Batavia performed, completely or in part, by free Christian natives (*inlander*) instead of by slaves".[149] He did not contribute in writing for the Society's transactions (*Verhandelingen*) himself, but dispatched a living orangutan from Borneo to the Royal Zoo in the Netherlands in 1775, through his father at the Cape, thus providing material to the European debates on man's position in the natural world, including that of coloured races, sometimes thought to be intermediate between man and ape.[150]

As opperhoofd in Japan, he was confronted with the dwindling success of the Company, making endless efforts to obtain a larger quota of copper for export. His education helped him—evidently also for more private purposes—to befriend high-ranking Japanese hungry for knowledge about the rest of the world. He further endeared himself to them by having his slaves learn how to play Japanese musical instruments.[151] When he died, he left a large collection of Dutch, French and English books, including legal works and dictionaries, but also travelogues, for example *Cook's Voyage around the World*, geographical descriptions and lighter reading, such as the *Arabian Nights*, and poetry. He was even in the possession of Raynal's *Histoire Philosophique des Deux Indes* [Philosophical History of the East and West Indies] (the ten-volume edition of 1780) and Mary Wollstonecraft's work on the French Revolution.[152] Some of these may have been among the books former opperhoofd Isaac Titsingh had promised to send him in 1794 on his return to Europe.[153] Hemmij's 12 slaves, ranging in age from 12–42 when they arrived in 1792, were sent back to Batavia after his death.[154]

What is striking was Hemmij's versatility and relentless efforts to keep in contact with the rest of the world and with people who mattered to him. Persons like him entertained close links to Batavia and the other posts in Asia, as well as to Europe. They were also remarkably well informed and certainly not cut off from what happened in the metropolis, as is often supposed.[155] His originating from the Cape added just another link to his already vast network.

Mansell Upham has called him "Hemmy the free-thinker, classical scholar, enlightened jurist, champion for truth and social justice, worldly proto-globalist, free-trader, opportunist and modern 'person of colour'"[156] and yet, in spite of his personal background, open mind, cosmopolitism and contact to ideas that could have led to abolitionist feelings, I have not come across one single critical remark or effective action against the institution of slavery either in his published work, his Dagregisters or his private correspondence with Titsingh. Therefore, it should not come as a complete surprise that ordinary men, less cultivated and less well-connected than Gijsbert Hemmij, completely lacked such feelings at that time. The few who did harbour such feelings, like Dirk van Hogendorp, campaigned in vain. After that, it took more than half a century and global change for persons like Wolter van Hoëvell to finally mobilize anti-slavery adherents and press for abolition.

Conclusion

One of the most conspicuous features of Dutch abolitionism is that the trajectory towards final abolition—1860 in the Dutch East Indies and 1863 in the Caribbean—took so long and the mobilization of anti-slavery sentiments came so late. Before 1840, Dutch conservative policymakers were mainly preoccupied with getting Dutch finances in order, leaving no room for moral objections. Pragmatism and self-interest were more important. A feeling of national malaise and abhorrence for politics prevailed amongst the general public. Even in the final stage, after amendments to the liberal Constitution in 1848 had created more room for public opinion and participation in the political discourse, and when broader segments of society, inspired by *Uncle Tom's Cabin* and a growing flow of factual information about the situation in the colonies, started to rally for its cause, abolitionism has never grown into such a broad national movement as in Britain.

This elitist character is more reminiscent of the French case. Abolitionism largely remained a parliamentary matter in which discussions about the financial compensations to the slave-owners and the period of slave apprenticeship after abolition in 1863 further delayed the process, although the decision to abolish slavery itself was reached in 1853 or even earlier in 1842, and slavery had already become a morally embarrassing issue for conservatives, anti-revolutionaries and liberals alike.

As elsewhere, the manner and pace of Dutch abolitionism were determined by a variety of interacting local, external and global factors, some adverse to and some favouring swift abolition. For example, Dutch slave trade had been put to an end in 1814 under British pressure, and as one of the conditions for the restoration of Dutch rule over Batavia after the British interregnum. On the other hand, the Dutch aversion for radicalism held foreign interference at bay as much as possible, in spite of the efforts of the British abolitionists. A negative impact was also felt from the Haitian Revolt and the economic difficulties faced by Britain and France after emancipation. However, in the end liberal forces gained the upper hand, assisted by better and faster means of transport of people and ideas and global opinion disapproving of slavery.

This embarrassingly slow pace towards abolition may also be one of the reasons why, until recently, Dutch slavery and abolitionism have not appeared in the national historical narrative. It was mainly due to campaigns by Caribbean descendants of slaves in the Netherlands that these topics came to be acknowledged, which shows that further knowledge is of much social relevance.

In this article I have given an overview of Dutch abolitionism, based on the most recent research in this field, and have focused on the "enigma" of late Dutch abolition. In order to describe the outlook and mindset of ordinary Dutchmen in the colonies responsible for the slow change in perception of slavery, I have concentrated on Dutch slavery on Deshima, about which hardly anything has been published up till now in spite of rich Dutch and Japanese source material. Through a detailed description of the character of slavery on Deshima and by retrieving some of the attitudes from Dutchmen on the spot, I hope to have contributed to the quantitative research of Dutch slavery in the Indian Ocean World and to have encouraged a better understanding of how and why these Dutchmen were able to take slavery for granted and ignore its moral implications for so long.

Notes

1. Jan Pietersz Coen, 10 Oct. 1616, *Bescheiden omtrent zijn Bedrijf in Indië* [Records of His Undertakings in the East Indies], vol. 1, ed. Herman Th. Colenbrander ('s Gravenhage: Martinus Nijhoff, 1919), p. 218.

2. Abraham Barrau, "De Waare Staat van den Slaaven-handel in onze Nederlandsche Colonien" [The True State of the Slave Trade in the Dutch Colonies], *Bijdragen tot het Menschelijk Geluk* 3 (1790): 370–1.

3. A list of publications on the Dutch slave trade and slavery in the Atlantic is beyond the scope of this article. Please refer to the publications of Ernst van den Boogaart, Pieter C. Emmer, Cornelis Ch. Goslinga, Henk den Heijer, Martin A. Klein, Wim Klooster, Suzanne Miers, Gert van Oostindie, Johannes M. Postma and Alex van Stipriaan. Often cited general works are Johannes M. Postma, *The Dutch in the Atlantic Slave Trade, 1600–1815* (Cambridge: Cambridge University Press, 1990); Pieter C. Emmer, *The Dutch Slave Trade, 1500–1850* (Oxford: Berghahn Books, 2006); Rik van Welie, "Patterns of Slave Trading and Slavery in the Dutch Colonial World, 1596–1863", in *Dutch Colonialism, Migration and Cultural Heritage*, ed. Gert Oostindie (Leiden: KITLV Press, 2008), pp. 155–259 and "Slave Trading and Slavery in the Dutch Colonial Empire: A Global Comparison", *Nieuwe West Indische Gids* 82, 1–2 (2008): 47–96. See also Gert Oostindie and Jessica Vance Roitman, "Repositioning the Dutch in the Atlantic, 1680–1800", *Itinerario* 36, 2 (2012): 129–60.

4. The numbers stem from Postma, *Dutch in the Atlantic Slave Trade*, pp. 302–3.

5. For the history of the WIC, see Henk den Heijer, *De Geschiedenis van de WIC* [The History of the West India Company] (Zutphen: Walburg Pers, 1994).

6. The "Trans-Atlantic Slave Trade Database Project" has given impetus to this field of study as well.

7. See, for example, James O. Horton and Johanna C. Kardux, "Slavery and the Contest for National Heritage in the United States and the Netherlands", *American Studies International* 42, 2–3 (2004): 51–74; *Dutch Colonialism*, ed. Oostindie; Gert Oostindie, "Slavernij, Canon en Trauma: Debatten en Dilemma's" [Slavery, Canon and Traumas: Debates and Dilemmas], *Tijdschrift voor Geschiedenis* 121, 1 (2008): 4–21; Wim Klooster, ed., *Migration, Trade and Slavery in an Expanding World: Essays in Honour of Pieter Emmer* (Leiden: Brill, 2009); Gert Oostindie, *Postcolonial Netherlands: Sixty-five Years of Forgetting, Commemorating, Silencing* (Amsterdam: Amsterdam University Press, 2010); Ulbe Bosma et al., ed., *Postcolonial Migrations and Identity Politics* (Oxford: Berghahn, 2012).

8. For example, the National Slavery Monument in the Oosterpark in Amsterdam, erected in 2002. See also Gert Oostindie, ed., *Facing up to the Past: Perspectives on the Commemoration of Slavery from Africa, the Americas and Europe* (Kingston: Randle Publishers, 2001). The Dutch version of this book was presented to a member of the Dutch cabinet as a plea for a monument and to arouse awareness about Dutch slavery. See also Gert Oostindie, "The Slippery Paths of Commemoration and Heritage Tourism: the Netherlands, Ghana, and the Rediscovery of Atlantic Slavery", *New West Indian Guide* 79 (2005): 55–77.

9. See www.ninsee.nl/, accessed 4 Mar. 2015. Public funding was terminated in 2012.

10. For example, the NTR documentary *De slavernij* (in five parts), broadcast in 2011, which has drawn criticism as being too much a product of "white perspective".

11. For example, *Black is Beautiful: Rubens tot Dumas* in the Nieuwe Kerk in Amsterdam in 2008 (catalogue published by Waanders Uitgevers, Zwolle in 2008).

12. For example, Dirk J. Tang, *Slavernij: Een Geschiedenis* [Slavery: A History] (Zutphen: Walburg Press, 2013), which was published in commemoration of the Dutch slavery abolition in 1863.

13. For the text of the canon and further information see http://entoen.nu/en, accessed 4 Mar. 2015. Other related "windows" are: "the Dutch East India Company (VOC) 1602–1799: Overseas Expansion", "Max Havelaar 1860: Scandal in the East Indies", "Surinam and the Netherlands Antilles since 1945: Decolonisation in the West" and "Indonesia 1945–1949: A Colony Fights for Freedom".

14. For an overview of exhibitions and events held in 2013, see http://www.herdenkingslavernijverleden2013.nl/, accessed 4 Mar. 2015.

15. A search for "Zwarte Piet" or "Black Pete" on the Internet displays an astonishing amount of hits on this topic. See also Allison Blakely, *Blacks in the Dutch World: The Evolution of Racial Imagery in a Modern Society* (Bloomington, IN: Indiana University Press, 1993), pp. 39–49; John I.A. Helsloot, "*Zwarte Piet* and Cultural Aphasia in the Netherlands", *Quotidian: Journal for the Study of Everyday Life* 3 (2012): 1–20.

16. For the most recent demographic data and historical developments, see the population figures published by the Central Bureau for Statistics (https://www.cbs.nl/en-GB/menu/themas/bevolking/cijfers/default.htm, CBS Population Figures). Until the end of World War II the Netherlands was primarily white, but has grown into a multicultural society in which more than one in ten inhabitants is of non-Western background.

17. Van Welie, "Patterns of Slave Trading", p. 158.

18. Kerry Ward, *Networks of Empire, Forced Migration in the Dutch India Company* (Cambridge: Cambridge University Press, 2009), p. 26. She

mentions, however, an early study on slavery in the Indonesian Archi-
pelago: S. Kalff, *De slavernij in Oost-Indië* [Slavery in the East Indies]
(Baarn: Hollandia-drukkerij, 1920), pp. 3–34 and the pioneering work
on slavery and bondage in South Asia: Anthony Reid, ed., *Slavery,
Bondage and Dependency in Southeast Asia* (St Lucia: University of
Queensland Press, 1983). Other older publications are *"Slavernij"*
[Slavery], *Encyclopaedie van Nederlandsch-Indië* [Encyclopaedia of the
Dutch East Indies], vol. 3 ('s Gravenhage: Martinus Nijhoff, 1919), pp.
800–8; Frederik de Haan, *Oud Batavia: Gedenkboek* [Old Batavia: Com-
memorative Volume] (Batavia: G. Kolff, 1922–23), vol. 1, pp. 451–68.

19.   For example, Gwyn Campbell, Markus P.M. Vink, James F. Warren and
Rik van Welie for the Indian Ocean; Sinnapah Asaratnam for India;
Wil O. van Dijk for Birma [Burma]; Kate Ekama, Gerrit J. Knaap,
Remco Raben, Alicia Schrikker and Lodewijk J. Wagenaar for Ceylon;
and Nordin Hussin on Melaka. With regard to the slave trade and
slavery in and around Batavia and in other parts of the Indonesian
Archipelago, see works by Susan Abeyasekere, Peter Boomgaard, James
J. Fox, Hans Hägerdahl, Eric A. Jones, Bondan Kanomoyoso, Gerrit
J. Knaap, Alfons van der Kraan, Hendrik E. Niemeijer, Remco Raben,
Anthony Reid, Heather Sutherland, Gelman J. Taylor and Phillip Winn.
After submission of this article, a remarkable increase of scholarly
interest in Dutch slavery has occurred. Please refer to Reggie Baay,
Daar werd wat gruwelijks verricht: Slavernij in Nederlands-Indië [Some-
thing Horrifying was Carried Out: Slavery in the Dutch East Indies]
(Amsterdam: Athenaeum-Polak & Van Gennep, 2015) and Matthias
van Rossum, *Kleurrijke Tragiek: De Geschiedenis van Slavernij in Azië
onder de VOC* [Colourful Tragedy: The History of Slavery in Asia under
the VOC] (Hilversum: Verloren, 2015).

20.   For example, publications by James Armstrong, Anna J. Böeseken,
Robert J. Ross, Robert C.-H., Schell, Mansell Upham, Kerry R. Ward
and Nigel Worden.

21.   It goes without saying that the Durban "World Conference against
Racism, Racial Discrimination, Xenophobia and Related Intolerance" in
2001 has also given a large impetus to studies on slavery in the Dutch
Empire.

22.   See, for example, Gert van Oostindie, "Squaring the Circle: Commemo-
rating the VOC after 400 Years", *Bijdragen tot de Taal-, Land- en
Volkenkunde* 159, 1 (2003): 135–61; Anne Marieke van der Wal,
"Waarom wordt slechts de helft van ons slavenverleden herdacht?"
[Why is only Half of Our Slave Past Commemorated?], *Volkskrant*,
1 July 2013. For a general history of the VOC, see Pieter van Dam,
Beschrijvinge van de Oost-Indische Compagnie 1639–1701 [A Descrip-
tion of the East India Company, 1639–1701], 7 vols, ed. F.W. Stapel

et al. ('s Gravenhage: Martinus Nijhoff, 1927–54); Femme S. Gaastra, *The Dutch East India Company: Expansion and Decline* (Zutphen: Walburg Press, 2003).

23. The original text was: "Let us be happy together! Let us be optimistic! Let us say: the Netherlands are back on track! That same VOC mentality of crossing borders, dynamism! Do we not?" (28 Sept. 2006).

24. Nigel Worden, "The Changing Politics of Slave Heritage in the Western Cape, South Africa", *Journal of African History* 50 (2009): 34–6.

25. Markus Vink, "'The World's Oldest Trade': Dutch Slavery and Slave Trade in the Indian Ocean in the Seventeenth Century", *Journal of World History* 14, 2 (2003): 168. Vink's findings have been specified by Rik van Welie in *Patterns of Slave Trading*; Ulbe Bosma and Remco Raben, *Being "Dutch" in the Indies: A History of Creolisation and Empire 1500–1920* (Singapore: NUS Press, 2008), p. 47; Remco Raben, "Cities and the Slave Trade in Early-Modern Southeast Asia", in *Linking Destinies: Trade, Towns and Kin in Asian History*, ed. Peter Boomgaard et al. (Leiden: KITLV Press, 2008), pp. 119–40.

26. Vink, "The World's Oldest Trade", p. 139.

27. Van Welie, *Patterns of Slave Trading*, pp. 192–207, Vink, "The World's Oldest Trade", pp. 140–6; Hendrik E. Niemeijer, *Batavia: Een Koloniale Samenleving in de 17e Eeuw* [Batavia: A Colonial Society in the 17th Century] (Amsterdam: Uitgeverij Balans, 2005), pp. 53–5; Peter Boomgaard, "Human Capital, Slavery and Low Rates of Economic and Population Growth in Indonesia, 1600–1910", in *The Structure of Slavery in Indian Ocean Africa and Asia*, ed. Gwyn Campbell (London: Frank Cass, 2004), pp. 88–91; Raben, "Cities and the Slave Trade", pp. 125–34.

28. Vink, "The World's Oldest Trade", p. 146. See also Nigel Worden, "Indian Ocean Slavery and its Demise in the Cape Colony", in *Abolition and its Aftermath in Indian Ocean Africa and Asia*, ed. Gwyn Campbell (London: Routledge, 2005), pp. 29–38.

29. Els M. Jacobs, *Merchant in Asia: The Trade of the Dutch East India Company during the Eighteenth Century* (Leiden: CNWS Publications, 2006), p. 418, n. 6.

30. See also Gerrit J. Knaap, "Slavery and the Dutch in Southeast Asia", in *Fifty Years Later: Antislavery, Capitalism and Modernity in the Dutch Orbit*, ed. Gert Oostindie (Leiden: KITLV Press, 1995), p. 193; Vink, "The World's Oldest Trade", pp. 133–5.

31. Raben, "Cities and the Slave Trade", p. 133.

32. Ibid., p. 131.

33. For Company slaves, see Pieter van Dam, *Beschrijvinge*, 3, pp. 201–4; De Haan, *Batavia*, vol. 1, pp. 352–4.

34. Depopulation on the Banda Islands became the most conspicuous symbol of ruthless VOC government. For a revaluation, see Phillip

Winn, "Slavery and Cultural Creativity in the Banda Islands", *Journal of Southeast Asian Studies* 41, 3 (2010): 365–89. See also Jan Lucassen, "A Multinational and its Labor Force: The Dutch East India Company, 1595–1795", *International Labor and Working-Class History* 66 (2006): 24–6.

35. For demographical data from the censuses of Batavia and the surrounding region, see the appendices in Remco Raben, "Batavia and Colombo: The Ethnic and Spatial Order of Two Colonial Cities 1600–1800", unpublished PhD dissertation (Leiden: Universiteit Leiden, 1996); Hans Gooszen, "Population Census in VOC-Batavia 1673–1792", unpublished manuscript (2008, deposited at Data Archiving and Networked Services, DANS, www.dans.knaw.nl, accessed 4 Mar. 2015).

36. For Batavia see S. Abeyasekere, "Slaves in Batavia: Insights from a Slave Register", in Reid, *Slavery, Bondage and Dependency*, pp. 286–314.

37. Knaap, "Slavery and the Dutch", pp. 200–1; *Encyclopaedie van Nederlandsch-Indië*, vol. 3, p. 805.

38. Gert van Oostindie, "History brought Home: Post-colonial Migrations and the Dutch Rediscovery of Slavery", in *Migration, Trade and Slavery*, ed. Klooster, p. 312. For slave legislation, see, for example, James J. Fox, "'For Good and Sufficient Reasons': An Examination of Early Dutch East India Company Ordinances on Slaves and Slavery", in *Slavery, Bondage and Dependency*, ed. Reid, pp. 246–62; Jacobus A. van der Chijs, ed., *Nederlandsch-Indisch Plakaatboek, 1602–1811* [Book of Dutch East India Proclamations, 1602–1811] (Batavia: Landsdrukkerij, 1885–1900), 17 vols. For an overview of the most important regulations until the end of the 17th century, see van Dam, *Beschrijvinge*, 3, pp. 205–8. For the legal practices in Dutch Asia focused on the slaves, see Eric Jones, *Wives, Slaves and Concubines: A History of the Female Underclass in Dutch Asia* (DeKalb: Northern Illinois University Press, 2010), pp. 69–89, 96–8.

39. The most important older studies concerning Dutch abolitionism and abolition are: Riemer Reinsma, *Een merkwaardige episode uit de geschiedenis van de slavenemancipatie* [A Remarkable Episode in the History of Slave Emancipation] ('s Gravenhage: Van Goor & Zonen, 1963); Maarten Kuitenbrouwer, "De Nederlandse Afschaffing van de Slavernij in Vergelijkend Perspectief" [The Dutch Abolition of Slavery in a Comparative Context], *Bijdragen en Mededelingen betreffende de Geschiedenis der Nederlanden* 93 (1978): 69–100; Jozef R. Siwpersad, *De Nederlandse regering en de afschaffing van de Surinaamsche slavernij (1833–1863)* [The Dutch Government and the Abolition of Surinamese Slavery (1833–1863) (Groningen: Bouma's Boekhuis, 1979); Albertus N. Paasman, "Reinhart: Nederlandse Literatuur en Slavernij ten tijde van de Verlichting" [Reinhart: Dutch Literature and Slavery During the

Period of Enlightenment], unpublished PhD dissertation (Amsterdam: Universiteit Amsterdam, 1984); Johanna M. van Winter, "Public Opinion in the Netherlands on the Abolition of Slavery", in *Dutch Authors on West Indian History: A Historiographical Selection*, ed. Marie A.P. Meilink-Roelofsz (The Hague: Nijhoff, 1982), pp. 100–28; as well as the chapter on abolition and emancipation in Postma, *The Dutch in the Atlantic Slave Trade*. See also Emmer, *Dutch Slave Trade*, Gwyn Campbell, "Introduction: Abolition and its Aftermath in the Indian Ocean World"; Nigel Worden, "Indian Ocean Slavery and its Demise in the Cape Colony", *Abolition and its Aftermath*, pp. 1–25, 29–49.

40. See Oostindie, ed., *Fifty Years Later* with contributions a.o. by Gert Oostindie, "Introduction: Explaining Dutch Abolition", pp. 1–23; Seymour Drescher, "The Long Goodbye: Dutch Capitalism and Antislavery in Comparative Perspective", pp. 25–66 and "Epilogue: Reflections", pp. 243–61; Maarten Kuitenbrouwer, "The Dutch Case of Antislavery: Late Abolitions and Élitist Abolitionism", pp. 67–88; Angela Sens, "Dutch Antislavery Attitudes in a Decline-Ridden Society, 1750–1815", pp. 89–104; Robert Ross, "Abolitionism, the Batavian Republic, the British, and the Cape Colony", pp. 179–91; Gerrit J. Knaap, "Slavery and the Dutch", pp. 193–206, and Pieter C. Emmer, "The Ideology of Free Labor and Dutch Colonial Policy, 1830–1870", pp. 207–22.

41. Oostindie, "Introduction", *Fifty Years Later*, p. 15. See also Angelie Sens, '*Mensaap, Heiden, Slaaf*': *Nederlandse Visies op de Wereld rond 1800* [Ape, Pagan, Slave: Dutch Conceptions of the World around 1800] (Den Haag: Sdu Uitgevers, 2001). For the typical circumstances in the 18th-century Netherlands, see also Margaret C. Jacob and Wijnand W. Mijnhardt, *The Dutch Republic in the Eighteenth Century: Decline, Enlightenment, and Revolution* (Ithaca: Cornell University Press, 1992); Joost Kloek and Wijnand Mijnhardt, *1800: Blauwdrukken voor een Samenleving* [1800: Blueprints of a Society] (Den Haag: Sdu Uitgevers, 2001).

42. Oostindie, "Introduction", *Fifty Years Later*, p. 13.

43. Maartje Janse, *De Afschaffers: publieke opinie, organisatie en politiek in Nederland 1840–1880* [The Abolishers: Public Opinion, Organization and Politics in the Netherlands 1840–1880] (Amsterdam: Wereldbibliotheek, 2007), p. 13.

44. For the presence of slaves in the Netherlands, see Dienke Hondius, "Access to the Netherlands of Enslaved and Free Black Africans: Exploring Legal and Social Historical Practices in the Sixteenth-Nineteenth Centuries", *Slavery and Abolition* 32, 3 (2011): 377–95; Blakely, *Blacks in the Dutch World*, pp. 225–74. On the free soil principle, see also Sue Peabody, "Free Soil: The Generation and Circulation of an Atlantic

Legal Principle", *Slavery and Abolition: A Journal of Slave and Post-Slave Studies* 32, 3 (2011): 331–9.

45. Janse, *Afschaffers*, p. 53. See also Maartje Janse, "Réveilvrouwen en de strijd voor afschaffing van de slavernij (1840–1863)" [Women of the *Réveil* Movement and their Fight for the Abolition of Slavery (1840–1863)], *Documentatieblad van de Nederlandse Kerkgeschiedenis na 1800* 59 (2003): 11–21 and "Representing Distant Victims: The Emergence of an Ethical Movement in Dutch Colonial Politics 1840–1880", *Bijdragen en Mededelingen betreffende de Geschiedenis der Nederlanden* 126, 1 (2003): 53–80.

46. Drescher, "Long Goodbye", p. 37. See also Gert Oostindie, "Introduction", *Fifty Years*, pp. 1–23.

47. David Brion Davis, *The Problem of Slavery in Western Culture* (Ithaca, NY: Cornell University Press, 1966), pp. 108, 165.

48. G.A. Bredero's *Moortje* (Amsterdam, 1617), ed. P. Minderaa, C.A. Zaalberg and B.C. Damsteegt (Leiden: Martinus Nijhoff, 1984), line 233, p. 143.

49. Emmer, *Dutch Slave Trade*, pp. 13 16; Markus P.M. Vink, "Freedom and Slavery: The Dutch Republic, the VOC World, and the Debate over the 'World's Oldest Trade'", *South African Historical Journal* 59 (2007): 28–30.

50. Vink, "Freedom and Slavery", p. 37.

51. See, for example, Davis, *Problem of Slavery*; Paasman, *Reinhart*, pp. 98–108, 211–2; Sens, "Dutch Antislavery Attitudes", pp. 94–6; Vink, "Freedom and Slavery", pp. 30–44.

52. Paasman, *Reinhart*, pp. 109–16, 212–6; Sens, *Mensaap, Heiden, Slaaf*, pp. 97–9; Vink, "Freedom and Slavery", pp. 35–7.

53. Often cited is Nicolaas de Graaff, *Oost-Indise Spiegel* [The East Indian Mirror] (1701), ed. Marijke Barend-van Haeften and Hetty Plekenpol (Leiden: KITLV Press, 2010). For an overview of other visitors, see Barend van Haeften, *Oost-Indië Gespiegeld: Nicolaas de Graaff, een Schrijvend Chirurgijn in Dienst van de VOC* [East India Mirrored: Nicolaas de Graaff, a Writer-Surgeon in the Service of the Dutch East India Company (VOC)] (Zutphen: WalburgPers, 1992), pp. 131–90. For examples of such cruel treatment, see Niemeijer, *Batavia*, pp. 190–206; Jones, *Wives, Slaves and Concubines*, pp. 126–48.

54. See Adrienne Zuiderweg, "Nieuwsgaring in Batavia tijdens de VOC" [News Gathering in Batavia under the VOC], *Tijdschrift voor Tijdschrift-studies* 28 (2010): 108–26; Marie A.P. Meilink-Roelofsz, *Van Geheim tot Openbaar: Een Historische Verkenning* [From Secrecy to Publicity: A Historical Investigation] (Leiden: Universitaire Pers, 1970).

55. See Gerrit J. Knaap, "Slavery and the Dutch", p. 198.

56. Dirk van Hogendorp, *Kraspoekol, of De Slaavernij: Een Tafereel der Zeden van Neerlands-Indië* [Kraspoekol, or Slavery: A Tableau of Morals in the Dutch East Indies] (Delft: Roelofswaert, 1800). See also Ann Kumar, "Literary Approaches to Slavery and the Indies Enlightenment: Van Hogendorp's Kraspoekol", *Indonesia* 43 (1987): 43–65; Christine Levecq, "Het Denken over de Oost-Indische Slavernij" [East Indian Slavery Thought], *Indische Letteren* 12 (1997): 147–62. Hogendorp's eventful and colourful career as well as his anti-slavery writings and activities are too extensive to describe here in detail. See, for example, Gerrit J. Schutte, *De Nederlandse Patriotten en de Koloniën: Een Onderzoek naar hun Denkbeelden en Optreden 1770–1800* [The Dutch Patriots and the Colonies: An Investigation of their Opinions and Actions 1770–1800] (Groningen: Tjeenk Willink, 1974), pp. 178–89. One of the latest publications on Van Hogendorp is Edwin van Meerkerk, *De Gebroeders Van Hogendorp: Botsende Idealen in de Kraamkamer van het Koninkrijk* [The Brothers Van Hogendorp: Clashing Ideals in the Delivery Room of the Kingdom] (Amsterdam: Atlas Contact, 2013).

57. See Arend H. Huussen, Jr, "The Dutch Constitution of 1798 and the Problem of Slavery", *Tijdschrift voor Rechtsgeschiedenis* 67, 1 (1999): 107.

58. G. Th. Raynal, *Histoire Philosophique et Politique des Etablissements et du Commerce des Européens dans les Deux Indes* [A Philosophical and Political History of the Settlements and Trade of the Europeans in the East and West Indies] (La Haye, 1770 and later editions).

59. For the *patriotten* in the colonies see Schutte, *Nederlandse Patriotten*.

60. Huussen, "The Dutch Constitution of 1798", pp. 99–114.

61. See Sens, "Dutch Antislavery Attitudes", pp. 92–3 and *Mensaap, Heiden, Slaaf*, pp. 117–123.

62. Jean Gelman Taylor, *The Social World of Batavia: European and Eurasian in Dutch Asia* (Madison: University of Wisconsin Press, 1983), pp. 98–9.

63. Knaap, "Slavery and the Dutch", pp. 198–9.

64. Postma, *Dutch in the Atlantic Slave Trade*, p. 290.

65. Knaap, "Slavery and the Dutch", p. 199; Wolter R. van Hoëvell, *De Emancipatie der Slaven in Neêrlands-Indië: Eene Verhandeling* [The Slave Emancipation in the Dutch East Indies: A Treatise] (Groningen: C.M. van Bolhuis Hoitsema, 1848), Chapter III.

66. *Encyclopaedie van Nederlandsch-Indië*, 3, p. 804.

67. Janse, *Afschaffers*, p. 295.

68. Ibid., p. 57.

69. Ibid., p. 52.

70. Kuitenbrouwer, "Dutch Case of Antislavery", p. 71.

71. See Janse, *Afschaffers*, pp. 58–62.

72. Ibid., pp. 74–88. The archive of this association was recently discovered.

73. See Janse, *Afschaffers*, p. 32.

74. Ibid., pp. 65–7.

75. Ibid., pp. 67–9.

76. Ibid., pp. 88–9.

77. For his activities in Batavia, see Paul van 't Veer, *Geen blad voor de mond: Vijf radikalen uit de 19de eeuw* [Speaking Out: Five Radicals in the 19th Century] (Amsterdam: Arbeiderspers, 1958); Hans Groot, *Van Batavia naar Weltevreden: Het Bataviaasch Genootschap van Kunsten en Wetenschappen, 1778–1867* [From Batavia to Weltevreden: The Batavian Society of Arts and Sciences, 1778–1867] (Leiden: KITLV Press, 2009), pp. 289–347; Van Hoëvell, *De Emanipatie der Slaven*, pp. 289–347. For a discussion on this last work, see Levecq, "Denken over Oost-Indische Slavernij", pp. 155–8.

78. See also Ann Stoler, *Along the Archival Grain: Epistemic Anxieties and Colonial Common Sense* (Princeton, NJ: Princeton University Press, 2009), pp. 73–95.

79. Van Hoëvell, *Emancipatie der Slaven*. This treatise was originally written in 1847 at the request of the Governor-General in Batavia.

80. Wolter R. van Hoëvell, "Eene slaven-vendutie" [A Slave Auction], *Tijdschrift voor Nederlandsch-Indië* 15 (1853): 184–91.

81. For sentimentalism in the anti-slavery debates, see Janse, *Afschaffers*, pp. 100–3 and "Representing Distant Victims", pp. 59–68.

82. Janse, *Afschaffers*, pp. 91–7.

83. Ibid., pp. 103–14.

84. Ibid., p. 113.

85. Kuitenbrouwer, "Dutch Case of Antislavery", p. 74.

86. Wolter R. Van Hoëvell, *Slaven en Vrijen onder de Nederlandsche Wet* [Slaves and Free Men under Dutch Law], 1, 2 (Zaltbommel: Joh. Noman en Zoon, 1854). Kuitenbrouwer, "Dutch Case of Antislavery", p. 75. See also Janse, *Afschaffers*, p. 118.

87. See for example, Winter, *Public Opinion*, pp. 117–26; Janse, *Afschaffers*, pp. 120–4.

88. Emmer, *Dutch Slave Trade*, p. 128.

89. Knaap, "Slavery and the Dutch", p. 202.

90. See, for example, Thio Termorshuizen, "Indentured Labour in the Dutch Colonial Empire 1800–1940", in *Dutch Colonialism*, ed. Oostindie, pp. 261–314.

91. Previous studies about the slaves on Deshima, which have also made use of Dutch sources, are: Ryuto Shimada, "Jūhasseiki-matsu Nagasaki Dejima ni okeru Ajiajin Dorei: Oranda Higashi Indogaisha no Nihon Bōeki ni kansuru Hitotsu no Shakaishiteki Bunseki" [Asian Slaves on

Nagasaki Dejima at the End of the 18th Century: A Social-Historical Analysis of the Japan Trade of the Dutch East India Company], in *Chi'ikikan no Rekishi-sekai: Idō, Shōtotsu, Yūgō* [The World of Inter-Regional History: Migration, Collusion, Fusion], ed. Takeo Suzuki (Tokyo: Waseda Daigaku Shuppanbu, 2008), pp. 339–63; Michiko Kondō, "18 Seiki ikō Dejima ni okeru Marēkei Jūjin no Katsudō: Gakki Ensō ni yoru Nihonjin Hinkyaku e no Motenashi o Jirei to shite" [The Activities of the Malay Inhabitants of Dejima from the 18th Century Onwards: The Example of Entertaining Japanese Guests with Music], *Bunka Ronshū* 17 (2010): 75–111. For the Japanese image and awareness of Africa, including references to the slaves on Deshima and how they are depicted in Japanese sources, see Midori Fujita, *Afurika Hakken: Nihon ni okeru Afurika-zō no Hensen* [The Discovery of Africa: Changes in the Japanese Perception of Africa] (Tokyo: Iwanami Shoten, 2005). The Deshima slaves also feature in a few studies about Japanese images of blacks, such as Gary P. Leupp, "Images of Black People in late Mediaeval and Early Modern Japan, 1543–1900", *Japan Forum* 7, 1 (1995): 1–13; John G. Russell, "Excluded Presence: Shoguns, Minstrels, Bodyguards, and Japan's Encounters with the Black Other", *Zinbun* 40 (2007): 15–51.

92. For a general overview of Dutch–Japanese relations, see Leonard Blussé et al., ed., *Bridging the Divide: 400 Years The Netherlands–Japan* (Leiden: Hotei Publishing, 2000).

93. *Dagregisters, 1641–1833* and *1843–60*, NA (National Archive in the Hague), NFJ (*Nederlands Faktorij Japan* 1.04.21) 55–259 and 1613–24. For the tables of contents in English for the years 1641–70 and 1700–1800, see *The Deshima Dagregisters: Their Original Tables of Contents*, 13 vols (Leiden: Institute for the History of European Expansion, 1986–2010) and *The Deshima Diaries: Marginalia, 1700–1800*, 2 vols (Tokyo: Japan–Netherlands Institute, 1992, 2004).

94. For the case of 1792, see the following paragraph.

95. For example, Mosis, a black servant from Batavia in 1684 and of Titus, a slave of Opperhoofd David Drinkman who was to be taken to Edo in 1735 to serve as a translator on account of their fluency in Japanese (*Dagregister*, 9 Jan., 12 Apr. 1684 and 18 Nov. 1734: NA, NFJ 97 and 145).

96. *Dagregister*, 11 Aug. 1641 (NA, NFJ 55).

97. For example, in 1660, when seven black boys were counted (*Dagregister*, 27 Oct. 1660: NA, NFJ 74).

98. "Monsterrol van het schip *Zeeland*" [Muster-roll of the Ship *Zeeland*] *1787* (NA, NFJ 1484).

99. Shimada, "Jūhasseiki-matsu Nagasaki Dejima", pp. 348–54.

100. "Monsterrollen van voor Batavia of Deshima bestemde Schepen" [Muster-rolls of Ships Bound for Batavia or Deshima] *(1781–94)* (NA, NFJ 1475–89).

101. "Monsterrol van het schip *Mars*" [Muster-roll of the Ship *Mars*], *1781* (NA, NFJ 1475).

102. Deshima housed around 15–20 resident Dutchmen during the off-season. See Reinier Hesselink, "People on Deshima around 1700", in Blussé et al., *Bridging the Divide*, p. 48.

103. For muster rolls from 1831–42, see NA, NFJ 1452–63, and from 1844–56, NA, NFJ 1749–58 and 1902.

104. Shimada, "Jūhasseiki-matsu Nagasaki Dejima", p. 353.

105. For example, a certain Pieter from Sadraspatnam, who had hidden in a Chinese wankang afraid to be chastised for drunkenness (*Dagregister*, 14 May 1695: NA, NFJ 108).

106. See Fujita, *Afurika Hakken*, pp. 1–42.

107. For example, a "large *kaffer*, who could play a little on the violin", who was asked to entertain a highly-ranked Japanese guest (*Dagregister*, 1 Oct. 1647: NA, NFJ 70).

108. Kōkan Shiba, *Kōkan Saiyū Nikki* [Kōkan's Diary of a Ship to the West], in *Shiba Kōkan Zenshū* [The Complete Works of Kōkan Shiba], vol. 1 (Tokyo: Yasaka Shobō, 1992), p. 321.

109. "Attestatieboekjes, Particuliere Instrumenten, Protocollen" [Certificates, Private Deeds, Notarial Records] (1701–1860) (incomplete) (NA, NFJ 1560–72, 1573–89 and 1943–50).

110. See, for example, the registration paper of a certain Antonij from Bengal who had been renamed Fortuijn when he came into the possession of Junior Mate Pieter de Smet in June 1747 for 60 rijksdaalders in Batavia. Fortuijn was then resold on Deshima on 23 Oct. (before the departure of the ships) to Carpenter Eelke Riskes for 80 rixdaalders ("Minuutboek" [Collected Original Deeds] 174–46: NA, NFJ 1574).

111. *Vendue Rol* [Sales List] of the possessions of Assistant Jan Fauvarcq, 21 Sept. 1786 (*Minuutboek 1786*: NA, NFJ 1588). He had owned two slaves, Pedro and September, valued at 230 and 160 rixdaalders.

112. "Memorie voor een aankomend opperhoofd" [Memorandum for the Next *Opperhoofd* (Head of the Trading Post)] (Document No. 76 in the Collection of Private Papers of Hendrik Doeff: NA 2.21.054, Collectie Aanwinsten).

113. Gentaku Otsuki, *Ransetsu Benwaku* [A Clarification of Misunderstandings in Theories about the Dutch] (1799) in Chūryū Morishima, *Kōmō Zatsuwa/Ransetsu Benwaku* [A Miscellany about the Red-hairs], ed. Tsutomu Sugimoto (Tokyo: Yasaka Shobō, 1972), p. 194.

114. For examples from the Dagregisters, see Shimada, "Jūhasseiki-matsu Nagasaki Dejima", p. 356.

115. For pictorial sources of Deshima, see Nagasaki-shi Deshima Shiseki Seibi Shingikai, ed., *Deshima-zu: Sono Keikan to Hensen* [Illustrations of Deshima: Its Appearance and Transformation] (Tokyo: Chūō Kōron Bijutsu Shuppan, 1987). For Nagasaki prints, see Willem van Gulik, *The Dutch in Nagasaki: 19th-century Japanese Prints* (Amsterdam: Uitgeverij Stichting Terra Incognita, 1998) and for other representations of Dutchmen and their slaves, see the catalogue "Oranda Shumi: Sakoku-shita no Ekizochishizumu" [The Craze for Holland: Exoticism during the Period of Isolation] (Tokyo: Tobacco & Salt Museum, 1996). At the end of the 18th century, these representations were part of a craze for all things Dutch.

116. Nigel Worden, *Slavery in Dutch South Africa* (Cambridge: Cambridge University Press, 1985), pp. 119–37.

117. Taneo Morinaga, ed., *Hankachō: Nagasaki Bugyō Hanketsu Kiroku* [The *Hankachō*: Criminal Records of the Governor of Nagasaki] (1660–1867), 11 vols (Nagasaki: Hankachō Kankōkai, 1958–61).

118. See, for example, *Dagregister*, 13 Aug. 1649 or 27 Feb. 1778 (NA, NFJ 62 and 188).

119. See the example of the freed slave Esau Fransz from Batavia who had raped 10–12-year-old Floris from Bengal in 1718, or an anonymous slave who had been caught "indulging himself with a goat" in 1764 (*Dagregister*, 15 July 1718 and 1 June 1764: NA, NFJ 128 and 174).

120. See, for example, *Dagregister*, 14–21 May 1695 and 2–3 Dec. 1755 (NA, NFJ 108, 166). Another case in 1752, not mentioned in the Dagregister, concerns a slave who went on a drinking spree in the red-light district of Yoriai-machi, dressed in Japanese clothing together with a Japanese day labourer (Morinaga, *Hankachō*, 2, pp. 130–1).

121. See, for example, *Dagregister*, 22 and 23 June 1748 or 11–22 Jan. 1760 (NA, NFJ 158, 170).

122. See, for example, *Dagregister*, 1 Dec. 1689, 23 Jan. 1719, 24 Sept. 1733, 20 Apr. 1744 and 19 Mar. 1745 (NA, NFJ 103, 129, 143, 154 and 155).

123. For a list of the cases which could not be put under wraps on Deshima and which have been tried by the Nagasaki authorities, see Fujita, *Afurika Hakken*, pp. 46–7.

124. See, for example, *Dagregister*, 3 Mar. 1719, 29 Jan. 1760, 11 Dec. 1755 and 2 Jan. 1756 (NA, NFJ 129, 170, 166).

125. For the part on slaves' legislation in the Batavian Statutes see Van der Chijs, *Nederlandsch-Indisch Plakaatboek*, vol. 1, pp. 572–6.

126. Stoler, *Archival Grain*, pp. 40–1, 44.

127. For such Japanese descriptions, see Fujita, *Afurika Hakken*, pp. 49–72.

128. *Dagregister*, 2, 3 Mar. 1744 (NA, NFJ 154).

129. *Dagregister*, 22, 23 Mar. 1792 (NA, NFJ 203).

130. *Dagregister*, 4 Apr. 1794 (NA, NFJ 205).

131. This intercultural effect was already noted by Michiko Kondō, who focused on the musical performances by the slaves (see Kondō, "18 Seiki ikō Dejima", pp. 78, 85, 91, 98).

132. For Japanese slavery, see Hidemasa Maki, *Kinsei Nihon no Jinshin Baibai no Keifu* [A Chronology of Human Traffickking in Early Modern Japan] (Tokyo: Sōbunsha, 1970); Thomas Nelson, "Slavery in Medieval Japan", *Monumenta Nipponica* 59, 4 (2004): 463–92. Although trafficking of slaves was officially banned at the end of the 16th century, such trade did not fully disappear and slave-like conditions, such as those of the girls in the brothels continued to exist. See Chapter 8 by Yuriko Yokoyama in this volume; Yōko Matsui, "The Debt-servitude of Prostitutes in Japan during the Edo Period, 1600–1868", in *Bonded Labour and Debt in the Indian Ocean World*, ed. Gwyn Campbell and Alessandro Stanziani (Brookfield: Pickering & Chatto, 2013), pp. 173–85.

133. Kai Hirokawa, *Nagasaki Kenbunroku* [A Record of Personal Observations of Nagasaki] (Nagasaki: Nagasaki Bunkensha, 1973, 1st ed., 1797), pp. 89–90. The translation of the citation is based on Russell, "Excluded Presence", p. 26.

134. *Dagregister*, 9 Aug.–23 Sept. 1782; *Justitieele Papieren d'Anno, 1782* [Judicial Papers of the Year 1782] (NA, NFJ 192 and 1526). For a discussion of this case, see Shimada, "Jūhasseiki-matsu Nagasaki Dejima", pp. 357–8.

135. *Dagregister*, 26 Aug. 1782.

136. *Dagregister*, 13 Aug. 1782.

137. *Dagregister*, 21 Oct. 1783 (NA, NFJ 194).

138. Shiba, *Kōkan Saiyū Nikki*, p. 321.

139. Chūryū Morishima, *Kōmō Zatsuwa* in *Kōmō Zatsuwa/Ransetsu Benwaku*, (1st ed., 1787), p. 20.

140. Fujita, *Afurika Hakken*, p. 62; Leupp, "Images of Black People", pp. 1, 4–6; Russell, "Excluded Presence", pp. 26–7.

141. On Hemmij see the biographical notes in Gysbert Hemmy, *Oratio Latina, De Promontorio Bonae Spei, 1767*, tr. and ed. K.D. White (Cape Town: South African Public Library, 1959) and *De Testimoniis: The Testimony of the Chinese, Aethiopians and other Pagans, as well as of the Hottentots inhabiting the Cape of Good Hope, likewise about the Complaints of East Indian Slaves*, tr. and annot. Margaret L. Hewett (Cape Town: University of Cape Town, 1998). See also Mansell Upham, "'This Corner of the World Smiles for Me above all Others': Gysbert Hemmy from Africa—A Reappraisal", *Quarterly Bulletin of the National Library of South Africa* 63, 1 (2009): 17–30; Isabel Tanaka-van Daalen, "Het Graf van Gijsbert Hemmij bij de Tennenji Tempel in Kakegawa" [The Grave of Gijsbert Hemmij at the Tennenji Temple in Kakegawa],

unpublished report for the occasion of the restoration of Hemmij's grave (2004).

142. See Jan Feenstra Kuiper, "Some Notes on the Foreign Relations of Japan in the Early Napoleonic Period (1798–1805)", *Transactions of the Asiatic Society of Japan* 2, 1 (1923): 55–82.

143. *Oratio Latina, De Promontorio Bonae Spei*, pp. 27–8.

144. See also John Hilton, "The Roman-Dutch Law of Evidence at the Cape (Book Review on M.L. Hewett (trans. and ed.), De Testimoniis: A Thesis by Gysbert Hemmy on the Testimony of the Chinese, Aetheiopians, and Other Pagans", *Scholia: Studies in Classical Antiquity* 10 (2001): 120–5.

145. Hemmy, *De Testimoniis*, pp. 66–7.

146. J.C. Beaglehole, ed., *The Journals of Captain Cook and his Voyages of Discovery* (Cambridge: Cambridge University Press, 1967), 3, 2, p. 17 (18 Oct. 1776).

147. Yvette Ranjeva-Rabetafika et al., "Of Paper and Men: A Note on the Archives of the VOC as a Source for the History of Madagascar", *Itinerario* 24, 1 (2000): 58.

148. For details, see Upham, "This Corner of the World", p. 18.

149. *Verhandelingen van het Bataviaasch Genootschap* [Proceedings of the Batavian Society] 2 (1780): 24. For the Batavian Society see Groot, *Van Batavia naar Weltevreden*. For slave-related articles of the Society, see also Sens, *Mensaap, Heiden, Slaaf*, pp. 110–2.

150. Arnout Vosmaer, *Beschrijving van de Aap-soort, gen. Orang-Outang, van het eiland Borneo, leevendig overgebragt in de Diergaarde van den Prinse van Oranje* [A Description of the Ape Species, Named Orang-Outang, from the Island Borneo, brought Alive to the Zoological Garden of the Princess of Orange] (Amsterdam, 1778), p. 13. See also Sens, *Mensaap, Heiden, Slaaf*, p. 48.

151. Kondō, "18 Seiki ikō Dejima", pp. 87–90.

152. For Hemmij's book inventory, see Kiyoshi Matsuda, *Yōgaku Soshikiteki Kenkyū* (Kyoto: Rinsen Shoten, 1998), pp. 353–69.

153. Frank Lequin, ed., *De Particuliere Correspondentie van Isaac Titsingh (1783–1812): Text, Brieven* [The Private Correspondence of Isaac Titsingh (1783–1812)] (Alphen aan den Rijn: Canaletto, 2009). Letter of 10 June 1794, p. 397.

154. "Monsterrol van het Schip *Erffprins*", *1792* [Muster-roll of the Ship *Erffprins*, 1792] and *Dagregister*, 21 Nov. 1798 (NA, NFJ 1487 and 210).

155. A similar attachment to the mother country was already noted in the case of VOC employees in Ceylon by Alicia Schrikker, *Dutch and British Colonial Intervention in Sri Lanka, 1780–1815: Expansion and Reform* (Leiden: Brill, 2007), p. 100.

156. Upham, "This Corner of the World", p. 24.

CHAPTER 5

The Persian Gulf and Britain: The Suppression of the African Slave Trade

Behnaz A. Mirzai

Introduction

To most indigenous peoples of the Persian Gulf region during the 19th century, the notion of abolishing slavery was seen as "an alien idea...[that] came from Britain".[1] Nonetheless, abolitionism was to give shape to—and profoundly impact—the development of legislation and policy in the region for nearly a century. It is important to note, however, that the anti-slavery discourse that emerged from 18th-century socio-political and humanitarian idealism in Europe was not equivalent to that which shaped the abolitionist mandate in the Persian Gulf region. Instead, it was inexorably linked to Britain's imperial ambitions. That is, the anti-slavery campaign was implemented alongside the establishment of geopolitical dominance over maritime trade routes in the region, and as such, was legislated in order to safeguard the commercial interests of the British East India Company.[2] Since Britain most decidedly ruled the waves throughout the 19th century, the only effective challenge to its hegemony in the Middle East came from the "Great Game" in Iran's border regions.[3]

The Persian Gulf States in the 19th Century

As an important seaborne link connecting Arabic, Iranian, Indian and African communities, the Persian Gulf was home to a heterogeneous group of states in the late 18th century: the Ottoman Empire, Iran and various Arab states including Oman. Slavery was a reality within all these societies, but the culture and nature of this institution differed in some important ways from that found contemporaneously in the Americas or Sub-Saharan Africa.[4] Among these were the Islamic protocols and cultural mores that governed the ownership of slaves and their place in society: indeed, they were afforded certain rights and privileges such as the possibility of liberation and social integration.[5]

The dynamic political landscape to be found today among the Gulf States has largely emerged in response to foreign interactions and influences. Since the 16th century, the Portuguese, Dutch, French and British all sought to establish bases in the region as part of commercial expansion and imperial ambitions. This was not surprising since it was the source of important commodities: everything from precious gems and dates to medicinal drugs and the ubiquitous Persian carpet found important markets in Europe.[6] Trade flowed in the opposite direction too and was reliant on Gulf ports like Bandar 'Abbas, as the Scottish author Henry James Whigham noted in 1903:

> Bunder Abbas is at present a port of entry and exit for about half a million pounds' worth British-Indian trade, and the principal merchants of the place are British-Indian subjects. In the event of Persia adopting ordinary modern methods of transport that trade might indefinitely increase and would continue to be largely British-Indian, provided the railway system was in the hands of no hostile Power.[7]

It was the discovery of oil in 1908 that was the game-changer for the region: not only did it add an unparalleled dimension to the geopolitical importance of the Gulf, but the wealth derived from its production transformed these societies.[8] Until they were formally emancipated around this time, slaves played a crucial role in making the traditional economic sectors lucrative.

The Abolitionist Debates

The abolitionist mandate in Iran culminated in the edict by Reza Shah in 1929 that formally outlawed slavery and was part of a larger modernization process that had been initiated by the Qajars in the

19th century. Scholars and historians all agree that the root of the expression of this mandate lies in European and North American philosophy, jurisprudence, social reformism and political economics. Robin Blackburn's *The Overthrow of Colonial Slavery, 1776–1848* provides one of the most comprehensive studies on the history of anti-slavery in the modern period.[9] Blackburn argues that while the roots of primitive abolitionism reach back to the Middle Ages, philosophical attacks on the institution of slavery were rare until the mid-18th century.[10] One such example was that of Jean Bodin in the late 16th century who, inspired by the French municipal tradition of *affranchisement* or the proclamation of a town being incompatible with bondage, proposed one of the first documented discussions criticizing slavery by saying it was against nature and common sense. More arcane was the 1567 English judgement that prevented a traveller from bringing a Russian slave into the country on the grounds that the slave's breath would pollute the air. By the end of the 17th century, although both the Holy Office of the Portuguese Empire (1686) and the French *Code Noir* (1688) condemned slave trading and emphasized the rights of people of colour, neither proclamation received formal judicial backing. In general, the horrors of slavery and its trade led to demands that slaves' conditions improve—but not overthrow of the institution itself. In the mid-18th century, Scottish philosopher Francis Hutcheson argued that slavery and the slave trade were a violation of human justice, Christian morality and liberty. His anti-slavery ideas suggested a reform rather than abolition of the institution. Scottish jurist George Wallace's anti-private property views reflected his proposition of the abolition of slavery even at the expense of economic loss. His radicalism was followed by Rousseau and American Quaker Anthony Benezet, who opposed the cruelty and immorality of the slave trade, in the second half of the 18th century. Political economists such as Adam Smith viewed slavery as costly and unprofitable because of its high mortality and low fertility rates, adding that slaves did not work efficiently in the Atlantic World. Anti-slavery sentiments in Western Europe from the late 18th century onwards developed a uniquely bourgeois flavour, with an emphasis on social responsibility, social order and emergent capitalist sensibilities.[11] Most vocal in Britain and North America were those who belonged to the dissenting, non-established churches, such as the Quakers and the later Methodists.

Although the first decree banning a branch of the Atlantic slave trade was issued by Portugal in 1761,[12] Britain led the European abolitionist mandate, beginning with a parliamentary injunction challenging participation in the slave trade in 1779. Before the late 1780s, the debate remained limited to political expediency and had little impact. The establishment of an abolitionist committee in 1787, for instance, focused on the economic unprofitability of slavery and abhorred the blatant racist philosophical justifications for it. The parliament's first regulation of the slave trade was passed in 1788.[13] Meaningful change was not possible until the movement was directed by popular support for political and social reform. This emerged gradually through the late 18th century and was fuelled by responses to events like the slave revolt in St Domingue in 1791. Examples such as these piqued humanitarian outrage against the institution of slavery and helped shift European attitudes.[14] As Blackburn notes: "popular pressure did not directly produce abolition but it did encourage ruling authorities to present themselves as guarantors of elementary personal freedom".[15] Noble as these sentiments were, these kinds of attitudes easily grew out of imperial and colonial idealism. As Suzanne Miers explains:

> [Abolitionism] was an integral part of the belief in what came to be seen as Britain's civilizing mission—an ideological package, which included the spreading of British democratic ideas, British views of freedom, British commerce, and the Christian religion to the "backward races" of the world.[16]

This philosophical ambiguity possibly explains the slow pace of legislation at the end of the 18th century. Thus, the bill of 1792 that called for the gradual end of the slave trade by 1796 was never realized.[17] It was not until the Abolition Act of 1808 that restricted the participation of British ships in the Atlantic slave trade, that abolitionist legislation was able to have a far-reaching international and domestic impact elsewhere in the world.[18] Finally, the Abolition of Slavery Bill of 1833 outlawed slavery in Britain and its colonies.[19]

Abolitionism and the British East India Company

British support for banning all aspects of the seaborne slave trade in the Persian Gulf must be seen as part of a larger policy designed to safeguard commercial and political hegemony in and around India.[20]

Historian Cooper Busch links slavery, piracy, trade and communication as all part of this bigger picture:

> It was in connection with India that Britain had originally taken interest in the Gulf: safeguarding lines of communication from local pirates or other European powers, Britain had kept watch on the Gulf and acted, as needs be, with varying force.[21]

Over the course of the 19th century, Britain emerged increasingly as a suzerain in the region—from ruling the Trucial States to exercising considerable authority over various royal dynasties in Iran.[22] These "British satellites" were governed by a network of diplomats and bureaucrats through the British Residency of the Persian Gulf, an institution that was established in the late 18th century with an administrative base at Bushehr.[23] Its directives, however, came from London.

Because naval supremacy in the Persian Gulf and the Indian Ocean region guaranteed the East India Company's success, Britain's maritime infrastructure was fiercely protected. Thus, as other countries increasingly sought to compete with or actively challenge this dominance throughout the 19th century, British foreign policy responded accordingly. It became increasingly important to interfere in the domestic affairs of the individual Gulf States.[24]

Abolition of the African Slave Trade in the Persian Gulf

Anti-slavery legislation became an effective political tool within this context. It was first employed in the second decade of the 19th century when, in 1812, the Ottoman Empire banned the sale of Indians.[25] Next, the British brokered the General Maritime Treaty between several Gulf rulers—Abu Dhabi, Sharjah, Umm al Qaywayn, Bahrain and 'Ajman—in 1820. Signed at Ras al-Khaimah, Article 9 indicated that the "carrying off of slaves, men, women or children, from the Coasts of Africa or elsewhere, and the transporting of them in vessels, is plunder and piracy, and the friendly Arabs shall do nothing of this nature".[26] Although they signed the treaty, the general consensus among these Gulf States (as by Iran and the Ottoman Empire) was that the legislation was not only a pretext for British interference in their internal affairs, it was designed to justify punitive policies like the search-and-seizure policy of boarding seaborne vessels if slave dealing was suspected.

In 1822, the British concluded a treaty with Oman's Sayyid Sa'id (r. 1806–56) to ban the sale of slaves to Christian nations; they also established a base in East Africa, ostensibly for regulating the terms. Further treaties were signed in 1839 and 1845.[27] The former allowed the British to cordon off an area from Cape Delgado in Mozambique to Puzim on the coast of Makran. Slaves travelling across this boundary, not within it, and out of the restricted zone could be confiscated. The vessels on which they were found could also be impounded.[28] Yet while the agreement deterred dealers from sailing across the Arabian Sea to India with their bounty, they could still conduct overland slave-trading activities between East Africa and the Persian Gulf. It was not until 1847 that the Sultan concluded an agreement to punish those exporting slaves from his African holdings into his Asian territories.

Analysis of the legislation reveals the importance Britain attached to being able to maintain the presence of its warships in the Persian Gulf. In order to realize the abolitionist objective more fully, the British were also eager to control the slave trade in Iran—a policy similar to that which they had negotiated with the Omani sultan. A letter from Justin Sheil, the East India Company officer and diplomat, to Haji Mirza Aqasi, Muhammad Shah's prime minister, in 1847 illustrates the reasoning:

> On the basis of this decree, the export and trade of blacks from the countries of the Imam of Masqat in Africa, and also their importation into his country in Asia was prohibited. In order to enforce this decree, warships of the British government confiscate the Imam's vessels that trafficked in the trade of black men and women. The trustees of the British government drew attention to the need for the Iranian government to issue a *firmān*, such as the agreement of the 15th of Muharram with the Imam of Masqat, to prohibit the black trade in the ports of Iran and the sea of Oman. The *firmān* should indicate that the British government can carry out your Kingship's order in the same way as they do under the agreement with the Imam of Masqat.[29]

Indeed, one year later, in 1848, the Shah issued a firmān banning the importation of African slaves by sea into Iran.[30]

Elsewhere in the Gulf, agreements were signed. In 1838–39, treaties were signed with the Trucial Shaykhs.[31] Bahrain, the centre of the pearl-fishing and trading activities, signed an anti-African slave trade treaty in 1847.[32]

Reaction of Gulf States to Abolitionist Legislation

It is worth noting that almost all of these agreements were only grudgingly acceded. The anti-British feelings occasioned by these interventions and intrusions inspired distrust and resistance to the abolition of the African slave trade.[33] Samuel M. Zwemer, an American missionary and resident of Bahrain, stated that Britain's only concern was commerce and the suppression of the slave trade, which brought no reforms: "To be 'protected' means here strict neutrality as to the internal affairs and absolute dictation as to affairs with other Governments."[34] In many ways, perpetuation of the slave trade was becoming an emblem of independence. Whigham, who visited the Gulf in the early 20th century, stated:

> I can see nothing to lose and everything to gain by winning over the Arabs of the interior. Their one objection to us is that we put down the slave trade, a policy on our part which they can so little understand.[35]

In spite of the humanitarian rhetoric, abolitionist pressure prompted a knee-jerk reaction by many in the Gulf as an affront to established social mores and religious teachings. For instance, not only did religious scholars in the Hijaz (western Saudi Arabia) suggest that their challenge of the treaties signed in 1847 and 1857 banning the trade in African slaves in the Ottoman Empire was akin to taking a stand against the domination of the Turks and Western values,[36] they kept the land route from Saudi Arabia to the east of the country and beyond open for the transportation of African slaves.[37]

The analysis of the practice of slavery and resistance to abolition in the Middle East is unique in that it offers an array of insights into the culture and mores of those societies but it also provides an accurate, non-romanticized glimpse into them, far from preconceived notions. Most importantly, slavery was decidedly not an integral feature of these societies' modus vivendi. Bernard Lewis argues that, for Muslims, "to forbid what God permits is almost as great an offense as to permit what God forbids".[38] Chouki El Hamel, a historian who has examined Qur'anic texts pertaining to slavery, asserts: "No single verse in the Qur'an calls for the acceptance of slavery as a normal social practice"[39] and the only way to acquire slaves was through war or jihad as self-defence—but even then, the practice was governed by many provisions and regulations. The practice of liberating slaves was well established in Middle Eastern societies since the advent of Islam. Indeed, Qur'anic instructions and customary laws provided guidelines and encouraged emancipation as a valuable and rewarding act, and in some cases made it mandatory.[40] It should be noted that the practice of slavery was neither recommended as an obligatory act in Islam nor was its suppression forbidden;[41] instead, various schools of Islamic law established different guidelines.

Since the enslavement of Muslims by Muslims was contrary to Islamic law, it is clear that slavery in these societies tended to be perpetuated by political motives rather than by religious injunction. By adopting sectarian loyalties and adhering to the teachings and customs of a specific Islamic denomination, Middle Eastern rulers were able to distance themselves from their political rivals and mobilize their people and resources against foreign threats. History abounds with examples, but it is notable to consider the Wahhabis of the Saudi Arabia who were hostile to the Shi'as, 'Ibadis and Sufis.[42] Similarly, there are accounts of Shi'a Iran's enmity to the Sunni Ottoman Empire and 'Ibadi Oman[43] during the abolitionist negotiations with the British. For example, in 1847, the Shah declared: "Turks are Sunni and they are in opposition to the Iranians. The Imam of Masqat is also Khariji, and one level better than Kafir [unbeliever]. Then, we, who are the leader of Shi'as will not follow them."[44]

Following political pressures and diplomatic negotiations, Muhammad Shah issued a decree in 1848 prohibiting the importation of African slaves into Iran by sea.[45] The British, seeking to obtain fuller control over sea traffic in the Persian Gulf, were not satisfied with this royal edict. As such, they enforced another agreement in 1851 that gave their warships the right to search Iranian merchant ships. Notably, the implementation and overseeing of the regulations was given to Iranian officials just as was the granting of freedom to slaves found on board and punishment of the culpable ship owners. Similarly, it was the responsibility of the Iranian government to provide certificates to un-freed and former slaves, allowing them to travel across the Gulf or to India.[46] By 1882, the British had assumed full authority at sea, and were granted by treaty the right to search Iranian ships in the Gulf without indigenous supervisors necessarily being present.[47] Having procured the authority to freely manoeuvre in these waters, they could now fully safeguard their interests by restricting the movement of otherwise sovereign nations. Yet, prima facie, the British succeeded in safeguarding their commercial interests —indirectly—through treaties with Persian Gulf rulers who relied for enforcement on their superior naval power.

Abolition and Its Aftermath

The ramifications of abolition on the Persian Gulf region were far-reaching. First and perhaps most importantly, the ban did not bring about an end to slave ownership and trading; rather, it only restricted their transportation by sea. Instead, because the British assiduously "found it necessary to abstain from active interference with domestic slavery in the Persian Gulf"[48] (as J.G. Lorimer pointedly observed in the first decade of the 20th century), a devastating consequence of the ban was a steep increase in the enslavement of indigenous peoples, especially among local ethnic groups such as the Baluchis in southwestern Iran.[49] British Resident Arthur P. Trevor noted the situation in 1921:

> My object in writing this letter is to ascertain what line the Government of India desires me to take in regard to this Baluch slave traffic. I noticed that the slave trade engagement of 1847 signed by the Shaikhs on the Trucial Coast (no. XLI, page 178, Aitchison, Volume XII, part 2) is headed "Engagement for the abolition of the African Slave Trade" and though the words "and elsewhere" are inserted after the word "Africa" in the body of the engagement I think the latter is really meant to refer to African slaves. Further, while the engagement contemplates the seizure of vessels engaged in the traffic by HM cruisers, the Shaikhs do not undertake any co-operation themselves. On the other hand, under article 3 of Agreement of 1839 (no. XL, page 177, Aitchison, Volume XII, part 2) the Shaikhs of the Trucial Coast agree to treat and punish as pirates any persons convicted of selling males, or females who are "hoor" or free, and this clause would naturally cover Baluchis and Mekranis who are "hoor" although it seems originally to have been inserted to meet the case of Somalis.[50]

This increase is largely attributable to continued demand, especially for labour by slave markets in the Arab states.[51]

Second, slaves also became an important commodity in the burgeoning arms trade of the later 19th and early 20th century.[52] Emrys Chew characterizes the situation as such:

A nineteenth-century triangular trade in guns, slaves, and ivory would redefine the political economy of the western Indian Ocean. The collapse of imperial rule in Southwest Asia, the ambitions of local chiefs, and Britain's growing dominance in the emerging industrial world economy opened a period of profound upheaval for the Persian Gulf region.[53]

Amidst escalating political instability in southern Iran, Baluchis were often exchanged for rifles.[54] Politician Arthur Arnold described finding almost all the men and boys in the area armed in 1876: "The donkey-drivers carried long guns slung at their backs; the peasant who were scratching the earth in patches with wooden ploughs, were armed in the same way...."[55] In spite of Naser al-Din Shah's decree in 1881 prohibiting this trade on Iranian soil, the traffic in arms and slaves continued from India via Iran to Herat and from Zanzibar to Masqat and Iran.[56] So alarmed was the international community that the Brussels Conference ratified, in 1891, an act to stem the flow of slaves and contraband weapons throughout the Indian Ocean and Persian Gulf. Article I specifically included: "Restriction of the importation of fire-arms, at least of modern pattern, and of ammunition throughout the entire extent of the territories infected by the Slave Trade."[57]

Third, abolition can also be closely linked to various impacts associated with fugitive and liberated slaves, ranging from a master's discontent at losing a slave to issues associated with relocating populations of liberated slaves and even political unrest. Areas under the jurisdiction of the British (such as telegraph stations, consulates and vessels) were traditionally considered safe havens for runaway slaves. In the 1880s, following the escape of slaves to the British telegraph station at Jask and their return to the owners, Edward C. Ross, the Resident in the Persian Gulf, ordered that:

> Runaway slaves should not in future be admitted to premises owned in Persia by the British Government, as the result would be a great influx of slaves, leading to political complications, into the British stations. These instructions were approved by the Government of India, with the proviso that exception should be made in cases where, owing to the slaves being placed in imminent danger or otherwise, considerations of humanity might dictate an opposite course.[58]

Qeshm, the largest island in the Persian Gulf, was another popular destination for fugitive slaves. It had been turned, by the British, into naval headquarters and a coal depot in 1891, with Bas'idu and Bandar Singau becoming the principal stations.[59]

Finally, the British also had to deal with situations arising from previous abolitionist agreements. Thus, in compliance with the treaty of 1873, the Sultan of Oman freed 70 slaves who fled enslavement amongst the Rind communities of Baluchistan and sought sanctuary at the British telegraph station at Gwadar along the Makran coast in 1892. Enraged that the British would not repatriate their fugitive slaves, the Rinds cut telegraph lines and threatened to continue civil disobedience if their demands were not met. From 1892–93, several hundred fugitive slaves took refuge at Gwadar.[60]

When it became too complicated to release them into the community, the British often chose to send liberated slaves to other territories or countries. This was not always, however, a well-received solution. Thus, while India had traditionally been the preferred destination, the government in Bombay demanded an end to the practice in 1889. Sarawak, the Fiji Islands and Borneo were similarly reticent. Thus, in 1897, a decision was made to send emancipated slaves to East Africa. Many were relocated in the Zanzibar Archipelago to work on Omani plantations.[61] Relocations like this, however, often resulted in a high mortality rate due to mistreatment and abuse. For instance, an estimated 35 per cent of the liberated slaves who went to Aden died from lung disease in the 1860s.[62]

Such situations illustrate the extent to which the British sought to resolve the various challenges arising from the liberation of slave populations, while at the same time not putting at risk their political and economic interests. Thus, in 1876, it was decreed that fugitive slaves on board British vessels should not be returned to their owner regardless of being within or outside the territorial waters of a state where slavery was legal.[63] Harking back to its relationship with the East India Company, the British government authorized the expenditure of liberating slaves in the Persian Gulf from the Indian budget. This arrangement was reversed in 1883, when the Indian government announced that henceforth such costs were to be debited from the Queen's Treasury. Up until 1900, fines levied against offenders involved in the slave trade by local governments were credited back to London to cover the expenses associated with abolition and liberation.[64]

Although they initiated the process, the British largely abstained from interfering in the socio-political mechanisms attendant in deconstructing the institutional apparatus of slavery in order (ostensibly) to avoid provoking civic unrest. As Miers explains:

> The administrators were not impervious to the injustice of slavery, but as a matter of practical politics, they were content to pass laws allowing slaves to leave their owners, without taking steps to enable them to turn legal manumission into reality.[65]

Therefore, liberation and building the post-emancipation society became a matter for local rulers. At the micro level, the process was often linked to parochial concerns such as loss of income or investment. But ultimately, changes in lifestyle, modernization and industrialization, along with the disappearance of traditional aspects of Islamic society such as the harem, helped eradicate the institution of slavery as a social category in the Middle East.[66]

It was, however, not until Muhammad Reza Shah Pahlavi came to power that full emancipation was possible. The efforts of the Qajars in brokering relations with Britain as part of negotiating the realization of the abolitionist mandate admittedly set the stage, but the Pahlavi regime was able to realize the process in 1929. In large part, the transition of society from slavery to wage labour was a direct result of the emergent oil industry. Indeed, not only had a semi-industrial society emerged by the mid-20th century, there were plenty of employment opportunities for all Iranians, including the descendants of slaves. Similarly, economic circumstances profoundly influenced social and migratory patterns, with the expansion of markets allowing former slaves to detach more easily from their former masters.

The institution of slavery was also abolished in Middle Eastern societies: Bahrain in 1937, Kuwait and Qatar 1952, Yemen and Saudi Arabia in 1962, the Trucial States (United Arab Emirates) in 1963 and Oman in 1971.[67]

Conclusion

While British support for the suppression of the African slave trade in the Persian Gulf during the 19th century should be viewed as the continuation of a policy that had begun in Europe and the Americas, it emerged in unique circumstances. The imposition of various abolitionist agreements and treaties on local governments in the Gulf served as a strategy to safeguard the British interests in the region—especially those of the East India Company. Mastery of the region was therefore essential and depended on the kind of naval authority that would facilitate the establishment of military and political superiority as well as guarantee commercial privilege. This was brokered through the abolitionist mandate that, through various legislative injunctions, gave the British increasing control over the Persian Gulf and Indian Ocean throughout the 19th century.

The socio-political and economic impacts associated with abolition and emancipation were considerable but were gradually accommodated by all levels of society. Descendants of former slaves have, overall, achieved modest vertical mobility in Gulf societies, especially as a result of the burgeoning oil industry since the early 20th century. Not only did this create opportunities for employment, it profoundly transformed—and continues to impact—the social categories and expectations within society.

Notes

1. Ehud R. Toledano, *The Ottoman Slave Trade and its Suppression: 1840–1890* (Princeton, NJ: Princeton University Press, 1982), p. 91. See also Robin Blackburn, *The Overthrow of Colonial Slavery, 1776–1848* (London: Verso, 1990), p. 35.
2. J.E. Peterson, "Britain and the Gulf: At the Periphery of Empire", in *The Persian Gulf in History*, ed. Lawrence G. Potter (New York: Palgrave Macmillan, 2009), p. 278.
3. It was in this theatre that the limitations and complications associated with the abolitionist mandate may said to have been most apparent, as Emrys Chew notes: "The 'Great Game' was staged by Britain and Russia with varying degrees of intrigue and intensity between 1828 and 1907" (*Arming the Periphery: The Arms Trade in the Indian Ocean during the Age of Global Empire* [Hampshire: Palgrave Macmillan, 2012], p. 105).
4. Toledano, *The Ottoman Slave Trade*, p. 5.
5. Gwyn Campbell, "Female Bondage and Agency in the Indian Ocean World", in *African Communities in Asia and the Mediterranean: Identities between Integration and Conflict*, ed. Ehud R. Toledano (Trenton: Africa World Press, 2012), p. 56. In spite of these guarantees, a number of factors—ranging from ethnic and denominational to demographic and environmental—often meant that political and economic interests overshadowed shared Islamic attitudes and tolerances.

6. Before the oil industry became the main economic driver for the region, much of the global output of date palm and pearls (especially on Kharg Island and in Bahrain) came from the Gulf States (Paul Popenoe, "The Distribution of the Date Palm", *Geographical Review* 16, 1 (Jan. 1926): 117–21; D. Wilson, "Memorandum Respecting the Pearl Fisheries in the Persian Gulf", *Journal of the Royal Geographical Society of London* 3 (1833): 283–6). See also William Ashton Shepherd, *From Bombay to Bushire, and Bussora* (London: Richard Bentley, 1857), pp. 113, 117, 159.

7. British imports represented 84 per cent of the total trade of Bandar Abbas (equal to £629,268) in 1899 (H.J. Whigham, *The Persian Problem* [New York: Charles Scribner's Sons, 1903], p. 66). The total value of imports from Britain into the Gulf in 1900 was £1,500,000 (ibid., pp. 62, 338).

8. J.V. Harrison was commissioned to go to Makran by the Anglo-Persian Oil Company to survey the region from 1918 until 1933 (J.V. Harrison, "Coastal Makran", *The Geographical Journal* 97, 1 [Jan. 1941]: 1).

9. Blackburn, *The Overthrow of Colonial Slavery*.

10. For instance, Blackburn shows that the Spanish ban on the enslavement of Indians in its colonies during the 1540s actually "paved the way for extensive imports of African slaves". He adds that their Spanish captors justified this decision by suggesting that Africans were "more capable of enduring the rigours of bondage" (ibid., p. 39).

11. Ibid., p. 60.

12. Ibid., pp. 36–62.

13. Ibid., pp. 138, 156.

14. See Bernard Lewis, *Race and Slavery in the Middle East* (New York: Oxford University Press, 1990), p. 78.

15. Blackburn, *The Overthrow of Colonial Slavery*, pp. 40, 54.

16. Suzanne Miers, *Slavery in the Twentieth Century: The Evolution of a Global Problem* (Walnut Creek, CA: AltaMira Press, 2003), p. 10.

17. Blackburn, *The Overthrow of Colonial Slavery*, p. 146.

18. David Brion Davis, *Inhuman Bondage: The Rise and Fall of Slavery in the New World* (New York and Oxford: Oxford University Press, 2006), pp. 157–74, 233.

19. Blackburn, *The Overthrow of Colonial Slavery*, p. 457.

20. Miers notes that Britain's "interests were limited to ending the maritime slave and arms trades, protecting British subjects, and preventing naval hostilities between the rulers" (*Slavery in the Twentieth Century*, pp. 10, 164). See also Peterson, "Britain and the Gulf", pp. 278, 279; Mahmmud Mahmmud, *Tarikh-i Ravabet-i Siasi-yi Iran va Englis* [The History of Political Relations of Iran and Britain], vol. 2 (Tehran: Eqbal, 1367), p. 530.

21. Briton Cooper Busch, *Britain and the Persian Gulf, 1894–1914* (Berkeley and Los Angeles, CA: University of California Press, 1967), p. 9.

22. Alasdair Drysdale and Gerald H. Blake, *The Middle East and North Africa: A Political Geography* (New York: Oxford University Press, 1985), p. 68; Miers, *Slavery in the Twentieth Century*, p. 165.

23. Robert A. Huttenback, *The British Imperial Experience* (New York: Harper & Row, 1966), p. 75; J.B. Kelly, *British and Persian Gulf 1795–1880* (Oxford: Clarendon Press, 1968), p. 348; Arnold P. Kaminsky, *The India Office, 1880–1910* (Westport: Greenwood Press, 1986), p. 159; Jerry Dupont, *The Common Law Abroad: Constitutional and Legal Legacy of the British Empire* (Littleton, Col.: F.B. Rothman Publications, 2001), p. 851; Chew, *Arming the Periphery*, p. 104.

24. The treaty with Oman in 1798, which forced "the total exclusion of French and Dutch trade, and especially French influence, from Muscat", exemplifies this: indeed, Oman's vast empire had historically controlled trading networks from East Africa to southern Iran, from the Indian Ocean and Arabian Sea to the Persian Gulf (Whigham, *The Persian Problem*, p. 14); see also Abdul Sheriff, *Slaves, Spices and Ivory in Zanzibar: Integration of an East African Commercial Empire into the World Economy, 1770–1873* (Athens, OH: Ohio University Press, 1987), pp. 235–8.

25. Lorimer reported that the Pasha of Baghdad ordered enslaved Indians who had been bought in Basra to be returned (*Gazetteer of the Persian Gulf, Oman, and Central Arabia*, vol. 1, part 2 [Calcutta: Superintendent Government Printing, 1908–15], p. 2481).

26. Arnold T. Wilson, *The Persian Gulf* (London: George Allen & Unwin, 1959), p. 216.

27. A final treaty was concluded with Sa'id's successor Turki in 1873 (Lorimer, *Gazetteer of the Persian Gulf*, vol. 1, part 2, p. 2478; vol. 1, part 1A, p. 499).

28. *Fugitive Slaves*, Parliamentary Papers, House of Commons and Command (House of Commons: Session 8 Feb.–15 Aug. 1876), p. 28: 208; Wilson, *The Persian Gulf*, p. 217; Lorimer, *Gazetteer of the Persian Gulf*, vol. 1, part 2, p. 2477.

29. Justin Sheil to Haji Mirza Aqasi, Q1263 (1847). 2. 5, VUK (Vezarat-i Umur-i Khareja-yi Iran [Ministry of Foreign Affairs of Iran], Markaz-i Asnad [Center of Documents], Tehran, Iran); Correspondence, the British government to the Iranian government, Jamadi al-Awwal 16, 1264, Q1264.6.6, VUK.

30. The Shah to Haji Mirza Aqasi, 1264, Q1264.5. 38, VUK.

31. The Shaykhs of Sharjah, 'Ajman, Dubai, Abu Dhabi, and Umm al Qaywayn; Wilson, *The Persian Gulf*, p. 218.

32. Wilson, *The Persian Gulf*, p. 246.

33. Fereydun Adamiyat, *Amir Kabir va Iran* [Amir Kabir and Iran] (Tehran: Khawrazmi, 1362), p. 516; Kelly, *British and Persian Gulf*, p. 594; Ann Lambton, *Qajar Persia* (London: I.B. Tauris, 1987), p. 213.

34. Whigham, *The Persian Problem*, p. 35.

35. Ibid., p. 174.

36. Toledano, *The Ottoman Slave Trade*, pp. 129–35; Lewis, *Race and Slavery*, p. 80.

37. Lady Mary Sheil, *Glimpses of Life and Manner in Persia* (New York: Arno Press, 1973), p. 245.

38. Lewis, *Race and Slavery*, p. 78.

39. Chouki El Hamel, *Black Morocco: A History of Slavery, Race, and Islam* (New York: Cambridge University Press, 2013), p. 42.

40. Y. Hakan Erdem, *Slavery in the Ottoman Empire and its Demise, 1800–1909* (Oxford: St Martin's Press, 1996), p. 152.

41. Esma'il Ra'in, *Daryanavardi-yi Iranian* [Iranian Navigation], vol. 2 (Tehran: Sekka, 1350), p. 685.

42. Jerzy Zdanowski, *Slavery and Manumission* (Reading: Ithaca Press, 2013), p. 30.

43. 'Ibadi or 'Ibadiyah is a branch of the Khawarej. They were opposed to the Shi'i thoughts and believed that Ali, the son-in-law of the prophet, and his followers were heretics.

44. Adamiyat, *Amir Kabir va Iran*, p. 517.

45. Autographed note from Muhammad Shah to Haji Mirza Aqasi, 1263, Q1262.5.38, VUK; Ra'in, *Daryanavardi-yi Iranian*, vol. 2, p. 685; Lorimer, *Gazetteer of the Persian Gulf*, vol. 1, part 2, p. 1974.

46. The 1851 agreement between the British and Iranian governments, Isfahan, Shawwal 1267, Q1263.6.24.2, VUK.

47. Ra'in, *Daryanavardi-yi Iranian*, vol. 2, p. 705.

48. Lorimer, *Gazetteer of the Persian Gulf*, vol. 1, part 2, p. 2512.

49. Ibid., vol. 2B, p. 1137.

50. A.P. Trevor to Bray, Delhi, Dec. 31, 1921, R/15/1/221, BL (British Library, London, UK).

51. Zdanowski, *Slavery and Manumission*, p. 22; Lorimer, *Gazetteer of the Persian Gulf*, vol. 2B, p. 1137.

52. Denis Wright, *The English among the Persians during the Qajar Period 1787–1921* (London: Heinemann, 1977), p. 70.

53. Chew, *Arming the Periphery*, p. 40.

54. Navarra at Jask to D.P.G. at Karachi, 23 Aug. 1921, R/15/1/221, BL; A.S. in Jask to the director in Karachi, 12 June 1921, R/15/1/221, BL.

55. Arthur Arnold, *Through Persia by Caravan*, vol. 2 (London: Tinsley Brothers, 1877), p. 183.

56. Lorimer, *Gazetteer of the Persian Gulf*, vol. 1, part 2, pp. 2556–7; Busch, *Britain and the Persian Gulf*, p. 271; Wright, *The English Among the Persians*, p. 71.

57. Political Department, General Act of the Brussels Conference, Bombay Castle, 8 June 1891, R/15/1/199, BL.

58. Lorimer, *Gazetteer of the Persian Gulf*, vol. 1, part 2, p. 2513.

59. Whigham, *The Persian Problem*, p. 52.

60. Lorimer, *Gazetteer of the Persian Gulf*, vol. 1, part 1A, p. 620 and vol. 1, part 2, pp. 2512, 2486.

61. Between 1900 and 1902, 35 manumitted slaves were sent from Masqat to Zanzibar. Lorimer, *Gazetteer of the Persian Gulf*, vol. 1, part 2, p. 2491.

62. Matthew Scott Hopper, "The African Presence in Arabia: Slavery, the World Economy, and the African Diaspora in Eastern Arabia, 1840–1940", unpublished PhD dissertation (Los Angeles, CA: University of California, 2006), p. 76.

63. Lorimer, *Gazetteer of the Persian Gulf*, vol. 1, part 2, p. 2487.

64. Ibid., p. 2491.

65. Miers, *Slavery in the Twentieth Century*, p. 166.

66. Muhammad Taqi Lesan al-Mulk Sepehr, *Nasekh al-tawarikh tarikh-i Qajariya* [Effacement of the Chronicles of the History of Qajar], vol. 1 (Tehran: Asatir, 1377), p. 317.

67. Notwithstanding, slave trading persisted during the 1920s and 1930s throughout the region—but the British withheld this information from the League of Nations. Miers, *Slavery in the Twentieth Century*, pp. 164–6, 267, 341–7; Behnaz A. Mirzai, "The 1848 Abolitionist *Farmān*: A Step towards Ending the Slave Trade in Iran", in *Abolition and its Aftermath in Indian Ocean Africa and Asia*, ed. Gwyn Campbell (London and New York: Routledge, 2005), p. 100; Zdanowski, *Slavery and Manumission*, p. 328; Lewis, *Race and Slavery*, p. 79.

CHAPTER 6

The End of the Coolie Trade in Southern China: Focus on the Treaty Port of Amoy

Ei Murakami

Introduction

During the mid-19th century, while Western European countries were proceeding to abolish the slave trade, indentured emigration substituting for the slave trade emerged at treaty ports in China. In this article, contracted emigration between the 1840s and 1870s, from southern China to areas other than South East Asia, is referred to as the "coolie trade".[1] The article reconsiders the role of Britain and local Qing officials who led the abolition of the coolie trade.

With the global expansion of emigration, interest in the subject has increased. Similarly, studies on the Chinese diaspora are now gaining greater focus. However, research on the coolie trade was already underway by the 1980s. Persia Crawford Campbell examined the coolie trade as practised throughout the British Empire, while Elliott Campbell Arensmeyer studied the British government's role in the trade and its relationship with British merchants.[2] From the Qing perspective, Qing government policy towards the coolie trade has also attracted the attention of scholars.[3] Furthermore, the emigration system,[4] resistance to the coolie trade[5] and the rescue of kidnapped women[6] are all topics that have been studied, along with the situation in the emigrants' destination countries.[7]

Although considerable research has been carried out on this topic, some issues remain unresolved. For instance, most previous studies focused on the coolie trade and therefore overlooked the relationship between its emergence and changes in the governance or socio-economic dynamics of China's coastal areas during the mid-19th century. In general, they focused on the government's role in countries such as China and Britain in abolishing the coolie trade. However, this implies disregarding the role of British consuls and local Chinese officials in the process of abolition. Few studies have been concerned with how local Chinese officials, who were powerless to control the region, coped with the coolie-trade problem during the mid-19th century, when social order collapsed.

In this article, we address a number of important developments in the coolie trade. First, we survey the reasons for its rise in Amoy, while considering socio-economic conditions in the coastal area and the problems associated with the trade at the time. Second, we analyse the attitude of various groups towards the coolie trade. Third, we examine how it declined in the treaty ports. In particular, we concentrate on the roles of British diplomats and local Qing officials.

Our analysis focuses on the treaty ports of Amoy because it was here that the coolie trade both started and declined earlier than elsewhere. Its decline in Amoy led to its expansion in Guangdong and greatly influenced its development. Furthermore, Amoy was also the main port for emigration to South East Asia and the most important city for Chinese emigrants during the modern period.

We employ British Foreign Office archives as our primary sources because trade in 19th-century Amoy was funded mostly by British capital and undertaken by British merchants.[8] Few Chinese documents describing the trade in Amoy exist from this period since local Chinese officials declined to draft them.

Rise of the Coolie Trade

In response to pressures from the anti-slavery movement, Britain abolished the slave trade in 1807 and passed the Bill of Emancipation in 1833.[9] Many European countries soon followed suit.[10] However, the demand for labour continued to increase on the plantations of Latin America. In North America and Australia, the discovery of gold

Map of the Coastal Area of South China

created new demand for labour. In addition, in Peru, large numbers of labourers were needed to collect guano. Since there were insufficient white workers to meet the demand, Asian labour was brought in. This development underpinned the origin of the coolie trade.[11]

In essence, the coolie trade was a form of contract emigration, where the contractors (coolies) worked for a fixed period under set conditions. Initially, the counterparty bore the transportation fees. Contractors incurred the debt, and several of their rights were restricted.[12] Migrants were recruited between November and March because this was the monsoon period and an off-season for farming.[13] Although they changed over time, the embarkation locations were typically Amoy, Swatow, Hong Kong, Macau and their surrounding districts. The principal destinations for emigrants were the West

Indies, where labour was required to replace slaves, and the United States, Canada, Peru[14] and Australia, all of which saw an increase in labour demand.

Between 1845 and August 1852, approximately 6,255 coolies departed from Amoy: four British ships carried 3,946 coolies; two Spanish ships carried 850; and French, American and Peruvian ships carried the remainder. Their destinations were principally Australia (2,666) and Cuba (990).

Why did the coolie trade emerge during this period? First, the region had a strong tradition of emigration to Taiwan and South East Asia. Second, the trafficking of women and children to Taiwan and South East Asia existed before the treaty ports opened, and it continued afterwards.[15] Third, many Cantonese middlemen were good at foreign languages and introducing migrants to foreigners because of their experience in the opium trade, that had expanded in Guangdong since the end of the 18th century. Furthermore, Qing control over he coastal areas had been hindered by piracy and the opium trade since the early 19th century. Once the treaty ports opened, rampant smuggling in and around those ports prevented order being restored, and Cantonese and Fujianese pirate activity boomed. A silver shortage resulted in a financial depression in China during the 1840s and the first half of the 1850s. These factors underpinned the expansion of the coolie trade.[16]

Several previous studies have pointed to problems associated with the coolie trade, including instances of cruelty in the barracoons (barracks for temporary confinement) where coolies were housed; poor conditions and high mortality rates during sea voyages; and overall poor treatment, including long working hours, low pay and mistreatment upon arrival (especially in Cuba and Peru).[17]

The greatest problem was the recruitment of emigrants by brokers. Coolie emigration was made less attractive because their real wages were probably lower than the wages of those who remained in Amoy, and communication between the emigrants and their families at home was cut off. Therefore, if they relied solely on ordinary methods the brokers could hope to recruit only "poor-quality" labourers, who did not provide what was required of them by their chosen destination.[18] Faced with an increasing demand for labour, brokers began securing "good-quality" labour by resorting to illegal means, such as seduction, fraud, gambling, human trafficking and kidnapping.[19]

Human trafficking around Amoy had never been locally problematic and it did not lead to friction. Why, then, did the illegal acts committed by coolie brokers begin to cause so many problems?

Although the trafficking of lower-class men and women was not a serious problem for the local community, coolie brokers began indiscriminately kidnapping individuals on whom families depended for their livelihood, who served as successors in the family line or who were relatives of local leaders, rather than kidnapping the weak or "superfluous".[20]

Unsurprisingly, the hostility towards the brokers intensified. Underlying the 1852 Amoy riot was a belief that once foreigners started trading, they would begin to buy people, which in turn would attract bandits (*jianfei*) who would kidnap innocent civilians.[21] In short, residents were hostile towards brokers, believing them to be bandits. British officials who were dispatched during this particular incident also regarded brokers as "men of the lowest possible character"[22] and viewed them with contempt similar to that towards the coolies. The antipathy felt towards the Cantonese owing to their role as brokers was especially strong. For instance, after the Amoy riot a man in Amoy petitioned for compensation, following an incident in which the British shot and killed innocent people while protecting "Cantonese vagabonds".[23]

As discussed above, the antagonism towards brokers (lower-class people in coastal areas and the Cantonese) who colluded with and were protected by foreigners was similar to the attitude of Qing officials towards traitors (*hanjian*) in the opium trade before and during the Opium War. However, there was a significant difference between the coolie and opium trades in that those involved in the former tended to have lower-class origins and excluded those involved in the opium trade, such as merchants, officials and soldiers. In sum, the coolie trade, combined with ruthless acts by coolie brokers, damaged the stability of treaty ports and their hinterland. Along with smuggling and piracy, this was the main issue affecting coastal-area governance following the opening of the treaty ports.

Attitudes towards the Coolie Trade

On 22 November 1852, a riot broke out in Amoy, caused principally by the coolie trade run by Syme, Muir & Co. The riot was triggered by Francis Darby Syme's request for the release of Lin Huang, a broker arrested by local Qing officials and taken to the police station (*canjiang yamen*) on 22 November. On the same day, all of Amoy's shops closed, vagabonds gathered from neighbouring villages, and both the gentry and the officials petitioned the circuit intendant of Amoy (Amoy Taotai) to control the coolie trade. On 23 November, British marines fired on the mob, killing 12 people and wounding between about 12 and 16 others. In the wake of this incident, negotiations between the British consul and the circuit intendant and sub-prefect of Amoy (*Xiamen haifang tongzhi*) resulted in the opening of the British consular court and a guilty conviction for Syme. Fines provided compensation payments for those killed or wounded, and the incident finally ended.[24] While the Amoy riot was a relatively small-scale incident, the related debate helps illustrate attitudes towards the coolie trade in the treaty ports.

Foreign Merchants

The British, the most numerous of all foreign merchants, were divided into two groups. The first comprised merchants such as James Tait and Syme, who were engaged in the coolie trade. The second group, including Jardine, Matheson & Co. and Dent & Co., regarded the coolie trade as an obstacle to other types of trade.[25] While Jardine, Matheson & Co. also profited from the coolie trade by providing ships to Tait & Co. for coolie emigration,[26] their disapproval likely stemmed from the lower profits of the coolie trade as compared with other types of trade.

British Diplomats

British diplomats, including the British consuls in China, were overwhelmingly against the coolie trade because of its resemblance to the slave trade. However, it was difficult for them to legally control the trade because no rules existed permitting Chinese emigration or controlling emigration in general. Furthermore, they had to consider the profits of planters (plantation owners) in British colonies.

However, it was the British consuls' duty to ensure that Britons in China observed the treaty. The British response to the Amoy riot illustrates this obligation. In that case, in their sentencing of Syme the consular courts found that he had breached the Treaty of Nanjing and the Supplementary Treaty signed at Bogue by asking local officials to release a broker employed by him. Based on this breach, the court fined Syme.[27] Furthermore, British minister John Bowring believed that Syme's action also breached clause 13 of the "General Regulations, Under Which the British Trade is To Be Conducted At the Five Ports", and therefore trespassed on consular jurisdiction.[28]

From the viewpoint of Frederick Harvey, the man dispatched by Bowring during the Amoy riot, the relationship between foreigners and the Chinese in Amoy was good. He therefore opposed the coolie trade because it risked damaging this relationship.[29] Like most British merchants, Bowring agreed.[30] The British home government came to hold the same view.[31]

Local Qing Officials

At first, local Qing officials overlooked the coolie trade, as illustrated by the presence of a barracoon near the maritime customs office in Amoy.[32] However, their greatest point of contention with foreign merchants was their trespassing on the power of local officials. When Harvey met local Qing officials after the Amoy riot, they complained primarily about the actions weakening their authority, such as when British merchants sent messages to local officials or visited their office in person to obtain the release of captured brokers.[33] In fact, even though British diplomats were concerned about breaches of the treaty and local officials were angered by challenges to their authority, both viewed Syme's acts as having encroached on their authority. Hence, they shared a mutual concern.

Moreover, it was important for local Qing officials to stabilize the area under their jurisdiction. They also aimed to avoid conflict with Britain and to prevent the riot from spreading when the sub-prefect's proclamation ordered Amoy's inhabitants to notify him of the identity of the person who had put up a poster inflaming hostility towards foreigners.[34] They were concerned, therefore, about deteriorating security and the escalation of problems instigated by the worsening conflict with Britain. It was clear that to stabilize local control, it would first be necessary to control the coolie trade.

However, because the Qing central government had banned emigration abroad, local Qing officials had no intention of inspecting passenger ships. Thus, the sub-prefect declined the offer for him and the British consul to examine these ships together.[35] Local Qing officials also lacked the power to control the brokers. Therefore, to control the coolie trade, it was important for them to cooperate with foreign consuls along with the local people.

Gentry and Merchants in Amoy

While the gentry and merchants in Amoy strongly opposed the coolie trade, they also wished to avoid stirring up anti-foreign movements and setting off a conflict with foreigners. According to an American missionary's testimony, a number of respectable Chinese men held meetings and some called for the destruction of the English *hongs* (merchant houses) and for attacks on the coolie ships. However, they ultimately repudiated these suggestions because their success would be only temporary: a British warship would arrive within a few days and the mobs would plunder local shops after attacking foreign firms.[36] Therefore, the gentry and merchants understood that good foreign relations were essential to bringing peace to the area. In this respect, their response differed from that of the gentry around Guangzhou, who led the anti-foreign movement.

Considering brokers and the local people, the conflict in the coolie trade appears to have been one between the following two groups: (a) some foreign merchants, major Cantonese brokers and Fujianese brokers; and (b) local people, gentry, merchants, local Qing officials, British diplomats and foreigners in Amoy. Overall, group (a) was clearly weaker than group (b). In addition, those comprising group (a) did not trust each other. In contrast, group (b) included local officials and leaders who shared a mutual interest in stabilizing society and opposing illegal acts by foreign merchants and the coolie trade. Furthermore, anti-foreign movements were uncommon around Amoy, and there was frequent negotiation between local Qing officials and the British consul. Both local Qing officials and the British consul regarded the coolie-trade problem as a serious one, and it was considered important to address it through diplomatic channels. Negotiations relating to the Amoy riot provided a good opportunity. In what follows, we evaluate how the coolie trade changed following the Amoy riot.

Decline of the Coolie Trade

Cooperation between China and Britain

Previous studies have claimed that the Amoy coolie trade declined following the riot there.[37] However, the Small Sword Society revolted in May 1853, with the insurgents occupying Amoy until November of that year. This resulted in stagnation in both the coolie trade but also trade in general. We cannot therefore conclude that the coolie trade declined after the events of 1852. In fact, on 2 March 1855, Tait & Co. transported 240 coolies from Jinmen Island near Amoy to Swatow.[38] Similarly, the French were still transporting coolies to their colonies of Guadeloupe and Martinique,[39] and 2,489 coolies were recruited in Amoy and 5,332 in Swatow in 1855. Therefore, despite the move to Swatow, the coolie trade in Amoy continued.[40]

Clearly, it was important to control the brokers in order to abolish the coolie trade. However, Martin Crofton Morrison, the British consul in Amoy, reported on 17 March 1857:

> The "Brokers' Village" above alluded to is on the seashore 8 or 9 miles distant from Amoy in the Prefecture of Chang-Chow and beyond the jurisdiction of the Amoy officials. I have requested the Taotai to bring its existence to the notice of the proper authorities, but I believe its inhabitants are sufficiently powerful to set them at defiance.[41]

The power of local Qing officials to act against the brokers was obviously limited. For example, they interrupted the arrest of a major coolie broker belonging to an influential clan. It was difficult to control the coolie trade because the organization of brokers was on a micro scale and often only temporary. Accordingly, it became important to employ the help of foreign consuls in order to control the major brokers forming the core of the coolie-trade organization.

In 1855, a widow named Ye petitioned the circuit intendant, claiming that her son had been deceived, brought to Amoy, sold by a British firm (possibly Tait & Co. or Syme, Muir & Co.) and handed over to a British ship. On 24 July, under orders from the circuit intendant, the sub-prefect stated that he could not arrest the brokers because they were hiding in British firms. He then asked the British consul to hand over the brokers and the kidnapped victims.[42] This example illustrates the relationships between the widow and the circuit intendant, the circuit intendant and the sub-prefect, and the sub-prefect and the British consul. Local Qing officials may have used widows to put pressure on the British consul because the kidnapping of a widow's son was considered serious.

Another example involves the sub-prefect's correspondence on 26 April 1857, in which several provincial graduates (*juren*), stipend students (*linsheng*), government students (*shengyuan*),[43] students by purchase fourth class (*jiansheng*)[44] and Confucian apprentices (*tongsheng*) accused a crimp named Yan Qing of kidnapping for the coolie trade. The sub-prefect requested the British consul to arrest Yan Qing.[45]

As this chain of interactions demonstrates, it became more difficult for British merchants to protect their brokers, and consequently brokers' activities were increasingly restricted. At the same time, the British consuls applied direct pressure on British merchants. For instance, when Syme, Muir & Co. attempted to resume the coolie trade using a ship called the *Zetland*, British consul Charles Alexander Winchester warned that the British authorities would not assist if any problems arose. He also urged the firm to engage only in legal emigration.[46] As a result, Syme, Muir & Co. gave up recruiting coolies in Amoy.[47] Tait & Co. followed suit owing to the difficulties involved.[48] By the late 1850s, British firms had begun withdrawing from the coolie trade.

To assert institutional control over ships, on 14 August 1855 the British government issued an Act for the Regulation of Chinese Passenger Ships, which came into effect on 1 January 1856. This affected all British passenger ships departing for British colonies from Hong Kong, ports in China or the Chinese coast. The Act stipulated that ships were permitted to sail only after emigration officers had certified that the ship was properly manned, equipped, fitted and ventilated and had ascertained that emigrants were willing, knew their destination and comprehended the nature of their contracts.[49] This Act was generally ineffective at fully controlling the coolie trade because it covered only British ships, and was ignored in Hong Kong.[50] Nonetheless, in some areas the Act did have a significant impact.

British consuls performed the role of emigration officers.[51] On 27 February 1857, the British consul inspected *Goldstream*, a British ship chartered by a Spaniard named Armero. The coolies on board, who did not wish to emigrate, were liberated.[52] Similarly, when the consul inspected the British ship *Cleopatra* on 29 May 1858, the coolies, though contracted, were hesitant to leave but disembarked.[53] The British consul now had the legal right to control emigrants, and this limited the unrestricted coolie trade. An article in the *China Mail* on 24 December 1857 confirmed that the coolie trade in Amoy had declined because of the new law.[54]

Because of the Act, the *Cleopatra* set sail from Amoy at the end of May 1858 having failed to secure a sufficient number of emigrants. Another ship, the *Scotia*, which arrived in June of that year, later moved to Macau owing to a similar difficulty in recruiting coolies.[55] In 1857 and 1858, Syme, Muir & Co. moved all their passenger ships to either Swatow or Macau,[56] a further indication that, by then, the coolie trade involving British ships in Amoy had completely ceased.

Handling Foreign Ships

Despite the success of the British Emigration Act, it was still important to address trade by non-British ships because, following the Act's implementation, the coolie trade stopped using British ships and began deploying vessels from other nations.[57] The conduct of other countries also evoked general anti-foreign sentiment in China.

From this point on, cooperation with the US progressed smoothly, which was critical in the coolie trade. For example, in 1860, following a report by the British consul, who had been under pressure from a local Qing official, the American consul inspected an American ship named the *Ann* and released 46 coolies.[58] However, ships belonging to Portugal and Spain were still a problem because Portugal controlled Macau, the centre of the coolie trade, and Spain controlled Cuba, the destination for coolie ships.

Difficulties began to arise in the recruitment of coolies by Spanish and Macau ships at the end of May 1859. On 15 June 1859, the circuit intendant told Morrison, British consul in Amoy, that the British and Luzon ships anchored outside the port of Amoy had purchased people and colluded with vagabonds in the coastal area. He requested that they collaborate to control the trade and rescue the coolies by dispatching warships.[59]

In response to the circuit intendant's request, Morrison replied that the ships were not of British origin and suggested that the intendant instead negotiate with the Spanish and Portuguese consuls. However, early in July, missionaries warned foreign merchants that the Amoy locals were enraged by the incidence of kidnapping. Several influential Chinese men also visited Morrison, warning him that another Amoy riot could occur. In fact, Morrison revealed that the brokers' activities were more violent at this time than in 1852.[60]

Government students and local leaders in Amoy now petitioned the magistrate of Tongan county, informing him of their miserable situation, because criminals in Amoy were deceiving and kidnapping people in pursuit of profits from the purchase of coolie labour by Luzon ships. They also wrote that, despite foreigners' promises not to purchase people again following the strike in November 1852 (that is, the Amoy riot), foreign ships had recently resumed this practice. If the officials had not told the foreign consuls and banned the practice, the area would have remained destabilized by local anger.[61] In fact, foreigners had made no such promise after the Amoy riot. Local elites imagined that event in this petition.

The magistrate of Tongan county then asked the British consul to return the people kidnapped and to outlaw kidnapping.[62] The British consul informed the Spanish consul of his intention to mediate with the Qing officials. The Spanish consul agreed to inspect the passenger ship before its departure, witnessed by the British consul and the Qing officials. However, the ship was cleared without having been inspected by the Qing officials, and the problem disappeared.[63]

In this incident, local officials pressured the British consul, emphasizing the feelings of the locals. In addition, with the British consul's assistance, local officials and residents tried to influence activities by non-British ships and merchants. The British consul therefore adopted the role of mediator. In part due to such pressure, the coolie trade conducted by Spanish and Portuguese ships also gradually moved to Macau. It failed from 1867–69 owing to opposition from the American consul, despite Spain's attempts to resume the trade in Amoy.[64]

Decline of Cantonese Power

Cantonese brokers disappeared after the Amoy riot, illustrating the difficulty in carrying out this role in the area around Amoy. The coolie trade instead used native Fujianese and their ships. As in the case of the broker Jiang Yinshui in 1858 and in the 1860 incident aboard the *Ann*, all brokers were now from Tongan county (that is, Fujianese).[65] In the case of Jiang Yinshui, four people became major brokers in a partnership (*hegu*) and shared the profits.[66] This shows that even with minimal capital, any Fujianese could become a major broker through partnerships.

As the case of Jiang Yinshui demonstrates, the social status of these brokers changed and people at the lowest levels of society with little capital could now become brokers. In fact, Jiang Yinshui had lost his father and had been working as a labourer before becoming a broker. As a result, the organization of brokers became smaller in scale, reducing opportunities to resume a large-scale coolie trade.

However, coolie-trade expansion was possible due to the growth in Cantonese piracy during the early 1850s. For example, armed *lorchas* (ships operated by the Cantonese pirates) dispatched from Macau attacked villages and kidnapped villagers in Guangdong province.[67] Clearly, there was a close relationship between piracy and the coolie trade. Indeed, the comprador of Syme, Muir & Co. was involved in piracy[68] and it is likely that the coolies sold in Guangdong province were transported on either West Coast boats or Cantonese lorchas.

In fact, records exist of an incident relating to the release of coolies from a Cantonese lorcha. This came to light in April 1858, when a poor Chinese woman notified the British consulate that her son had been kidnapped. Although the British consul subsequently notified the circuit intendant and a Qing navy soldier was also abducted by the same Cantonese lorcha, local officials would not intervene because the lorcha was heavily armed and had foreigners on board. The circuit intendant requested assistance from the British consul and a gunboat was dispatched. The consul searched the lorcha and released 150 abductees; 22 brokers were handed over to the Qing officials for punishment.[69] This is clear evidence of the association of Cantonese pirates with the coolie trade.

However, during the late 1850s, Cantonese pirates declined in number due to their suppression by the British navy.[70] This damaged the coolie trade because it was carried out mainly by the Cantonese, and led to the expulsion of the Cantonese network from the coastal area of Fujian. The Cantonese coolie trade now concentrated in Guangdong province, where the trade continued for some time.

As discussed, the coolie trade in Amoy declined due to various factors: close cooperation between the British consul and the local officials; the Act for the Regulation of Chinese Passenger Ships; and the suppression of Cantonese pirates. This contrasts with the experience in Guangzhou, where the coolie trade expanded rapidly until 1859.[71]

Conclusion

The coolie trade in Amoy began because of the port's tradition of emigration, connections between foreigners and Chinese that began in the early 19th century and the chaos prevailing in coastal areas during the mid-19th century. Coolie brokers committed illegal acts, including kidnapping, to secure good labourers. This led to considerable opposition that eventually ended the coolie trade. The Amoy riot was a good opportunity for China and Britain to cooperate in the region. This cooperation had an impact on the coolie trade, leading to the expulsion of the Cantonese involved (major brokers and pirates, for instance) and pressure being put on ships belonging to countries other than Britain.

The cooperation between local Qing officials and foreign diplomats expanded into Guangdong province with the introduction of controlled emigration in response to military pressure, from the allied British and French armies occupying Guangzhou during the Second Opium War. Emigration then expanded to Swatow.[72] However, the coolie-trade problem did not immediately dissipate in the coastal areas of Guangdong. This was because of the presence of coolie trade bases in Hong Kong and Macau, and because the network of Cantonese brokers was more efficient in Guangdong than in Fujian. The coolie trade in Guangdong finally ended in March 1874 due to its cessation in Macau.

During the process of suppressing the coolie trade, local Qing officials exploited the emotions of the local people and requested that the British consul control British merchants and act as an intermediary between themselves and other foreign countries. For example, they asked the consul to pressure non-British foreign merchants, and local officials entrusted the inspection of emigrants to the British consul. For instance, in 1860 the British consul first proposed the joint inspection of passenger ships to the sub-prefect. While the sub-prefect declined on grounds of illness,[73] it is also apparent that he did not intend to inspect the ships. Although this was partly because foreign emigration was banned at that time, this attitude remained unchanged after the treaties of Tianjin and Beijing, which allowed Chinese emigration abroad. In fact, there was no supervision by Qing officials of emigrants before embarkation even in 1883,[74] and the situation whereby the Qing entrusted emigration services to foreign countries continued for some time. Under this condition, British consuls had responsibility for emigration services, leading to a decline in the coolie trade and, ultimately, a concentration of emigration to South East Asia.

In addition to the coolie trade, China's cooperation with and delegation of services to Western countries and the utilization of

Western institutions, such as their maritime customs and the British navy, brought about a decrease in smuggling and the suppression of piracy. This led directly to the re-establishment of order by the Qing government in the treaty ports system.[75]

Until now, studies on the role of Western countries, such as Britain, in introducing modern institutions to China's treaty ports during the late Qing period have viewed them either positively—as bringing modernization—or negatively—since they were enforced through imperial power. This is because most studies have tended to emphasize the leading role of Britain and other Western countries and neglected the proactive role of local Chinese officials and people. However, it would be better to argue that Western countries were "entrusted" with services by the Qing government, especially local Qing officials. The unequal treaties imposed on China at the time became fertile ground for such a delegation by admitting the privilege of foreigners. However, such a delegation had already been used in China, especially when controlling local areas lacking government power and resources. In fact, the only change after the opening of the treaty ports was that the Chinese government began to use foreign contractors alongside its Chinese private contractors, including the gentry, influential merchants, guilds and lineages. Hereafter, in analysing the role of treaty ports it is important to emphasize the role of the Chinese, who were agents of Western countries, and to analyse the role of foreign countries and their citizens in governing China; those foreign countries and citizens ultimately became agents of the Qing government.

Notes

1. There were great differences between the emigration to South East Asia and the emigration to areas beyond. The former did not cause serious disruption to local societies because emigrants could keep in contact with their homeland, and the emigration system was more reliable. Ei Murakami, *Umi no Kindai Chūgoku: Fukkenjin no Katsudō to Igirisu/Shinchō* [Maritime History of Modern China: Local Fujian Actors and the British and Chinese Empires] (Nagoya: Nagoya Daigaku Shuppankai, 2013), pp. 283–4.

2. Elliott Campbell Arensmeyer, "British Merchant Enterprise and the Chinese Coolie Labour Trade: 1850–1874", unpublished PhD dissertation (Hawaii: University of Hawaii, 1979); Persia Crawford Campbell,

Chinese Coolie Emigration to Countries within the British Empire (London: Frank Cass, 1923).

3. Robert L. Irick, *Ch'ing Policy Toward the Coolie Trade, 1847–1878* (Taipei: Chinese Materials Center, 1982); Ching-hwang Yen, *Coolies and Mandarins: China's Protection of Overseas Chinese During the Late Ch'ing Period (1851–1911)* (Singapore: Singapore University Press, 1985); Zhuang Guotu, *Zhongguo Fengjian Zhengfu de Huaqiao Zhengce* [The Chinese Feudal Government's Policies towards Overseas Chinese] (Xiamen: Xiamen Daxue Chubanshe, 1989).

4. Wang Sing-wu, *The Organization of Chinese Emigration 1848–1888: With Special Reference to Chinese Emigration to Australia* (San Francisco, CA: Chinese Materials Center, 1978).

5. For the Amoy riot see Junko Ozawa, "1852 nen Amoi Bōdō nitsuite" [The Amoy Riot of 1852], *Shiron (Tōkyō Joshi Daigaku)* 38 (1985); Ng Chin-keong, "The Amoy Riots of 1852: Coolie Emigration and Sino-British Relations", in *Mariners, Merchants and Oceans: Studies in Maritime History*, ed. K.S. Mathew (New Delhi: Manohar, 1995). For the attack on foreigners in Shanghai, see Kani Hiroaki, "Kanpō Kyūnen Shanhai niokeru Gaikokujin shugekijiken nitsuite" ["On the Anti-foreign Incident in Shanghai in 1859"], *Tōyōshi Kenkyū* 43, 3 (1984). Yoshiyuki Nishisato, *Shinmatsu Chūryūnich Kankēshi no Kenkyū* [The Relationship between China, Ryūkyū and Japan during the Late Qing Period] (Kyoto: Kyōto Daigaku Gakujyutsu Shuppankai, 2005) examines the riot aboard the *Robert Bowne* in the context of the history of Ryūkyū.

6. Hiroaki Kani, *Kindai Chūgoku no Kūrī to "Choka"* [Coolies and "Slave Girls" of Modern China] (Tokyo: Iwanami Shoten, 1979).

7. Watt Stewart, *Chinese Bondage in Peru: A History of the Chinese Coolie in Peru, 1849–1874* (Westport, CT: Greenwood Press, 1970); Setsuko Sonoda, *Nanboku Amerika Kamin to Kindai Chūgoku: Jyūkyūsēki Transnashonarumaigrēshon* [Overseas Chinese in the Americas and Modern China: Transnational Migration in the Nineteenth Century] (Tokyo: Tokyo Daigaku Shuppankai, 2009).

8. FO663 (Great Britain, Foreign Office Archives, Embassy and Consular Archives, China, Amoy, National Archives, Kew, UK)/10, Robertson to Bonham, No. 28, 15 Apr. 1853.

9. On the abolition of the slave trade in Britain, see Chapter 3 by Kumie Inose in this volume.

10. On the abolition of slavery in France, see Chapter 2 by Sue Peabody in this volume.

11. Kani, *Kindai Chūgoku*, pp. 6–8; Sonoda, *Nanboku Amerika Kamin*, pp. 44–54.

12. Campbell, *Chinese Coolie Emigration*, pp. 24–160.

13. *BPP, China* (Irish University Press, *Area Studies Series, British Parliamentary Papers*, China, 42 vols (Shannon: Irish University Press, 1972), vol. 3, Correspondence with the Superintendent of British Trade in China, upon the Subject of Emigration from that Country (hereafter "Emigration"), Encl. No. 1 in No. 8, Elmslie to Bowring, 25 Aug. 1852, p. 8 (18).

14. *Maria Luz*, a Peruvian ship that had stopped at Yokohama, triggered the abolition of *yūjo* in Japan (see Chapter 8 by Yuriko Yokoyama in this volume) and negotiations on treaties between China and Peru relating to the control of coolie emigration (Sonoda, *Nanboku Amerika Kamin*, pp. 61–3).

15. According to Qing officials, 50,000 people emigrated from Fujian every year, and at least 5,000 men moved to the Straits Settlements. The number of emigrants to South East Asia was much larger then than the coolie trade. FO663/9, Encl. No. 3 in No. 127, 26 Aug. 1852, Note by Dr Winchester.

16. Murakami, *Umi no Kindai Chūgoku*, pp. 265–8.

17. Kani, *Kindai Chūgoku*, pp. 11–2. In 1874, the Chinese government sent commissions to Peru and Cuba to investigate conditions among the Chinese there. In 1876, English, French and Chinese versions of the report on the Chinese in Cuba were published, exposing the poor conditions faced by Chinese labourers in that country (Sonoda, *Nanboku Amerika Kamin*, pp. 69–102).

18. Murakami, *Umi no Kindai Chūgoku*, pp. 268–70.

19. Wang, *The Organization of Chinese Emigration*, pp. 56–64.

20. Murakami, *Umi no Kindai Chūgoku*, pp. 268–70.

21. FO228/903 (Great Britain, Foreign Office Archives, Embassy and Consular Archives, China, Amoy, National Archives, Kew, UK), Chinese Enclosure, proclamation issued by the gentries and merchants of Amoy.

22. *BPP, China*, vol. 3, *Emigration*, Encl. No. 7 in No. 14, Harvey to Bowring, p. 41 (53).

23. FO228/903, Petition by Chen Sha.

24. Ozawa, "1852 nen Amoi Bōdō"; Ng, "The Amoy Riots of 1852", pp. 423–40.

25. Campbell, *Chinese Coolie Emigration*, pp. 102–3; *BPP, China*, vol. 3, *Emigration*, Encl. No. 8 in No. 14, pp. 68–9, 80–1.

26. Arensmeyer, "British Merchant Enterprise", pp. 69–76.

27. *BPP, China*, vol. 3, *Emigration*, Encl. No. 5 in No. 14, Minutes of Consular Court of Amoy, p. 38 (50).

28. FO663/9, Bowring to Backhouse, No. 67, 29 Dec. 1852.

29. *BPP, China*, vol. 3, *Emigration*, Encl. No. 7 in No. 14, Harvey to Bowring, p. 42 (54).

30. *BPP, China*, vol. 3, *Emigration*, No. 12, Bowring to Malmesbury, 14 Dec. 1852, p. 29.
31. Arensmeyer, "British Merchant Enterprise", pp. 177–8.
32. *BPP, China*, vol. 3, *Emigration*, No. 2, Bowring to Malmesbury, 17 May 1852, p. 2 (12).
33. *BPP, China*, vol. 3, *Emigration*, Encl. No. 7 in No. 14, Harvey to Bowring, p. 43 (55).
34. FO228/903, Papers relating to Coolie traffic at Amoy brought by Mr Harvey.
35. FO663/9, Encl. No. 10 in No. 177, Nov. 1852 to FO, Account of the Interview at the Marine Magistrate on the 14th instant.
36. *BPP, China*, vol. 3, *Emigration*, Encl. No. 8 in No. 14, *Minutes of Evidence*, p. 70 (82).
37. Ozawa, "1852 nen Amoi Bōdō", pp. 59–60.
38. FO228/188, Winchester to Bowring, No. 46, 3 Mar. 1855.
39. FO228/188, Winchester to Bowring, No. 32, 14 Feb. 1855.
40. FO228/211, Encl. No. 2 in Backhouse to Bowring, No. 18, 31 Jan. 1856.
41. FO228/233, Morrison to Bowring, No. 14, 17 Mar. 1857.
42. FO663/62, Sub-prefect Li to British Vice Consul, 24 July 1855.
43. Students eligible to participate in the provincial examination, the first major stage in the civil-service recruitment examination system.
44. Men permitted to study at the national university without having passed at any level of the civil-service recruitment examination system, in recognition of their contribution of grain or money to the state.
45. FO663/65, Sub-prefect Li to British Consul, 26 Apr. 1857.
46. FO228/188, Winchester to Bowring, No. 23, 30 Jan. 1855.
47. FO228/188, Winchester to Bowring, No. 32, 14 Feb. 1855.
48. FO228/211, Backhouse to Bowring, No. 15, 22 Jan. 1856.
49. 18 & 19 Vict., c. 104.
50. Campbell, *Chinese Coolie Emigration*, pp. 115–6; Kani, *Kindai Chūgoku*, p. 25.
51. FO228/250, Malmesbury to Bowring, No. 28, 17 Apr. 1858.
52. FO228/233, Morrison to Bowring, No. 14, 17 Mar. 1857.
53. FO228/251, Morrison to Bowring, No. 49, 16 June 1858.
54. *China Mail*, 24 Dec. 1857, p. 206.
55. FO228/251, Morrison to Bowring, No. 49, 16 June 1858.
56. FO228/265, Morrison to Bruce, No. 14, 22 June 1859.
57. Wang, *The Organization of Chinese Emigration*, p. 167.
58. FO228/285, Gingell to Bruce, No. 20, 21 Feb. 1860; FO663/19, Haifang Yu to Gingell, No. 5, 10 Feb. 1860.
59. FO663/65, Circuit Intendant Chen to British Consul, 14 June 1859.
60. FO228/265, Encl. No. 2 in Morrison to Bruce, No. 18, 16 July 1859.

61. FO663/65, Chen, Magistrate of Tongan County, to the British Consul in Sept., in the ninth year of the Xianfeng era.

62. Ibid.

63. FO228/265, Encl. No. 1 in Morrison to Bruce, No. 18, 16 July 1859; FO228/265, Encl. No. 2 in Morrison to Bruce, No. 18, 16 July 1859.

64. Irick, *Ch'ing Policy*, pp. 239–50.

65. Jiang Yinshui was arrested by Qing local officials on suspicion of kidnapping 150 people for the purpose of selling them abroad. FO228/251, Encl. 3 in Morrison to Bowring, No. 46, 2 June 1858; FO228/285, Encl. 4 in Gingell to Bruce, No. 20, 21 Feb. 1860.

66. FO228/251, Encl. 2 in Morrison to Bowring, No. 46, 2 June 1858.

67. Wang, *The Organization of Chinese Emigration*, p. 78.

68. Murakami, *Umi no Kindai Chūgoku*, pp. 161–2.

69. FO228/251, Gingell to Bowring, No. 26, 8 Apr. 1858; FO663/65, Circuit Intendant Si to British Consul, 29 Apr. 1858.

70. Murakami, *Umi no Kindai Chūgoku*, pp. 166–9.

71. Campbell, *Chinese Coolie Emigration*, pp. 117–8.

72. Irick, *Ch'ing Policy*, pp. 89–140.

73. FO228/285, Gingell to Bruce, No. 87, 4 Dec. 1860.

74. FO228/721, Encl. in Forrest to Parkes, No. 18, 25 Oct. 1883.

75. Takashi Okamoto, *Kindai Chūgoku to Kaikan* [China and the Maritime Customs System in Modern Times] (Nagoya: Nagoya Daigaku Shuppankai, 1999), pp. 179–203; Murakami, *Umi no Kindai Chūgoku*, pp. 145–81.

CHAPTER 7

Freedom Across the Water: British Emancipation of Slavery and Maritime Marronage in the Danish West Indies

Amitava Chowdhury

Introduction

In 1847, William Gilbert, a former slave in the Danish West Indies, wrote the following words to the Danish monarch, King Christian VIII:

> Sir: I taken my pen in hand a runaway slave, to inform your excelcy of the evil of slavery. Sir Slavery is a bad thing and if any man will make a slave of a man after he is born free, i should think it an outrage becose I was born free of my Mother wom and after I was born the Monster, in the shape of a man, made a slave of me in your dominion....[1]

Gilbert was situated in Boston, Massachusetts where his freedom was secure, since slavery had been declared unconstitutional in the previous century, perhaps the reason why he escaped to Boston in the first place; but he had aspirations to visit his birthplace, St Croix, in the Danish West Indies, where, at the time of writing this letter, slavery was extant.[2] While Gilbert was a freeman in Boston, it is doubtful whether his freedom would have been recognized in St Croix if he chose to return or visit the island, especially because he had escaped the regime of slavery as a runaway. Gilbert writes:

> i have a writ to my freedom I have my freedom now but that is not all Sir, i want to see my Sisters & my Brothers and i now ask your excelcy if your excelcy will grant me a free pass to go and come when ever I fail dispose to go and come to Ile of St. Croix or Santacruce the West Indies.[3]

Gilbert knew that visiting St Croix without a free pass would jeopardize his chances of returning to Massachusetts as a freeman. His letter to the king, therefore, was a personal and specific appeal— an appeal to extend the right of his freedom beyond the free soil of Massachusetts so that he could visit his family and kindred in the island he had left as a runaway. Gilbert continues, "I ask in arnist for that pass for the tears is now gushing from mine eyes as if someone had poar water on my head and it running down my Cheak."[4]

There is no evidence in the archives that Gilbert's appeal was ever answered, but his letter came in the wake of a decade of petitions, intrigues, adventures and ameliorative ordinances that finally brought slavery to an end in the Danish West Indies in 1848, almost 14 years after British emancipation and a decade after British abolition of the apprenticeship system in 1838. It is precisely at this time, after the abolition of slavery (and apprenticeship system) in the British colonies that freedom and slavery were incongruously juxtaposed in the liminal waters of the Virgin Islands. Such a collocation of contrasting institutions of labour reveals the fragility of freedom in the post-emancipation Caribbean world. In this article, I aim to bring out the trans-imperial consequences of British emancipation that resulted in the uneven terrain of enslavement and liberty, giving freedom a very curious geographical meaning.

In the intervening period between 1834 and 1848, an increasing number of slaves ran away from the Danish islands to the British territories in the hope of gaining freedom by virtue of stepping on a soil free from bondage.[5] Prior to British emancipation, maritime marronage[6] was a frequent phenomenon in the West Indies, and on numerous occasions, slaves sailed away from the British islands to French and Danish islands.[7] However, after 1834, the unusual proximity of the British territory of Tortola and the Danish island of St John made frequent escape all the more enticing and possible within the broader circle of maritime marronage from the wider

Caribbean basin to the British islands. The steady stream of Danish maritime maroons on the one hand, created diplomatic impasse between the Danish and British colonial governments that brought out the ambiguities and paradoxes of British legal regimes surrounding slavery and freedom, and on the other hand, it ultimately weakened the system of slavery in the Danish territories. In fact, considerations of neighbourly relations played an important role in most decisions surrounding slavery, marronage and freedom in the post-emancipation Caribbean World. For instance, when a certain Mr Hodge—a British citizen but resident of French St Martin and a slave owner—proposed to free all of his slaves in return for adequate compensation in the form of land in the British territories, the British authorities, although sympathetic to the idea, found the proposal to be not "politic" in light of their friendly relationship with the surrounding foreign islands, especially the Danish, where the enslaved were clamouring for freedom.[8] The question of bondage and freedom, thus, was intricately entwined with the practicalities of diplomatic discourses. The stream of maritime maroons not only depleted the slave population and created a drain on colonial economy, but also the very act of running away led to sweeping ameliorations in the conditions of the enslaved in a way that would not have been possible in the absence of freedom in the British territories.[9] In a very real sense, the lure of freedom across the water brought about by British emancipation ultimately made freedom a reality in the Danish West Indies.

Marronage in the Danish West Indies

In the Danish West Indies, marronage was not a new phenomenon, and similar to other locales where slavery existed, running away was a concomitant part of slavery in the Danish colonies from the beginning. We know from contemporary sources and various later accounts that the slave system in the Danish islands was particularly harsh with a very high mortality rate in the 18th century.[10] The mode of marronage and the choice of a hiding place usually depended on the state of development of an island colony and its topography.[11] In the early phase of colonial settlement, when the administrative reach of the colonial apparatus was incomplete, the fugitive slaves attempted to hide in the island peripheries—on remote mountaintops, in inaccessible forests and in other difficult-to-reach areas.[12] But as the colonial economy developed and agriculture and habitation covered the greater part of the islands, the runaway slaves had to seek alternative avenues. Many slaves often passed as free in the towns, hid amongst relatives and friends and often had temporary hideouts in the cane fields, between December and June, when the cane was high enough to hide a makeshift hutment.[13] Neville A.T. Hall describes another alternative as "cultural marronage", which is best conceptualized as a system of accommodation, where the enslaved population withdrew from the affairs of plantation life and wove their lives around their own cultural mores.[14] Many of the maroons, if they were not captured in the meanwhile, ended up in Maronbjerg, where by the 1770s they had set up a rather thriving maroon village.[15]

Others, however, took to maritime marronage, and in the context of the Danish Caribbean, this was the most common form of running away.[16] Taking advantage of the geographical peculiarities of the Caribbean area, the slaves made use of makeshift boats and set sail to nearby islands.[17] Most of these early maritime maroons ended up in Spanish Puerto Rico. In these early days before intensification of plantation culture, Puerto Rico proved to be quite attractive for the maroons. The Spanish authorities not only welcomed them, received them and treated them mildly, there is evidence to show that they indeed encouraged the Danish slaves to leave for Puerto Rico.[18] Escaped slaves were granted freedom after one year, or after conversion to Catholicism, and were often granted a plot of land.[19] Such tempting news of freedom across the sea made maritime marronage a frequent affair and a cause for major headache for the Danish planters.

The slaves manufactured dugout canoes; they occasionally stole and even seized boats to reach Puerto Rico. The evidence for such means comes from numerous legislations passed in the Danish Virgin Islands, restricting access to boat use and elaborate registration requirements for boat owners.[20] In fact, as early as 1706, the Privy Council of St Thomas ordered all trees large enough to provide timber for canoes to be cut off.[21] When all else failed, some slaves swam across the narrow straits and reached other islands in search of a new life. Reports from Danish residents in St Croix in the mid-18th century show how prevalent the phenomenon of marronage was, and in some instances 20–25 slaves ran away each night.[22] Continuous efforts at curtailing maritime mobility of the fugitive slaves through restrictive boat ownership legislation ultimately proved ineffective.

Between 1742 and 1767, a series of diplomatic arrangements between the Danish and Spanish authorities were implemented, but maritime marronage continued in spite of such arrangements for some more time until a rigid plantation structure appeared in Puerto Rico in the early 19th century when the previous lenient treatment meted out to the escaped slaves was replaced by a harsh slave regime. By the late 18th century, maritime marronage from the Danish islands to Puerto Rico had declined and the escaped slaves sought other methods of running away from their bondage.[23]

In the early 19th century, a large number of the fugitive slaves tried to pass off as freemen in the towns and ports of Danish West Indies. By now, a large number of small towns and ports had arisen in different parts of the Caribbean, and those who were lucky enough to reach some of the Danish port towns were able to sail off to other locations and were not limited to the Spanish colonies any longer.

In Search of Freedom across the Water

In March 1802, David Tams and Hans Jonathan, two slaves purchased in St Croix and brought over to Copenhagen, escaped. In a series of events reminiscent of the famous Somerset case (and several other habeas corpus cases in Britain), Tams and Jonathan refused to go back to the West Indies when they were eventually recaptured.[24] The prisoners claimed through their attorneys that their status as enslaved individuals ended the moment they set foot in Denmark, a land free from slavery.[25] The legal precedent created by the Somerset case of 1772, made it impossible in Britain to forcibly return an ex-slave back to the colonies. Such a legal atmosphere influenced the juridical circles in Denmark hence the attorneys invoked the habeas corpus writ in support of Tams and Jonathan. While the appeal of Tams and Jonathan reveals the import and influence of the Somerset case in the Atlantic World, the results of the lengthy legal deliberations appear ironical and even baffling. This, therefore, brings us to the question of free soil in Denmark and the juridical philosophy surrounding the question. What was the nature of the "transatlantic gap" in the Danish Atlantic, and what was the nature of the contradictions between metropolitan and colonial laws related to slavery? Just as fugitive slaves found their way to Puerto Rico and other Caribbean destinations, many ended up in Denmark as well. They were either escaped slaves passing as free who had taken up employment as maritime labourers on board Danish boats, or they were taken there by their masters with the intention of bringing them back to the Virgin Islands after a limited period of sojourn, as was the practice in the French and British Atlantic.

The complicated juridical procedure of the Tams and Jonathan case involved several legal experts in Denmark, and the foremost among them was a legal philosopher of immense repute, Anders Ørsted.[26] Faced with the conflict between metropolitan legal system and that of the colonies, Ørsted proceeded to evaluate the case in a radically different way than what Judge Mansfield had done in Britain. Instead of asking the question whether the slaves became free by stepping on the soil of Denmark, Ørsted raised the issue of security of property. Ørsted argued that if the property right (in slaves, or otherwise) had been granted by the Danish King in Danish territories abroad such rights could not be seized away in the metropole.[27] However, this right in property acquired in the colonies and maintained in the metropole, was restricted and limited in the Danish legal system by the fact that slavery was illegal in Denmark. Ørsted's ambiguous conceptualization of the legal problem on the one hand ensured the sanctity of the master's property rights, and on the other maintained that a contract for sale of slaves could not be executed in Denmark; such contracts executed elsewhere, when translated as property rights, remained valid in Denmark. In short, the principle of free soil celebrated in the Somerset case in 1772 did not take hold in Denmark, ironically a country that abolished the slave trade before any other European nation. This, then, is the general fabric of the concept of "free soil" in the Danish context. Unlike the British colonies, where gradual emancipation and amelioration made slavery somewhat less odious in the 19th century, and where the fundamental contradiction between the metropolitan and colonial legal systems eventually rendered slavery untenable in the empire, the congruity between the metropolitan and colonial laws insofar as the stance on free soil is concerned, made it possible for slavery to survive longer in the Danish colonies. Some have argued that it was the very influence of Ørsted's legal philosophy that made slavery last as long as it did in the Danish Virgin Islands.[28]

In the days following Ørsted's decision, slaves continued to run away to near and distant places, they continued to be rounded up and punished, and they frequently succeeded in escaping further enslavement in another corner of the world. What was a trickle of what we may term "maroon emigration", until the 1830s, suddenly became a torrent when slavery was abolished in the British Empire, and shortly afterwards, when apprenticeship proved to be untenable. This, of course, owes to the fact that freedom existed across the sea in what had now become a soil free of slavery in nearby Tortola, slightly distant Jamaica, and further away in Grenada and elsewhere.

Diplomatic Consequences of British Emancipation

The Danish Governor General's response to such increased maritime marronage was initially to claim that the slaves in the Danish Virgin Islands were indeed far better off than the freed in the British territories. Peter von Scholten, the Governor, wrote back to Copenhagen, "I have on all occasions…impressed on the Negroes that it is only by their own good conduct…that the government will be enabled to ameliorate their condition."[29] And when the slaves in St John seemed to be particularly inclined to embark on an insurrection, von Scholten observed:

> in the event of insurrection on the part of the slaves our physical power would soon be diminished to such a degree that we could not without a great sacrifice exert the necessary force to bring them back to order and obedience, the only plan is to obviate this as much as possible by moral means in which purposes in my opinion the best and the fittest method at this moment is to improve the condition of the negroes to such a degree that they themselves by the knowledge they acquire may easily perceive that their condition is in every respect better than what is to be found in all other colonies, and especially where they are enfranchised.[30]

As the evidence shows, von Scholten was willing to improve the conditions of the slaves to a status better than that enjoyed by the ex-apprentices in the British territories, but the thought of absolute emancipation remained inadmissible for the time being.[31] Meanwhile, he gave the order of shoot at sight for all maritime maroons in the Danish West Indian port towns.[32] This rather anachronistic and extreme inflexibility in an Atlantic World ripe with the knowledge and practice of abolition, freedom and free soil, rhymes with the equally absurd, ambiguous and anachronistic decision made in Copenhagen by Ørsted a generation earlier. This peculiarly inflexible juridical philosophy and legal intransigence sits rather oddly with the extraordinarily proactive abolition of Danish slave trade in the 1790s.

Escape from slavery and gaining freedom by stepping on British free soil continued to be the fate of a few fortunate maritime maroons in the early years of the 1840s. In real numbers, the loss to the planters was hardly significant, but what was deemed meaningful was the legal implication of the proximity of free soil and the perceived danger of an imminent exodus. Von Scholten wrote to the President of Tortola and the authorities in Grenada, asking them to capture and return all Danish fugitive slaves who had landed on British soil. This is precisely where the story becomes most complex. On the one hand was the question of diplomatic relations with Denmark and associated questions of security, safety and sovereignty, and on the other the very meaning of freedom as interpreted and translated in the Atlantic theatre. Lord Glenelg, the Colonial Secretary, wrote with his characteristic fierceness, "I have considered as inadmissible the proposal that fugitive slave criminals fleeing to the British colonies should be tried by the British tribunals for the crimes committed by them in the Danish colonies."[33]

While on face value this may be deemed as a celebration of the free soil principle, hidden beneath a few lines is the subtext of a legal license that rendered access to freedom for the fugitive to be problematic. Glenelg wrote that if a fugitive slave was proved to have been guilty of murder or other heinous crimes, appropriate measures would be taken to restitute the fugitive back to foreign authorities.[34] In reality, therefore, just the *claim* of extreme criminality was sufficient ground for denying freedom through free soil to the Danish slaves fleeing to British waters. Following Glenelg's instructions, the colonial authorities in the British Caribbean were seen to be exchanging notes claiming that the laws of their colonies did not offer any obstacle to bringing the fugitive offender to justice".[35] The problem of applicability of the principle of free soil to the Danish fugitives thus often made out Danish fugitives to be "offenders" in the eyes of British colonial law.

In 1841, when six Danish slaves escaped from St John to Tortola, the Governor General of the Danish territories requested the slaves to be restituted.[36] This, of course, is one of numerous such requests and incidents involving maritime maroons in the Virgin Islands, but in this particular instance, the demands on diplomatic pragmatism and the "law of nations" created a gulf within British administrative ranks. The initial desire of the British authorities was to seek a compromise by finding the Danish fugitives to be "guilty in the Danish possessions of crimes to which the laws of all civilized countries attach severe punishment".[37] Such a conclusion would have maintained the diplomatic status quo at the expense of the fugitive slaves, but the Queen's advocates ultimately found the slaves to be not guilty of any serious crime. "Having possessed themselves of a boat the property of their master, for the purpose of escaping from slavery" could hardly be considered to be a serious crime worthy of punishment in the British post-emancipation regime.[38] The six fugitives, as a result, were not given up to the Danish.

A narrow strait separated the uneven terrain of freedom and rights on one side and enslavement and force on the other within the Virgin Islands. This created an asymmetric world that maritime maroons tried to turn in their favour. While some succeeded and others were captured, recaptured or restituted, the meaning and attraction of freedom across the water ultimately painted the imagination of the enslaved population in the Danish West Indies. In November 1842, when Archdeacon Davis visited the Danish island of St Croix, a young boy named Oscar introduced himself and sought protection as a British subject.[39] Oscar, who was enslaved in St Croix, claimed to be born of a freewoman in Barbados, and thus claimed to be free according to British laws. Upon investigation, however, it was found that Oscar was born and sold in French St Martin, and thus his claim to freedom on the basis of British subjecthood could not be sustained. We do not know whether Oscar believed the story he recounted in front of the archdeacon or if he lied, but it is clear that the ironies of asymmetric freedom in a small geographical corner even captured the desire and imagination of a small boy unfortunate enough to find himself a slave in a curiously anachronistic setting.

Concluding Thoughts

This study reveals a highly uneven nature of legal regulations regarding slavery and freedom in the Atlantic World when compared across imperial borders. The principle of free soil firmly established in the British Isles in 1772 and extended to the colonies in 1834, provided an enormous opportunity for freedom for slaves across the boundaries in the Danish Caribbean. It remains a fact that a large number of slaves emancipated themselves by taking advantage of the

British free soil. But such freedom was not automatic, not without contest and always intensely fragile. Faced with diplomatic pressure, political expedience, planter security and imperial solidarity, the desired principle of free soil, the British "moral capital" was sometimes upheld but often readily and summarily sacrificed. While it was a reality for some, for many others, "freedom across the water" remained an illusion. In the post-emancipation Atlantic World, the meaning of freedom, therefore, remained an idea that was actively nurtured, and yet was often contested and always negotiated.

Notes

I wish to thank Paul Olsen and Erik Gøbel of the Statens Arkiver in Copenhagen. Thanks also to the Weatherhead Initiative on Global History, Harvard University for a visiting fellowship that provided me with the opportunity to complete this work.

1. William F.A. Gilbert to King Christian VIII, Copenhagen, Denmark, 12 Aug. 1847. Rigsarkivet, Generaltoldkammeret, Vestindiske Journaler, 1848, no. 141. Postponed cases. Quoted in Neville A.T. Hall, "Maritime Maroons: Grand Marronage from the Danish West Indies", *William and Mary Quarterly* 42, 4 (1985): 497–8.
2. It is difficult to know with certainty whether Gilbert's birthplace was St Croix. Nevertheless, his impassioned appeal reveals that he had the strongest ties with the island.
3. Ibid.
4. Ibid. On the concept of free soil, see Sue Peabody, "An Alternative Genealogy of the Origins of French Free Soil: Medieval Toulouse", *Slavery & Abolition* 32, 3 (2011): 341–62. The reference to free soil in the British context in this article adapts from Peabody's formulation of the concept in the French Atlantic World. Free soil here refers to a land and regime free from slavery where the status of enslavement effected elsewhere was generally not recognized.
5. See Chapter 7: "Maritime Maroons: Grand Marronage", in *Slave Society in the Danish West Indies: St. Thomas, St. John, and St. Croix*, ed. Neville A.T. Hall and B.W. Higman (Baltimore, MD: Johns Hopkins University Press, 1992), pp. 124–38. [This is a reproduction of Hall, "Maritime Maroons" but owing to the presence of some differences, I have chosen to cite from both.]; Karen Fog Olwig, "Caribbean Place Identity: From Family Land to Region and Beyond", *Identities Global Studies in Culture and Power* 5, 4 (1999): 435–67.

6. Marronage: act of running away or becoming a fugitive slave. Maritime maroons: fugitive slaves who escaped by water. See Hall, "Maritime Maroons".

7. See The National Archives, UK (henceforth TNA) CO 71/76, Governor MacGregor to Viscount Goderich, 1 Mar. 1833.

8. See TNA CO 239/68, Governor of Antigua to Lord Stanley, 22 Sept. 1842.

9. Ibid. The Danish were preparing for eventual emancipation whereas the French considered the question of emancipation to be inadmissible.

10. Christian Georg Andreas Oldendorp and Johann Jakob Bossart *Geschichte der Mission der evangelischen Brüder auf den caraibischen Inseln S. Thomas, S. Croix und S. Jan:...enthaltend die Geschichte der Mission von 1732. bis 1768* [A History of the Mission of the Evangelical Brothers on the Caribbean Islands of St. Thomas, St. Croix, and St. John, including a History of the Mission from 1732 to 1768], vol. 2. Laux, 1777. See Bo Ejstrud, "Maroons and Landscapes", *Journal of Caribbean Archaeology* 8 (2008): 1–14; and Hall and Higman, ed., *Slave Society*, p. 85.

11. See Amitava Chowdhury, "Theoretical Reflections on Maroon Archaeology in Mauritius", *Revi Kiltir Kreol* 3 (2003): 55–59 and "Maroon Archaeological Research in Mauritius and its Possible Implications in a Global Context", in *The Archaeology of Slavery: Toward a Comparative Global Framework*, ed. Lydia Wilson Marshall (Carbondale, IL: CAI, Southern Illinois University, 2014), pp. 255–75. See also *Maroon Societies: Rebel Slave Communities in the Americas*, ed. Richard Price (Baltimore, MD: Johns Hopkins University Press, 1996).

12. Holly A. Norton, "The Challenge in Locating Maroon Refuge Sites at Maroon Ridge, St. Croix", *Journal of Caribbean Archaeology* 7 (2007): 1–17. See also Daniel Hopkins, Philip Morgan and Justin Roberts, "The Application of GIS to the Reconstruction of the Slave-plantation Economy of St Croix, Danish West Indies", *Historical Geography* 39 (2011): 85–104; Hall and Higman, eds., *Slave Society*, p. 127.

13. Hall and Higman, eds., *Slave Society*, pp. 127, 131–3.

14. Neville A.T. Hall, "Review of *Cultural Adaptation and Resistance on St John* by Karen Olwig", *Hispanic American Historical Review* 67, 1 (1987): 147–8; Olwig, "Caribbean Place", p. 444.

15. Hall, "Maritime Maroons", p. 485; Ejstrud, "Maroons and Landscapes", p. 2.

16. Hall, "Maritime Maroons", p. 482.

17. Evidence for such acts of marronage is plentiful in the colonial archives. Ibid.

18. Hall, "Maritime Maroons", p. 484.

19. Waldemar Westergaard, *The Danish West Indies under Company Rule (1671-1754): With a Supplementary Chapter, 1755-1917* (New York: Macmillan, 1917); Richard Haagensen, *Beskrivelse over Eylandet St. Croix i America i Vestindien* [Description of the Island of St. Croix in America in the West Indies] (København, 1758); Hall, "Maritime Maroons", pp. 484, 486; Lomarsh Roopnarine, "Maroon Resistance and Settlement on Danish St. Croix", *Journal of Third World Studies* 27, 2 (2010): 101.

20. Hall, "Maritime Maroons", p. 482; Roopnarine, "Maroon Resistance", p. 104.

21. Ibid.

22. Hall, "Maritime Maroons", p. 485.

23. Ibid., p. 486.

24. See Jes Bjarup, "The Concept of a Person according to Anders Sandøe Ørsted", *Quaderni Fiorentini* 11/12 (1982): 461–74. See also Knud Waaben, "A.S. Ørsted og negerslaverne i København" [A.S. Ørsted and Negro Slaves in Copenhagen], *Juristen* 46 (1964): 321–43. For the famous Somerset case, see William R. Cotter, "The Somerset Case and the Abolition of Slavery in England", *History* 79, 255 (1994): 31–56; Daniel J. Hulsebosch, "Nothing but Liberty: Somerset's Case and the British Empire", *Law & History Review* 24 (2006): 647.

25. Bjarup, "Concept of a Person", p. 461; on free soil, see further Sue Peabody, "The French Free Soil Principle in the Atlantic World", *Africana Studia* 14, 1 (2010): 17–27; Ada Ferrer, "Haiti, Free Soil, and Antislavery in the Revolutionary Atlantic", *The American Historical Review* 117, 1 (2012): 40–66.

26. See Bjarup, "Concept of a Person", p. 462.

27. Ibid., p. 470.

28. Ibid., p. 472.

29. TNA CO 318/141, 16 July 1839. Peter Carl Frederik von Scholten's proclamation (7 May 1838).

30. Ibid.

31. See again TNA CO 239/68, Governor of Antigua to Lord Stanley, 22 Sept. 1842 for further evidence on Danish ameliorative measures.

32. Hall and Higman, eds., *Slave Society*, p. 135.

33. TNA CO 318/143, Lord Glenelg's circular to the governors in the British Caribbean, Jan. 1839.

34. Ibid.; TNA CO 318/144, 16 July 1839, Normandy to Colebrooke.

35. Ibid.; TNA CO 101/88, 14 May 1839, MacGregor to Normandy.

36. TNA CO 239/66, Lord Leveron to James Stephen, 29 Jan. 1841.

37. Ibid.

38. Ibid.

39. TNA CO 239/68. Spring Rice to Stanley, 14 Nov. 1842.

CHAPTER 8

The *Yūjo* Release Act as Emancipation of Slaves in Mid-19th-Century Japan

Yuriko Yokoyama

Introduction

> Kashiku insists that she does not want to remain as a *yūjo* (prostitute) any longer no matter what happens to her. Please, with the mercy of the Tokyo municipal government, grant her the status of normal citizen.[1]

On 2 November 1872 Kashiku, a lowly *yūjo* in the Shin-yoshiwara *yūkaku* (licensed red-light district) of Edo and Takejiro, a servant, petitioned the municipal government of Tokyo, asking for the release of Kashiku from her status as a *yūjo*, explaining that they were engaged to be married. Quoted above is an excerpt from the petition, and although we do not know who wrote it, the clumsy handwriting and awkward sentences reveal their background. At the bottom of the document, the nail prints of both petitioners are substituted for proper seals. Nail prints were used by women and lower-class males not authorized to use seals. In Japan, the Meiji Restoration had restored imperial rule in 1868 at the time of the demise of the *bakufu*—the Tokugawa shogunate—and the commencement of Meiji government. The new government promoted various modernization measures, including a transformation of the policy regarding prostitution following the enactment of *Yūjo Kaihō Rei* (*Yūjo* Release Act) in October 1872. Yūjo detained in the brothels welcomed the Act, thinking it a blessing, and Kashiku's letter shows the effect the Release Act typically had on them. A desperate Kashiku tried twice to obtain release, but her dream never came true. What were her motives?

One should not regard the status of yūjo as something equivalent to slavery merely because such individuals were kept in poor conditions, and indeed in the field of early modern Japanese history only a few studies recognize yūjo as a form of slavery. Therefore, this article opts not to define slavery and look for evidence to support the idea that that was what yūjo was; instead it will clarify specifically what led people in the 19th century to believe it was and to strive for "emancipation". Consideration of the particular features of the various regions and states, peoples' ages and genders will make for a more fruitful discussion, but of course if a person was kept in servitude for an extended period of time based on a social system in a traditional society, and if that person could be sold as a commodity, it would be reasonable to regard anyone caught up in such a position as being effectively a slave. However, this article explores the society that gave birth to such status and the reality of each social system supporting it, and then examines how the logic of emancipation developed.[2] In doing so, we will focus on the following three aspects.

First, we consider the self-determined actions of yūjo, such as Kashiku's response to the Release Act. Considering who they were, their reactions to the Act are very important. For a comparative historical study of the emancipation of slaves all over the world,[3] it is well worth paying close attention to who individual yūjo were.

Second, we will explain the origins of the Release Act and its historical meaning in Japan in the light of the status system on which Japanese society was still based in the Edo period. Both the dissolution of the status system and the emancipation of slaves—which were closely related to each other—occurred in various countries about the time of the 19th century. In Japan, too, the Yūjo Release Act was enacted in the context of the abolition of the status system. Therefore, this article takes the status system into consideration in exploring why this Act was passed.

Third, we will stress the fact that in the 19th century the emancipation took place as much under the influence of a global movement as in local contexts, or nationwide.[4] In Japan, especially, the emancipation of yūjo would never have occurred had it not been for the impetus provided by the emerging concept of human rights, more

Figure 8.1 Photograph of the Brothel in Shin-yoshiwara in the Meiji Period. (Photo Database of Nagasaki University)

particularly in the form of the movement against the Contagious Diseases Acts led by Josephine Butler in the latter half of the 19th century, and the widespread international criticism of the coolie trade.

Was a Yūjo a "Slave"?

Brothel Structure: Ranks in Brothels and the Yūjo

This section examines the reality of yūjo who were actually forced into sexual activity under indefinite obligations of slavery that resulted from what was, practically, human trafficking. To begin with, we present an overview of what a typical Edo brothel looked like (see also Figure 8.1).

Figure 8.2[5] is a map of Shin-yoshiwara during the Tenpō era (1830–44), when it featured six *chou* (communities) consisting of the Shin-yoshiwara area (Edo chou 1-choume, 2-choume, Sumi chou, Ageya chou, Kyomachi 1-choume and 2-choume). It shows the structures inside them—privately owned houses, leased land or shops, also held under lease agreements. Edo chou 1-choume shown on the upper side of the map was populated with large-scale, high-class

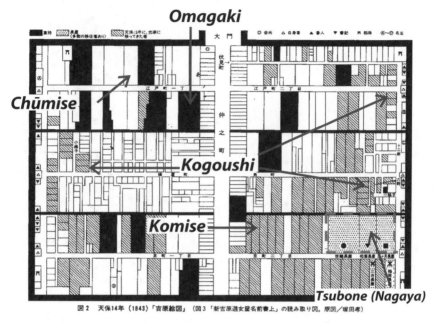

図2 天保14年（1843）「吉原絵図」（図3「新吉原遊女屋名前書上」の読み取り図。原図／塚田孝）

Figure 8.2 Shin-yoshiwara. (Nobuyuki Yoshida, *Mibunteki Shūen to Shakaibunka Kōzō* [Class Marginality and Sociocultural Structure]. Kyoto: Burakumondai Kenkyūsho, 2003, p. 414)

brothels called *ōmagaki* (large) brothels, whereas smaller *kogoushi* brothels were clustered on the leased lands of Edo chou 2-choume, Sumi chou and Kyomachi 1-choume. Finally, Kyomachi 2-choume at the bottom right of the map was occupied mainly by the lowest-status *tsubone* (small) brothels, some of which were known as *nagaya* (back-alley tenements).

Table 8.1 shows the number of yūjo living in Shin-yoshiwara and sorted by their ranks as at the end of the Tokugawa era. In 1847, only 1.7 per cent of yūjo were high-ranking *yobidashi* (a high-ranking prostitute who was not required to be displayed at the *harimise*—a place to display the prostitutes for customers: she greeted customers and entertained them with her entourage before intercourse), who had their own prostitutes of lower rank and did not offer themselves at the harimise. The latticed front porches of the brothels are shown in Figure 8.3. Most yūjo did, however, appear at the harimise, where they were selected directly by clients. The environment in which the lowest-status brothels, known as tsubone or kogoushi, did business was particularly bad. As shown in Figure 8.2, tsubone brothels

Table 8.1 *Yūjo* Ranks

Year		Rank	Charges*	Number of yūjo	Proportion (%)
1847	(High) Not Harimise	*Yobidashi* *Shinzo-tsuki* (*yūjo* with an attendant *yūjo*)	Kin 3 Bu–1 Ryō	87	1.7%
	(Middle) Harimise	*Yūjo* with her own room	Kin 2 Shu–Kin 2 Bu	3670	71.8%
	(Low) *Kogoushi* *Tsubone*	*Kogoushi, tsubone* (*yūjo* with her own bed)	–	1354	26.5%
	Total			5111	100%
1871	Not Harimise	*Yobidashi*	Gin 72–84 Monme	0	0%
	(Middle) Harimise	*Shinzo-tsuki* (*yūjo* with an attendant *yūjo*)	Gin 24–48 Monme	221	13.4%
		Yūjo with her own room		794	48.2%
	(Low) *Kogoushi* *Tsubone*	*Kogoushi, tsubone* (*yūjo* with her own bed)	Gin 15 Monme	633	38.4%
	Total			1648	100.00%

Notes: *Currencies
Kin (gold): One ryō equals four bu equals sixteen shu
Gin (silver): One ryō in gold equals about sixty monme

Sources: Morisada Kitagawa, *Kinsei Hūzoku Sh*i (*Morisada Mankō*), vol. 3, ed. Hideki Usami [Iwanami Bunko] (Tokyo: Iwanami Shoten, 1999); "*Tokyo Shishikō Shigai Hen*", vol. 51, ed. Tokyo Prefecture, 1960.

typically operated in nagaya, the internal structure of which can be seen in Figure 8.4. In the centre of the passage running through a nagaya stood a wall to hide the faces of customers from other visiting customers at the other side of the brothel.[6] Inside the building, yūjo engaged in prostitution in a small space separated by *karakami* (paper board) partitions (Figure 8.5), with the area behind the partition acting as the living space of the brothel keepers. In 1847, 26.5 per cent of yūjo were working in kogoushi and tsubone, although the number of high-ranking yūjo was decreasing, until by 1871 the highest-ranking yobidashi had ceased to exist altogether. In the same year, the low-ranking yūjo, such as kogoushi and tsubone, accounted

Figure 8.3 Photograph of a *harimise* in Yoshiwara in the Meiji Period. (Photo Database of Nagasaki University)

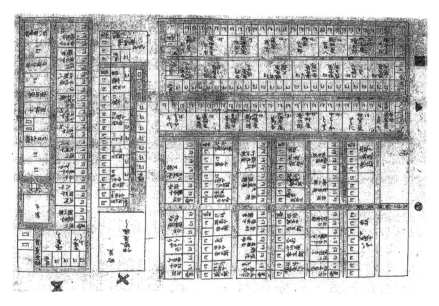

Figure 8.4 The Structure of Nagaya in 1842. (Yoshida, *Mibunteki Shūen*, p. 417)

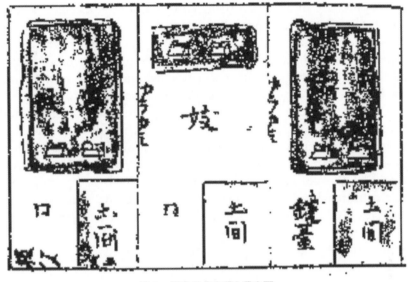

図6　足見せの為帯を示す図

一二の度口に、みせ、店よ人の人口せ上り見、帝市、一二世刊に二二の役に以ともみよる、
みとけ明存一枚を附てく、「守其名簿」号刊、二上の会別哲凞凞。ほうも！

Figure 8.5 Inside a *Tsubone* Brothel. (Yoshida, *Mibunteki Shūen*, p. 424)

for 38.4 per cent of the yūjo population. Many of the yūjo in Shin-yoshiwara brothels are said to have died in their twenties for various reasons, many of them of syphilis, while there was at least one recorded double suicide,[7] confirming the harsh living and working conditions to which the yūjo were subjected.

Yūjo as Merchandise

Yūjo were usually sold to brothels by their natural "owners" (*hito-nushi*, most often their parents) under the rules of fixed-term service known as *miuri-boko*. At the conclusion of a contract of sale, a ransom was paid to the hitonushi, and the yūjo was obliged to repay the ransom from the earnings of her prostitution. In addition, however, the miuri-boko included peculiar terms not found in ordinary fixed-term apprenticeship contracts.[8] First, a hitonushi exercised a patriarchal right to sell his daughters or wives, but at the conclusion of a contract he relinquished his right over the person sold and transferred it to the brothel. In other words, the contract constituted the virtual purchase of a human being, who was then expected to never again go back to her family home. Under the terms of miuri-boko, a system to increase the debt of the yūjo was operated so that an employer could bind the yūjo beyond the period of the original contract. A yūjo's daily garments, cosmetics, bedding and food were provided at her own expense, and considerable amounts of money were thus added to the original ransoms as personal debts of the yūjo. Also, in an ordinary apprenticeship, any losses and damage caused by an apprentice were to be covered by the hitonushi or a joint guarantor, while damages caused by yūjo were their own liability instead of that of the hitonushi or other guarantors who had relinquished their patriarchal rights. As a result of these methods, most yūjo debts were steadily increased, making escape from what amounted to debt bondage next to impossible. Then, in addition to earnings from the services of yūjo, brothels were entitled to increase their profit by treating the yūjo as "live goods".

Let us examine the case of Kashiku, mentioned earlier (Table 8.2). She was born into a farming family but after her parents died when she was seven, she was sold to an inn in the Kanto region. In 1871, she became a yūjo in the Shin-yoshiwara red-light district after being repeatedly resold among other premises in similar districts. Once she started to earn money as a yūjo her ownership was transferred many times, with the size of her ransom increasing from 75 ryō to 80 ryō in gold, suggesting that the debt increase was due to reselling and to the extension of her term of servitude.

Furthermore, it was by no means rare for a yūjo to be mortgaged against a loan to her brothel. Table 8.3 shows the mortgages held by the Bukkōji temple,[9] which was located in Kyoto and lent money in Edo.[10] The temple financed many lay enterprises, including brothels in Edo. Almost all other debtors mortgaged their furniture, fixtures and fittings or wooden buildings, which could be relocated or taken apart and sold as lumber, but brothels mortgaged their yūjo. For example (Table 8.3, No. 6), in 1859 Harumoto-ya Kanejirō, a brothel in Shin-yoshiwara Kyomachi 1-choume, borrowed 30 ryō in gold as a nominal loan from the officer of the Bukkōji temple, submitting the bond below which states that Harumoto-ya mortgaged three yūjo whose names were Wakamatu (若松), Ippon (一本) and Suminoe (住の江). It can be confirmed that they were real women by reference to the Yoshiwara Saiken published in 1859, which confirms, too, that yūjo were treated as merchandise.

Table 8.2 The Chronology of Kashiku

Date	Age	Events
		Born in Yuriage Village, Makino-higashi, Kambara-gun, Echigo (now Niigata Prefecture).
	7	Following her parents' death and removal from her place of birth, became a resident *yūjo* at Fukudaya Inn at Yashū-kassenba *shuku* (post town).
	13	Was sold to Beni-ya Inn in Shinagawa post town for 75 ryō. Resold 6 months later to Fujimoto-ya Inn in Senju post town for 75 ryō.
		After 18 months, was resold as a resident *yūjo* under the care of Masagoro Hashi-ya in Yokocho, Fukagawa, for 75 ryō.
15 November 1871		Was resold to Kunijiro of Sanshu-ya at Kyo machi 2-*choume*, Yoshiwara, for 80 ryō (for a fixed term of 5 years and 6 months).
8 October 1872		The Release Act enacted. Was returned to Masagoro Hashiya (the *hitonushi*) but later resold after the "emancipation" to a brothel in Shin-yoshiwara and was forced to work as a prostitute there.
2 November 1872		Directly petitioned Masagoro and the ward mayor for release based on her engagement with Takejiro, a servant at Ebiya in Shin-yoshiwara, but her petition was rejected.
11 January 1873		Fire broke out in Shin-yoshiwara. Evacuated to Edo-chou 1-*choume*.
14 January 1873		Stayed with Kikujiro, a hairdresser, in Ougibashi-chou, Fukagawa. On Kikujiro's advice, briefly returned to Masagoro's residence, then went back to Kikujiro's home.
2 February 1873		Sadakichi Kasuya, Kikujiro's master, offered to pay off the 15 ryō debt and to act as intermediary. Kikujiro and Kashiku jointly petitioned Tokyo's municipal government.
3 February 1873		Investigation carried out by the ward mayor of the 12th minor ward in the 5th greater region.
3 February 1873		Tokyo's municipal government completed its investigation and ruled that Kashiku should be sent back to Masagoro. Both parties accepted the terms.

Source: "Shougikaihou" 604.A2.12, Tokyo Metropolitan Archives.

Table 8.3 Mortgages (*Myōmokukin* Loans) Held by the Bukkōji Temple

No.	Date	Debtor (1, Address; 2, Status; 3, Name)	Occupation	Amount (ryō in gold)	Mortgage	Source: Yamada-ke monjo (no.)
1	July 1849	(1) Asakusa minamiumamichi machi (2) Lease on Sukejirō's tenement (3) Kōhei	Not brothel	10	Nijukken mizuchaya (teahouse), 3 ken wide by 4.5 ken deep in yard of Sensouji temple.	88-1
2	June 1850	(1) Nannba *chou* (2) Lease on Yasusaburō's land (3) Kitarō	Not brothel		One-storey house, 2.5 ken wide by 5 ken deep.	88-1
3	17 December 1851	(1) Mikawa *chou* (2) Leased land (3) Rihei	Not brothel		House and all of furniture with Tatami and cupboard.	88-1
4	December 1851	(1) Kandamyoujinsita odaidokoro *chou* (2) Landlord (3) Heikichi	Landlord	10	Nagaya, 12 ken wide by 2.5 ken deep.	89-1
5	July 1858	(1) Shin-yoshiwara Edo *chou* 2-*choume* (2) Landowner (3) Tomoe-ya Tokubei	Brothel	50	*Yūjo*, real name: Sue; professional name: Yaeume (八重梅), ransom 32 ryō, apprenticeship 6 years 8 months. *Yūjo*, real name: Hana; professional name: Masakoto (政琴), ransom 25 ryō, apprenticeship 6 years.	74-1-3

Table 8.3 continued

No.	Date	Debtor (1, Address; 2, Status; 3, Name)	Occupation	Amount (ryō in gold)	Mortgage	Source: Yamada-ke monjo (no.)
6	March 1859	(1) Shin-yoshiwara Kyo machi 1-*choume* (2) Lease on Seiemon's land (3) Harumoto-ya Kanejirō	Brothel	30	*Yūjo*, real name: Take; professional name: Wakamatu (若松), ransom 30 ryō, apprenticeship 5 years 5 months. *Yūjo*, real name: Take; professional name: Ippon (一本), ransom 38 ryō, apprenticeship 7 years 6 months. *Yūjo*, real name: Sano; professional name: Suminoe (住の江), ransom 39 ryō, apprenticeship 6 years.	74-1-4-4
7	1859	(1) Shin-yoshiwara Edo *chou* 2-*choume* (2) ? (3) Okada-ya Sōbei	Brothel	100	*Yūjo*, real name: Hide; professional name: Hamaura (濱浦), ransom 7 ryō, apprenticeship for 18 years 3 months. *Yūjo*, real name: Yasu; professional name: Nagayama (長山), ransom 8 ryō, apprenticeship for 19 years 2 months. *Yūjo*, professional name: Somekawa (染川). *Yūjo*, real name: Yone; professional name: Momotose (百年), ransom 32 ryō, apprenticeship for 11 years 4 months. *Yūjo*, professional name: Wakahito (若人).	74-1-4-3

Source: Yamada Shouzaemon-ke Archives, Nakano City Museum in Nagano Prefecture.

The Mortgage Bond Submitted[11]

1. Indentured term as a prostitute from September 1856 (Ansei 3, the seventh month of the year of the dragon) to January 1862 (the first month of the next year of the dog), a period of exactly five and a half years.

Yūjo, real name: Take, professional name: Wakamasu (若松)
Ransom: 30 ryō in gold.

1. Her indentured term as a prostitute from July 1855 (Ansei 2, the seventh month of the year of the rabbit) to December 1862 (the twelfth month of the next year of the dog), a period of exactly seven and a half years.

Yūjo, real name: Take, professional name: Ippon (一本)
Ransom: 38 ryō in gold.

1. Her indentured term as a prostitute from March 1856 (Ansei 3, the third month of the year of the dragon) to March 1862 (the third month of the next year of the dog), a period of exactly six years.

Yūjo, real name: Sano, professional name: Suminoe (住の江)
Ransom: 39 ryō in gold.

The above were indentured by Kanejirō, resident of a "street-front property" in Kyomachi 1-*choume*, Shin-yoshiwara.

According to the attached bond, I (Kanejirō) have incurred a debt of 30 ryō in gold and mortgaged these three *yūjo* as security. This is clear and definite.

The documents of their contract to be sold for prostitutes have been received in trust by sureties in the presence of you. If I fail to pay my debt or pay late, I'll give three *yūjo* to sureties immediately and they will pay it off. Furthermore if any *yūjo* should be indentured by another brothel or anything should happen to her [that is, she expires of illness or dies suddenly or accidentally], I will substitute something as collateral for her, of course; if it should be insufficient, sureties will be sure to pay it off completely.

In addition, if these *yūjo* were doubly mortgaged, you could take me to court by all means.

So, for posterity, this is a mortgage contract.

In Ansei 6 (1859, the year of the sheep), March

Kanejirō (seal)

Surety Kōhei (seal)

Resident of street-front property in Kyomachi 2-*choume*

Surety Sadakichi (seal)

Resident of street-front property in Kyomachi 2-*choume*

To Mr Seki Saigu, the officer of the Bukkōji temple

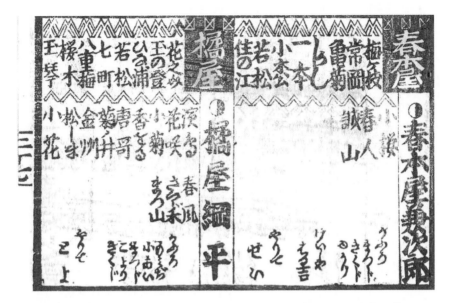

Figure 8.6 The *Yūjo* List in Brothel, Harumoto-ya. (NDL Digital Collection 856-29)

This document shows that Harumoto-ya Kanejirō, a middle-class brothel, mortgaged three yūjo for a loan of 30 ryō in gold. Furthermore, one of the sureties, Kōhei, who also was in a middle-class brothel and lived next door to Kanejirō (Figure 8.6), agreed to clear Kanejirō's debt instead of getting the three yūjo if Kanejirō should fail to repay his loan. All this refers then to a loan concerning human trafficking, and if Kanejirō had sold them under foreclosure, their new owner, Kōhei, would have imposed the sum of the charges on the yūjo as new ransoms to be redeemed by them selling their sexual services. From the examples given in Table 8.3, it is clear that yūjo, roughly equal to furniture, houses or land, were a commodity for trading and could be treated as collateral for a loan, although the duration was limited to the period of apprenticeship.

Yūkaku is generally regarded as the place where "yūjo sold sex" in the Edo period, although actually it was the place where not only sexual services were provided but "brothels required yūjo to sell sex" and where the entire human being was traded. In other words, from the viewpoint of the commercialization of sex, *yūkaku shakai*[12] was de facto a system under which humans were trafficked as merchandise for sexual purposes. Consequently, a kind of sexual-debt slavery was legalized and was extremely difficult to escape from without some unexpected piece of luck.

A Chain Binding the Yūjo: Abusive Control

In the preceding section, we looked at the fact that debt constituted one of the direct factors that bound yūjo to the yūkaku. In this section, we examine violence, another factor that for the yūjo had the same effect.

First, to confirm the state of violence we include a passage from the "*Umemoto-ki*",[13] a record of the testimony transcribed by Nizaemon Takeshima, headman of Shin-yoshiwara. It presents the verbal evidence of the yūjo Shigemoto concerning an arson attack that occurred in Shin-yoshiwara in 1849.

> Normally we were given only two meals a day, never three. Those two meals were the most meagre ones imaginable, consisting of a porridge made by boiling down old rice with the bean husk or trimmed tips of brooms, with some salt added. Because of the bad smell of the porridge, we found it hard to even have a mouthful of it. When we hesitated to swallow it, we were severely abused. When there were no men to buy us, we were chastised for having been lazy. Even if we had an occasional customer, unless he ordered food and wine we were severely bullied for having failed to do a good job. No word of approval was ever heard, unless we managed to get a prodigal man on many "Shimai Days" [a fixed day on which the customer "bought up" the *yūjo* for the entire day] and to get the full payment for them. Failing that, we were tied to the box in the "hairdressing room" [the changing room] and thumped and thumped indiscriminately with the "hook" [an oak club which had inserted into its centre an iron bar with an iron hook at its tip] or with a broken arrow. Moreover, we were forced to sell ourselves to the customers in the most unspeakable fashion. We were even denied minimum food. Being certain we would die from such rough treatment, we were deeply determined to wreak our grudge and revenge without reserve with our fellow *yūjo*, sixteen in all. We were resigned to accept what legal punishment there was. To make sure that there were no traitors, *yūjo* Sakuragi told us yesterday, the fourth, of the need to have everyone sign her name, instead of jointly affixing our seals on the document. Firmly convinced that was precisely what was required, I had ready the formal lengthwise-folded "hanshi" paper and had

each of the sixteen *yūjo*, beginning with Fukuoka, write her name on it, in the same order as that in which each of them appeared in the *harimise* to be chosen and bought by customers. [...] Today, the fifth, at about five o'clock in the afternoon, taking advantage of the time when our employer, Sakichi, was taking a nap, the sixteen of us talked over the matter once again before proceeding. One of us set the ceiling on fire, the part above the staircase outside. Seeing the fire, passers-by created an uproar and somebody lost no time in putting it out.

According to that evidence, the 16 yūjo, beginning with Shigemoto, committed the arson at Umemoto-ya, the house of the brothel on Kyomachi 1-choume, in 1849 (the second year of the Kaei era) in an attempt to escape from the cruel treatment there. They revealed that they had set the fire at a spot facing the street, which was certain to be seen immediately by passers-by, and they themselves were ready to prevent the fire from spreading the moment it was noticed. It was not that they set the fire spontaneously, but rather they acted with premeditation. From the fact that the 16 yūjo had conspired for some time, one can conclude that the incident was caused not by the anger of one individual but by a rebellion of the entire group of yūjo at Umemoto-ya against their cruel treatment there. Moreover, judging by the contents of the documentation of the arson, we may conclude that the direct cause of this act was not evil treatment in general but rather the extreme violence inflicted on the yūjo, such as tying them to the box in the "hairdressing room" and beating them, as well as thrashing them with a broken arrow or the "hook". One of the yūjo, named Kohina, asserted that

> rather than being killed by the cruelty of our employer Sakichi, it was better to serve the punishment imposed by the law in a magistrate's court by throwing ourselves on the mercy of the headman as soon as we had put out the small fire that we had set. We had no intention at all of setting a large fire.

The arson was therefore a revolt of the yūjo against the violence that they sensed would ultimately have cost them their lives.

Table 8.4 lists all the fires that occurred in Shin-yoshiwara during the mid-19th century. More than half of them were deliberately set by yūjo. Though the circumstances might have differed, it cannot be denied that the violent and cruel treatment at the yūkaku was ultimately at the root of these incidents of arson.

Table 8.4 Fires in Shin-yoshiwara *Yūkaku* in the Mid-19th Century

No.	Date	Start and spread of the fire	Cause and process
1	5 December 1845	Kyo machi 2-*choume* Almost all of Shin-yoshiwara destroyed.	According to a rumour, the fire was started by *yūjo* Tamagoto (16 years old) and two other *yūjo* (16 and 14 years old) held by the Kawatsu-ya brothel. They were subsequently arrested.
2	5 August 1849	Kyo machi 1-*choume* Incipient fire.	*Yūjo* Kohina and 16 *yūjo* held by the Umemoto-ya brothel started the fire and subsequently surrendered to the magistrate.
3	26 September 1860	Kyo machi 2-*choume* Shin-yoshiwara *yūkaku* completely destroyed.	The fire was started by *yūjo* Kozakura, held by the Kinoji-ya brothel. Once the fire had taken hold, she raised the alarm.
4	14 November 1862	Kyo machi 2-*choume* Shin-yoshiwara yūkaku completely destroyed.	Cause unknown.
5	26 January 1864	Shin-yoshiwara *yūkaku* completely destroyed.	A fire broke out in the Oguchi-ya brothel.
6	11 November 1866	Three *chous* of Shin-yoshiwara destroyed.	*Yūjo* Yaegiku (14 years old), held by the Omasu-ya brothel, started the fire.

Source: "Tokyo Shisikou Hensai Hen", vol. 5; "Umemoto-ki" (included in Kanou-Bunko, National Diet Library).

In addition to yūkaku, bakufu tacitly allowed *meshimori-onna* or *chatate-onna* to prostitute themselves in *hatago-ya* (inns) near post stations and *chaya* (teahouses) in several urban areas in the 18th century. Moreover, clandestine prostitutes were found in *okabasho* (hill place), where men could pay for sexual services.

As another example of violence, let us consider Hatsu, a meshimori-onna who was a prostitute under tacit permission and living in a Kizaki-shako inn on Nikko-reiheishi Road.[14] In her letter of petition, Hatsu described the *seme-sekkan* (violent chastisement) meted out to her. Although documentation of violence such as this was uncommon, it should not be thought of as an isolated incident:

> One morning in July last year, I fell sick and became bedridden for about thirty days. As soon as I started to feel a little better and was out of bed around mid-August, I was forced to take in customers. And when I had no customers to attend to during the day, I was sent into the hills to cut firewood. As I was forced to work day and night, I could not fully recover from illness. Because I was violently chastised whenever I asked my master to give me a rest, I endured the toil just to avoid the painful chastisement.[15]

So far, we have looked at the reality of yūjo, who were sold as commodities by hitonushi and physically detained under debt and violence. However, what was the reason for the violence to the yūjo described above? In the Edo era, the shogunate, as a rule, forbade human trafficking as well as the exercise of violence in general, unless there were legitimate reasons. In spite of such restrictions, violence was tolerated in licensed quarters, such as yūkaku. As reasons for that situation, we must consider three aspects of Edo society.

One of them is the fact that yūjo were considered merchandise in yūkaku society, as we have already seen. As a rule, the owner of any merchandise was free to treat his property however he chose, which might conceivably have been seen as a ready justification for violence.

Second, we should also focus on the fact that violence to yūjo was encouraged by the rights of patriarchal household heads, legally considered family heads. Society in the Edo era was founded on *mura* (village) and *chou* (town) communities as status groups, each of which was aggregated from individual households, so-called *ie*.[16] The management rights of the head of the *ie* in relation to the members of their mura and chou neighbourhoods were officially approved. Indeed, there was a case in which the head of the brothel in Shinyoshiwara chou enrolled his yūjo as his adopted daughter in the register of residents.[17] As her father, he had the right to exercise violence on her as his adopted daughter. It seems obvious that such inclusion of yūjo by the head of a patriarchal household, ie, constituted the basis for the rise of violence there.

The two examples given above are factors that emerged from the relationship between the brothels and their yūjo. As the third aspect, we should focus on the fact that violence was tolerated publicly in the chou neighbourhood and by the brothels guild. In Shin-yoshiwara yūkaku, 76 articles and regulations were stipulated in 1795 (the seventh year of the Kansei era) by the chou community and the brothels guild, with the guidance of the magistrate. They were titled the "Shin-yoshiwara Licensed Quarters Provisions Act and Deed". Included in the provisions is the text of the following article:

> At the *yūkaku*, there are those who have no choice but to chastise the *yūjo*. Needless to say, we are engaged in the trade of selling 'bodies', so there is no alternative but to punish in order to keep things under control.

These words clearly demonstrate the view that the "chastisement "of yūjo in yūkaku, in other words violence, was indispensable in the operation of the yūkaku; in fact, they are extremely significant in showing the justification for violence there. Moreover, the Provisions Act and Deed were submitted to magistrates of the Edo period and subsequently formed the basis of regulations governing the business operations of Shin-yoshiwara yūkaku. Seen like that, we must con-clude that the violence in the yūkaku was not a violation of principles but rather something condoned by magistrates and regional societies.

So then, we now know that yūjo were bought and sold commer-cially by hitonushi and restricted by both debt and physical violence, which naturally exerted a powerful effect on the practice of the sex trade. Additionally, in the Edo era that state of affairs was assumed to be normal by public authorities, the chou neighbourhood and the brothels guild.[18]

The following section looks more closely at the chou that played a major part in bringing about such a servile position for yūjo.

Yūjo and Chou: The Roles and Privileges of Shin-yoshiwara Chou

The servile position of yūjo in Japan is considered to date from the 16th century, when early modern castle cities began to develop "red-light districts". The Edo bakufu strictly forbade the operation of brothels in any ordinary part of a castle city but authorized red-light districts (*yūjo machi* or yūkaku) to engage exclusively in the business of prostitution. The general principle of Edo society did not recognize women as *chonin*, official members of the chou community. Therefore yūjo, being women, were not considered parties who could themselves engage in any of the business operations of the red-light districts. Because prostitution was a business permitted by the Edo bakufu in red-light districts as communities, one should remember that yūjo were recognized as constituting a business method or tool, rather than as being themselves parties to the prostitution business. The structure of red-light districts meant that the district as a community was responsible for the organization and operation of prostitution facilities and was in charge of the detention, management and control of the entire yūjo population within its own community. The red-light districts were also responsible for the maintenance of the servile position of yūjo. The whole of that complex establishment of control over yūjo can therefore be said to have formed the fundamental characteristics of red-light districts since their establishment.[19] While the stylized contract form of *miuri-boko*[20] became generalized after the late 17th century,[21] the framework in which not only the individual brothels owned yūjo but also that the red-light district as a community assumed control over the entire yūjo population came into being once the red-light districts had been established.

Now, let us see how Shin-yoshiwara chou actually controlled and managed its yūjo population. This discussion will focus on the Shin-yoshiwara chou community.

According to recent studies in women's history, prostitution in Japan began as a business sometime during the ninth and tenth centuries, followed by the official opening of prostitution facilities under the name of yūkaku at around the end of the 16th century or the beginning of the 17th century.[22] The reality of licensed districts, founded as parts of castle cities under the supervision of a unified government or powerful lord, was that they were exclusive business precincts for the sole trade of prostitution, where brothels were clustered into a space surrounded by walls and a moat. In Edo, Jinemon Shoji took the initiative in building the Yoshiwara yūkaku with the permission of the Edo government, and the area became the official red-light district in 1612.[23] Every red-light district in Japan, including Shin-yoshiwara[24] chou, maintained its original features as professional precincts until the end of the Edo shogunate.[25] Likewise, the function of the Shin-yoshiwara yūkaku as a licensed community remained effective in managing and controlling its yūjo population. The following paragraphs show the detailed duties undertaken by the red-light district.

First, supervision of all yūjo in Shin-yoshiwara was the responsibility of the entire Shin-yoshiwara community, accompanied by the detection of and crackdown upon *baita* (unlicensed clandestine prostitution) everywhere except Shin-yoshiwara yūkaku in Edo, for which the Shin-yoshiwara community equipped itself with its own force, prepared to mete out a violent response. In the 17th century they mobilized up to 100 men, who were sometimes involved in pitched battles.[26] The maintenance of order in the prostitution trade in the entire Edo city through the suppression of baita was the most important responsibility of Shin-yoshiwara chou.

The second notable fact was that, in most cases, any baita detected and repressed by Shin-yoshiwara became the property of the community. From 1720 onwards, anyone caught engaging in baita was penalized by being placed under a three-year obligation as the property of Shin-yoshiwara. While this amounted to penal detention from the baita's point of view, for the Shin-yoshiwara chou community it meant a share in the distributed earnings—and use—of the baita. Such ownership of baita may be regarded as an extension of the Shin-yoshiwara community's obligation to control baita in the entire Edo city.

The third matter concerns *syūjoninbetu-aratame* (family registration). In general, the census of community residents was an important responsibility of every town, and at every census the town's residents were registered as town members in *ninbetsu-chou* (records of individuals). How, then, were yūjo in Shin-yoshiwara recorded as individuals? In principle, registration in the ninbetsu-chou treated a house as a unit, which listed all family members including, first of all, the master of the house then members of his family then servants and finally temporary residents.[27] Therefore *nenki-boko-nin* (fixed-term apprentices) were in general registered as servants of their master's house. Since most yūjo were taken to the red-light district under the terms of *nenki-boko*, they should theoretically have been registered as servants of the house they were working for. However, yūjo were excluded from the registration laws as *Seigai-no-mono* (persons not meeting the registration criteria).[28] Instead, they were registered in the *Yūjo ninbetsu-chou*, a register completely independent from the ordinary register of community members of Shin-yoshiwara chou. That indicates that yūjo were not residents of a town but subject to handling and control for the benefit of the community and its members.

Fourth, the violence employed for monitoring and controlling yūjo is thought to have been used mainly by the employees of each brothel, although Shin-yoshiwara chou as a community had its own guards in charge of preventing escape, arson and so forth. Therefore, yūjo were under the twofold control of the violent power of their respective brothel and of the town it was in.

The town of Shin-yoshiwara consisted of five smaller chou and it is clear that the overall role of the town was to segregate yūjo from ordinary citizens and to control and regulate all yūjo (licensed prostitutes) and baita (unlicensed clandestine prostitutes) in the capital city of Edo. Day-to-day control and regulation of the prostitution business in Edo was the *yaku* (official duty) of Shin-yoshiwara, and in return, the town was granted the exclusive privilege of running the prostitution business. That brought with it the institutionalization of the servile status of yūjo.

Was the way in which a town was sustained with its official duties and privileges unique to Shin-yoshiwara? Research since the 1980s on early modern Japanese society's status system has successfully clarified the historical significance of the relationship between official duties and privileges. Those studies also established the following points as common ground.

First, status groups were not political orders arranged by the feudal authorities, but indicated groups of people formed with reference to their social division of labour (business status) and ownership attributed to their respective duties (for example, a patch of field for peasants, townhouses for town dwellers, skills and business premises for craftsmen).

Second, in order to stabilize their business status, class groups often received secured privileges by bearing duties (peasants paid agricultural tax, town dwellers provided labour called *cho-nin sokuyaku*, and *senmin* (social outcasts) tended livestock and served as executioners).

Third, the samurai (feudal warriors) class conformed to their own autonomous rules and oversaw their lands, and, eventually, established the widespread discourse that Tokugawa society can be understood in terms of a rigid, four-tier hierarchy of *shi-nō-kō-shō* (warriors, farmers, artisans, merchants).

In the same way as other chou communities in Edo that took on duties and were given privileges,[29] Shin-yoshiwara chou were urban communities that assumed responsibility for controlling and regulating prostitution in Edo and were guaranteed in return the privilege of running their own prostitution business. Therefore, it can be said that, in private terms, yūjo were women bound by debts and sexual coercion and subject to patriarchal rights, including abusive control exercised by brothels, whereas in public terms they were the subject of repression by the Shin-yoshiwara communities because of their status as prostitutes and were placed in a servile position and so treated differently from ordinary citizens. In other words, the repression and servitude of yūjo were maintained by private contract between brothels and hitonushi as well as by the public and status system function of the Shin-yoshiwara chou, which was in charge of controlling prostitution in the city of Edo. We can see, from this, the slavish nature of the debt-bound yūjo in the Edo era.

Yūjo Release Act and Yūjo

The Yūjo Release Act of 1872 and its Details

Following the Meiji Restoration in 1868, the Meiji government tried to reorganize the status system by integrating various status groups into three classes: warriors and lords, citizens, and outcasts. However, the leaders of the government could hardly avoid seeing the difficulties confronting them. Ultimately, in 1871, they took the plunge, issuing an edict, *haihan chiken* (abolition of feudal domains and establishment of prefectures), to reform its state regime and adopt a policy to dissolve the status system.[30] The result was difficulty in keeping unchanged the yūkaku, which had ensured yūjo servitude under the community as one of the status groups. Of course, as we will see, neither the new government nor the Tokyo government had any intention of actually prohibiting prostitution itself. Many of its officials, including those at a high level, had been accustomed to enjoy themselves in yūkaku, even while they engaged in the *sonnō jōi* (Revere the Emperor and Expel the Barbarians) Movement for the Meiji Restoration.[31] Therefore, it should be emphasized that they still needed to control prostitution but using a method other than the status system. This section examines the enactment of the Yūjo Release Act in response to the new situation, and the reactions of yūjo.

Usually, the Yūjo Release Act refers to the Grand Council of State's Decree No. 295 of 2 October 1872 (A) and the Ministry of Justice's Decree No. 22 of 9 October 1872 (C). However, the unnumbered order by the Tokyo government concerning the Grand Council of State's Decree No. 295 on 7 October 1872 (B) also carries significant meaning, and the three orders are closely related to each other. The cabinet, especially, not to speak of the Tokyo government, was concerned with yūkaku, an important means to the maintenance of sexual order in Tokyo, the new capital. However, there were sharp differences of opinion within the cabinet on many issues, so in order to examine the actual details of the above constituents of the Release Act each is discussed separately as below. The word "release" or emancipation, used here, is a historical term referring to the act of release from their servitude as prostitutes, who had until then been subject to the terms of miuri-boko, the rules governing trading in people as commodities.

(A) Grand Council of State's Decree No. 295 of 2 October 1872

Since ancient times, the trade in humans and abuse of them indefinitely or for a limited period of time at the disposal of their masters has been prohibited as unacceptable acts against human ethics. The common practice of virtually trading people and binding them in servile positions under terms such as *nenki-boko* [fixed-term apprenticeship] and others should no longer be tolerated, and thus shall be strictly forbidden from now on.

[Two articles abbreviated]

About *yūjo* and *geisha* (entertainers),[32] etc., I hereby order the release of all *nenki-bokonin* [fixed-term apprentices]. Any lawsuits over debts concerning this matter shall be entirely disregarded.

(B) Unnumbered Order of Tokyo Government of 7 October 1872[33]

With regard to the ransoms concerning the *yūjo* and female entertainers who have been ordered to be released for the time being, the former *yūjo* must, upon promptly settling the amount with the parties (*hitonushi*) and upon making the necessary payment, report to the authority by the 15th.

(C) Ministry of Justice Decree No. 22 of 9 October 1872 [the Tokyo municipal government had been notified of this order on 8 October)[34]

With regard to the Minister's Decree No. 295 of 2 October, it should be understood as follows:

Although the trade in humans has been prohibited since ancient time, it has in reality been widely practiced under terms such as *nenki-boko*. In view of this, any capital money required for hiring prostitutes and entertainers should be regarded as illicit. Hence, any individual filing for claims concerning this matter shall forfeit his money upon investigation.

Similarly, prostitutes and entertainers are deprived of their basic human rights and, therefore, in this sense, should be regarded as something equivalent to livestock. There is no ground for a person to demand repayment from livestock. For these reasons, any unpaid money in return for loans or sold goods to prostitutes and female entertainers does not require repayment.

Decree (A) above clearly demands the "emancipation" of prostitutes and female entertainers, based on the principle of non-trafficking of humans and prohibits lawsuits over related debts. Faced with this shocking decree, the Tokyo municipal government issued Order (B) on 7 October 1872 to order that the debt problem be solved through "settlement". Order (B) can be described as a notice of recommendation for settlement, based on an assumption that the financial obligation remains intact even if yūjo are physically released, as well as on a tacit understanding that completion of negotiation on equal terms between brothels and yūjo, who had been privately controlled through abusive restraint by their employers, would never be achieved. In short, it was a supplemental law to secure the continued operation of brothels based on advance debt, which shows that the Tokyo government depended, for its maintenance of regional governance, on those who represented the interests of the region, such as the brothels in yūkaku. Additionally, some members of the Tokyo government had themselves been officials of the Edo magistrate.

In contrast to Decree (A) and Order (B), which failed to effect the emancipation of yūjo, the Ministry of Justice Decree (C) contained a ground-breaking element that enabled yūjo to be released immediately from their ransoms. Decree (C) laid down that individuals subjected to trade are effectively being treated as livestock, that no one can demand repayment of debt from livestock, and that ransom is therefore money extorted illicitly and for which no one can legitimately claim repayment. Finally, it was concluded that anyone filing any complaint should forfeit the entire ransom because it had been illegally demanded anyway.

Under the provisions of Decree (C), all ransoms incurred before 9 October 1872 were invalid, and yūjo were to be awarded unqualified "emancipated" status. After their "emancipation", the position of main party to the prostitution business was transferred from the brothels to the yūjo themselves, and every decision about whether their services should be sold or not, or where they should be sold, were to be made also by the yūjo. Similarly, the brothels were now defined as room-rental businesses, and thus regarded as leasing the spaces where the actual prostitution took place. The order had a dramatic effect. For example, in Shinyanagi-chou, the red-light district in Kofu City, Yamanashi Prefecture, 37 of the 136 yūjo (27 per cent) decided to remain in their brothels while 99 left the district.[35] A month after their emancipation in Shin-yoshiwara, Tokyo, "of approximately 3,500 emancipated *yūjo* fewer than ten per cent returned to Shin-yoshiwara".[36] The "emancipation" was in practice executed by returning yūjo to their hitonushi (parents or original employers); the possibility that they might be resold was therefore still implicit, indicating the limitations of "emancipation". However, the mass departure of yūjo from the red-light districts under the Release Act carries a great significance. Moreover, the responses of yūjo who decided to remain in their existing quarters also had a substantial impact on the brothel communities. In particular, as described in the following section, the behaviour of emancipated yūjo provoked hostility and confusion among brothels, which endangered the very existence of yūkaku.

The Battle for a Better Life and Emancipation

In the later days of modern-age Shin-yoshiwara, the difference in business models between brothels was significantly broadened, and the discrepancy in financial power became very large between the major brothels concentrated around Edo-chou 1-choume and the tsubone brothels clustered around Kyomachi. Among those various prostitution businesses, the *Yūjoya Nakama* (brothel association) organized by the major brothels held controlling power in the community.[37]

Many of the powerful brothels owned dozens of yūjo and had sub-
ordinated the lower-class brothels; the class of the yūjo was clearly
reflected in their working environment. After the enactment of the
Release Act, their new behaviour created a deep rift in the brothel
community based on class order; the following depicts some of the
developments in detail.

Soon after the Release Act, "there are very few yūjo in this red-
light district, and many of them are still taking breaks".[38] Another
section of the same document states, "Since the release order was
issued, yūjo and geisha have been spending their days playing and
taking breaks". As these descriptions show, many yūjo started taking
"breaks", which in reality meant a rejection of the prostitution ordered by the brothels, now "room-lease business operators".

After "emancipation", yūjo avoided being sent back to their
hitonushi by zegen and "many of them started to dilly-dally, avoiding
being taken back by zegen".[39] A zegen was a broker trading in yūjo,
who earned money primarily by arranging for their resale. Most
zegen were outlaws and typically known as kyōkaku (professional
gamblers). The yūjo of Shin-yoshiwara petitioned for the dissolution
of their relationships with these zegen. In response to yūjo pleas,
kochou (administrative officials in charge of local communities) ap-
pealed to the municipal government to regulate zegen, although without success.

Because the living conditions of yūjo were determined by the
class of room-lease business (former brothels) they were subject to,
those yūjo who decided to remain in their quarters began to be selec-
tive and move into new rooms if they could. As a result, the hostility
and disruption worsened between ōmagaki (literally, a big rough
fence; a high-ranking brothel was called so because of its big fence
at the front entrance) businesses and komise (lower-class brothels)
businesses, such as the former kogoushi and tsubone houses. As taxes
and licence fee were imposed on all such businesses regardless of
their place on the business scale, the discontent and anger of komise
businesses towards the Tokyo municipal government were intensified.
For example, a petition of February 1874 by a komise room-lease
business in Shin-yoshiwara for the reduction of the room-lease licence fee stated that "the government has until now discriminated
between classes for everything" but "under the new rule, yūjo are no
longer employees but have the freedom to rent wherever they want at
their own will", meaning that "yūjo concentrate in houses with better

rooms, meaning fewer *yūjo* in lower-class houses. Despite that, the government requires us to pay an equal amount of tax, which leaves us at our wits' end".[40] Here, we can see the situation in which the voluntary transfer of yūjo to rooms offering better conditions had a financially detrimental effect on lower-class room-lease businesses, causing the crumbling of the fundamental order in the red-light districts, which was centred on the brothel association consisting of major, or *ohmise*, businesses.

The shift described above was seen not only in Shin-yoshiwara but also surfaced in post towns along major routes, such as Naito-shinjuku and Shinagawa-juku. The situation became so serious for komise businesses that when an in-house yūjo went home, the komise business in Shin-yoshiwara would "have to close down when only one or two *yūjo* go home due to sickness or other business".[41]

In December 1873, when the Tokyo municipal government established *Kashizashiki-tosei-kisoku* (rules concerning businesses utilizing leased rooms) and *Shougi-kisoku* (rules concerning prostitutes and female entertainers) and determined the amount of tax payable, some yūjo complained about the amount of tax compared with the profits they made. To such complaints, room-lease businesses expressed their frustration because

> *yūjo* do not reflect on their own ugly looks (because of which they can never work at upper-class establishments) but instead always complain that they have to pay the same amount of tax as the ones who have moved to upper-class houses.[42]

The room-lease businesses were in a plight, as discontent intensified over the distribution of post-tax profit between the lease businesses and yūjo, who would often transfer to another house if a business could not accept their terms. As a result, most of the lower-class room-lease businesses experienced a miserable time.

The new government also obliged yūjo to be tested for syphilis. In response, "those who are listed below insisted that they are no longer in the business and went home without taking the test".[43]

The Case of Kashiku

In order to examine the reactions of yūjo, let us look more closely at the case of Kashiku, whose story introduced this article (see Table 8.2). As the Release Act took effect in Shin-yoshiwara, Kashiku was returned to Masagoro Hashiya, her former hitonushi, who ran a brothel in Fukagawa. In an attempt to resell Kashiku to Shin-yoshiwara, Masagoro insisted that he had to pay 15 ryō in gold to cover the cost of her clothes and bedding and threatened her that she would "become a *yūjo* again in Yoshiwara if she cannot repay the fifteen-ryō in gold". As briefly mentioned in the introduction to this article, Kashiku's response was to maintain that she was engaged to a man named Takejiro, a servant in a brothel in Shin-yoshiwara, and filed with Takejiro a joint petition addressed to the kochou, but the petition was dismissed by the Tokyo municipal government. A desperate Kashiku then escaped from the red-light district the following January (1873) during the fire at Shin-yoshiwara and sought the protection of Kikujiro, a hairdresser in Fukagawa who was one of her regular customers. Although Kikujiro at first persuaded Kashiku to go back, he set his mind on rescuing her after Kashiku attempted a second escape. Kikujiro's hairdresser master Sadakichi Kasuya also generously proposed to settle the 15-ryō debt and to serve as mediator in the hope of supporting his young apprentice's love. The Tokyo municipal government, however, ruled in the end that the 15-ryō loan was Kashiku's personal debt and instructed that settlement must be reached through negotiation. Master Sadakichi's negotiation attempts did not fare well, and, more or less as a last resort, Kashiku and Kikujiro jointly petitioned the municipal government, stating,

> I have been a *yūjo* all my life, and such life has brought nothing but misery. If Masagoro resells me in payment for my debt, I shall be doomed to fall into a further predicament. Please, be merciful for my sake and order my transfer to the care of Kikujiro.[44]

Despite her pleas, Kashiku's petition was dismissed, ultimately ruining her hopes. Kashiku was likely finally to have been forced back into prostitution.

From the various reactions among yūjo following the Release Act, the following points can be extracted for discussion. First, the annulment of ransoms and the introduction of a new legal principle that "prostitution is a business run by a *yūjo*'s own will" presented conditions in which yūjo could seek a better life and achieve their own "emancipation", such as escape from the restraint they lived under to a better business environment or they could, if they wished, reject work. At the same time, the action yūjo (sexual products) took in search of that "emancipation" had a shocking impact on the established order in red-light districts. The Release Act must have given yūjo, who had been keenly aspiring to be "emancipated", the hope and courage to act decisively, and the action they took struck a significant blow at the red-light districts for so long established throughout the Edo era.

The second point for discussion focuses on the types of force that could oppose the authority of the Shin-yoshiwara-chou community, which had been the dominant power in the red-light district. Clients came from diverse backgrounds, as Kashiku's case clearly shows, and lower-class workers, such as a hairdresser's apprentice, servant or day workers were often very important customers. Although of lowly social standing, they were craftsmen in possession of—in Kashiku's case, hairdressing—tools and skills and a clear business territory known as *dedoko* (hairdressing stall) or other *chouba* (spaces used exclusively for business operations). They were also proud people who were willing to fight injustice in support of the weak.[45] Therefore, they sometimes took action in support of yūjo. However, as far as their relationship with chou (small communities making up the city) was concerned, their social standing was not always sufficiently autonomous. In the case of Edo's hairdressers, or *kamiyui*, their business territory was strictly defined by each chou, and hairdressers were not allowed to choose their clients freely. Therefore, a hairdresser always had to obtain the support and permission of his chou. In other words, business existence was utterly dependent on the support of communities of townspeople, and as long as Shin-yoshiwara chou remained one of those communities, it would not have been possible for a hairdresser, as a lower-class craftsman, to oppose the authority and might of his community. It should also not be forgotten that these were among the men visiting brothels to enjoy the services of the prostitutes, so to that extent, although they exploited the prostitutes, they had mutual interests with Shin-yoshiwara chou and its brothels.

Third, we must explain the apathy of the new national government and the subordinate Tokyo municipal government to the true "emancipation" of yūjo in spite of the Yūjo Release Act. The following section looks at why these governments were ineffective in realizing the spirit of the new act despite the fact that they issued the act in definitively drastic terms.

Regions and Nations in the 19th Century: The Place of the Yūjo Release Act in World History

Domestic and International Background to the Enactment of the Yūjo Release Act

As the premise in discussing the reason for the inactivity of national and Tokyo municipal governments concerning the actual emancipation of yūjo, let us first distinguish between domestic and international factors affecting the background to the enactment of the Yūjo Release Act. Since 1872, the movement to reform the long-standing prostitution policy had operated at the national-government level, mainly at the prompting of the Ministry of Justice.[46] The move reflected the fact that it was impossible to maintain the old policy based on status-system duties and privilege exclusively within the red-light district while nationally promoting full-scale modernization by abolishing the status-dependent system. The progress of the status-system abolition policy at the time was probably at the phase where the existing style of administration, by which a specific town controlled prostitutes and segregated them from ordinary citizens in its registration practice, was no longer tolerated. As noted earlier in this article, licensed districts in the Edo era were maintained and operated under the principle of duty and privilege, and in tackling the challenge of abolishing the status system the national government saddled itself with the necessity to drastically revise that social foundation. The abolition of governance based on the autonomous intermediate groups that have taken various different forms at the end of the trajectories of many premodern societies creates a challenge commonly faced by many nations and regions in the process of modernization. To that extent, the Yūjo Release Act can be defined as an aspect of modernization normally experienced by modernizing countries. For the government that enacted the Release Act, the ultimate goal was to abolish the administration of prostitution as being dependent on the status system, while the actual "emancipation" of yūjo—let alone the abolition of prostitution generally—was scarcely on their radar, so to speak. They intended simply to build a new order of prostitution not reliant on the old system. However, they thought it absolutely essential to maintain prostitution itself and in reality made no attempt to relieve the servitude of yūjo. Apparently, the new policy's intention was to liberate yūjo from control by compulsion and allow them to work for themselves, but obviously that did not materialize. It is little wonder then that both the Japanese government and the Tokyo municipal government treated Kashiku and other yūjo so cold-heartedly.

Furthermore, it should be added that more than a few red-light districts prospered from foreign clients, and quite a number of high-ranking Japanese government officials themselves enjoyed the entertainment of licensed districts. On the other hand, the government, constrained by confrontation with overseas powers, probably recognized that the condition of the red-light districts, where human trafficking was practised openly, was a hindrance to their wish to maintain their dignity before the international community. In 1872, such were the circumstances in which reform of the organization of prostitution was undertaken within the competent government departments.

The international factor that propelled the enactment of the Yūjo Release Act was the *Maria Luz* incident, which touched on the relevance of coolie labour trade and Japanese yūjo and became a cause célèbre in the debates on slavery taking place throughout much of the 19th-century world.[47] The *Maria Luz* case was a legal dispute between the Japanese government, the British government in support of Japan, the Peruvian government, and concerned a coolie who had escaped from a ship—the *Maria Luz*—near the port of Yokohama.[48] One focus of the dispute was whether yūjo status constituted slavery equivalent to that of coolies. At that time, Peru was in need of labour for domestic development projects, and as an alternative solution following the ending of the African slave trade in the 1810s and Peru's own abolition of slavery for indigenous people in 1854, its national government attempted to import coolies as a new source of labour.[49] However, when one of these coolies escaped from the Peru-bound *Maria Luz* near the port of Yokohama, the servile status of coolies became the focus of international criticism. In an attempt to find a breakthrough, the Peruvian government insisted that the coolie trade should be deemed legal as long as yūjo business was treated as legal. After the Meiji restoration, the Japanese government, feeling itself belittled by the international community (*bankoku-taiji*), was desperately seeking a way at the earliest to establish a civilized society and renegotiate the unequal treaties imposed by the West. At such time, Peru's allegation that Japan engaged in domestic slavery came as a shock. Under such internationally sensitive circumstances, the Yūjo Release Act materialized earlier than originally intended, and with more drastic content, including the cancellation of ransom debt. The enactment of the Release Act became one of the Japanese government's most urgent tasks to save the country's face before the international community.

The Significance of the Yūjo Release Act in World History

The Yūjo Release Act, enacted in great haste in the early phase of the country's modernization, was therefore intended to supersede the existing governance system dependent on an early modern status system. However, its goal was not the reform of actual prostitution practices nor the outright rejection of prostitution. Domestically, the law was a method by which to modernize its organization, while internationally it was a measure to create the impression of a country with a modernized society that rejected human trafficking and slavery, in accordance with the prevailing trend of the 19th century. That said, the Yūjo Release Act was a movement manifested as a closely intermingled, indivisible part of the 19th century's world movement. It also bears witness to the fact that the 19th-century world was a place where systems were transformable only as entire structures, while intentional and accidental factors were complexly entwined in the process. The following discussion briefly explains this fact.

The allegation made by Peru, as mentioned above, was rooted in the debate over prostitution taking place in Britain at the time, without which the claim would never have been made. Against a backdrop of the global expansion of capitalism, the British government had introduced the Contagious Diseases Acts (enacted in 1864, amended in 1866 and 1868, and repealed in 1886) to require syphilis inspections at military garrisons and ports visited by British navy vessels and merchantmen. In the midst of heated debates in Britain, the acts were facing fierce protests led by Josephine Butler, a feminist activist in support of prostitutes' dignity, who maintained that forced inspection constituted what we would now call human-rights abuse.[50] In the case of *Peru* v. *Japan and Britain*, the government of Peru was represented by a British lawyer who discovered that, from the viewpoint of the existence of a slavish nature and human dignity, the coolie case was, despite its apparent irrelevance, identical to the yūjo system, where a de facto system of slavery took its form from private —and legitimate—contracts. Although, in complete disagreement with Butler's human-rights approach, the British lawyer had meant to advocate the continuance of slavery by labelling the coolie's case as being identical to that of yūjo, the fact that the legally servile condition of yūjo was now officially pointed out forced the Japanese government into a corner, finally compelling it to enforce the Yūjo Release Act in full. In other words, as a consequence of the negative mediation accidentally rendered by Peru's allegation, the feminist movement in Britain successfully condemned the Japanese government. As a result, the Yūjo Release Act went further than originally intended by the Japanese government and incorporated provisions including the immediate cancellation of ransom debt. The fact that the yūjo Kashiku believed in the possibility of her "emancipation" and that more than 3,000 yūjo in Shin-yoshiwara were released, although in some cases only temporarily, was indeed the fruit of the Release Act and brought about by its comprehensive nature, especially its unambiguous requirement for the immediate annulment of ransom debt. In that sense, the Yūjo Release Act can be seen to have been enforced due to movements for liberalism and feminism founded on the idea of human rights developed in opposition to British capitalism. It certainly affected Japan as the least developed capitalist country of the time, triggering as it did a global migration of people, including coolies, in the 19th century. The enactment of the Yūjo Release Act, a rather trivial incident occurring at the eastern end of the Eurasian continent, had its significance as an answer to the political problem originating in an inconsistency between domestic politics and society. At the same time, it was a reaction by Japan to the dilemma and development of the 19th century's new human-rights thinking with regard to slavery.

Conclusion

Emancipation logics and realities have characteristics unique to their respective regions in the world. However, the question of who was responsible for controlling and maintaining slaves should be one of the main focuses in discussing any form of slavery in any region at any time. Through examining the yūkaku (red-light districts) in Japan, it was found that the method of control and maintenance was distinctly characterized by the traditional class-based social structure of early-modern Japan, and that emancipation would have been impossible without rejecting that existing method of control. In other words, emancipation was inseparable from the structural transformation of a society that had always embraced slavery. In that regard, in the case of Japan, where efforts at modernization began to take place in the mid-19th century, the enactment of the Yūjo Release Act can be regarded as the rejection of a status-based social and economic control system.

Also, it should be pointed out once again that the process towards the enactment of the Yūjo Release Act suggests that the 19th-century world created a framework in which countries influenced each other in relation to common problems and debates, including human-rights ideas on the one hand and the problems of slavery on the other. Just as in the case of the relationship between Shin-yoshiwara chou and yūjo, which cannot be examined without regard to the world historical view, the 19th-century world seems to have been one where even the relationship between a domestic region and its national government cannot be explained without examining the international structure of the period and the transformation in it that may have affected and redefined the region-nation relationship itself.

Notes

1. From "Shougikaihou" [Release of Prostitutes], 604.A2.12, Tokyo Prefecture Historical Materials, Tokyo Metropolitan Archives.

2. Yuriko Yokoyama, "19 Seiki Toshi Shakai ni Okeru Chiiki Hegemony no Saihen: Onna-kamiyui, Yūjo no Seizon to 'Kaiho' o Megutte" [Reorganization of the Local Hegemony in the Urban Society in the 19th Century: Focusing on Subsistence and Release of Female Hairdressers and Prostitutes], *Rekishigaku Kenkyu* 885 (2011): 12–21.

3. See the discussion in Alice Bellagamba et al., ed., *African Voices on Slavery and the Slave Trade* (Cambridge: Cambridge University Press, 2013).

4. See the discussion in Daniel Botsman, "Freedom without Slavery? 'Coolies', Prostitutes, and Outcastes in Meiji Japan's 'Emancipation Moment'", *American Historical Review* 116, 5 (2011): 1323–47; Tadao Hama, *Haichi Kakumei to Furansu Kakumei* [Haiti Revolution and French Revolution] (Sapporo: Hokkaidō daigaku shuppankai, 1999).

5. See Nobuyuki Yoshida, *Mibunteki Shūen to Shakaibunka Kōzō* [Class Marginality and Sociocultural Structure] (Kyoto: Burakumondai Kenkyūsho, 2003), p. 414.

6. I am grateful to Professor Ryota Matsumoto for showing me the structure of the nagaya and the role of the wall that appears as a line on the map.

7. See Nishiyama Matsunosuke, "Kuruwa", in *Nishiyama Matsunosuke chosakushū 5: KinseiHūzoku to shakai* [A Selection from Nishiyama Matsunosuke's Works, vol. 5, Manners and Society in Early Modern Japan], Nishiyama Matsunosuke (Tokyo: Yoshikawa Kōbunkan, 1985).

8. Kiyoshi Shimojū, *"Miuri" no Nihonshi: Jinshin Baibai kara Nenkiboko e* [Japanese History of Human Trade: From Human Trafficking to *Nenkiboko*] (Tokyo: Yoshikawa Kōbunkan, 2012).

9. Nominal loans, termed *myōmokukin* loans (*myōmokukin kashitsuke*), were one way in which high-ranking temples, such as imperial monasteries or temples connected with the court nobility, could raise funds. They cited a reason (*myōmoku*) for needing to raise funds, such as building repairs, and then offered loans to commoners as a means to raise that money. As a result of this policy, the Bukkōji temple, which was one of Kyoto's imperial monastery temples (*monzeki*), began lending money to brothels in the Shin-yoshiwara red-light districts. On nominal loans, see Toshiaki Miura, *Kinsei Jisha Myōmokukin no Shitekikenkyū* [A Historical Study of Nominal Loans by High-ranking Temples and Shrines] (Tokyo: Yoshikawa Kōbunkan, 1993).

10. Approximately 90 per cent of commoners in Edo rented their dwellings or back-alley tenements, and could not therefore take out mortgages on land. See Daniel Botsman, "Recovering Japan's Urban Past: Yoshida Nobuyuki, Tsukada Takashi, and the Cities of the Tokugawa Period", *City, Culture and Society* 3, 1 (2012): 9–14.

11. *Yamada-ke monjo*, 74-1-3; Nakao City Museum, Nagano Prefecture.

12. Meaning the society around the yūkaku, where the brothels held hegemony over *zegen* (brokers), *chaya* (teahouses) and *tazusawaritosei* (small merchants subservient to the brothels), and strengthened their connections and ties with other areas for prostitution. See the discussion of yūkaku in Nobuyuki Yoshida, "Yūkaku shakai" [Society around the Yūkaku], in *Mibunteki Shūhen to Kinsei Shakai 4: Toshi no Shūhen ni Ikiru* [Class Marginality and Early Modern Society 4: Living on Urban Periphery], ed. Takashi Tsukada (Tokyo: Yoshikawa Kobunkan, 2006), pp. 49–51.

13. National Diet Library, Kanō Bunko, 11973-8.

14. Kizaki-shuku was a post station. Nikkō-reiheishi Road extended from Kuragano-shuku to Nikkō.

15. Misako Usami, *Shukuba to meshimori-onna* [Post Station and Meshimori Onna] (Tokyo: Dousei-sha, 2000), pp. 143–50.

16. See the definition of "ie" and patriarchy by Osamu Otō, *Kinseinōmin to Ie, Mura, Kokka; Seikatsushi/Shakaishi no Shiten kara* [Early Modern

Peasantry and Family System, Village and State: From the Perspective of Life History and Social History] (Tokyo: Yohikawa Kōbunkan, 1996), pp. 1, 271.

17. See the case of yūjo Kashiku later in this article, and Yuriko Yokoyama, "Geishougi Kaihourei to Yūjo: Shin-yoshiwara Kashiku Ikkenn no Shoukai wo Kanete" [The Release Act and Yūjo: Introducing the Kashiku Documents], *Tokyo Daigaku Nihonshigaku Kenkyu Kiyo* [Studies in the Social History of Early Modern Japan, Bulletin of the Department of Japanese History, Faculty of Letters, University of Tokyo (Supplement)] (2013): 159–71.

18. The role of the brothels guild deserves a study all of its own.

19. This idea was suggested by Takashi Tsukada, *Mibunsei Shakai to Shimin Shakai: Kinsei Nihon no Shakai to Hō* [Status-based Society and Civil Society: Society and Law in Early Modern Japan] (Tokyo: Kashiwa Shobō, 1992).

20. See Amy Stanley, *Selling Women: Prostitution, Markets, and the Household in Early Modern Japan* (Berkeley, CA: University of California Press, 2012), pp. 57–8.

21. Shimojū, *"Miuri" no Nihonnshi*, pp. 148–54.

22. Sōgōjoseishi Kenkyūkai, ed., *Jidai wo Ikita Joseitachi: Shin-nihon Josei Tūshi* [Women lived the Times: New Overview of History of Women] (Tokyo: Asahi Shimbun Publications, 2010), pp. 228–325.

23. Ibid., p. 236.

24. Yoshiwara yūkaku was relocated in 1657 (the third year of the Meireki era) and renamed Shin-yoshiwara.

25. Generally, any other unauthorized place for prostitution, for example *shukuba* (post station), was not officially recognized and had no privileges in sexual matters.

26. Takashi Tsukada, *Kinsei Mibunsei to Shūen Shakai* [Early Modern Class System and Marginal Society] (Tokyo: University of Tokyo Press, 1997), pp. 128–312.

27. Yuriko Yokoyama, *Meiji Ishin to Kinnsei Mibunsei no Kaitai* [The Meiji Restoration and Abolishment of Status System] (Tokyo: Yamakawa Shuppansha, 2005), pp. 30–46.

28. *Tenpōdō Gokaiseishojitome 10, Tempō Senyoruishu, Kyūbaku hikitugisho* [Collection of Orders and Precedents in Tempō Period (1830–44)], National Diet Library. See Sakamoto's discussion in Tadahisa Sakamoto, *Tenpō Kaikaku no Hō to Seisaku* [Law and Society in Tempo Reform] (Tokyo: Sōbunsha, 1997), pp. 156–62.

29. Excepting Shin-yoshiwara chou, chou communities in Edo gradually lost their characteristics as professional precincts and came to substitute their real and respective duties by making cash payments. Shin-yoshiwara chou retained its official duties and privileges. See the

discussion in Nobuyuki Yoshida, *Kinsei Kyodai Toshi no Shakai Kōzō* [Social Structure of Early Modern Megalopolis] (Tokyo: University of Tokyo Press, 1991).

30. Yokoyama, *Meiji Ishin to Kinsei Mibunsei no Kaitai.*

31. For example, in 1862 some anti-shogunate royalists, including Shinsaku Takasugi and Kaoru Inoue, stayed the night at the famous inn, Dozō Sagami, which had many *meshimori-onna* (prostitutes), and left to carry out an arson attack on the British legation in Shinagawa.

32. In Edo, some geisha, females and males, were in a situation similar to that of yūjo, who were often trafficked as nenki-bōkōnin. For geisha, see Ashita Saga and Nobuyuki Yoshida, ed., *Shirīzu Yūkaku Shakai 1: Santo to Chihōtoshi* [The World of the Pleasure Quarters 1: Three Cities and Local Towns] (Tokyo: Yoshikawa Kōbunkan, 2013).

33. "Tokyohu Shiryou" [Historical Documents of Tokyo Metropolitan], Naikaku Bunko, National Archives.

34. "Meiji 5 nen Hourei Zensho" [Statute Book of Meiji 5th].

35. "Shougikaihou", 606.A2.14, Tokyo Prefecture Historical Materials, Tokyo Metropolitan Archives.

36. "Shougikaihou", 606.A2.12, Tokyo Prefecture Historical Materials, Tokyo Metropolitan Archives.

37. Yoshida, "*Yūkaku Shakai*", pp. 49–51.

38. "*Tokyohu shiryō*", Naikaku Bunko, National Archives.

39. Ibid.

40. "Geishougi torishimari shorui" [Historical Documents about the Regulation of Prostitutes and Geisha], 606.A7.6, Tokyo Prefecture Historical Materials, Tokyo Metropolitan Archives.

41. Ibid.

42. Ibid.

43. Ibid.

44. "Shougikaihou", 606.A2.12, Tokyo Prefecture Historical Materials, Tokyo Metropolitan Archives.

45. Nobuyuki Yoshida, *Kinsei Toshi Shakai no Mibun Kōzō* [The Structure of Status in the Urban Society in Early Modern Japan] (Tokyo: University of Tokyo Press, 1998), pp. 292–7.

46. "*Dajōruiten*", 2-168, National Archives. See Sumio Obinata, *Nihon Kindai Kokka no Seiritsu to Keisatsu* [Birth of Modern State of Japan and Police] (Tokyo: Azekura Shobō, 1992), pp. 280–5.

47. For the *Maria Luz* incident, see Tomoko Morita, *Kaikoku to Chigai Hōken* [The Opening of Japan and Extraterritorial Rights] (Tokyo: Yoshikawa Kōbunkan, 2004).

48. For the trade in exporting coolies from China, and the attitude of British officials, see Chapter 6 by Ei Murakami in this volume.

49. Setsuko Sonoda, *Nanboku Amerika Kamin to Kindai Chugoku Jyūkyūseki Transnashonarumaigrēshon* [Overseas Chinese in the Americas and Modern China: Transnational Migration in the Nineteenth Century] (Tokyo: University of Tokyo Press, 2009).

50. For Josephine Butler, see Judith R. Walkowitz, *Prostitution and Victorian Society: Women, Class, and the State* (Cambridge: Cambridge University Press, 1980) [Japanese tr. Tomomi Nagatomi, *Baishun to Bikutoria Cho Shakai* (Tokyo: Sophia University Press, 2009)].

CHAPTER 9

The End of Slavery in French West Africa

Martin A. Klein

Introduction

In Chapter 2 in this volume, Sue Peabody talks about France's two abolitions. This article focuses on a third abolition. It did not happen in any single year, though there were landmark pieces of legislation in 1903 and 1905, and their centennials were largely ignored in both France and Africa. The first abolition, in 1794, was never really implemented in Africa and annulled when Napoleon re-established slavery in 1802. The slaves of St Louis and Gorée were freed by the British in 1807, and when the French returned, some of them moved to the new British settlement of Bathurst in the Gambia.[1] The second emancipation during the revolution of 1848 was clear, simple and seemed decisive, but French colonial governors did their best to prevent the colony from becoming a refuge for slaves from elsewhere and to limit its application when French sovereignty was extended outside the two island bastions. The most definitive action to free the slaves came in 1903 and 1905 with two acts, which did not actually make slavery illegal, but enabled slaves to leave their masters. Thus, in much of French West Africa, began the process of emancipation.[2]

Slavery in West Africa

As in all slave societies, there were a number of different types of slaves in West Africa during the mid-19th century. The largest number were probably agricultural slaves, some of them owned by smallholders, but the majority were on large estates, particularly in

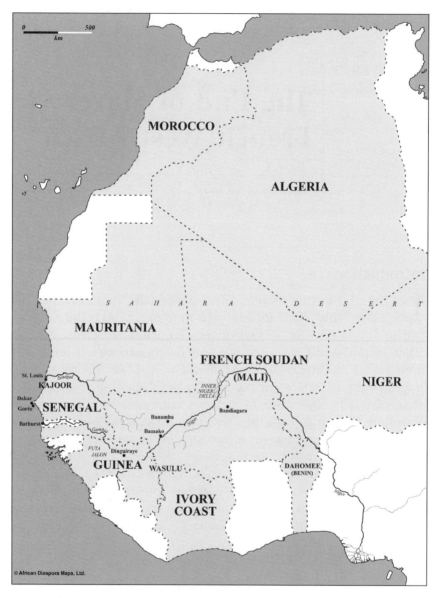

Map of French West Africa during the Partition

the savannah regions and near the capital cities of most regimes. They were the largest source of wealth in what we can class as slave societies.[3] They produced commodities like palm oil and peanuts for European markets, and among other things, grain and cloth for the

desert side trade between Saharan nomads and savannah agricul-
turalists. They also produced a grain surplus that enabled Muslim
elites to devote themselves to study and warrior elites to devote themselves to politics, warfare and the production of slaves.[4] The closing
of the Atlantic slave trade began with the termination of the slave
trade by the British in 1807 and the French in 1831, but the Atlantic
trade continued into the 1860s.[5] The Saharan slave trade was reduced
by the gradual closing of Mediterranean markets during the 19th
century, but a limited trade into and across the Sahara remained well
into the colonial period.[6] In spite of this, slavery and the slave trade
within Africa continued to grow until the beginning of the colonial
period. The demands of European markets, growth of markets within
Africa, development of more powerful weapons and a Muslim revolution all led to an increase in warfare and in enslavement as the century went along. The last third of the 19th century was the bloodiest
period in African history.

Most slaves within West Africa were women, in part because
women and children were more easily enslaved, but also because
women were more highly valued.[7] After a military victory, women
were the most important kind of booty. Some became the concubines of the rich and powerful, their functions being the provision
of pleasure to more privileged sexual partners and the production of
offspring.[8] Others were awarded to soldiers, for whom they farmed
and provided domestic services. There were usually enough women for
male slaves to receive partners, and in fact, some slaves had more
than one wife. Though not all women were happy with the male
slaves to whom they were assigned, partnering them with slaves was
a way to get them to accept their slave status.[9] There were, however,
other kinds of slaves. Most of the soldiers in Africans states and in
the French army that eventually conquered them were slaves. Most
kingdoms also had numerous slave officials. Slave warriors and officials were tied into the ruling dynasties and, thus, a privileged group
within society.

Slaves were also clearly important in the cities. A majority of the
population was servile both in coastal entrepôts and in the cities that
developed in the interior on the nodes of the commercial routes.[10]
These slaves fulfilled many economic roles, were freer than the agricultural slaves and were better off. The beginning of the French
Empire was two small island towns, St Louis in the mouth of the
Senegal river and Gorée, in what is now Dakar harbour. The various

companies that were granted monopolies of the slave trade from this section of the coast did not want their employees cohabiting with African women nor did they want responsibility for even small urban agglomerations. Their employees, however, like most European men living abroad without female companions, wanted both sexual partners and the pleasures of domestic life. The result was a form of temporary marriage, *marriage à la mode du pays*, which produced both a class of female entrepreneurs and offspring, who learned to operate within both French and African cultures.

These women, known as *signares*, invested in slaves, boats and urban property.[11] Both towns traded. From St Louis, annual convoys went upriver every year when the river was high, to engage in the gum trade of the middle river and the slave trade from what is now Western Mali. From Gorée, boats cruised the facing coast, known as the Petite Côte, and the rivers along the Atlantic coast from the Gambia to Sierra Leone. Most of the crews of these boats were made up of slaves, as were the captains of the boats and the *maitres de langues*, who traded with polities along the river. They were mostly men, though every boat had one *pileuse* who prepared food for the crew. What this meant is that a large part of the able-bodied male slave population was away from their owners much of the year and that they were entrusted with money, goods and property. Many of them were also trained for off-season labour as artisans: masons, shipbuilders, carpenters, weavers and sailors.

The slave-owners, called *habitants*, were mostly *métis*, at least until well into the 19th century. The most important owned up to 80–90 slaves, but many owned only a small number. What is crucial is that the slaves had a considerable measure of autonomy, marketable skills and close relations with the families of their owners. Many had knowledge of commerce and were the progenitors of a class of Muslim traders that eventually predominated in the commercial communities of St Louis, Gorée, Dakar and Rufisque. A majority of the population of St Louis and Gorée was made up of slaves. The colony of Senegal also operated with very few French men. In 1835, there were only 151 white French men in the colony.

The Emancipation of 1848

In France, abolition sentiment flowed not from a mobilization of religious groups, but from Enlightenment thought and revolutionary ideology.[12] The emancipation acts of both 1794 and 1848 were produced by revolutionary governments, and the colonial legislation of 1903 and 1905 was brought in by Republican colonial administrators pushed by progressive governments in France. Though abolitionism was based originally on a belief in the rights of man, there was also, during the 19th century, an increasing belief in the superiority of free labour.[13] Not all French people shared these commitments. In particular, those involved in colonies were, for the most part, hostile to abolition. There was generally a tension between Paris and its colonial governors, with metropolitan governments somewhat more anxious to distance themselves from slavery, particularly in the latter part of the century. Public opinion on this issue was not important before 1848,[14] but it became important under the Third Republic. There was also, often, a tension in the colonies, between senior administrators and those who administered in the field in Senegal and Algeria. Most colonial administrators were not hostile to slavery and many felt that coercion was necessary to get their subjects to work. The "bush" administrators also often had a sense of isolation and a fear of revolt. Finally, the bush administrators were often influenced by chiefs and other slaveholders on whom they depended in order to administer their districts. Senior administrators were more concerned about abolitionist sentiment in France. Some also became convinced that freeing the slaves would create a labour reserve.[15]

Though public opinion was not much concerned with slavery during the early 19th century, the abolition of slavery had been discussed in France for many years, though not with Senegal in mind.[16] Most slaves on French lands were in the Caribbean or the Indian Ocean. The abolition of the slave trade in 1818 had been imposed on the French after the defeat of Napoleon and was not enforced until the late 1820s. With the July Revolution of 1830, the government of King Louis Philippe began seriously enforcing the law against the slave trade. No French slave ship is known to have left the shores of Senegambia or the upper Guinea after 1831.[17] The Orleanist regime was, however, hesitant about attacking slavery itself. Though many key figures in the regime supported emancipation, only minor measures were taken. For example, an 1831 law provided for the imprisonment of slave traders and the confiscation of their ships.[18]

Nothing was done about the abolition of slavery until the fall of Louis Philippe in February 1848 brought a more radical group to power, which included Victor Schoelcher, the most important French abolitionist.[19] He proposed a law abolishing slavery. It was quickly accepted and probably without much discussion because the idea of slavery was offensive to most French people on the revolutionary left. The law itself was simple and clear. Article 1 stated: "Slavery will be completely abolished in all French colonies and possessions." Article 7 provided that "the soil of France frees the slave who touches it". It became illegal for any French citizen to possess, buy or sell slaves or participate in any way in such operations. The penalty was loss of French citizenship. Provision was made for indemnities to be paid to slave-owners, though at the time, bonds had to be issued because the money needed was not available. Within St Louis and Gorée, emancipation went well though there were vigorous protests from the signares and some slave-owners tried to move their slaves out of St Louis.[20] The day the law went into effect, slaves gathered on the shore for what seems to have been a spontaneous ritual cleansing. They then gathered in front of the government offices to dance and sing the praises of the government. For those slaves who worked for wages, the process was simple. They no longer had to share their wages, though they often continued to depend on their former masters for housing and jobs.[21] Some continued to live in the households of their former masters. About 200 found themselves without visible means of support and lived for a while in tents. In the long run, the former slaves and their children benefited from the growth of St Louis, its role as the port for the conquest of the Soudan and its situation as the capital of a growing colony.

The problem was not within the boundaries of the tiny colony, but outside. Senegal's neighbours and trading partners were all slave-holding societies. Fearing a massive flight of slaves to St Louis and Gorée, Governor Baudin warned neighbouring states to remove their slaves from St Louis if they did not wish to see them freed.[22] These states, at the same time, responded quickly, perhaps egged on by traders from St Louis. A delegation of chiefs from Kajoor threatened war if their slaves were freed.[23] When Baudin pleaded that he could not feed his tiny colony without food from the mainland, François Arago, the minister of colonies responsible for Schoelcher's law, reminded him that "he was invested with police powers necessary for the surveillance of Blacks who come into our cities to seek their emancipation and even to expel them from our territory if their presence becomes dangerous to good order".[24] Trarza, a Mauritanian polity on the north back of the Senegal River, suspended the profitable gum trade.[25] The chiefs of Cape Verde villages refused to sell fish to Gorée.[26] As a result, Baudin told local police to expel slaves from friendly states.[27] The result was the insulation of St Louis and Gorée from any tensions within local slave systems. Within a year, Louis Napoleon had been elected President and the revolutionaries yielded power. As President and then as Emperor Napoleon III, he had no interest in restoring slavery, but his regime had strong imperialistic tendencies and was generally sympathetic to the demands of its colonial proconsuls.

Faidherbe and Conquest

One of these was Major Louis Faidherbe, who was appointed Governor of Senegal in 1854 at the request of a group of Bordeaux merchants.[28] Faidherbe's programme was to establish French control over commerce and strategic parts of the mainland, starting with villages within cannon range of French posts. Faidherbe recognized that if slavery were illegal in conquered areas, it would be very difficult to find collaborators. From the first, French colonialism depended on indigenous collaborators both to conquer and to govern. To solve his problem, Faidherbe turned in 1855 to Frederic Carrère, head of the judicial service. Carrère came up with two legal formulas: first, that the Schoelcher law did not apply to those areas conquered after 1848 and second, that the residents of conquered areas on the mainland were not citizens but subjects and therefore not subject to French law.[29]

Faidherbe then followed through with a series of laws. An 1855 decree guaranteed the right of subjects to keep their slaves while reiterating that French citizens could not.[30] An 1857 circular held that when France was at war, slaves fleeing enemy states would be received and freed. However, slaves fleeing states at peace with the French would be expelled "as vagabonds dangerous for order and public peace" on the complaint of their masters.[31] The minister of colonies insisted that slaves not be delivered to their masters, but it became practice for the administration to inform the masters when and where the expulsion would take place. In the same year, Faidherbe reformed a system of wardship originally created by Baudin to deal with young slaves. Under the reformed system, children could be purchased on condition that they would be "freed" within 24 hours of their arrival in St Louis. Those freeing these children became their guardians. The system became a major source of domestic child labour for both French and African families in St Louis. Faidherbe wrapped this programme in abolitionist rhetoric, arguing that France had to tolerate slavery in order to eventually end it.[32] Faidherbe's heirs did not find the time ripe for half a century.

This pattern of two steps forward and one step back remained important up to 1905, and to some degree even after. The key factors were the commitment to expansion of governors, all of whom were military officers until 1883, their need for African collaborators and the pressure of an increasingly anti-slavery public opinion in France. There was no colonial ministry until 1894, only a department in the Navy Ministry. For a generation, slavery was rarely an issue, first because of the support of the Napoleonic regime for colonial governors, and then because the Franco-Prussian war of 1870–71 immobilized France. When the issue erupted again, it was because courts and prosecutors in Senegal depended not on the Navy Ministry but on the Ministry of Justice. In 1875, a new prosecutor, Darrigrand, began bringing charges of slave trading against *habitant*s, men who moved slaves into and out of St Louis buying and selling in violation of the law.[33] The governor, Brière de l'Isle, tried to influence Darrigrand, and unable to do so, tried to get him transferred.[34] The situation in France had changed. The media and public opinion were more developed and the government was, for the moment, less committed to colonial expansion. In addition, information about the situation in Senegal was fed to the Paris press, perhaps by Darrigrand, but certainly by a Protestant mission that protected runaway slaves. In 1880, Schoelcher, who had become a senator, gave an important speech in which he denounced the situation.[35] Under abolitionist pressure, after several years of governors trying to parry the pressures of public opinion, Governor René Servatius decreed that any slave making it to territories of direct administration could claim liberty papers.[36] This, however, was not what it seemed. Subsequent administrators tried to make it difficult for slaves to make it to areas where they could claim their freedom. This was a period when peanut exports were booming and slaves were being imported into Senegal from what is now Mali to produce those peanuts. It was also a period when Fulbe chiefs were fleeing Senegal with their slaves for fear of seeing those slaves liberated. As a result, in 1889, large parts of Senegal were converted into protectorates under treaties in which France committed itself to protecting traditional culture.[37] This meant protecting slavery. An increasing number of slaves were freed in the 1880s and 1890s, but never over several thousand a year.[38] The creation of protectorates effectively slowed the emancipation process.

Conquest of the Soudan

The situation in Senegal was ambiguous, with forward and backward moves alternating, but the conquest of interior areas involved a passionate embrace of slavery by the soldiers of the Third Republic. Support for the conquest of the African interior was strongest in the naval infantry, the marines, who had provided many of the governors of Senegal before 1883.[39] To carry out their goals, commanders needed soldiers and allies. The core of the army was the *tirailleurs sénégalais* (Senegalese riflemen), originally organized by Faidherbe. Faidherbe thought that by making military service attractive he could recruit free men, but very few enlisted. Military service in West Africa was primarily dependant on slave soldiers. Well before the conquest began, French officers were buying slaves and "freeing" them on condition of a 14-year military engagement.[40] From the first the French army had many African slave soldiers, but they quickly learned that they could rely on these soldiers. They were certainly more reliable than the French *disciplinaires*, sent out to Africa as a punishment.

Even with cheaper African soldiers, however, they never had enough men. France conquered the huge area of French West Africa with an army that never contained over 4,000 men and frequently had many fewer. They had supremacy in weapons. French field artillery could batter a hole in fortifications, but they then needed the men to charge through those holes. This depended on strategic alliances. Their ability to make strategic alliances was facilitated by the bitter religious wars of the previous half-century. Jihad largely displaced rulers who were not Muslim or lax Muslims and who were often persecuted orthodox Muslims. In almost every area controlled by one of the Muslim victors, the deposed had withdrawn, waiting for an opportunity to return to power. For all sides of the various conflicts, slaves were the ultimate prize. In French commercial reports from the savannah lands, slaves were by far the most valuable item of trade, often worth more than all other items of trade combined.[41]

These slaves were then the most important form of booty. Furthermore, a majority of the adults were women. When spoils were divided after a battle, French officers often took some of the prettiest. Many who have written about the motives of the French military in Africa have stressed the desire for military action and promotions. Reading some of the very limited accounts of life in the Soudan, I would suggest that a major motive was freedom from the sexual restraints of French Catholic society.[42] Some also went further and accumulated slaves as an investment. Most of the slaves, however, were distributed to allied chiefs, African agents and the soldiers. On the trail, the French generally travelled with what one missionary called their "battalion of women", who carried equipment, made camp, cooked and were sexual partners for the soldiers. There were also new chiefs. Archinard, the most important of the French generals, created kings. Mademba Sy was a Senegalese, who had been in charge of constructing the telegraph line to the Soudan.[43] Aguibou, one of the sons of a major jihad leader, Al Haj Umar Tal, was moved from Dinguiraye in Guinea to Bandiagara, east of the inner Niger delta. Each of these men used the transitional years of the colonial conquest to raid and build up a force of slaves to enable him to live a proper royal life.

The End of Legal Slavery

Then suddenly it was over. In 1898, the French captured Samori Ture, their most important military opponent, and seized the mighty fortress of Sikasso built by Tieba Traoré, another African leader. There were still resisters and rebels to deal with but, by and large, French West Africa was under their control. Though the soldiers were still in control of the Saharan areas, civilian rule was gradually imposed. In 1899, William Ponty, who had been a civilian aide to Archinard, was appointed Delegate-General for Haut Sénégal-Niger, the new name for the Soudan. Once out of the shadow of the soldiers, Ponty moved slowly but resolutely, being careful at first to not attack slavery itself. The Soudan went overnight from being a happy hunting ground for slaving officers to becoming the most anti-slavery French colony. Ponty started by distributing a speech by Albert Decrais, Minister of Colonies, calling for an end to the trade and making clear that the end of slavery was a French goal.[44] He then asked for the enforcement of some laws that had been ignored. Most importantly, slave caravans were to be stopped, their slaves placed in liberty villages and the slave traders were to be jailed for 15 days and fined 100 francs for every slave.[45] Several months later, he distributed a more radical circular arguing that France could no longer officially recognize the difference between slave and free:

> Today, we ask you, Messieurs, to be unrelenting in sending from your offices any person coming to claim an escaped slave and ask you henceforth in such affairs to treat all natives as "men". In the same order of ideas, we should attribute to those improperly called domestic slaves the rights which servants attached to a family have among us.[46]

It is doubtful that many administrators actually did as Ponty suggested, at least not right away. Most administrators were not ideologically opposed to slavery and even if they were, were reluctant to alienate the elites of the *cercles* (a French administrative district, especially an administrative subdivision in a French colony) they ruled. Many insisted that slaves should be freed only when they had been mistreated. In 1903 there were few cases involving slavery brought before the courts, and in many cercles, none at all. The largest number involved either enslavement or theft of a slave, the effort by a man to convince a slave woman to run away with him. This policy of distancing the French state from slavery did, however, within a few years become official policy. But an increasing number of slaves ran away. Some used forced labour levies to escape. Twelve of Aguibou's wives fled his harem.[47]

Ponty had clearly thought about the necessity of doing something about slavery. He was years ahead of most of his colleagues, who were either hostile to any action against slavery or afraid of the consequences. In 1902, Ernest Roume was appointed Governor-General. An official in the finance and colonial ministries, he had no African experience, but he seems to have had a clear programme for Republican reforms and the support of progressive governments in France. He was succeeded in 1908 by Ponty, who eventually died at his post in 1915. Both of them shared a commitment to Republican values and the development of education, administration and a modern system of justice, but they had very different backgrounds, Roume in the elite Ecole Polytechnique and in the corridors of power and Ponty in field administration. Both were also politically able and capable of tempering commitment with astute political caution.

It was during the Roume and Ponty years that France took action on slavery, as much because of a practical commitment to a free labour society as to an ideological opposition to slavery. They were briefly seconded in their efforts by Camille Guy, a liberal governor of Senegal.[48]

In January 1903, Victor Prom, an employee of a French commercial house, purchased a small girl upriver for Amadu Fall, a Senegalese friend, and sent her back to St Louis where Fall got liberty papers for her—as had been done for 45 years. Prom, who made many such purchases, was charged with slave-trading under the same 1831 law that Darrigrand had used successfully.[49] When the court acquitted him, Roume ordered an appeal to the Cour de Cassation, the French appeals court, which held that the law was applicable only to maritime trade. Roume, Guy and Colonial Minister Gaston Doumergue were startled, Roume because he suddenly found himself without a law that he could use in cases of the slave trade and Guy and Doumergue because a form of slave trade was suddenly legal within Senegal.[50] Furthermore, it soon became clear that the registers of those freed under the *tutelle* or wardship system Prom had used were poorly maintained and that there was little supervision. With instructions from Doumergue, Guy prepared a decree that ended the programme and returned the children to their parents, or if the parents were unknown, assigned them to a public institution or training school.[51]

The same month, November 1903, Roume took a tour of Senegal, which confronted him with the magnitude of the problem. Policies differed from cercle to cercle and, in some places, slaves were being openly traded. He asked that all laws dealing with slavery and the slave trade be enforced.[52] A new law code known as the *indigenat* was also proclaimed that month. The only provision dealing with slavery was an article that held that "Native justice will apply to any matter of local custom except where it is contrary to the principles of French civilization". If slavery was not adequately treated in the code itself, it was an important part of the letter Roume's Secretary General, Martial Merlin, sent out with the code. Jurisdiction in all cases of enslavement and slave trading was removed from the chief's court and assigned to administrators. The principles to be followed were clearly laid out. Administrators were to work towards the suppression of servile statuses. Administrators were told to be prudent, but their approach was clear:

Do not hesitate then in rejecting definitively any claim by would-be masters who call on rights over the person of other natives based on slavery, whoever they may be. You will warn others who may try to seize those they claim as slaves that such an act will expose them to legal action. To those who come to claim against their masters or simply to claim their liberty, you will explain if they are adults or at least in a condition to understand their situation, that they are free under the law and that French authority will insist on respect for their freedom.

Merlin also insisted that children be given to their parents or provided for if that was not possible, and he suppressed liberty papers because they were no longer necessary in a society where everyone was free.[53] It is probable that most administrators and even lieutenant governors chose prudence rather than follow Merlin's instructions. Some administrators still distributed freed children to local notables. In all of this, Merlin ably seconded Roume. He was later to become a conservative governor-general, but on the slavery issue, he seems to have felt that decisive action was important.

Roume also moved to develop legislation dealing with slavery. The first thing was to distribute a question to every administrator in French West Africa. There were 20 questions, which covered both slavery and the trade and requested suggestions on how to deal with the problem. The reports varied in quality.[54] Only one administrator, J.C. Brevié, actually interviewed slaves. Many administrators answered questions with a cavalier brevity; most minimized the harshness of slavery and many were very hostile to doing anything. "Suppress the slaves," Victor Allys in Tivouane wrote, "and the fields will remain uncultivated and the colony will be ruined."[55] As in other societies debating emancipation, there was a widespread belief that slaves would not work without coercion, and that the result of emancipation would be vagabondage and prostitution. The questionnaires are still the best source available for the study of slavery.[56]

At the same time, memos were passing back and forth between Roume, his Chief Prosecutor and other high officials. The problem was that the 1831 law applied only to the maritime trade and the 1848 law had only one sanction, loss of French citizenship, which was not a threat to either subjects or to some citizens from the coastal towns. Roume's superiors in Paris were also committed to doing something. Roume had been convinced by many of the discussions that slavery in Africa was benign and administrators should try to arbitrate conflicts.[57] The decree, which was presented to the President of the Republic and proclaimed on 12 December 1905, was clear. It did not actually abolish slavery, though many write about it as if it did. It abolished enslavement and all transactions between persons: sale, exchange, inheritance or gift. One reason for this misinterpretation of what the law actually said is that Roume presented it to the Government Council as if it had abolished slavery. "There is no longer", he claimed, "an institution of slavery in any form whatever."[58] The colonial government could no longer return slaves to their masters and administrators had to assure those who claimed their liberty that they already had it. Many administrators and lieutenant governors were not pleased. The Lieutenant Governor of the Ivory Coast explained to Roume and his administrators why the law could not be applied everywhere.[59] The Lieutenant Governor of Guinea simply recommended caution, but most administrators knew what that meant.[60] The Mauritanian circular insisted on an end to slave-raiding, but then listed reasons for prudence. The military men in Mauritania then simply ignored the decree.

The Exodus

At this point, slaves took the situation in their own hands. It all began around Banamba, the most important market for slaves in western Mali, and the centre of a closely cropped zone of slave-worked plantations. Founded only in the 1840s, Banamba was populated largely by slaves who remembered an earlier home. In the spring of 1905, when slaves were supposed to be preparing for the rains, they began to leave. By April, armed vigilantes were patrolling the paths and the slaves were travelling in groups. Ponty was on leave but in May, Roume sent in a company of *tirailleurs* (riflemen) and asked acting Lieutenant Governor Fawtier to arbitrate, and if necessary to arrest those who were fomenting trouble. Even though he was working on the anti-slavery decree, he was afraid to compromise public order. The Resident successfully arbitrated an agreement, which involved mostly confirming rights slaves thought had long been theirs, such as the right to two days to work their own lands.[61]

The following spring, the slaves started to move again. Masters seized their children and their property. This was their right under customary law, but the slaves were angry. This time, Ponty insisted that they be allowed to leave as long as they paid their taxes and indicated where they were heading. About 3,000 slaves left Banamba during the months of April and May. Most of them were heading to areas in the southern savannah. About 40 per cent went back to Wasulu, which had been intensively slaved by Samori's warriors. This was not, however, easy. For most, it was a walk of 30–35 days, with little food except what they could scavenge. The commandant in Bamako wrote that the "emaciation and misery of most of these unfortunates deprived for many days of sufficient nourishment, despoiled of their modest savings by shameless masters can only arouse the most profound pity".[62] Many stopped where they could find work and feed themselves, sometimes to continue after the harvest.

Slaves continued to leave Banamba the following year. As the files of slaves heading home passed through other areas and traders and soldiers spread the news, departures took place in one area after another. Often they went on for two or three years. Between 1906 and 1911 or 1912, there was a massive redistribution of population, perhaps over a million people, many more than were involved in France's 1848 abolition. Where masters tried to stop them, they often fled in large groups. To be sure, the same numbers did not leave in all areas. François Manchuelle and Andrew Clark have argued that few left eastern Senegal until later.[63] In desert areas under military rule, administrators refused to enforce new laws and slavery remained an issue into the 21st century. In spite of the industriousness of the former slaves, many administrators continued to fear the consequences. In Masina, the inner delta of the Niger, which was the breadbasket of the Soudan, the slaves were the cultivators. Their Fulbe masters devoted themselves to study, politics and pastoralism. From 1908–14, colonial administrators tried to negotiate a new contact relationship between masters and slaves based on the control of land and payment of rent.[64] The masters, however, continued to insist that they owned their slaves. In some areas, administrators turned a blind eye to masters' efforts at using force to keep slaves in place, but it was hard to totally stop the movement. Some slaves were killed, including several women returning to claim children in villages. Parallel to this, there were efforts to find and reclaim relatives. Notables could often use the French to arrange the return of lost relatives. Other groups sent people back to the slave village to bring out older people.

The interesting question is how they did it.[65] Some of the areas they returned to had been depopulated. Often, the communities they once lived in were no longer there. In other areas, small communities had difficulty absorbing the influx. Land had returned to bush and had to be cleared. They needed weapons to protect themselves against predators. They needed seed and tools. Many of the returning slaves did not make it all the way home, but found somewhere else where they could earn their livelihood. Even those who made it home found that they had to migrate to get money to pay the taxes the French insisted on and to buy the tools, guns and seeds they needed. They often went to Senegal to work the peanut fields. As early as 1903, there are reports that administrators no longer needed to use coercion to recruit porters.[66] French rule in Guinea was brutal but unlike central Africa, that brutality was not tied to the exploitation of rubber, which was produced by peasants and carried to market by ex-slave porters.[67] Some panned for gold. Some also got land from Muslim religious fraternities, particularly the Mourides of Senegal.[68] As in other areas where slaves were freed, their behaviour disproved the myth of the lazy slave. The one thing slaves knew how to do was to work. Their goal was to work for themselves and not for others. As Ponty recognized, the freed slaves became a reservoir of labour, a large part of the new working class.

Across West Africa, many liberty villages were set up to receive slaves fleeing France's enemies; many returning slaves used these liberty villages. It was possible to place women and children in the village while the male slaves tried to find earlier homes, and if that was not possible, places to settle. For most administrators, this was not a question of human rights. Former slavers rarely remained in liberty villages because they had to work for the French without pay. Slavery was ended for many, but forced labour was crucial to French rule until 1946.[69] Many slaves did not remember their homes and some had forgotten their clan names. It was often necessary to assign returnees arbitrarily to a clan. Some slave groups did not try to return home, but merely to move away from their masters and find land to work. With the famines of 1912 and 1913, the large-scale movements ended, though some took place in later years. When the tirailleurs returned from World War I, soldiers of slave origin often refused to return to subservient relationships, often leading kin to new settlements free of the control of former masters.[70] After World War II, there were again migrations in the desert-side areas of the Soudan.

Those Who Stayed

Massive as the exodus was, most slaves remained with or near their masters.[71] There had long been a distinction between those enslaved during their lifetime and the newly enslaved. Such distinctions existed in many slave societies, for example, distinctions in the Americas between *bozales*, newly arrived slaves seen as barbaric, and Creole slaves, who spoke the dominant language and participated in the master's culture. The vast majority of the slaves who remained were, to use the Mandinka term *woloso*, "born in the house". These *woloso* already worked for themselves in exchange for a payment to their masters. For all of these slaves, there was a complicated process of renegotiation. The masters no longer had the whip hand. The slaves could leave, though they were often kept in place by kinship links and ties of clientship. They no longer had another home. Sometimes they lacked the networks that facilitated migration but those who did leave were often innovative, seeking out new kinds of work.

Networks were important. People who migrated either to the cities or to Europe usually went to someone and often lived in dormitory-style residences in which those of slave ancestry often did menial work. Lotte Pelckmans describes how linkages between slaves and slave-owners in an isolated area in the bend of the Niger were reproduced in Bamako.[72] Though former slaves were more likely to seek education, those nobles who sought an education were better able to convert political linkages into good jobs, and as a result to maintain a social hegemony. Descendants of slaves found it useful to maintain links, even though the jobs and perks they received sometimes opened them up to personal abuse.

But masters also gave concessions. The amount of labour or the annual payment the freed slaves owed was gradually reduced in all areas. In many areas, it became a token payment. In most of 20th-century West Africa, there was a struggle for the control of the former slave population. In the beginning, it was for control of their labour, but with time, in most areas the labour of former slaves was no longer a major issue. Former slaves were farming for themselves and developing new skills but masters clung to social distinctions, sometimes at a cost. These social distinctions were important. So too was the control of the machinery of the state. In cash crop areas, chiefs had an interest in letting former slaves and descendants of slaves acquire land, but discriminated against them in other ways.

Almost all of the forced labour was done by former slaves, and in societies that had large populations of former slaves, only former slaves were recruited into the French army during World War I. Echenberg estimates that about three-fourth of the African forces during World War I were of slave origin.[73]

The key variable was the options that the freed slaves had. In the Senegalese peanut basin, a market economy was well developed by the 1880s. There is little discussion in the archives of mass departures, in part because slave holdings were widely dispersed, but not large. Oral informants suggest that a large number of slaves left their masters between 1905 and 1914. There was work available in the cities and on the railroad. In areas where land was freely available, former slaves could find land. This process increased after World War I, as slaves often cleared land outside their villages. They were still attached to the village for tax purposes but essentially farmed for themselves. One of my informants, Biraan Ture, moved out of his village in the 1920s, and as he cleared land and put it into cultivation, he gradually moved members of his family to the village.[74] When I interviewed him in 1975, he claimed to be 102 years old. His hamlet contained 40–50 people divided into four households. He was wealthy enough to make the pilgrimage to Mecca, selling seven cows to do so. He still had obligations. He was supposed to make a small payment called *assaka* to his master every year, and he had to "buy" his freedom under traditional law before making the pilgrimage. Slave descendants often earn more money than their masters because of their willingness to work hard and their eagerness to learn new skills. In Senegal, for example, former slaves from the Futa Jallon became charcoal makers. Elsewhere, they often became taxi drivers or mechanics.

Honour

In most areas, relations between former slaves, former masters and their dependents were masked by unwritten rules of social behaviour.[75] For instance, I was told that it is considered bad manners to confront descendants of slaves with the fact that you know their social status. In one case, the nephew of the village chief, who had attached himself to me, blurted out in the middle of an interview, "Who's your master?" The informant immediately clammed up. In another case, there was a rather able Peace Corps volunteer who assured me that there were no "slaves" in the village where he had lived for 18 months. In the middle of the interview, he was surprised when the elder I was interviewing explained to him that one entire section of the village is inhabited by descendants of slaves. Other cases, however, illustrated that there were subtle mechanisms at play. Before going to Mecca, Biraan Turé was expected to buy under traditional law the freedom he already exercised. The going rate was then about 18,000 francs CFA, then worth about US$70. By accident, I was interviewing Biraan's master and there was a contradiction between what he said and what Biraan had told me. When I pointed this out, the master retorted angrily that Biraan had come into his hut, plunked 18,000 francs on his table and said that he was going to Mecca. He was not supposed to do that; he was supposed to come deferentially and ask his "master" to set a price. The reason that my friend, the Peace Corps volunteer, did not know that there were "slaves" in the village was that he never became aware of difference between diverse kinds of deference, that is, between the young and the old, between wives and husbands, and towards people in authority. Of course, there are societies where abuse is common, slavery is still real and deference is visible.[76] Discrimination can also be situational. In Senegal in the 1970s, many slave descendents were elected to the boards of cooperatives.[77]

Stigma

Throughout West Africa, and even in the diaspora, people of slave descent are bound by taboos. Islam and marriage are the most important battlegrounds, though sometimes in ambiguous ways. People of slave descent cannot serve as imams or sit in the front of the mosque, and in many areas, it is inappropriate for the descendent of slaves to wear a starched white *boubou* (classic Senegalese robe worn by both men and men).[78] And yet, the response of freed slaves was always to seek validation through Islam, in particular, through the study of the Quran. Jeremy Berndt has written about slave clerics in central Mali who can preside over services for other slave descendants, but not if a free person is present.[79] Similarly, marriage is possible between a free man and a slave woman, but not between a male slave descendant and a free woman.

The difficult question is why the stigma persists. There are two components to this question. One is why descendents of slaves continue to operate within a social order that discriminates against them. The second is why the descendents of slave-owners cling to the status that owning slaves conferred on them. I had started out with a neo-Marxist approach that saw slavery largely in terms of labour and the ability of elites to extract profit from slave ownership, but masters all over cling to the status of slave masters even when it no longer provides economic benefits. Why? The answer is largely in terms of codes of honour that mark many societies in West Africa. Within these codes, the noble is seen as brave, generous and discreet. He or she is refined, speaks softly and does not speak openly of sexual matters. The slave is crude, loud and dependent.

People of slave descent are encouraged to behave in ways that confirm these stereotypes. Thus, they are expected to cook at rites of passage like weddings and naming societies, after which they can ask for and are given gifts. In fact, begging confirms the noble's image of his generosity but provides income for the slave descendant. Many nobles informed me that they gave more to their "slaves" than they received from them. I was sceptical of this until I realized that this was an important boundary-setting device. Dancing has also been an issue in Muslim areas because of its link to sexuality. Traditionally, slave women were sexually exploited, which somehow dishonoured the woman more than the man who used her. Slave women were also often expected to do erotic dances. While the dances done by young people are not more erotic than Western disco dancing, they are offensive to many strict Muslims. Many villages have banned dancing while others have limited it to people of slave and caste descent. Other people will gather and watch, but not participate. Once again, this sets a boundary. There are other, subtler, ways this distinction plays out. Thus, Paul Riesman writes that in the village he studied, Fulbe men liked to visit the attached slave village, enjoying the greater conversational licence the slave descendents had.[80]

Of course, slaves in most of West Africa have been able to walk away. Pelckmans and Amadou Sehou have written about slaves who seek manumission under traditional law.[81] Their doing so is criticized by two other groups of slave descendants, one who totally reject their own servility and the other who consider their servility God's will, and accept and internalize their own inferiority. At the same time, the extension of electoral democracy has made possible the organization of slave descendants in those countries where servility remains strongest. Timidria in Niger and SOS-Esclaves and El Hor in Mauritania have fought continuing discrimination against people of slave descent.[82] In Senegal, Endam Bilali has been organized in the socially conservative areas of the Senegal River. Eric Komlavi Hahonou has written about the Gando of northern Benin, who were once regarded as people who internalized their own inferiority but today are voting for candidates to public office from their own community.[83]

Conclusion

Paul Lovejoy and Jan Hogendorn have described the decline of slavery as a *Slow Death of Slavery*.[84] That is in essence what happened everywhere, but much slower in many areas and rarely finished, even today. Emancipation was virtually non-existent in the desert, though groups like the Haratin in Mauritania and the Bella in Mali and Niger were able to exploit differences between their nomadic and colonial masters.[85] Enslavement became more difficult though the warrior Bidan of Mauritania continued, for years, to kidnap Senegalese children and chiefs in isolated areas raided for slaves into the middle of the 20th century. There was no single moment when slavery ended. Slave raiding and slave trading disappeared in many areas and became isolated forms of criminal behaviour in others.

Emancipation took place as part of a global movement. People in Great Britain and other Western European countries became convinced that slavery was immoral and its perpetuation was not in their interest. Most colonial administrators did not share that belief. Many would have perpetuated slavery indefinitely, but the violence associated with slavery was dysfunctional for economic development and their own advancement was determined by colonial budgets determined in Europe, where anti-slavery ideology held sway. These changes made it possible for slaves to take the initiative. Changes in colonial policy designed in the metropole created the opportunity but slaves took advantage of that opportunity, both in fleeing servile relationships and in pushing the boundaries of their exploitation. After the departure of those who remembered another home, many struggled to redefine their relationship with their masters. These struggles played out in different ways in different areas but, overall, it was slaves who pushed the processes of change and slave descendants who are pushing it today.

Notes

1. James Searing, *West African Slavery and Atlantic Commerce: The Senegal River Valley, 1700–1860* (Cambridge: Cambridge University Press, 1998). See also Boubacar Barry, *Senegambia and the Atlantic Slave Trade*, tr. Ayei Kwei Armah (Cambridge: Cambridge University Press, 1998).

2. Much of this is covered in Martin A. Klein, *Slavery and Colonial Rule in French West Africa* (Cambridge: Cambridge University Press, 1998). See also Trevor Getz, *Slavery and Reform in West Africa: Toward Emancipation in Nineteenth Century Senegal and the Gold Coast* (Athens, OH: Ohio University Press, 2004). On the events of 1848 in Senegal, see Mbaye Gueye, "La fin de l'esclavage à St. Louis et Gorée en 1848" [The End of Slavery in St. Louis and Gorée in 1848], *Bulletin de l'Institut Français d'Afrique Noire* 28 (1966): 637–67; Roger Pasquier, "A Propos de l'émancipation des esclaves au Sénégal en 1848" [Concerning the Emancipation of Slaves in Senegal in 1848], *Revue Française de l'Histoire d'Outre-Mer* 54 (1967): 188–208.

3. Martin A. Klein and Paul Lovejoy, "Slavery in West Africa", in *The Uncommon Market: Essays in the Atlantic History of the Slave Trade*, ed. Jan Hogendorn and Henry Gemery (New York: Academic Press, 1980); Patrick Manning, *Slavery and African Life: Occidental, Oriental and African Slave Trades* (Cambridge: Cambridge University Press, 1990). The concept of slave society comes from Moses Finley and is similar to the Marxist concept of a slave mode of production. Moses Finley, "Slavery", *International Encyclopedia of the Social Sciences* (New York: Macmillan, 1968), pp. 307–13.

4. Lamine Sanneh, "Slavery, Islam and the Jakhanke People of West Africa", *Africa* 46 (1976): 80–97 and "The Origins of Clericalism in West African Islam", *Journal of African History* 17 (1976): 17–49.

5. David Eltis, *Economic Growth and the Ending of the Transatlantic Slave Trade* (New York: Oxford University Press, 1987). Senegambia did not participate in this trade after 1831.

6. Elizabeth Savage, ed., *The Human Commodity: Perspectives on the Trans-Saharan Slave Trade* (London: Frank Cass, 1992).

7. Marie Rodet, *Les migrantes ignorées du Haut-Sénégal (1900–1946)* [Forgotten Migrants of Upper Senegal (1900–1946)] (Paris: Éditions Karthala, 2009); Martin A. Klein, "La traite transatlantique des esclaves et le développement de l'esclavage en Afrique occidentale" [The Transatlantic Slave Trade and the Development of Slavery in West Africa], in *Esclavage et Dépendances Serviles: Histoire comparé* [Slavery and Servile Outbuildings: History Compared], ed. Myriam Cottias et al. (Paris: Harmattan, 2006), pp. 35–54; Claire Robertson and Martin A.

Klein, ed., *Women and Slavery in Africa* (Madison, WI: University of Wisconsin Press, 1883).

8. Martin A. Klein, "Sex, Power and Family Life in the Harem", in *Women and Slavery*, vol. 1, *Africa, the Indian Ocean World and the Medieval North Atlantic*, ed. Gwyn Campbell et al. (Athens, OH: Ohio University Press, 2007), pp. 63–82.

9. On the tensions involved in slave marriage, see Richard Roberts, *Litigants and Households: African Disputes and Colonial Courts in the French Soudan, 1895–1912* (Portsmouth, NH: Heinemann, 2005); Rodet, *Les migrantes ignorées*.

10. Martin A. Klein, "Slavery in the Cities of the Slave Trade", in *Looking for the Tracks*, ed. Alice Bellagamba et al. (Trenton, NJ: African World Press, forthcoming); Michael Marcson, "European–African Interaction in the Precolonial Period: Saint Louis, Senegal, 1758–1854", unpublished PhD dissertation (Princeton, NJ: Princeton University, 1976); Amanda Sackur, "The Development of Creole Society and Culture in Saint Louis and Gorée", unpublished PhD dissertation (London: University of London, 1999); Robin Law, *Ouidah: The Social History of a West African Slaving Port, 1727–1892* (Athens, OH: Ohio University Press, 2005); Kristin Mann, *Slavery and the Birth of an African City: Lagos, 1760–1900* (Bloomington, IN: Indiana University Press, 2007). On slaves in the cities, see Jean-Louis Boutillier, "Les Trois Esclaves de Bouna" [The Three Slaves of Bouna], in *L'Esclavage en Afrique précoloniale* [Slavery in Precolonial Africa], ed. Claude Meillassoux (Paris: Maspero, 1968), pp. 252–80; Edmond Bernus, "Kong et sa région" [Kong and its Region], *Etudes eburnéennes* 8 (1960): 239–324.

11. George Brooks, "The Signares of St. Louis and Gorée: Women Entrepreneurs in Eighteenth Century Senegal", in *Women in Africa*, ed. Nancy Hafkin and Edna Bay (Stanford, CA: Stanford University Press, 1976), pp. 19–44.

12. See Chapter 2 by Sue Peabody in this volume. On the difference between the British and French anti-slavery movements, see Seymour Drescher, *Capitalism and Antislavery: British Mobilization in Comparative Perspective* (London: Macmillan, 1986).

13. This argument has been made primarily for Great Britain but it can be extended to Continental Europe. See Howard Temperley, "Capitalism, Slavery and Ideology", *Past and Present* 75 (1977): 94–118; David Brion Davis, *Slavery and Human Progress* (Oxford and New York: Oxford University Press, 1984), pp. 107–16. See also Nelly Schmidt, *Abolitionnistes de l'esclavage et réformateurs des colonies, 1820–1851: Analyse et documents* [Abolitionists of Slavery and Reformers of the Colonies, 1820–1851: Analysis of Documents] (Paris: Éditions Karthala, 2000), pp. 267–81.

14. Lawrence C. Jennings, *French Anti-Slavery: The Movement for the Abolition of Slavery in France, 1802–1848* (Cambridge and New York: Cambridge University Press, 2000), p. 187.

15. For a discussion of the ideological imperatives of the early 20th-century regimes, see Alice Conklin, *A Mission to Civilize: The Republican Idea of Empire in France and West Africa, 1895–1930* (Stanford, CA: Stanford University Press, 1997).

16. On abolition in France, see Nelly Schmidt, *Victor Schoelcher et l'abolition de l'esclavage* [Victor Schoelcher and the Abolition of Slavery] (Paris: Fayard, 1994); Marcel Dorigny, ed., *Les Abolitions de l'esclavage de L.F. Sonthonax à V. Schoelcher, actes du colloque international tenu à l'Université de Paris VIII les 3, 4 et 5 février 1994* [Slavery Abolitions from L.F. Sonthonax to V. Schoelcher, conference proceedings, University of Paris, 3, 4 and 5 February 1994] (Paris: Presse Universitaire de Vincennes, 1998). For more citations on French abolition, see Chapter 2 by Sue Peabody in this volume.

17. Martin A. Klein, "Slaves, Gum, and Peanuts: Adaptation to the End of the Slave Trade in Senegal, 1817–1848", *William and Mary Quarterly* 66 (2009): 894–913.

18. Jennings, *French Anti-Slavery*, p. 32. On further measures in the 1840s, see Chapter 2 by Sue Peabody in this volume.

19. Schmidt, *Schoelcher*.

20. Mbaye Guèye, "La fin de l'esclavage"; Roger Pasquier, "A propos de l'émancipation des esclaves", pp. 188–208.

21. Mohammed Mbodj, "The Abolition of Slavery in Senegal, 1820–1890: Crisis or the Rise of a New Entrepreneurial Class?" in *Breaking the Chains: Slavery, Bondage and Emancipation in Modern Africa and Asia*, ed. Martin A. Klein (Madison, WI: University of Wisconsin Press, 1993).

22. Baudin to misc. rulers, 15 Feb. 1848, Archives de la République du Sénégal (ARS), 3B 64, cited in Mamadou Diouf, *Le Kajoor au XIXe siècle: Pouvoir ceddo et conquête coloniale* [Kajoor in the 19th Century: Ceddo Power and Colonial Conquest] (Paris: Éditions Karthala, 1990), p. 152.

23. Gov. Baudin to Min., 22 Aug. 1848, Archives Nationales, Section Outre-Mer (ANSOM), Sénégal XIV 15a.

24. Min. to Commissaire de la République, 7 May 1848, ARS, K 8.

25. Report of 18 Apr. 1849, ANSOM, Sénégal XIV 15a.

26. Gov. Baudin to Min., 2 Feb. 1849, ANSOM, Sénégal XIV 15a.

27. Gov. to Dir. Des Colonies, 26 Dec. 1848 and 12 Feb. 1849, ANSOM, Sénégal XIV 15a.

28. Leland C. Barrows, "The Merchants and General Faidherbe. Aspects of French Expansion in Senegal in 1950's", *Revue Française d'histoire*

d'outre-mer 61 (1974) and "Louis Léon Cesar Faidherbe (1818–1889)", in *African Proconsuls: European Governors in Africa*, ed. Peter Duignan and L.H. Gann (Stanford: Hoover Institution, 1978), pp. 51–79.

29. Minutes of Conseil d'administration meeting of 10 Apr. 1855 and Gov. to Min., 25 Apr. 1855, ANSOM, Sénégal XIVb. See also François Renault, *L'abolition de l'esclavage au Sénégal: l'atitude de l'administration française* [Abolition of Slavery in Senegal: The Attitude of the French Administration] (Paris: Société Française de l'Histoire d'Outre-Mer, 1972), pp. 83–7.

30. Decree of 18 Oct. 1855, ARS, K 11.

31. Decree of 14 Nov. 1857, ARS, K 11.

32. Minutes of Conseil d'Administration, 5 Dec. 1857, ANSOM Sénégal, 15b.

33. Darrigrand to Gov., 28 May 1875, ANSOM, Sénégal XIV 6. See also Klein, *Slavery and Colonial Rule*, pp. 60–1.

34. Gov. to Min., 27 Aug. 1878 and 1 Feb. 1879, APRS, K 11.

35. *Journal Officiel de la République Française*, 2 Mar. 1880.

36. Circular to Commandants du Cercle, 8 Jan. 1884, ARS, K12.

37. Klein, *Slavery and Colonal Rule*, pp. 66–7.

38. Ibid., pp. 71–4.

39. A.S. Kanya-Forstner, *The Conquest of the Western Sudan: A Study in French Military Imperialism* (Cambridge: Cambridge University Press, 1969).

40. Myron Echenberg, *Colonial Conscripts: The Tirailleurs Sénégalais in French West Africa, 1857–1960* (Portsmouth, NH: Heinemann, 1991), Chapter 2; Martin A. Klein, "Slaves and Soldiers in the Western Soudan and French West Africa", *Canadian Journal of African Studies* 45 (2011): 565–87.

41. Klein, *Slavery and Colonial Rule*, Chapter 5.

42. Ibid., pp. 83–4.

43. Richard Roberts, "The Case of Faama Mademba Sy and the Ambiguities of Legal Jurisdiction in Early Colonial French Soudan", in *Law in Colonial Africa*, ed. Kristin Mann and Richard Roberts (Portsmouth, NH: Heinemann, 1991), pp. 185–201.

44. Minister of Colonies Albert Décrais, 6 Jan. 1900, Archives Nationales du Mali (ANM), A 20.

45. Del. Gen. Ponty to all administrators, Haut Sénégal Niger, Circular of 18 Oct. 1900, ARS K 18. See also his letter to Gov. Gen., 15 Sept. 1900, ARS K15.

46. Del. Gen. Ponty, Circular of 1 Feb. 1901, ANM A 20.

47. Monthly reports, May to Sept. 1903, Bandiagara. ANM, 1 E 23. Similarly, when Moussa Molo decided to move from the Casamance into

the Gambia, the French claimed that many of his "wives" were slaves. When the British asked them if they wanted to accompany him, about 100 refused (Gov. Gambia to Colonial Office, 5 Oct. 1903. Public Record Office, CO 8/170). Alice Bellagamba, "Mussa Molo Baldeh of Fuladu: Memories of a Senegambian Slave Descendant and Slaver", paper presented at Annual Conference of African Studies Association, Baltimore, 21–24 Nov. 2013; Abderrahmane Ngaidé, *L'esclave, le colon et le marabout. Le royaume peul du Fuladu de 1867 à 1936* [The Slave, the Colonizer and the Marabout: The Kingdom of the Peul Fuladu, 1867–1936] (Paris: Harmattan, 2012).

48. On Roume and Ponty, see Alice Conklin, *A Mission to Civilize: The Republican Idea of Empire in France and West Africa, 1895–1930* (Stanford, CA: Stanford University Press, 1997), Chapters 2–4.

49. E. Joucla, "L'esclavage au Sénégal et au Soudan, état de la question en 1905" [Slavery in Senegal and the Soudan, State of the Question in 1905], *Bulletin de la Société des anciens élèves de l'école colonial* 19 (1905): 1–13.

50. Min. G. Doumergue to Gov. Gen. 31 Oct. 1903, ARS K 27; Lt. Gov. C. Guy to Gov. Gen. 22 Nov. 1903, ARS K 27 #28.

51. Arrêté of 24 Nov. 1903, ARS K 27.

52. Gov. Gen. Roume to Sec. Gen., 3 Dec. 1903, ARS, K 27.

53. Circular of 10 Dec. 1903, ANSOM Sénégal XIV 28 or ARS K 16/14. Part of it is reprinted in François Renault, *L'abolition de l'esclavage*, p. 100.

54. See Merlin's harsh assessment in the summary report he prepared for Roume. Report to Gov. Gen., ARS K 16. See also Jean-Louis Boutillier, "Les Trois Esclaves de Bouna".

55. Report on Slavery, Tivouane, 29 Jan. 1904, ARS K 18.

56. The vast majority of the questionnaires and the correspondence about them are available in ARS, K16 and K 18 to 22.

57. There was extensive correspondence between senior officials in Dakar and with Paris. See Procureur-Général to Gov. Gen., 3 Dec. 1903, ARS, K16. See also memos in ARS, K 24.

58. The speech was published in the *Journal Officiel de l'Afrique Occidentale Française* and in the *Bulletin du Comité de l'Afrique Française*, Jan. 1906, p. 15.

59. Lt. Gov. Ivory Coast to Gov. Gen, 16 Mar. 1906 and his circular of 10 Mar. 1906, ARS K 24.

60. Circular of 17 Mar. 1906, ANG, 2 A 3.

61. On the treatment of slaves in the Maraka cities, see J.C. Brevié, "Report on Slavery, Bamako", ARS K 19, describing the slaves as poorly fed, poorly clothed and mistreated. See Martin A. Klein and Richard

Roberts, "The Banamba Exodus of 1905 and the Decline of Slavery in the Western Sudan", *Journal of African History* 21 (1980): 375–94; Klein, *Slavery and Colonial Rule*, Chapter 10.

62. Political report, Bamako, May 1906, ANM 1 E 19.

63. François Manchelle, "Emancipation and Labor Migration in West Africa: The Case of the Soninke", *Journal of Africa History* 30 (1989): 89–106; *Willing Migrants* (Athens, OH: Ohio University Press, 1997); Andrew Clark, "Slavery and its Demise in the Upper Senegal Valley, 1890–1920", *Slavery and Abolition* 15 (1994): 51–71.

64. Klein, *Slavery and Colonial Rule*, pp. 179–84.

65. Ibid., Chapter 12.

66. Annual Report, Bougouni, 1903, 29 Feb. 1904, ANM, 1 E 23; Annual Report, Bamako, 1905, 2 Feb. 1906, ANM, 1 E 19.

67. See various political reports from Upper Guinea in Archives Nationales de la Guinée, 7 G 63 and Lt. Gov. Guinea to Gov. Gen., 30 Apr. 1910, ANG, 2 B 53.

68. There is extensive literature on the Mourides. See, especially, Donal Cruise O'Brien, *The Mourides of Senegal* (London: Oxford University Press, 1971); Jean Copans, *Les Marabouts de l'Arachide. La Confrérie mouride et les Paysans du Sénégal* [The Marabouts of the Peanut. The Mouride Confraternity and the Peasants of Senegal] (Paris: Harmattan, 1988); Cheikh Anta Babou, *Fighting the Greater Jihad: Amadu Bamba and the Founding of the Muridiyya of Senegal, 1853–1913* (Athens, OH: Ohio University Press, 2007).

69. Babacar Fall, *Le travail force en Afrique occidentale française (1900–1946)* [Forced Labor in French West Africa (1900–1946)] (Paris: Éditions Karthala, 1993).

70. Klein, *Slavery and Colonial Rule*, pp. 216–9.

71. Ibid., pp. 205–10.

72. Lotte Pelckmans, *Travelling Hierarchies: Moving In and Out of Slave Status in a Central Malian Fulbe Network* (Leiden: African Studies Center, 2011); Mirjam De Bruijn and Lotte Pelckmans, "Facing Dilemmas: Former Fulbe Slaves in Modern Mali", *Canadian Journal of African Studies* 39 (2005): 69–96.

73. Echenberg, *Colonial Conscripts*. On the legacy of military service for soldiers of slave descent, see Gregory Mann, *Native Sons: West African Veterans and France in the 20th Century* (Durham, NC: Duke University Press, 2006).

74. Martin A. Klein, "'He Who is Without Family will be the Subject of Many Exactions': A Case from Senegal", in *African Voices on Slavery and the Slave Trade*, ed. Alice Bellagamba et al. (Cambridge and New York: Cambridge University Press, 2013), pp. 65–70.

75. Martin A. Klein, "The Concept of Honour and the Persistence of Servitude in the Western Soudan", *Cahiers d'Études Africaines* 45 (2005): 831–52.

76. Benedetta Rossi, "Slavery and Migration: Social and Physical Mobility in Ader", in *Reconfiguring Slavery: West African Trajectories*, ed. Benedetta Rossi (Liverpool: Liverpool University Press, 2009) and "Without History? Interrogating Slave Memories in Ader (Niger)", in *African Voices on Slavery and the Slave Trade*, ed. Alice Bellagamba, Sandra Greene and Martin A. Klein (Cambridge and New York: Cambridge University Press, 2013), pp. 536–54.

77. On the way the democratic electoral process has made possible political action by slave descendants, see Eric Komlavi Hahonou, "The Struggle for Political Emancipation of Slave Descendants in Contemporary Borgou, Northern Benin", in *Bitter Legacy: African Slavery Past and Present*, ed. Alice Bellagamba et al. (Princeton, NJ: Markus Wiener, 2013), pp. 29–56. Hahonou, with Camilla Strandbjerg, has also produced an excellent ethnographic film on the Gando of Northern Benin: *Yesterday's Slaves: Democracy and Ethnicity in Benin* (2011).

78. Roger Botte, "Stigmates sociaux et discriminations religeuses: l'ancienne classe servile au Futa Jaloo" [Social Stigmas and Religious Discrimination: The Former Servile Class in Futa Jaloo], *Cahiers d'études africaines* 34 (1994): 109–36.

79. Jeremy Berndt, "Speaking as Scholars: The First Generation of Slave Moodibaabe in Gimbala, Central Mali", paper presented at Conference on Finding the African Voice, Bellagio, Italy, September 2007; Jeremy Berndt, "Closer than Your Jugular Vein: Muslim Intellectuals in a Malian Village, 1900 to the 1960s", unpublished PhD dissertation (St Evanston, IL: Northwestern University, 2008).

80. Paul Riesman, *First Find Your Child a Good Mother: The Construction of Self in Two African Communities* (New Brunswick, NJ: Rutgers University Press, 1992).

81. Lotte Pelckmans, "To Cut the Rope from One's Neck? Manumission Documents of Slave Descendants from Central Malian Fulbe Society", in *Bitter Legacy*, ed. Bellagamba et al., pp. 67–86; Amadou Sehou, "Some Facets of Slavery in the *Lamidats* of Adamawa in North Cameroon in the Nineteenth and Twentieth Centuries", in *Bitter Legacy*, ed. Bellagamba et al., pp. 182–90.

82. Eric Komlavi Hahonou and Lotte Pelckmans, "West African Anti-Slavery Movements: Citizenship Struggles and the Legacies of Slavery", *Vienna Journal of African Studies, Stichprobe* 20 (2011): 141–62.

83. Eric Komlavi Hahonou, "Slavery and Politics: Stigma, Decentralisation and Political Representation in Niger and Benin", in *Reconfiguring*

Slavery, ed. Benedetta Rossi, pp. 152–81; Eric Komlavi Hahonou, "The Struggle for Political Emancipation of Slave Descendants in Contemporary Borgu, Northern Benin", in *Bitter Legacy*, ed. Bellagamba et al., pp. 29–56. Forty years earlier, the Gando were seen as people who accepted their servility. See Bernd Baldus, "Responses to Dependency in a Servile Group", in *Slavery in Africa: Historical and Anthropological Perspectives*, ed. Suzanne Miers and Igor Kopytoff (Madison, WI: University of Wisconsin Press, 1977), pp. 435–58.

84. Paul Lovejoy and Jan Hogendorn, *Slow Death for Slavery: The Course of Abolition in Northern Nigeria 1897–1936* (Cambridge: Cambridge University Press, 1993).

85. Martin A. Klein, "Slavery and French Rule in the Sahara", in *Slavery and Colonial Rule in Africa*, ed. Suzanne Miers and Martin A. Klein (London: Frank Cass, 1999).

CHAPTER 10

The Abolition of Serfdom in Russia

Alessandro Stanziani

Historiography

Most discussions of Russian serfdom have focused on the origins of this institution (was the state[1] responsible for it or the land-owners?[2]) and on the question of its economic efficiency,[3] rather than on the interplay between the two overlapping aspects at the core of serfdom: a particular legal regime and specific economic relationships. There have been some remarkable exceptions, however, notably the contributions made by Michael Confino, Steven Hoch, Elise Kimerling Wirtschafter, Edgar Melton and David Moon.[4]

In turn, debates on the abolition of Russian serfdom were long imprisoned by teleological approaches to history: first Russian Marxist, then Soviet historiography sought confirmation of the "laws of capitalism" and hence saw the abolition of serfdom in 1861 as the passage from feudalism to capitalism.[5] Non-Marxist Western historiography, on the contrary, stressed the economic and political limitations of Russia after 1861. The limits of the reforms were thus identified with the poverty of the peasantry, slow development of the Russian economy and tensions between new market dynamics and persistent legal and political forms of exclusion.[6]

Since the mid-1980s, these views have been strongly challenged and a more positive image of the reforms of 1861 has emerged; post-Soviet Russian scholars and Western specialists have underlined the positive demographic and economic performance of Russia between 1861 and 1914 as well as the gradual evolution of Russian institutions towards a more liberal architecture.[7] In this new view, World War I and not limited reforms became the main cause of the revolution. Without the war, Russia would have followed a "normal" path and been fully integrated into the Western world.

In sum we find, on the one hand, those who stress the continuities between pre-reform and post-abolition Russia and on the other, those who emphasize the important changes introduced by the Emancipation Act of 1861. Only a few authors have tried to place the reforms within a longer process comprising several previous partial emancipation acts and several drafts of a general abolition between 1801 and 1859, accompanied by the long-term evolution of Russian society and economy between the mid-17th century and World War I.[8] This approach, therefore, puts the accent on structural factors and *longue durée* instead of single events such as the Crimean War to explain the abolition of serfdom. Alfred Rieber attributed a prominent role to the Crimean War, arguing that the defeat forced the army to reform its technique and forms of recruitment; then, as soldiers were mostly inexperienced and unmotivated peasants, the military reforms led to a wider reform of the whole social order.[9]

Without denying the impact of war, other authors such as Terence Emmons, Daniel Field and William Bruce Lincoln have stressed the role of political tensions between the state and the nobility and between small and large estate owners, as well as the Decembrists and other Westernizing thinkers and their impact on Russia.[10] According to this interpretation, political and intellectual debates rather than economic interests were behind the abolition of serfdom. These authors sought to challenge the conventional Marxist approach, which insisted on the primary role of economic structure underpinning politics, ideas and "superstructure". In their view, even if serfdom was not efficient,[11] the ultimate force underlying its abolition was not economic but political and came from above (the tsar and some enlightened nobles).[12]

In this article, we would like to suggest somewhat different explanations that partly complement the preceding ones. In particular, as suggested by a few other scholars and our own previous works,[13] this article will argue, first, that the abolition of 1861 must be viewed as part of a long-term process of reform starting at least in the 18th century and completed on the eve of World War I with Stolypin's reforms (1906–11). Second, though this process was mainly directed from above, it also benefited from contributions from below, in particular the participation of peasants and nobles in judicial activity in defence of their legal rights and their involvement in market activity, which was much greater than is usually acknowledged. Third, the impact of the abolition of 1861 can be better understood if we take into consideration the fact that, prior to that date, serfdom was not fading away nor, on the whole, was it unproductive or inefficient. A satisfactory rate of growth was recorded in 18th- and early 19th-century Russia and it increased after 1861.

These issues suggest two broader implications: on the one hand, the revisited history of serfdom, its abolition and aftermath confirms what many other historical experiences had already proved,[14] namely, that coercion and capitalism are compatible. On the other hand, the Russian case also shows that economic growth and capitalism can occur despite the lack of democracy.[15]

The Origins of Abolition: Economic Dynamics in 18th–19th-century Russia

Let us begin with the economic argument: was serfdom opposed to capitalism? Was it in crisis before 1861?

We know that landlords could demand either quit-rent or labour services (corvées) from peasants. Most Western, Russian and Soviet historiography has argued that quit-rent encouraged trade and economic growth, whereas labour service restricted both.[16] However, others maintain that trade and economic growth could also take place under a system of corvée labour or even slavery, in the strict sense.[17] Indeed, in 18th-century Russia, increasing agricultural prices (rising by a factor of two and a half) made service labour more profitable than quit-rent.[18] Grain exports rose and, as Boris Mironov has shown, Russian markets became more and more integrated into the international and European markets. However, the growth of exports did not take place at the expense of local and national markets; by 1760 the demand for grain in the heartland pushed prices up.[19] Russian local markets were therefore increasingly integrated into the national market during the second half of the 18th century.[20] Peasant activity in rural markets exceeded that of merchants and small urban traders.[21] Thus, contrary to traditional arguments, trade in estate production increased with *barshchina* (corvées), which was compatible not only with exports and long-distance trade, but also with the rise of local and national markets.

This trend continued during the first half of the 19th century. This period has usually been described as the deepening "crisis of serfdom" in terms of income growth, demographic trends and social unrest. However, in the last two decades, these views have been seriously challenged, and historians have revised upwards the rate of growth in agriculture and industry as well as overall economic activity.[22] Recent analyses sought to take into account the underestimation of birth rates in 18th- and 19th-century censuses as well as the annexation of new territories and the resettlement (legal and illegal) of the peasantry. Once these biases were corrected, the natural rate of population growth proved to be considerable: on peasant estates, it was about 0.70 per cent between 1678 and 1719, 0.62 per cent between 1719 and 1744, 0.97 per cent between 1744 and 1762, and 0.96 per cent over the next 20 years. It fell to 0.60 per cent between 1782 and 1795, rose again to 0.86 per cent between 1795 and 1811 but collapsed during the Napoleonic Wars to −0.42 per cent. During the first half of the 19th century, the natural rate of growth of Russia's peasant population increased again to 0.94 per cent in 1815–33, 0.59 per cent between 1833 and 1850, and 0.54 per cent between 1850 and 1857.[23] Certainly, the high birth rate corresponded to an equally high rate of death, particularly among children. This trend has usually been considered as evidence of the "backwardness" of Russia and its poverty. However, in recent years, this view has been seriously called into question: high child mortality actually had less to do with famine than with diseases resulting from lack of hygiene (particularly with regard to water), epidemics and wars.[24] In the decades before the abolition of serfdom, the population in some areas increased mainly because the rate of mortality dropped and children's exposure to disease also fell.[25] Both reflect increasing well-being and better hygienic practices.

These trends occurred at a moment when noble estates merged; the number of small estates declined while large properties became the rule, to such an extent that, in 1857, noble estates with less than 21 peasants accounted for barely 3.2 per cent of all estates; those with between 21 and 100 peasants made up 15.9 per cent, and the great majority of estates had between 100 and 500 peasants (37.2 per cent), 500 and 1,000 peasants (14.9 per cent), or even more than 1,000 peasants (28.7 per cent).[26] This process was linked to the increasing indebtedness of the estate owners and the limited capital markets available to them. The growing institutional pressure of a tsarist state favouring peasant emancipation (which we will discuss later) and the development of merchants also contributed to the concentration of estates.

Regional specialization progressed: central and other industrial and proto-industrial areas specialized in manufacturing,[27] while in rural areas of the Central Black Earth Region, the Volga and the steppe, the surface area of cultivated land expanded in the territory as a whole and inside the main estates.[28] This process had a profound influence on social relations. Contrary to the practices in the previous period and despite legal prohibitions, noble landlords now often rented peasants and craftsmen to non-noble merchants and manufacturers.[29] Social differentiation between peasants was more pronounced in rural and proto-industrial areas close to industrial districts, but they generally benefited from higher per capita income than those in agricultural regions. Their diversified economies provided protection against both crop failure and market downturns.

Now if we look at the statistics available since the first half of the 19th century, even if the average value of production seems lower than those on the large estates, the overall picture is not as dark as earlier commentators have argued. First, because the statistics underestimate peasant and landlord production: based upon interviews with producers and indirect evidence, the figures suffered from the producers' incentive to hide a portion of their production and income for fiscal reasons.[30] Statisticians were concerned with the "poverty of the peasantry" and exaggerated losses and crises in order to criticize autocracy and advocate social policies in support of the peasantry.[31] Even if the collected data is not corrected (some considered the underestimation to be about 20 per cent), the final picture still shows increasing productivity, well-being and commercialization from the 18th century onwards. Between 1718 and 1788, Russian aggregate national income increased fivefold, raising per capita income by 85 per cent. After 1788, the annexation of rich southern provinces further intensified this growth.[32]

Even the most pessimistic recent analyses show that, while Russia's main economic indicators were persistently below those of the main Western European countries, the gap between them was not significant and did not widen until collectivization. Prior to that date, it remained constant, and even decreased during certain periods in terms of yields and commercialization, for example in the second half of the 19th century.[33]

Other, more optimistic interpretations conclude that, by 1788, the average Russian was as rich as his English equivalent and only 15 per cent poorer than the average Frenchman, who at that time enjoyed the peak of his fortunes in the 18th century. During the Revolutionary and Napoleonic Wars, moreover, the Russian maintained his position, surpassing the Frenchman and rising with the Briton to the very top international level.[34] This means that contrary to the conventional images of historiography, Russian economic growth between the mid-18th century and the abolition of serfdom was far from negligible.

In short, landlords and the demesne economy did not correspond to the ideal type of a "feudal economy"; they were not devoted to unproductive tasks or supported monopolistic and parasitic attitudes, but instead sought to exploit imperfect competition to increase their profits. The peasant economy under serfdom corresponded neither to the Chayanovian model of a peasant willing to satisfy his family's needs and entering the market only when forced to do so, nor to the Kula model of peasants pushed to produce by the landlord, who took the entire production and sold it on the market. Peasants were already integrated into market activity and proto-industry was not necessarily residual (that is, an activity engaged in only after a period of time had elapsed and opportunities in agriculture had been fully exploited). "Anti-economic" cultural values have been used to oppose imaginary peasantries to proletarians or landlords to capitalists. In reality, Russian landlords were interested in profits, and peasants were integrated into markets to various degrees. That they did not transform in accordance with some Western model does not mean that they were backward, but simply that the historical transformation of markets and societies could take different forms. In short, there is no evidence that serfdom was in crisis at the moment of its abolition; thus economic variables can explain only a small part of the Emancipation Act. In order to understand it fully, we must turn to the social and political forces.

Institutional Evolution

It has often been said that Russian reforms were mostly "from above", that is, conceived and implemented by the state. Indeed they were, but we should be more cautious about the meaning of this process. From a strictly political and legal point of view, by definition, all abolition of un-free labour has been from above, with the exception of the Saint-Domingue (Haiti) revolution. Yet it is also true that the participation of civil society in this process was much more substantial in Britain than in France.[35] From this standpoint, the role of civil society in Russia cannot be compared to that of Britain: there were no private circles and political movements. Discussions of serfdom took place within intellectual circles—the Academy of Science, the Imperial Society of Economics—or in more or less restricted if not secret governmental commissions.

The very notions of "above" and "below" and civil society require close examination. We cannot enter into a general discussion of these terms here, but can offer more details on who concretely supported emancipation in Russia and why. Indeed, reforms of serfdom were a mix of cautious administrative action from above and some limited possibilities left to estate owners and the peasants themselves to defend their rights from below. Political stability, economic efficiency, paternalistic criticism of serfdom, and the concrete economic interests of the state and part of the nobility all contributed to the reforms.[36] We will start with the most neglected aspect, namely, participation from below. Historians have talked about the role of peasant unrest and the fear of the emancipation process it aroused among noble and state elites. These events were strongly emphasized by certain Soviet historians eager to demonstrate the revolutionary nature of the abolition of Russian feudalism; however, most of the unrest took place after 1861, for reasons we will explain later. It is worth stressing that a process of judicial litigation, which has been completely neglected by historiography, played a distinct role in the transformation of serfdom. Let us be clear: we are not arguing that the rule of law existed in Russia or that pre-emancipation Russia was legally and politically comparable to Western countries. What we are saying is that it is wrong to assert there was no law but merely coercion by the state and the nobles in the face of peasant unrest and violence. We maintain that a kind of legal order existed in Russia; peasants had some rights: they could not denounce physical violence by their landlord, but they could contest her/his property rights and thus deny their obligations to her/him. At the same time, peasants' rights and their ability to defend them were highly unequal and unfair compared with those of landlords. The latter enjoyed a privileged position in the local court system but, in turn, they could easily lose all their rights and privileges by will of the tsar. We must therefore try and understand how these hierarchical rights influenced social relationships and the evolution of serfdom.[37]

Numerous laws were adopted between the end of the 18th century and 1861 to facilitate the submission of cases to the peasant courts created in 1775 and challenge ownership rights to "inhabited estates". In general, illegal enserfment was an offence under the criminal code; whereas before 1845 the punishment was limited to a fine, after that date the usual penalty was imprisonment, in addition to emancipation without compensation.[38] Throughout the first half of the 19th century, conflicts between peasants, peasant-workers and estate owners over both peasants' obligations and landlords' title to ownership were on the agenda of the courts. Usually, peasants who won their cases in court were reclassified either as state peasants or as urban residents.[39] The arguments presented by the plaintiffs testify, first of all, to the peasants' knowledge of the legal rules governing the possession of estates, which we mentioned earlier. For example, in many cases, plaintiffs emphasized that the transfer of the estate took place through the intermediary of a non-noble (which was prohibited); in other cases, plaintiffs demonstrated that the landowner was not a noble but rather a merchant and, as such, prohibited from possessing serfs.[40] On these grounds, they contested their obligations vis-à-vis their landlords.[41] It should be noted that these rules sought not so much to protect the peasants as to identify the genuinely "entitled" owner: illegitimate owners were those who had no real title of nobility. From this standpoint, the main purpose of these rules was, as before, to grant the "real nobles" a monopoly on possessing and transmitting inhabited estates. At the same time this game was more complex: the peasants were not trying to prove that the estate owner was not a "real noble" but rather that she/he had no right to enserf them inasmuch as the peasants belonged to another legal category. The complexity of the legal classification of social groups (the estate system) was so extreme that it was possible to use such an argument. And, indeed, the proceedings brought by peasants became so numerous that between 1837 and 1840, the Senate decided to put a stop to cases involving serfs still living with their masters.[42] In all, between 1833 and 1858, the Senate recorded 15,153 cases of illegal ownership and illegal bondage, whereas the provincial courts we have examined (just a few provinces) dealt with 22,000 cases of this type.[43]

Of course, these positive outcomes (for the peasants) of litigation should not obscure the difficulties peasants faced in bringing proceedings against a landlord. The rulings of local courts often differed considerably and several judges deemed peasant petitions inadmissible and even refused to grant them the right to appeal.[44] A number of cases of corruption of judges by noble landowners were also recorded. Finally, the investigations of such proceedings went slowly and often took ten years to reach a conclusion. Measures aimed at changing this state of affairs were not adopted until the end of the 1840s, when a new law facilitated the legal proceedings of all those who considered their obligations towards estate owners illegal.[45]

In short, peasant emancipation through litigation was by no means a rare occurrence in Russia; the data we have quoted reflects a still limited analysis made on the ground at the Senate archives (the supreme jurisdiction) and a few local courts. There is no reason to think they did not exist in all the other areas. At the same time, even when overall data becomes available, we may presume that the percentage of the peasantry who gained their freedom through personal litigation was no more than 3–5 per cent at best. This is still far superior to what occurred in other pre-abolitionist societies: in France and Britain, litigation was won by slaves in exceptional cases, although they were highly debated and therefore had a major impact on the emancipation process. Indeed, the public impact of jurisprudential issues, above all in Britain and much less in France, was the result of a strong civil society rather than of legal rules particularly favourable to slaves. In other words, in Russia we find more legal rights attributed to serfs compared with slaves in the United States and the British Empire, but a far weaker civil society supporting those claims (at best, the case of France should be seen as intermediate).

Furthermore, in Russia, as in slave societies, an estate owner could voluntarily redeem a peasant's obligations and thus change her/his legal status. It was already possible in the 17th and 18th centuries for a noble landowner to free peasants from their obligations, with or without land. In the latter case—the most widespread—there were no legal restrictions: the civil authorities gave their consent and the will (in the case of emancipation after the landowner's death) was recognized as valid.[46] The noble landowner was responsible for paying the capitation or head tax on the peasant until the next revision, unless a special clause in the emancipation contract stipulated that the peasant would pay her/his own tax.[47] No systematic, province-by-province studies have been carried out on this practice, but useful information can be found in notarial archives (*krepostnye knigi*) and estate archives. The impression given by this huge mass of archives is that the number of voluntary acts of redemption increased during the 19th century in response to tax support and simplified legal procedures provided by tsarist rules.[48]

Although various forms of emancipation enacted by estate owners or conquered by peasants in the law courts became increasingly accepted, they nevertheless remained marginal. The tight political control from above corresponded to the central role assigned to administrative law and ultimately to the will of the tsar over civil, commercial and criminal law. Prior to 1861, most emancipations were the result of administrative acts. In fact, many laws were passed during the first half of the 19th century to facilitate administrative procedures for changing the legal status of private peasants. Why were such rules adopted and what effect did they have?

Administrative Emancipation

These rules actually reflected issues and concerns specific to some of the Russian elites, such as political stability, economic efficiency, paternalistic criticism of serfdom and the concrete economic interests of the state and part of the nobility. In varying degrees, all these variables prompted the reforms. In 1803, a decree created the *svobodnye khlebopashtsy* (free farmers). By will of a landowner, these individuals were exempt from any obligation to him except those resulting from the attribution to peasants of plots of land belonging to the owner. Between 1833 and 1858, 58,225 private peasants succeeded in changing their legal status on the basis of this law,[49] a figure that rose to 114,000 male peasants between 1803 and 1855.[50] In 1842, a special category of peasants was created with a temporary specified obligation (*obiazannye krest'yanie*) to landowners. From the adoption of this law until 1858, 27,173 male peasants (and thus their families) were affected by the decree.[51]

In 1841, peasants who had been freely transferred to monasteries or charity institutions by private nobles were also re-classified.[52] About 8,900 people thus changed category and became state peasants.

In 1844, two new laws facilitated the re-classification of *dvorovnye liudi* (servants); the first law freed the master from any responsibility regarding the payment of the taxes of these individuals.

The second facilitated a change in legal status when the landowner mortgaged his estate to certain credit institutions. In 1851 alone, 11,000 *meshchane* (merchants) from 11 provinces benefited from these rules.[53]

Many peasant-workers attached to private factories were also exempted from any obligation to the factory owners between 1840 and 1851; about 19,000 people were concerned. During the same period, 53,900 men working in the mines were transferred to state estates as peasants.[54]

Administrative reclassification sometimes occurred for other reasons. State and noble elites agreed that indebted landowners had to be helped to keep their lands from falling into the hands of "speculators" and "merchants". To this end, in 1841, a new law prohibited the succession of landless nobles or landless owners of peasants. Consequently, between 1841 and 1858, the number of landless nobles dropped from 17,700 to 3,633 and their peasants from 62,000 to 12,045 (even taking into account the possibility that some of the serfs may have been sold to other nobles).[55]

Mortgaged estates put up for auction were especially targeted. Local peasants were given priority (along with the state itself) to acquire lands. In all, between 1833 and 1858, the legal status of 343,575 male peasants changed because of these operations.

Other provisions allowed for changes in the legal status of peasants as a consequence of their landowners' political crimes. In the Western Borderlands, Poland and Western Ukraine, the estates of nobles who took part in uprisings were confiscated and their peasants (estimated at 264,000) entered the category of state peasants.[56]

Finally, massive changes in the legal status of peasants resulted from conscription and military service. Once a conscript had completed his military service, he was classified as *raznochintsy* (literally: people of various ranks, which meant a whole residual category of people that included peasants, merchants, official elites and clergy) and could therefore move about freely, settle in the city and so on. In this way, some 433,750 peasants changed their legal status from private to state peasants or even urban residents between 1833 and 1858 alone.[57]

The legal status of conscripts also affected their families; in particular, children born after the soldier entered service were placed under the guardianship of the Ministry of War and destined for military service. This rule gave rise to numerous disputes and petitions.

brought not only by peasants but also by nobles who saw themselves deprived of considerable manpower for the benefit of the army.[58] Roughly 12,000 children changed legal status between 1833 and 1858. Added to the reclassification of soldiers, the number of peasants whose legal status changed in connection with the status of a soldier or as the child of a soldier rose to about 450,000.[59]

In all, between 1833 and 1858, around a million men were released from the status of peasants of private owners as a result of administrative acts (the army plus the other cases mentioned), out of a total of about 10 million serfs. More than a quarter of all male peasants were switched to other categories and became either state peasants or urban dwellers. At the time, barely half of all private peasants still engaged in "corvées". This means that, in 1861, the end of "coerced labour" concerned barely a quarter of the Russian peasantry. From this point of view, the reforms of 1861 have to be seen in the broader context of several reforms implemented over a century and a half.

The Emancipation Act of 1861

Five years separated the decision made by Alexander II to abolish serfdom (1856) and its execution (1861). Support for the measure came, above all, from certain elite nobles close to the tsar, such as the Miliutin brothers, who promoted emancipation to solve military and domestic security problems (peasant unrest in particular). Reformers won the backing of many enlightened bureaucrats who had joined in previous years to prepare for the Emancipation Act with detailed economic, social and legal inquiries.[60] Most of them took inspiration from the decrees of partial emancipation of 1801, 1842, etc. mentioned earlier.

For various reasons, radical intellectuals and proponents of Westernization in general saw reform as a way to abolish coercion and bring Russia closer to Europe. From the late 18th century, Russian followers of Adam Smith, like Heinrich Storch (a Prussian working at Saint Petersburg University), advocated the gradual abolition of serfdom. This process could create, step by step, the material and cultural conditions for emancipating the serfs.[61] Then, after the Decembrist movement in mid-1825, the debate between Westernizers and Slavophiles drew further public attention to the discussion on serfdom. Both groups supported abolition; however, the former maintained it was necessary to educate the backward peasantry and move towards individual forms of property, whereas the latter defended the commune as an institution capable of reconciling local traditions with modernity.[62]

The opponents of reform were divided as well. First, it is wrong to assert that the nobility as a whole opposed emancipation. On the contrary, many large estate owners supported it at once for humanitarian, political and economic reasons. As landlords, they knew perfectly well they would benefit from the peasants' freedom; already, during previous decades, peasants frequently escaped from small estates where conditions were harsh and moved either to town or more often to large estates. As we have seen, the concentration process accelerated during the first half of the 19th century, sustained by the increasing freedom of movement granted to peasants, the effective development of trade, markets and proto-industry, and the intensified economic difficulties of small estate owners. From this angle, we can understand the hostility most provincial small estate owners expressed towards emancipation. Unlike huge estate owners, small landlords barely survived with a few serfs; the abolition of serfdom seemed to spell their final ruin.[63]

Another argument mobilized the opposition of numerous landlords: though partial reforms had taken place in the previous decades, the monopoly on land and the connection between land ownership and the social, political and legal status of the nobility had never been under attack. Now, with a general emancipation, there was a risk that the "bourgeois", merchants and urban dwellers might claim rights to the land.[64]

Thus, the major points under discussion in the years between 1855 and 1861 concerned the schedule of reforms and the role of landowners: should the reforms be gradual or immediate? What sort of compensation should be given to the noble estate owners and who should paid for it—the state, the peasants or both?

Other debates arose over the status of the freed peasants: should they have access to land and if so, how? Or should they be turned into proletarians? Which form of property should be instituted—communal tenure or individual property?

The last set of questions pertained to the scale and variation of reforms: should a single reform be adopted throughout the whole of Russia or different criteria be promoted according to local conditions?

The attitude of the secret commission established in 1857 was initially cautious. It proposed applying the decrees of 1803 and 1841 to the entire country, but the tsar and his brother Constantine Niko-laevich pushed for a more resolute approach.[65] The debate focused on peasant unrest and peasant views: some reports showed increasing peasant unrest, while others challenged this view. Moreover, some members of the elite attributed the unrest to lack of reform, while their opponents interpreted it as fear of reform. The tsar decided to establish local commissions to identify regional specificities, and on this basis, to detail local criteria for abolition. Provincial nobles actively participated to these commissions; no doubt they considered reform inevitable and therefore sought to play a prominent role in order to influence it. As a result, many commissions were deeply divided and presented a majority and a minority report. The views and suggestions differed widely from one commission to another. For example, estate owners from central agrarian areas were mostly concerned with the question of how much land they would keep and the labour services peasants would have to provide following abolition. In contrast, in proto-industrial areas, nobles attached the greatest importance to the peasants' actual redemption of their lands and the fees they would have to pay the landlords to gain access to markets, tools and credit.[66]

However, these reports and the divisions within and between local commissions were overcome by the simultaneous evolution of the central commission. While the provincial committees were at work, this commission drafted a new plan according to which freed peasants would gradually become landowners and no longer be subject to their previous masters but to the state authority. This shift was linked, first, to the deep division within the provincial committees, which the tsar and his closest advisers perceived as a source of political instability. They therefore seized the opportunity to proceed without the agreement of a majority of local owners. This choice was also made because, unlike the provincial nobility, the central state reformers gradually came to an agreement on a plan for emancipation. Last but not least, the tsar and his circle of advisers interpreted peasant unrest in Estonia in 1858 as acts of landless peasants and a sign for the need to quickly implement reforms.[67]

Confronted by this move, the representatives of the local nobles sent petitions to the tsar protesting against the attitudes of the "bureaucrats". However, they had still failed to agree on an alternative programme. Despite their divisions and political weakness, the nobles won some concessions; in particular, the amount of land to be given to freed peasants was reduced to a minimum. The provincial nobility also succeeded in ensuring that the state did not provide financial support to emancipated peasants in order to run their farms. In their eyes, the lack of resources meant that the peasants would need assistance from their former landlords and thus perpetuate their dependence. Central state reformers accepted this solution because of the major financial crisis of 1859 and the state's rising public debt.[68]

The official abolition of serfdom on 19 February 1861 was set forth in a long, complicated text, accompanied by a few other decrees detailing the main points. To add to the complexity, several further decrees referred to different areas of the empire. As a general rule, emancipation was divided into three steps: first, a transitional period of two years to implement the basic rules of emancipation and define the main criteria for the second step (allotments, the amount of land to be given to peasants in different areas, etc). Then the second step, an indefinite period during which peasants had to redeem their freedom and land allotment; the third and last step was redemption, which was supposed to complete the whole process within 49 years. In practice, the size of peasants' land allotments in the local statutes greatly varied depending on soil fertility, population density and agricultural practices. More land was assigned in the steppe and non-black earth lands than in black earth localities, where the land was more fertile and there was greater pressure from the population. Indeed, instead of a fixed amount of land per capita (or per family or per commune), each statute identified an interval within which the final amount of land should be determined. In general, local nobles imposed the shortest possible interval possible.

Local statutes also identified the amount of labour or fees peasant had to provide during the second phase. The amount of labour was set at 40 days a year for men and 30 for women, and it had to be performed primarily during the summer and other periods of heavy agricultural work. There was a complex arrangement that varied the amount according to the area, fertility of land, size of the allotment, etc. Rules for cash dues were even more complicated, depending on the distance from St Petersburg, major towns and markets, and the size of the allotment. As peasants were considered indebted until they had completed their redemption, the state and the estate owners retained their rights to restrict mobility and require formal consent for any market operation (selling, offering labour, etc).

In practice, in many localities, nobles abused their position and imposed unfair terms on the peasants; in many cases, landlords gave away their worst land and the peasants had to redeem it at the highest price.[69] Does this mean that the conditions of the peasantry worsened after abolition and that the act did not result in any real change?

The Aftermath of the Emancipation

It is important to distinguish the impact of the reform on political and civil rights on the one hand, and on the economy, on the other. From the first perspective, the abolition of serfdom was not accompanied by dissolution of the traditional estate order of the old regime (the *soslovie* system in Russia). The population and their rights were divided into a few main groups (peasants, landlords, priests, merchants) and a myriad of subgroups.[70] Nobles continued to enjoy special rules and privileges while peasants, despite their increasing legal rights, still had few political rights. Merchants and urban groups were allowed some rights at the local level but very few at the national level until after the revolution of 1905, when the tsar was forced to concede a constitution. In particular, the reforms of 1861–64 introduced local governments (*zemstvos*), which could levy local taxes and adopt public policies concerning health, social welfare, education and the local economy. The zemstvos played a major role in the evolution of political, social, intellectual and economic life in Russia until the revolution.[71] They achieved these goals in spite of major limitations in terms of rights and representativeness. The zemstvos initially linked political rights and the number of elective representatives from each estate (peasants, merchants, priests, nobles, etc.) to land ownership. Peasants and merchants acquired more and more property, as we will see in a moment, leading the tsarist government and the most reactionary factions among the nobility to change the elective principle in 1890. Land ownership as the sole criterion for eligibility to take part in local political life was counterbalanced first by minimum land and income requirements (below a certain amount, one had no right to be elected), and second, by a predetermined number of elective representatives from each order. This meant that the nobility had more representatives than merchants who, in turn, had more votes and hence more representatives than peasants.

However, these restrictive political measures ran up against increasing social and economic mobility. Conventional historiography stressed the limits of reforms, increasing poverty of the peasantry and persistent backwardness of Russia.[72] More recent historiography has provided a completely different picture. Russia experienced significant social transformation and economic growth between 1861 and 1914; revised population trends show that mortality and birth rates were lower than was previously thought.[73] There was a decline in the pauperization of the peasantry and the number and severity of large-scale famines;[74] the period from 1861 to 1914 was an era of steady improvement in both agricultural production and living standards.[75]

The rate of growth and commercialization of Russian agriculture also accelerated.[76] Between the 1880s and 1900, capitalism spread to the most remote corners of the empire through the grain trade,[77] and Russia's wheat market was fully integrated into global markets.[78] The contribution of agriculture to the national income rose at a rapid pace, comparable to that of contemporary Western European economies. In Paul Gregory's assessment, Russia experienced growth rates similar to those of Germany, France, America, Japan, Norway, Canada and the United Kingdom—1.35 per cent average annual productivity growth in agriculture between 1883–87 and 1909–13, which was three-quarters of the rate of industrial productivity growth and nearly equal to the 1.5 per cent rate of the economy as a whole.[79]

Net grain production rose to 3.1 per cent annually between 1885 and 1913; Russia produced more grain than any other country in 1861 and in 1913, was second only to the US.[80] The average annual growth rate of wholesale grain and potato production in European Russia from 1870–1913 was 2.5 per cent: 1.6 per cent for the first 30 years and 4.4 per cent after the turn of the century. Gregory estimated the rate of economic growth in the entire Russian empire including the frontier regions from 1883–87 through 1909–13 at 2.8 per cent, with some fluctuations within the intervals of that period.[81] The value of labour input increased between 1861 and 1913 by 42.6 per cent, or an average annual rate of 1.7 per cent.

Economic growth relied on the evolution of core Russian social institutions such as the peasant commune. It is no accident that over the past 20 years, when the history of enclosures in Britain and agriculture in Europe was being re-examined,[82] the image of the Russian commune was called into question as well.[83] Recent estimates for

Russia confirm there was no correlation between land redistribution practices and economic productivity.[84] Periodic redistributions had far less influence on productivity than endogenous investment decisions. When redistributing land plots, communes often took into account as key factors the quality of the soil and any improvements in its quality made by the previous tenant. Repartitions allowed land communes to respond to sudden, unexpected changes in their size brought about by epidemics or migrations, to recast the shape of the open fields and to bring order to field strips by reducing their number.[85]

Peasant land possessions more than doubled between the 1870s and World War I, and acquisitions were made not only by land communes but also, increasingly, by individual households. Between 1863 and 1872, Russian peasants bought lands to add to their communal allotments. Over three-quarters of all peasant acquisitions on the open market were made by individuals. This trend accelerated with the foundation of the Peasant State Bank, intended to encourage loans to peasants seeking to buy land. There was a twofold increase in peasant land properties between 1877 and 1905. In 80 per cent of the cases, the transactions were made by the peasant commune or by peasant associations. During the following years, between 1906 and 1914, the state sold 1.5 million *desiatines* (1 desiatine = 1.10 hectares) to peasants; landlords sold them one-fifth of their land, that is, 10.2 million out of 49.7 desiatines. Two-third of the purchases were made by peasant associations and land communes and one-third by individual households. Cossack and peasant ownership increased by 9.5 million desiatines, reaching a total of 170.4 million.[86] The dynamics of land acquisition thus further substantiate the assertion that peasant well-being increased between 1861 and 1914.

This revised view of Russian agriculture corresponds to the new assessments of Russia's industrialization. According to recent estimates, between 1881 and 1913 the share of industry in national income rose from 25 per cent to 32 per cent. The productivity of industrial labour was 28 per cent higher than that in agriculture.[87] The rate of urbanization was considerable,[88] largely attributable to the influx of peasant migrants who accounted for 93 per cent of all factory workers in Moscow in 1902[89] and most of whom worked in textiles. Industry remained geographically concentrated in the central provinces of Moscow and Vladimir as well as in and around the imperial capital. This means that despite an increasing rate of urbanization and regional specialization, the peasant worker was still the leading figure in the Russian economy.[90] According to the 1897 census, 23.3 per cent of the active population was employed in non-agricultural sectors, half of them in proto-industrial and craft activities and the rest in industry and services. Proto-industry and especially rural cottage industry were still serious competitors for urban industry, not only in terms of production but also in the size of the labour market.[91] This seems to confirm the contention of Olga Crisp and more recently of Leonid Borodkin, Brigid Granville and Carol Scott Leonard that the relatively low numbers of the industrial labour force were not due to internal passports or legal constraints on mobility[92] but to the strength of agriculture, its profitability and people's interest in staying in rural areas and leaving only for seasonal urban employment.[93]

Conclusion

The historiography of Russian serfdom and its abolition has constantly suffered from stereotypes and historical determinism: the passage from feudalism to capitalism, from un-freedom to freedom; the persistent opposition between absent estate owners and exploited, anti-market peasants; and the tension between lack of democracy and the weakness of market and economic development.

Market integration, trade and proto-industrial development were, in fact, central in the functioning of the Russian economy in the 18th and 19th centuries. It was not a feudal regime; it was not contemporary England either. Instead, Russia testifies to a process of economic modernization led by nobles and peasants. The institutions supporting this world were ordered in an extremely hierarchical system with the tsar at the top, then some nobles, then military officers and small estate owners, down to the peasant communes. The state never directly promoted serfdom but it gave landlords the right to profit from it. Yet peasants were not excluded like alien slaves; they were part of this society. They had limited but significant rights, which they used to negotiate with the landlord and sometimes even challenge her/his rights, as well as to move elsewhere.

From this point of view, the abolition of serfdom in 1861 completed an ongoing process, already underway at least by the end of the 18th century and finally achieved only on the eve of World War I.

Most of the reforms were from above, but the contribution of peasants and nobles to the process of emancipation, especially during the first half of the 19th century, should not be neglected. Peasants made use of unequal rules to defend their rights; they were unsuccessful in most of their attempts, but their insistence ultimately won the support of enlightened bureaucrats and landowners interested both in preserving the regime and in seizing the lands of small estate owners, held to be brutal, backward and dangerous for the whole aristocratic system. The reforms of 1861 constituted a step in a longer process, which made the system more open without destroying it. After 1861, the aim of tsarist elites was to prevent massive peasant proletarization and potential socialism, as well as limit the success of merchant groups. A process of relative modernization, supported by the peasant-workers on the one hand, and peasant communes and aristocratic landlords on the other, was at work after 1861. This solution proved to be effective; the gloomy forecasts of many contemporaries were contradicted by the country's economic performance and the high rate of growth and social progress in post-emancipation Russia. Thanks to these policies, the Russian Empire avoided the fate of the Ottoman Empire, but failed to attain the strength of the Prussian state. The history of Russia thus confirms the intuition Arno Mayer had several years ago: in Europe, the old regime made up of land aristocracies, peasants and political inequalities only collapsed with World War I.[94] Until that moment Russia was not outside Europe, as many observers have argued. Russia was not "otherness", but merely an extreme variation of Europe.[95] The point of fundamental divergence between Russia and Europe was therefore neither the French Revolution nor the first industrial revolution, but World War I and its aftermath.

Notes

1. Jerome Blum, *Lords and Peasants in Russia from the Ninth to the Nineteenth Century* (New York: Atheneum, 1964); Alexander Gerschenkron, *Economic Backwardness in Historical Perspective: A Book of Essays* (Cambridge, MA: Harvard University Press, 1962); Richard Hellie, *Enserfment and Military Change in Muscovy* (Chicago, IL: University of Chicago Press, 1971); Peter Kolchin, *Unfree Labor: American Slavery and Russian Serfdom* (Cambridge, MA: Harvard University Press, 1987).
2. Steven Hoch, *Serfdom and Social Control: Petrovskoe, a Village in Tambov* (Chicago, IL: University of Chicago Press, 1986).

3. Petr Struve, *Krepostnoe khoziaistvo. Issledovaniia po ekonomicheskoi istorii Rossii v XVIII i XIX vv.* (The Serf Economy: Studies on the Economic History of Russia, 18th to 19th Century) (Saint Petersburg, 1913); Ivan D. Koval'chenko, *Russkoe krepostnoe krest'ianstvo v pervoi polovine XIX v.* (Russian Serfdom during the First Half of the 19th Century) (Moscow: Nauka, 1967); Edgar Melton, "Proto-industrialization, Serf Agriculture, and Agrarian Social Structure: Two Estates in Nineteenth-century Russia", *Past and Present* 115 (1987): 73–81. See also Evsey Domar and M. Machina, "On the Profitability of Russian Serfdom", *The Journal of Economic History* 44, 4 (1984): 919–55.

4. Michael Confino, *Domaines et seigneurs en Russie vers la fin du XVIIIe siècle: Étude de structures agraires et de mentalités économiques* (Paris: Mouton, 1963) and *Systèmes agraires et progrès agricole en Russie aux XVIIIe–XIXe siècles: Étude d'économie et de sociologie rurales* (Paris: Mouton, 1969); Hoch, *Serfdom and Social Control*; David Moon, *The Russian Peasantry, 1600–1930* (London: Longman, 1996) and *The Abolition of Serfdom in Russia, 1762–1907* (London: Pearson, 2001); Elise Kimerling Wirtschafter, *Structures of Society: Imperial Russia's "People of Various Ranks"* (DeKalb, IL: Northern Illinois University Press, 1994); Elise Kimerling Wirtschafter, *Social Identity in Imperial Russia* (DeKalb, IL: Northern Illinois University Press, 1997).

5. The obvious reference was Lenin's *The Development of Capitalism in Russia*. Then Peter Lyashchenko, *History of the National Economy of Russia to the 1917 Revolution* (New York: Macmillan, 1949); Koval'chenko, *Russkoe*; Pavel Andreevich Zaionchkovskii, *Otmena krepostnogo prava v Rossii* [The Abolition of Serfdom in Russia], 3rd ed. (Moscow: Izd-vo Kniga, 1968), ed. and trans. Susan Wobst, Gulf Breeze, FL: Academic International Press, 1978.

6. Blum, *Lords and Peasants*; Gershenkron, *Economic Backwardness*; Geroid Tanquary Robinson, *Rural Russia under the Old Regime* (Berkeley, CA: University of California Press, 1970).

7. Lidia Zakharova, ed., *Velikie reformy v Rossii, 1856–1874* [The Great Reforms in Russia] (Moscow: Nauka, 1992); Ben Ekloff et al., ed., *Russia's Great Reforms, 1855–1881* (Bloomington, IN: Indiana University Press, 1994).

8. Moon, *The Abolition of Serfdom in Russia* and the *Russian Peasantry*; Alessandro Stanziani, *Bondage, Labor and Rights in Eurasia, 17th–20th Centuries* (New York and Oxford: Berghahn Press, 2014).

9. Alfred Rieber, "Alexander II: A Revisionist View", *The Journal of Modern History* 43, 1 (1971): 42–58.

10. Terence Emmons, *The Russian Landed Gentry and the Peasant Emancipation of 1861* (Cambridge: Cambridge University Press, 1968); William

Bruce Lincoln, *In the Vanguard of Reforms: Russian Enlightened Bureaucrats, 1825–1861* (DeKalb: Northern Illinois University Press, 1982); Daniel Field, *The End of Serfdom: Nobility and Bureaucracy in Russia, 1855–1861* (Cambridge, MA: Harvard University Press, 1976).

11. Koval'chenko, "Russkoe krepostnoe"; Melton, "Proto-industrialization".

12. Blum, *Lords and Peasants*; Hoch, *Serfdom and Social Control*; Boris Mironov, *The Social History of the Russian Empire*, 2 vols (Boulder, CO: Westview, 1999).

13. Ian Blanchard, *Russia's Age of Silver: Precious Metal Production and Economic Growth in the Eighteenth Century* (London and New York: Routledge, 1989); Moon, *The Abolition of Serfdom in Russia*; Stanziani, *Bondage, Labor and Rights in Eurasia*.

14. Robert Fogel, *Without Consent or Contract: the Rise and Fall of American Slavery* (New York: Norton, 1989); David Eltis, *Economic Growth and the Ending of Transatlantic Slave Trade* (Oxford: Oxford University Press, 1989); Stanley Engerman, *Terms of Labor: Slavery, Serfdom, and Free Labor* (Stanford, CA: Stanford University Press, 1999).

15. On this, see Alessandro Stanziani, *After Oriental Despotism: Warfare, Labour and Growth in Eurasia, 17th–20th Centuries* (London: Bloomsbury, 2014).

16. Gerschenkron, *Economic Backwardness*; Olga Crisp, *Studies in Russian Economy before 1914* (London: Basingstoke, 1976).

17. Blanchard, *Russia's Age of Silver*; Tracy Dennison, *The Institutional Framework of Russian Serfdom* (Cambridge: Cambridge University Press, 2011).

18. Mironov, *The Social History*.

19. Ibid.

20. Boris Mironov and Carol S. Leonard, "In Search of Hidden Information: Some Issues in the Socio-Economic History of Russia in the Eighteenth and Nineteenth Centuries", *Social Science History* 9 (Autumn 1985): 339–59; Boris Mironov, *Vnytrennii rynok Rossii vo vtoroi polovine XVIII–pervoi polovine XIX v.* [The Domestic Market in Russia during the Second Half of the Eighteenth–First Half of the Nineteenth Century] (Leningrad: Nauka, 1981).

21. Mironov, *Vnutrennyi rynok*, pp. 153–4.

22. Paul Gregory, *Russian National Income (1885–1913)* (Cambridge: Cambridge University Press, 2004).

23. Moon, *The Russian Peasantry*, p. 27.

24. Vladimir M. Kabuzan, *Izmeneniia v razmeshchenii naseleniia Rossii v XVIII–pervoi polovine XIX v.* [Changes in the Rate of Growth of the Russian Population during the Eighteenth and the First Half of the Nineteenth Centuries] (Moscow: Nauka, 1971); Alain Blum and Irina

Troitskaia, "La mortalité en Russie au XVIIIe et XIXe siècles. Estimations locales à partir des Revizii", *Population* 51 (1996): 303–28; Steven Hoch, "Famine, Disease, and Mortality Patterns in the Parish of Borshevka, 1830–1912", *Population Studies* 52, 3 (1998): 357–68.

25. Hoch, *Serfdom and Social Control*.

26. Aleksandr' Troinitskii, *Krepostnoe naselenie v Rossii po 10 narodnoi perepisi* [The Russian Serf Population according to the Tenth Census] (St Petersburg: Wulf, 1861), p. 45.

27. Irina V. Ledovskaia, "Biudzhet russkogo pomeshchika v 40-60kh godakh XIX v" [Estate Owners' Budgets in the 1840s–60s], in Akademiia Nauk SSSR, *Materialy po istorii sel'skogo khoziaistva i krest'ianstva SSSR*, vol. 8 (Moscow: Nauka, 1974), pp. 240–5; Moon, *The Russian Peasantry*.

28. Moon, *The Russian Peasantry*.

29. RGADA, Rossiikii Gosudastvenny Arkhiv Drevnikh Aktov (Russian State Archives of Ancient Acts), fond 342, opis' 3, delo 749. Aussi: RGADA, fond 1287 (Sheremetev), opis' 3, chast' 1, delo 107, 117, 1745.

30. Alessandro Stanziani, "Les statistiques des récoltes en Russie, 1905–1928", *Histoire et mesure* VII, 1/2 (1992): 73–98.

31. Alessandro Stanziani, "Les enquêtes orales en Russie, 1861–1914", *Annales ESC* 55, 1 (2000): 219–41.

32. For a full discussion of these materials, see Blanchard, *Russia's Age of Silver*, Chapter 5 and Appendix 2, revised in Ian Blanchard, "Le développement économique en perspective historique: l'avenir de la Russie à la lumière de son évolution à l'époque moderne (1700-1914)", in *Les enterprises et leurs réseaux: hommes, capitaux, techniques et pouvoirs xixe-xxe siècles. Mèlanges en l'honneur de François Caron*, ed. Michèle Merger and Dominique Barjot (Paris: Presse de l'Université de Paris-Sorbonne, 1998), pp. 381–92.

33. Carol Leonard, *Agrarian Reform in Russia* (Cambridge: Cambridge University Press, 2011), in particular Fig. 8.1 on p. 258.

34. Blanchard, "Le développement économique".

35. Seymour Drescher, *Capitalism and Anti-slavery* (London: Palgrave, 1987); *Abolitions: A History of Slavery and Antislavery* (Cambridge: Cambridge University Press, 2009).

36. Samuel Becker, *Nobility and Privilege in Late Imperial Russia* (DeKalb, IL: Northern Illinois University Press, 1985); Paul Dukes, *Catherine the Great and the Russian Nobility* (Cambridge: Cambridge University Press 1967); Robert E. Jones, *The Emancipation of the Russian Nobility, 1762-1785* (Princeton, NJ: Princeton University Press, 1973); David Lieven, *The Aristocracy in Europe, 1815-1914* (New York: Columbia University Press, 1994); William Bruce Lincoln, *The Great Reforms: Autocracy, Bureaucracy and the Politics of Change in Imperial Russia* (DeKalb, IL: Northern Illinois University Press, 1990); Walter M.

Pintner, *Russian Economic Policy under Nicholas I* (Ithaca, NY: Cornell University Press, 1967).

37. Recent important works on the role of the law in Russia are: Wirtschafter, *Social Identity*; Virginia Martin, *Law and Custom in the Steppe: The Kazakhs of the Middle Horde and Russian Colonialism in the Nineteenth Century* (Richmond, Surrey: RoutledgeCurzon, 2001). Most of the available literature on legal action in imperial Russia focuses on the post-1864 period: Richard Wortman, *Development of a Russian Legal Consciousness* (Chicago, IL: University of Chicago Press, 1976); William Wagner, *Marriage, Property and Law in Late Imperial Russia* (Oxford: Oxford University Press, 1994); Jane Burbank, *Russian Peasants Go to Court: Legal Culture in the Countryside, 1905–1917* (Bloomington, IN: Indiana University Press, 2004); Peter Solomon, ed., *Reforming Justice in Russia, 1864–1994: Power, Culture, and the Limits of Legal Order* (New York: Armonk, 1997); Ekaterina A. Pravilova, *Zakonnost' i prava lichnosti: administrativnaia iustitsiia v Rossii, vtoraia polovina XIX v.– oktiabr' 1917* [Legality and the Rights of the Person: Administrative Justice in Russia in the Second Half of the Nineteenth Century to October 1917] (St Petersburg: Izd-vo SZAGS2000).

37. Jones, *Emancipation of Russian Nobility*; Daniel Saunders, *Russia in the Age of Reaction and Reform, 1801–1881* (London and New York: Longman, 1992).

38. *Polnoe sobranie zakonov Rossiskoi Imperii* (hereafter PSZ) [Full Collection of Laws of the Russian Empire PSZ], sery II, vol. 20, n. 19283.

39. Decisions of Senate in that sense in PSZ (II), vol. 3, n. 2378, vol. 8, n. 6129, vol. 9, 6941, vol. 10, n. 8539, vol. 11, n. 9203, vol. 15, n. 13051, vol. 17, n. 15693, vol. 20, n. 19283, vol. 22, n. 20825.

40. TsGIAM (*Tsentral'nyi gosudarstvennyi istoricheskii arkhiv gorod Moskvy* [Central State Historical Archive of Moscow]), fond 54, 1783–1917, opis' 1, for example: dela 56, 284, 966, 1509.

41. On transfer to married women and involved questions (legal statute): TsGIAM, fond 54, opis 1 and 2; for example Opis 1, delo 284; RGIA *Rossiskii gosudarstvennyi istoricheskii archiv* [Russian State Historical Archive], fond 1149, opis' 2 delo 20 and delo 44. The issue was not always favourable to the peasants and workers.

42. RGIA, fond 1149, opis' 2, delo 90.

43. PSZ (II), vol. 20, n. 19283, vol. 22, n. 20825. RGIA, fond 1149, opis' 3, delo 125.

44. RGIA, fond 1149, opis' 2, delo 20.

45. Law of 1847, in PSZ II, vol. 22, n. 20825.

46. *Svod zakonov* [Law Collection], vol. 9, art. 674-680, 1833, art. 1148-84, 1857.

47. PSZ, I, vol. 20, n. 14294 (de 1775).

48. Notarial archives in RGADA, fond 615, opis' 1; fond 1253 and 1274.

49. Steven Hoch and Wilson Augustine, "The Tax Census and the Decline of the Serf Population in Imperial Russia, 1833–1858", *Slavic Review* 38, 3 (1979): 403–25.

50. Nikolai M. Druzhinin, *Gosudarstvennye krest'iane i reforma P.D. Kiseleva* [State Peasants and the Reform of P.D. Kiselev] (Moscow: Nauka, 1958).

51. Hoch and Augustine, "The Tax Census", p. 410.

52. PSZ, II, vol. 16, n. 14669, 19 June 1841.

53. Petr Keppen, *Deviataia reviziia: issledovanie o chisle zhitelei v Rossii v 1851 goda* [The Ninth Census: Study of the Number of Inhabitants in Russia in 1851] (St Petersburg: Tip. Imp. Akademii nauk, 1857): 6–7, 21, 62, 88, 95, 100, 127, 142–4, 152–9.

54. Pavel G. Ryndziunskii, *Gorodskoe grazhdanstvo doreformennoi Rossii* [Urban Citizenship in Russia before the Reforms] (Moscow: Nauka, 1958).

55. Hoch and Augustine, "The Tax Census", p. 420.

56. PSZ, II; vol. 11, n. 9053.

57. Hoch and Augustine, "The Tax Census".

58. TsGIAM, fond 16, opis' 2 ; delo 192; fond 54, opis' 1, delo 1618; fond 16, opis'2, delo 192; fond 54, opis' 1, delo 1618. Also TsGIAM, fond 16, opis' 227, dela? 227,938, 948, 976 980, 986, 1573, 1571, 1588, 1589.

59. Hoch and Augustine, "The Tax Census".

60. Lincoln, 1982.

61. Heinrich Storch, *Cours d'économie politique ou exposition des principes qui déterminent la prospérité des nations*, 5 vols (St Petersburg: A. Pliushar, 1815), booklet 5: 255, 258, 261, 279, 291–2.

    See also Alessandro Stanziani, "Free Labor-Forced Labor: an Uncertain Boundary? The Circulation of Economic Ideas between Russia and Europe from the Eighteenth to the Mid-nineteenth Century", *Kritika: Explorations in Russian and Eurasian History* 9, 1 (2008): 1–27.

62. On this debate, among the others: Esther Kingston-Mann, *In Search of the True West* (Princeton, NJ: Princeton University Press, 1999); Alexander Vucinich, *Social Thought in Tsarist Russia* (Chicago, IL: University of Chicago Press, 1976).

63. Terence Emmons, *The Russian Landed Gentry and the Peasant Emancipation of 1861* (Berkeley and Los Angeles, CA: University of California Press, 1968).

64. Ibid.

65. Field, *The End*; Zaionchkovsky, *Otmena*; Lidya Zakharova, *Samoderzhavie i otmena krepostnogo prava v Rossii, 1856–1861* [Autocracy and the Abolition of Serfdom in Russia, 1856–1861] (Moscow: Izdatel'stvo Moskovskogo Gosudarstvennogo Universiteta, 1984).

66. Emmons, *The Russian Landed Gentry*; Daniel Saunders, *Russia in the Age of Reaction and Reform, 1801–1881* (London and New York: Longman, 1992).

67. Zakharova, *Samoderzhavie*; Emmons, *The Russian Landed Gentry*.

68. Steven Hoch, "The Banking Crisis, Peasant Reforms, and Economic Development in Russia, 1857–1861", *American Historical Review* 96, 3 (1991): 795–820.

69. Boris Litvak, *Russkaia derevniia v reforme 1861 goda: Chernozemnyi tsentr 1861–1895 gg* [The Russian Countryside in the Reform of 1861: The Central Black-earth, 1861–1895] (Moskva: Nauka, 1972); Serguei Kashchenko, *Reforma 19 Fevralia 1861 goda na severo-zapade Rossii* [The Reform of 1861 in the North-west of Russia] (Moskva: Mosgosararkhiv, 1995).

70. Gregory Freeze, "The Soslovie (Estate) Paradigm In Russian Social History", *American Historical Review* 91, 1 (1986): 11–36.

71. Terence Emmons and Wayne Vucinich, *The Zemstvos in Russia: An Experiment in Local Self-Government* (New York and Cambridge: Cambridge University Press, 1992).

72. Robinson, *Rural Russia*; Gershenkron, *Economic Backwardness*.

73. Steven Hoch, "Famine, Disease and Mortality Patterns in the Parish of Boshervka, Russia, 1830–1932", *Population Studies* 52, 31 (1998): 357–68; "On Good Numbers and Bad: Malthus, Population Trend and Peasant Standard of Living in Late Imperial Russia", *Slavic Review* 53, 1 (1994): 41–75; and "Serfs in Imperial Russia: Demographic Insights", *The Journal of Interdisciplinary History* 13, 2 (1982): 221–46.

74. Stephen Wheatcroft, "Crisis and Condition of the Peasantry in Late Imperial Russia", in *Peasant Economy, Culture and Politics of European Russia, 1800–1921*, ed. Esther Kingston-Mann and Timothy Mixter (Princeton, NJ: Princeton University Press, 1991), pp. 101–27.

75. Elvira M. Wilbur, "Was Russian Peasant Agriculture really that Impoverished? New Evidence From a Case Study From the 'Impoverished Center' at the End of the Nineteenth Century", *Journal of Economic History* 43, 1 (1983): 137–44; Esther Kingston-Mann, "Marxism and Russian Rural Development: Problems of Evidence, Experience and Culture", *American Historical Review* 86, 4 (1981): 731–52; James Y. Simms, Jr, "The Crisis in Russian Agriculture at the End of the Nineteenth Century: A Different View", *Slavic Review* 36, 3 (1977): 377–98 and "The Crop Failure of 1891: Soil Exhaustion, Technological Backwardness, and Russia's Agrarian Crisis", *Slavic Review* 41, 2 (1982): 236–50.

76. Paul Gregory, *Russian National Income 1885–1913* (Cambridge: Cambridge University Press, 1982); Alessandro Stanziani, *L'économie en*

révolution. Le cas russe, 1870–1930 (Paris: Albin Michel, 1998); Peter Gatrell, *The Tsarist Economy, 1850–1917* (New York: St Martin's Press, 1986).

77. Ivan Koval'chenko and L. Milov, *Vserossiiskii agrarnyi rynok, XVIII–nachalo XX v.* [The All-Russian Agrarian Market, 18th–Early 20th Centuries] (Moscow: Nauka, 1974).

78. Barry K. Goodwin and Thomas J. Grennes, "Tsarist Russia and the World Wheat Market", *Explorations in Economic History* 35, 4 (1998): 405–30.

79. Gregory, *Russian National Income*, pp. 126–30, 168–94.

80. Robert Allen, *Farm to Factory: A Reinterpretation of the Soviet Industrial Revolution* (Princeton, NJ: Princeton University Press, 2003).

81. Gregory, *Russian National Income*, Table 6.3.

82. Donald McCloskey, "The Open Fields of England: Rent, Risk, and the Rate of Interest, 1300–1815", in *Markets in History: Economic Studies of the Past*, ed. David Galenson (Cambridge: Cambridge University Press, 1989), pp. 5–51.

83. Esther Kingston-Mann, "Peasant Communes and Economic Innovation: A Preliminary Inquiry", in *Peasant Economy, Culture, and Politics of European Russia, 1800–1921*, ed. Esther Kingston-Mann and Timothy Mixter (Princeton, NJ: Princeton University Press, 1991), pp. 23–51; Pavel' N. Zyrianov, *Krest'ianskaia obshchina Evropeiskoi Rossii 1907–1914 gg.* [The Peasant Commune in the European Russia, 1907–1914] (Moscow: Nauka, 1992); Judith Pallot, *Land Reform in Russia 1906–1917: Peasant Responses to Stolypin's Project of Rural Transformation* (Oxford: Clarendon Press, 1999).

84. Steven Nafziger, *Communal Institutions, Resource Allocation, and Russian Economic Development*, unpublished PhD dissertation (New Haven, CT: Yale University, 2006).

85. Pallot, *Land Reform*, p. 81.

86. *Ezhegodnik GUZiZ* [Yearbook of the Land Commission of the Ministry of Agriculture], 1907–16 (St Petersburg: Gosizdat).

87. Gregory, *Russian National Income*, p. 132.

88. Gatrell, *The Tsarist*.

89. David Pretty, "Neither Peasant nor Proletarian: The Workers of the Ivanovo-Voznesensk Region", unpublished PhD dissertation (Providence, RI: Brown University, 1997).

90. Jeffrey Burds, *Peasant Dreams and Market Politics: Labor Migration and the Russian Village, 1861–1905* (Pittsburgh, PA: University of Pittsburgh Press, 1998).

91. Gatrell, *The Tsarist*.

92. Leonid Borodkin et al., "The Rural/Urban Wage Gap in the Industrialisation of Russia, 1884–1910", *European Review of Economic History* 12, 1 (2008): 67–95.
93. Leonard, *Agrarian Reforms.*
94. Arno Mayer, *The Persistence of the Old Regime* (London: Pantheon, 1981).
95. On this, see Stanziani, *Bondage, Labor and Rights in Eurasia.*

Contributors

Amitava Chowdhury is Associate Professor of History, Queen's University, and Visiting Fellow at the Weatherhead Initiative on Global History, Harvard University. He is Managing Editor of the *Canadian Journal of Latin American and Caribbean Studies* and a collaborating member of the Indian Ocean World Center, McGill University. A historian and historical archaeologist, Chowdhury is primarily interested in the histories of plantation labour in the Caribbean and the Indian Ocean. His other research interests include diaspora theory and the theory and methodology of Global History.

Kumie Inose is a Professor in the Faculty of Letters, Konan University, Japan. She is a member of Science Council of Japan. She has published widely on modern British history, especially on the cultural history of the British Empire. She is the author of *Shokuminchi keiken no yukue: Alice Green no salon to seiki tenkanki no daiei-teikoku* (in Japanese: *Colonial Experience and Its Aftermath: Mary Kingsley and Alice Green at the turn of the century Britain*, Kyoto, 2004), *Daiei teikoku toiu keiken* (in Japanese: *Encountering the Empire*, as a part of the series of the Rise and Fall of the Powers and Civilization, Tokyo, 2007), and the chief-editor of *Igirisu bunkashi* (in Japanese: *British Cultural History*, Kyoto, 2010), and the co-editor of *Afurika to teikoku: koroniarizum kenkyu no shinshikou ni mukete* (in Japanese: *Africa and the Empire: Rethinking the Studies of Colonialism*, Kyoto, 2010).

Martin Klein is a Professor Emeritus from the University of Toronto where he taught African history. He is the author of *Slavery and Colonial Rule in French West Africa* (Cambridge, 1998) and the *Dictionary of Slavery and Abolition* (Scarecrow, 2002). He is co-editor with

Sandra Greene and Alice Bellagamba of *African Voices on Slavery and the Slave Trade* (Cambridge, 2013) and *Bitter Legacy: African Slavery Past and Present* (Markus Wiener, 2013). He edited *Slavery, Bondage and Emancipation in Modern Asia and Africa* (Wisconsin, 1993) and with Clare Robertson *Women and Slavery in Africa* (Wisconsin, 1983). He has been President of both the African Studies Association and the Canadian Association of African Studies. In 2002, he received the Distinguished Africanist Award from the African Studies Association.

Behnaz A. Mirzai is Associate Professor of Middle Eastern history at Brock University. Prior to her current appointment, she taught at Southern Methodist University from 2005 to 2006. She has authored several articles on slavery and the African Diaspora in Iran; edited a special issue of *Journal of Middle East and Africa* (2013) on the Baluchi and Baluchistan; co-edited *Slavery, Islam and Diaspora* (Trenton, 2009); and produced two documentary films *Afro-Iranian Lives* and *African-Baluchi Trance Dance*. She is currently working on a book manuscript tentatively titled "Slavery and Emancipation in Iran 1800–1929".

Ei Murakami is Associate Professor of Institute for Research in Humanities, Kyoto University, Japan. He is also the chief of the Research Center for Modern and Contemporary China, Institute for Research in Humanities. He has been organizing the research group for studying "Reorganization of Social and Economic Institutions in Modern China" (www.zinbun.kyoto-u.ac.jp/rcmcc/group2.html) since 2012. He obtained his PhD from the University of Tokyo in 2012. His main academic interests are socio-economic history of south China during the late Qing and the early Republican period, maritime history of East and South China Sea from seventeenth century to the present and history of overseas Chinese in Southeast Asia. He is the author of *Umi no Kindai Chūgoku: Fukkenjin no katsudō to Igisiru/Shinchō* (in Japanese: *Maritime History of Modern China: Local Fujian actors and British and Chinese Empires*, Nagoya, 2013).

Sue Peabody, Professor of History at Washington State University Vancouver, is author and editor of several books on French ideas and legal regulation of slavery and race, including: *"There Are No Slaves in France": The Political Culture of Race and Slavery in the Ancien*

Régime (New York, 1996), *The Color of Liberty: Histories of Race in France*, with Tyler Stovall (Durham, 2002) and *Le Droit des Noirs en France au temps de l'esclavage*, with Pierre Boulle, Autrement Mêmes (Paris, 2014). She has also edited, with Keila Grinberg (University of Rio de Janeiro), *Slavery, Freedom and the Law in the Atlantic World* (Boston, 2007) and a special issue of *Slavery & Abolition* (2011) on the Free Soil principle in Atlantic legal systems. Her new book will appear soon as *Madeleine's Children: Family, Freedom, Secrets and Lies in France's Indian Ocean Colonies*, the biography of a family held in slavery 1750–1850.

Alessandro Stanziani is full Professor at the EHESS, where he teaches global history, and Senior Researcher at the CNRS, Paris. He is the author of 7 monographs, 12 edited books and more than 100 articles and chapters. Among which: *Rules of Exchange. French Capitalism in Comparative Perspective, 18th–20th Centuries* (Cambridge, 2012), *Bondage, Labor and Rights in Eurasia, 17th–20th Centuries* (Oxford and New York, 2014), *Bâtisseurs d'Empire. Russie, Inde et Chine à la croisée des mondes* (Paris, 2012), *Labour, Coercion and Economic Growth in Eurasia, 17th–20th Centuries* (editor) (Leiden, 2012).

Hideaki Suzuki is an associate professor at Nagasaki University where he teaches history of global exchange. He received his doctoral degree from University of Tokyo in 2010 with the thesis to examine transformation of slave traders in the nineteenth-century western Indian Ocean. He has authored several journal articles on Indian Ocean World both in English and Japanese, especially focusing on slave traders and slavery, including "Enslaved Population and Indian Owners along the East African Coast: Exploring the Rigby Manumission List, 1860–1861", *History in Africa: A Journal of Method* 39, 1 (2012), "Indo-yō nishi-kaiiki to 'kindai': dorei no ryutsu wo jirei ni shite [Western Indian Ocean and 'Modern Era': A Case Study on Slave Distributions]" (in Japanese), *Shigaku Zasshi* 116, 7 (2007). He also contributed to several edited volumes including *African Voices on Slavery and the Slave Trade* cited in the section of Martin Klein.

Isabel Tanaka-Van Daalen is a joint researcher at the Center for the Study of Visual Sources of the Historiographical Institute, University of Tokyo. Her research concerns the Dutch-Japanese historical relations in the Edo period, in particular the Japanese interpreters working for the Dutch on Deshima. She is also preparing a PhD thesis in History at Leiden University on these interpreters, focusing on their non-official activities and their (private) dealings with the Dutch residents in Japan. During her more than 25-year-long career at the Japan–Netherlands Institute in Tokyo, she was involved, among other things, in the compilation of the Kodansha's Dutch-Japanese Dictionary and the English marginalia publications, holding the contents of the diaries written by the heads of the VOC trading post on Deshima. She has also published several genealogies of Japanese interpreter families. She has published a number of articles and chapters including "Communicating with the Japanese under *Sakoku*: Dutch Letters of Complaint and Attempts to Learn Japanese", in *Large and Broad: the Dutch impact on early Modern Asia: essays in honor of Leonard Blussé*, ed. Nagazumi Yoko, Toyo Bunko Research Library 13 (Tokyo: The Toyo Bunko, 2010), pp. 100–29.

Yuriko Yokoyama is a professor at the National Museum of Japanese History, Inter-University Research Institute Corporation National Institutes for the Humanities. She also teaches early modern Japanese history. She is the author of *Meiji ishin to kinsei mibunsei no kaitai* [The Meiji Restoration and Dissolution of Early Modern Status System] (Tokyo, 2006) and has published a number of journal articles including "Jyūkyū toshi shakai ni okeru chiiki hegemoni no saihen: Onna-kamiyui, Yūjo no Seizon to 'Kaihou' wo megutte" [Reorganisation of Regional Hegemony in the Nineteenth Century Urban Society: On the Survival and 'Emancipation' of Coiffures and Yūjo], *Rekishigaku Kenkyū* 885 (2011).

Bibliography

Abeyasekere, S., "Slaves in Batavia: Insights from a Slave Register", in Anthony Reid, *Slavery, Bondage and Dependency in Southeast Asia.* New York: St Martin's Press, 1963, pp. 286–314.

Ackerson, Wayne, *The African Institution (1807–1827) and the Antislavery Movement in Great Britain.* Lewiston, NY: E. Mellen Press, 2005.

Adamiyat, Fereydun, *Amir Kabir va Iran* [Amir Kabir and Iran]. Tehran: Khawrazmi, 1362.

Adélaïde-Merlande, Jacques, "La Commission d'abolition de l'esclavage" [The Abolition of Slavery Commission], *Bulletin de la Société d'histoire de la Guadeloupe* 53–54 (1982): 3–34.

———, *La Caraïbe et la Guyane au temps de la Révolution et de l'Empire* [The Caribbean and Guiana during the Revolution and the Empire]. Paris: Éditions Karthala, 1992, pp. 185–201.

Agbetu, Toyin, "Protest at Slavery Service", *Independent*, 28 Mar. 2007.

———, "My Protest was Born of Anger, Not Madness", *Guardian*, 3 Apr. 2007.

Allain, Jean, "Slavery and the League of Nations: Ethiopia as a Civilised Nation", *Journal of the History of International Law* 8 (2006): 213–44.

Allen, Robert, *Farm to Factory: A Reinterpretation of the Soviet Industrial Revolution.* Princeton, NJ: Princeton University Press, 2003.

Anderson, Bonnie S., *Joyous Greetings: The First International Women's Movement, 1830–1860.* Oxford: Oxford University Press, 2000.

Andrews, George Reid, *Afro-Latin America, 1800–2000.* New York and Oxford: Oxford University Press, 2004.

Anonymous, "Discours sur la nécessité d'établir à Paris une Société pour concourir, avec celle de Londres, à l'abolition de la traite & de l'esclavage des Nègres. Prononcé le 19 Février 1788, dans un Société de quelques amis, à la prière du Comité de Londres" [Speech on the Necessity to Establish in Paris a Society to Contribute, with that of London, to the Abolition of the (Slave) Trade and of Negro Slavery. Given on 19 February 1788, in a Society of Some Friends, at the Behest of the Committee from London]. Paris, s.d., 1788, in *La Révolution française et l'abolition de l'esclavage* [The French Revolution and the Abolition of Slavery], 12 vols. Paris: EDHIS, 1968, 6, 1, p. 1.

Anstey, Roger, "Capitalism and Slavery: A Critique", *Economic History Review*, 2nd ser. XXI, 2 (1968): 307–20.

———, *The Atlantic Slave Trade and British Abolition, 1760–1810*. London: Macmillan, 1975.

Arensmeyer, Elliott Campbell, "British Merchant Enterprise and the Chinese Coolie Labour Trade: 1850–1874", unpublished PhD dissertation. Hawaii: University of Hawaii, 1979.

Arnold, Arthur, *Through Persia by Caravan*, vol. 2. London: Tinsley Brothers, 1877.

———, *The Atlantic Slave Trade and British Abolition, 1760–1810*. London: Macmillan, 1975.

Baay, Reggie, *Daar werd wat gruwelijks verricht: Slavernij in Nederlands-Indië* [Something Horrifying was Carried Out: Slavery in the Dutch East Indies]. Amsterdam: Athenaeum-Polak & Van Gennep, 2015.

Babou, Cheikh Anta, *Fighting the Greater Jihad: Amadu Bamba and the Founding of the Muridiyya of Senegal, 1853–1913*. Athens, OH: Ohio University Press, 2007.

Badji, Mamadou, "L'abolition de l'esclavage au Sénégal: entre plasticité du droit colonial et respect de l'Etat de droit" [The Abolition of Slavery in Senegal: Between the Elasticity of Colonial Law and Respect for the State of Law], *Droit et Cultures* 52 (2006): 239–74.

Baldus, Bernd, "Responses to Dependency in a Servile Group", in *Slavery in Africa: Historical and Anthropological Perspectives*, ed. Suzanne Miers and Igor Kopytoff. Madison, WI: University of Wisconsin Press, 1977, pp. 435–58.

Bales, Kevin, *Disposable People: New Slavery in the Global Economy*. Berkeley, CA: University of California Press, 1999.

———, *Understanding Global Slavery: A Reader*. Berkeley and Los Angeles, CA: University of California Press, 2005.

Barrau, Abraham, "De Waare Staat van den Slaaven-handel in onze Nederlandsche Colonien" [The True State of the Slave Trade in the Dutch Colonies], *Bijdragen tot het Menschelijk Geluk* 3 (1790): 341–88.

Barrows, Leland C., "The Merchants and General Faidherbe. Aspects of French Expansion in Senegal in 1950's", *Revue Française d'histoire d'outre-mer* 61 (1974).

———, "Louis Léon Cesar Faidherbe (1818–1889)", in *African Proconsuls: European Governors in Africa*, ed. Peter Duignan and L.H. Gann. Stanford, CA: Hoover Institution, 1978, pp. 51–79.

Barry, Boubacar, *Senegambia and the Atlantic Slave Trade*, tr. Ayei Kwei Armah. Cambridge: Cambridge University Press, 1998.

Beaglehole, J.C., ed., *The Journals of Captain Cook and His Voyages of Discovery*. Cambridge: Cambridge University Press, 1967.

Becker, Samuel, *Nobility and Privilege in Late Imperial Russia*. DeKalb, IL: Northern Illinois University Press, 1985.

Bellagamba, Alice, "Mussa Molo Baldeh of Fuladu: Memories of a Senegambian Slave Descendant and Slaver", paper presented at Annual Conference of African Studies Association, Baltimore, 21–24 Nov. 2013.

Bellagamba, Alice, Sandra Green and Martin A. Klein, eds., *African Voices on Slavery and the Slave Trade*. Cambridge: Cambridge University Press, 2013.

Bénot, Yves, *La Révolution française et la fin des colonies, 1789–1794: postface inédite* [The French Revolution and the End of the Colonies, 1789–1794: A New Postface]. Paris: La Découverte, 2004 (Orig. Publ. 1987).

———, *La Guyane sous la Révolution française, ou, L'impasse de la révolution pacifique* [Guiana during the French Revolution, or the Dead End of the Peaceful Revolution]. Kourou: Ibis Rouge, 1997.

———, *La Démence Coloniale sous Napoléon* [Colonial Madness under Napoleon]. Paris: La Découverte, 1992 (Rpr. 2006).

Bénot, Yves and Marcel Dorigny, *Rétablissement de l'esclavage dans les colonies françaises, 1802: ruptures et continuités de la politique coloniale française, 1800–1830: aux origines d'Haïti* [Reestablishment of Slavery in the French Colonies, 1802: Ruptures and Continuities of French Colonial Policy, 1800–1830: From the Origins to Haiti]. Paris: Maisonneuve et Larose, 2003.

Berndt, Jeremy, "Speaking as Scholars: The First Generation of Slave Moodibaabe in Gimbala, Central Mali", paper presented at Conference on Finding the African Voice, Bellagio, Italy, Sept. 2007.

———, "Closer than Your Jugular Vein: Muslim Intellectuals in a Malian Village, 1900 to the 1960s", unpublished PhD dissertation. St Evanston, IL: Northwestern University, 2008.

Bernus, Edmond, "Kong et sa région" [Kong and its Region], *Etudes eburnéennes* 8 (1960): 239–324.

Bissondoyal, Uttama, ed., *L'Île de France et la Révolution française* [Île de France and the French Revolution]. Mauritius: Mahatma Gandhi Institute Press, 1990.

Bjarup, Jes, "The Concept of a Person according to Anders Sandøe Ørsted", *Quaderni Fiorentini* 11/12 (1982): 461–74.

Blackburn, Robin, *The Overthrow of Colonial Slavery, 1776–1848*. London: Verso, 1988.

———. *The Making of New World Slavery: From the Baroque to the Modern, 1492–1800*. London: Verso, 1997.

———, *The American Crucible: Slavery, Emancipation and Human Rights*. London: Verso, 2011.

Blackmon, Douglas A., *Slavery By Another Name: The Re-Enslavement of Black Americans from the Civil War to World War II*. New York: Doubleday, 2008.

Blakely, Allison, *Blacks in the Dutch World: The Evolution of Racial Imagery in a Modern Society*. Bloomington, IN: Indiana University Press, 1993.

Blanchard, Ian, *Russia's Age of Silver: Precious Metal Production and Economic Growth in the Eighteenth Century*. London and New York: Routledge, 1989.

_____, "Le développement économique en perspective historique: l'avenir de la Russie à la lumière de son évolution à l'époque moderne (1700–1914)", in *Les enterprises et leurs réseaux: hommes, capitaux, techniques et pouvoirs xixe–xxe siècles. Mèlanges en l'honneur de François Caron*, ed. Michèle Merger and Dominique Barjot. Paris: Presse de l'Université de Paris-Sorbonne, 1998, pp. 381–92.

Blanchard, Peter, *Under the Flags of Freedom: Slave Soldiers and the Wars of Independence in Spanish South America*. Pittsburgh, PA: University of Pittsburgh Press, 2008.

Blériot, Laurent, "La loi d'indemnisation des colons du 30 avril 1849, aspects juridiques" [The Law for the Compensation of Colonists of 30 April 1849, Juridical Aspects], *Revue historique des Mascareignes* 2, 2 (2000): 147–65.

Blum, Alain and Irina Troitskaia, "La mortalité en Russie au XVIIIe et XIXe siècles. Estimations locales à partir des Revizii", *Population* 51 (1996): 303–28.

Blum, Jerome, *Lords and Peasants in Russia from the Ninth to the Nineteenth Century*. New York: Atheneum, 1964.

Blussé, Leonard, Willem Remmelink and Ivo Smits, eds., *Bridging the Divide: 400 Years The Netherlands–Japan*. Leiden: Hotei Publishing, 2000.

Bongie, Chris, "A Street Named Bissette: Nostalgia, Memory, and the Cent-Cinquantenaire of the Abolition of Slavery in Martinique (1848–1998)", *South Atlantic Quarterly* 100, 1 (2001): 215–57.

_____, "'C'est du papier ou de l'Histoire en marche?' [Is it [Mere] Paper or is it History in Motion?]: The Revolutionary Compromises of a Martiniquan Homme de Couleur, Cyrille-Charles-Auguste Bissette", *Nineteenth-Century Contexts* 23, 4 (2002): 439–74.

Boomgaard, Peter, "Human Capital, Slavery and Low Rates of Economic and Population Growth in Indonesia, 1600–1910", in *The Structure of Slavery in Indian Ocean Africa and Asia*, ed. Gwyn Campbell. London: Frank Cass, 2004, pp. 83–96.

Boomgaard, Peter, Dick Koolman and Henk Schulte Nordholt, eds., *Linking Destinies: Trade, Towns and Kin in Asian History*. Leiden: KITLV Press, 2008.

Borodkin, Leonid, Brigitte Granville and Carol Scott Leonard, "The Rural/ Urban Wage Gap in the Industrialisation of Russia, 1884–1910", *European Review of Economic History* 12, 1 (2008): 67–95.

Bosma, Ulbe, ed., *Post-Colonial Immigrants and Identity Formations in the Netherlands*. Amsterdam: Amsterdam University Press, 2012.

Bosma, Ulbe and Remco Raben, *Being "Dutch" in the Indies: A History of Creolisation and Empire 1500–1920*. Singapore: NUS Press, 2008.

Bosma, Ulbe, Jan Lucassen and Gert Oostindie, eds., *Postcolonial Migrations and Identity Politics*. Oxford: Berghahn, 2012.

Botte, Roger, "Stigmates sociaux et discriminations religeuses: l'ancienne classe servile au Futa Jaloo" [Social Stigmas and Religious Discrimination: The Former Servile Class in Futa Jaloo], *Cahiers d'études africaines* 34 (1994): 109–36.

Botsman, Daniel, "Freedom without Slavery? 'Coolies,' Prostitutes, and Outcastes in Meiji Japan's 'Emancipation Moment'", *American Historical Review* 116, 5 (2011): 1323–47.

———, "Recovering Japan's Urban Past: Yoshida Nobuyuki, Tsukada Takashi, and the Cities of the Tokugawa Period", *City, Culture and Society* 3, 1 (2012): 9–14.

Boutillier, Jean-Louis, "Les Trois Esclaves de Bouna" [The Three Slaves of Bouna], in *L'Esclavage en Afrique précoloniale* [Slavery in Precolonial Africa], ed. Claude Meillassoux. Paris: Maspero, 1968, pp. 252–80.

Brooks, George, "The Signares of St. Louis and Gorée: Women Entrepreneurs in Eighteenth Century Senegal", in *Women in Africa*, ed. Nancy Hafkin and Edna Bay. Stanford, CA: Stanford University Press, 1976, pp. 19–44.

Brower, Benjamin Claude, "Rethinking Abolition in Algeria: Slavery and the 'Indigenous Question'", *Cahiers d'Études Africaines* 195, 3 (2009): 805–28.

Brown, Christopher Leslie, *Moral Capital: Foundations of British Abolitionism*. Chapel Hill, NC: University of North Carolina Press, 2006.

Brown, Christopher Leslie and Philip D. Morgan, ed., *Arming Slaves: From Classical Times to the Modern Age*. New Haven, CT: Yale University Press, 2006.

Buffon, Alain, "L'Indemnisation des planteurs après l'abolition de l'esclavage" [The Planters' Compensation after the Abolition of Slavery], *Bulletin de la Société d'histoire de la Guadeloupe* (1986).

Burbank, Jane, *Russian Peasants Go to Court: Legal Culture in the Countryside, 1905–1917*. Bloomington, IN: Indiana University Press, 2004.

Burds, Jeffrey, *Peasant Dreams and Market Politics: Labor Migration and the Russian Village, 1861–1905*. Pittsburgh, PA: University of Pittsburgh Press, 1998.

Burns, Arthur and Joanna Innes, ed., *Rethinking the Age of Reform: Britain 1780–1850*. Cambridge: Cambridge University Press, 2003.

Busch, Briton Cooper, *Britain and the Persian Gulf, 1894–1914*. Berkeley and Los Angeles, CA: University of California Press, 1967.

Campbell, Gwyn, "Introduction: Slavery and Other Forms of Unfree Labour in the Indian Ocean World", in *Structure of Slavery in Indian Ocean Africa and Asia*, ed. Gwyn Campbell. London: Frank Cass, 2004, pp. vii–xxxii.

————, "Introduction: Abolition and its Aftermath in the Indian Ocean World", in *Abolition and its Aftermath in Indian Ocean Africa and Asia*, ed. Gwyn Campbell. London and New York: Routledge, 2005.

————, "Slave Trades and the Indian Ocean World", in *India in Africa, Africa in India: Indian Ocean Cosmopolitanisms*, ed. John C. Hawley. Bloomington, IN: Indiana University Press, 2008, pp. 17–51.

————, "Female Bondage and Agency in the Indian Ocean World", in *African Communities in Asia and the Mediterranean: Identities between Integration and Conflict*, ed. Ehud R. Toledano. Trenton: Africa World Press, 2012, pp. 37–63.

Campbell, Gwyn and Alessandro Stanziani, eds., *Bonded Labour and Debt in the Indian Ocean World*. Brookfield: Pickering & Chatto, 2013.

Campbell, Persia Crawford, *Chinese Coolie Emigration to Countries within the British Empire*. London: Frank Cass, 1923.

Chew, Emrys, *Arming the Periphery: The Arms Trade in the Indian Ocean during the Age of Global Empire*. Hampshire: Palgrave Macmillan, 2012.

Chivallon, Christine, *Espace et identité à la Martinique: Paysannerie des mornes et reconquête collective, 1840–1960* [Space and Identity in Martinique: Peasantry of the Hills and Collective Reconquest]. Paris: C.N.R.S. Editions, 1998.

————, *L'esclavage, du souvenir à la mémoire: contribution à une anthropologie de la Caraïbe* [Slavery, from Recollection to Memory: Contribution to an Anthropology of the Caribbean]. Paris: Éditions Karthala, 2012.

Chowdhury, Amitava, "Theoretical Reflections on Maroon Archaeology in Mauritius", *Revi Kiltir Kreol* 3 (2003): 55–59.

————, "Maroon Archaeological Research in Mauritius and its Possible Implications in a Global Context", in *The Archaeology of Slavery: Toward a Comparative Global Framework*, ed. Lydia Wilson Marshall. Carbondale, IL: CAI, Southern Illinois University, 2014, pp. 255–75.

Christopher, Emma, Cassandra Pybus and Marus Rediker, ed., *Many Middle Passages: Forced Migration and the Making of the Modern World*. Berkeley, CA: University of California Press, 2007.

Clark, Andrew, "Slavery and its Demise in the Upper Senegal Valley, 1890–1920", *Slavery and Abolition* 15 (1994): 51–71.

Coen, Jan Pietersz, *Bescheiden omtrent zijn Bedrijf in Indië* [Records of His Undertakings in the East Indies], 7 vols, ed. Herman Th. Colenbrander W. Ph. Coolhaas. 's Gravenhage: Martinus Nijhoff, 1919–53.

Coleman Jr, Sterling Joseph, "Gradual Abolition or Immediate Abolition of Slavery? The Political, Social and Economic Quandary of Emperor Haile Selassie I", *Slavery and Abolition: A Journal of Slave and Post-Slave Studies* 29, 1 (2008): 65–82.

Combeau, Yvan, *La Réunion républicaine: l'avènement de la IIe et de la IIIe République 1848/1870* [Republican Réunion: The Arrival of the Second and the Third Republic, 1848/1870]. Le Port, La Réunion: Les Deux Mondes, 1996.

Confino, Michael, *Domaines et seigneurs en Russie vers la fin du XVIIIe siècle: Étude de structures agraires et de mentalités économiques*. Paris: Mouton, 1963.

———, *Systèmes agraires et progrès agricole en Russie aux XVIIIe–XIXe siècles: Étude d'économie et de sociologie rurales*. Paris: Mouton, 1969.

Conklin, Alice, *A Mission to Civilize: The Republican Idea of Empire in France and West Africa, 1895–1930*. Stanford, CA: Stanford University Press, 1997.

Copans, Jean, *Les Marabouts de l'Arachide. La Confrérie mouride et les Paysans du Sénégal* [The Marabouts of the Peanut. The Mouride Confraternity and the Peasants of Senegal]. Paris: Harmattan, 1988.

Cooper, Frederick, Thomas C. Holt and Rebecca J. Scott, *Beyond Slavery: Explorations of Race, Labor, and Citizenship in Postemancipation Societies*. Chapel Hill, NC: University of North Carolina Press, 2000.

Cotter, William R., "The Somerset Case and the Abolition of Slavery in England", *History* 79, 255 (1994): 31–56.

Coupland, Regiland, *Wilberforce*. Oxford: Oxford University Press, 1923.

———, "The Abolition of the Slave Trade", in *The Cambridge History of the British Empire*, ed. J. Holland Rose, A.P. Newton and E.A. Benians, vol. 2, *The Growth of the New Empire, 1783–1870*. Cambridge: Cambridge University Press, 1940.

Crisp, Olga, *Studies in Russian Economy before 1914*. London: Basingstoke, 1976.

Cruise O'Brien, Donal, *The Mourides of Senegal*. London: Oxford University Press, 1971.

Cubitt, Geoffrey, "Museums and Slavery in Britain: The Bicentenary of 1807", in *Politics of Memory: Making Slavery Visible in the Public Space*, ed. Ana Lucia Araujo. London and New York: Routledge, 2012, pp. 159–77.

Daget, Serge, *La Répression de la Traite des Noirs au XIXe Siècle: L'Action des Croisières Françaises sur les Côtes Occidentales de l'Afrique (1817–1850)* [The Suppression of the Slave Trade in the Nineteenth Century: The Activities of the French Fleet on the Eastern Coast of Africa (1817–1850)]. Paris: Éditions Karthala, 1997, pp. 36–55.

Davis, David Brion, *The Problem of Slavery in Western Culture*. Ithaca, NY: Cornell University Press, 1966.

———, *The Problem of Slavery in the Age of Revolution, 1770–1823*. Ithaca, NY: Cornell University Press, 1975.

———, *Slavery and Human Progress*. Oxford and New York: Oxford University Press, 1984.

———, "Looking at Slavery from Broader Perspectives", *American Historical Review* 105, 2 (2000): 451–66.

———, *Inhuman Bondage: The Rise and Fall of Slavery in the New World*. New York and Oxford: Oxford University Press, 2006.

De Bruijn, Mirjam and Lotte Pelckmans, "Facing Dilemmas: Former Fulbe Slaves in Modern Mali", *Canadian Journal of African Studies* 39 (2005): 69–96.

De Cauna, Jacques, ed., *Toussaint Louverture et l'indépendance d'Haïti* [Toussaint Louverture and Haitian Independence]. Paris: Éditions Karthala, 2004.

De Graaff, Nicolaas, *Oost-Indise Spiegel* [The East Indian Mirror], ed. Marijke Barend-van Haeften and Hetty Plekenpol. Leiden: KITLV Press, 2010. 1st ed., 1701.

De Haan, Frederik, *Oud Batavia: Gedenkboek* [Old Batavia: Commemorative Volume], 3 vols. Batavia: G. Kolff, 1922–23.

Dennison, Tracy, *The Institutional Framework of Russian Serfdom*. Cambridge: Cambridge University Press, 2011.

Den Heijer, Henk, *De Geschiedenis van de WIC* [The History of the West India Company]. Zutphen: Walburg Pers, 1994.

Devereux, W. Cope, *A Cruise in the "Gorgon;" or, Eighteen Months on H.M.S. "Gorgon", Engaged in the Suppression of the Slave Trade on the East Coast of Africa. Including a Trip up the Zambesi with Dr. Livingstone*. London: Bell and Daldy, 1869.

Diouf, Mamadou, *Le Kajoor au XIXe siècle: Pouvoir ceddo et conquête coloniale* [Kajoor in the 19th Century: Ceddo Power and Colonial Conquest]. Paris: Éditions Karthala, 1990.

Domar, Evsey and M. Machina, "On the Profitability of Russian Serfdom", *The Journal of Economic History* 44, 4 (1984): 919–55.

Dorigny, Marcel, ed., *Les abolitions de l'esclavage: de L.F. Sonthonax à V. Schœlcher, 1793, 1794, 1848* [Slavery Abolitions from L.F. Sonthonax to V. Schoelcher, 1793, 1794, 1848]. Saint-Dénis, France: Presses Universitaires de Vincennes; Paris: UNESCO, 1995.

———, ed., *Les Abolitions de l'esclavage de L.F. Sonthonax à V. Schoelcher, actes du colloque international tenu à l'Université de Paris VIII les 3, 4 et 5 février 1994* [Slavery Abolitions from L.F. Sonthonax to V. Schoelcher, conference proceedings, University of Paris, 3, 4 and 5 February 1994]. Paris: Presses Universitaires de Vincennes, 1998.

———, *Anti-esclavagisme, abolitionnisme et abolitions: débats et controverses en France de la fin du XVIIIe siècle aux années 1840* [The Abolitions of Slavery and Anti-Slavery, Abolitionism and Abolitions: Debates and Controversies in France, from the End of the 18th Century to the 1840s]. Quebec: Presses de l'Université Laval, 2008.

Dorigny, Marcel and Bernard Gainot, *La Société des Amis des Noirs, 1788–1799: Contribution à l'histoire des abolitions de l'esclavage* [The Society of the Friends of the Blacks, 1788–1799: Contribution to the History of the Abolitions of Slavery]. Paris: UNESCO, 1998.

Drescher, Seymour, *Capitalism and Antislavery: British Mobilization in Comparative Perspective.* London/New York and Oxford: Macmillan/Oxford University Press, 1986/87.

———, "British Way, French Way: Opinion Building and Revolution in the Second French Slave Emancipation", *American Historical Review* 96 (1991): 725–34.

———, "The Long Goodbye: Dutch Capitalism and Antislavery in Comparative Perspective", in *Fifty Years Later: Antislavery, Capitalism and Modernity in the Dutch Orbit*, ed. Gert Oostindie. Leiden: KITLV Press, 1995, pp. 25–66.

———, *Abolition: A History of Slavery and Antislavery.* Cambridge: Cambridge University Press, 2009, pp. 205–41.

———, "Capitalism and Abolition: Values and Forces in Britain, 1783–1814", in *Liverpool, the African Slave Trade, and Abolition: Essays to Illustrate Current Knowledge and Research*, ed. R. Anstey and P.E.H. Hair. Liverpool: Historic Society of Lancashire and Cheshire, 1976, pp. 167–95.

———, *Capitalism and Antislavery: British Mobilization in Comparative Perspective.* New York and Oxford: Oxford University Press, 1987.

———, *The Mighty Experiment: Free Labor versus Slavery in British Emancipation.* New York and Oxford: Oxford University Press, 2002.

———, *Econocide: British Slavery in the Era of Abolition* Pittsburgh, PA: University of Pittsburgh Press, 1977, 2nd ed. Chapel Hill, NC: University of North Carolina Press, 2010.

Druzhinin, Nikolai M., *Gosudarstvennye krest'iane i reforma P.D. Kiseleva* [State Peasants and the Reform of P.D. Kiselev]. Moscow: Nauka, 1958.

Drysdale, Alasdair and Gerald H. Blake, *The Middle East and North Africa: A Political Geography.* New York: Oxford University Press, 1985.

Dubois, Laurent, "Haunting Delgrès", *Radical History Review* 78 (Fall, 2000): 166–77.

———, *Avengers of the New World: The Story of the Haitian Revolution.* Cambridge, MA: Belknap Press, 2004a.

———, *A Colony of Citizens: Revolution & Slave Emancipation in the French Caribbean, 1787–1804.* Chapel Hill, NC: Published for the Omohundro Institute of Early American History and Culture, Williamsburg by the University of North Carolina Press, 2004b.

Dukes, Paul, *Catherine the Great and the Russian Nobility*. Cambridge: Cambridge University Press, 1967.

Dupont, Jerry, *The Common Law Abroad: Constitutional and Legal Legacy of the British Empire*. Littleton, Col.: F.B. Rothman Publications, 2001.

Echenberg, Myron, *Colonial Conscripts: The* Tirailleurs Sénégalais *in French West Africa, 1857–1960*. Portsmouth NH: Heinemann, 1991.

Ejstrud, Bo, "Maroons and Landscapes", *Journal of Caribbean Archaeology* 8 (2008): 1–14.

Ekloff, Ben, John Bushnell and Larisa Georgievna Zakharova, ed., *Russia's Great Reforms, 1855–1881*. Bloomington, IN: Indiana University Press, 1994.

El Hamel, Chouki, *Black Morocco: A History of Slavery, Race, and Islam*. New York: Cambridge University Press, 2013.

Eltis, David, *Economic Growth and the Ending of Transatlantic Slave Trade*. New York: Oxford University Press, 1987.

Emmer, Pieter C., *The Dutch Slave Trade, 1500–1850*. Oxford: Berghahn Books, 2006.

Emmons, Terence, *The Russian Landed Gentry and the Peasant Emancipation of 1861*. Berkeley and Los Angeles, CA: University of California Press, 1968.

Emmons, Terence and Wayne Vucinich, *The Zemstvos in Russia: An Experiment in Local Self-Government*. New York and Cambridge: Cambridge University Press, 1992.

Encyclopaedie van Nederlandsch-Indië [Encyclopaedia of the Dutch East Indies], 8 vols (vols 5–8: suppl.). 's Gravenhage: Martinus Nijhoff; Leiden: Brill, 1919–39.

Engerman, Stanley, *Terms of Labor: Slavery, Serfdom, and Free Labor*. Stanford, CA: Stanford University Press, 1999.

Erdem, Y. Hakan, *Slavery in the Ottoman Empire and its Demise, 1800–1909*. Oxford: St Martin's Press, 1996.

Emmons, Terence, *The Russian Landed Gentry and the Peasant Emancipation of 1861*. Cambridge: Cambridge University Press, 1968.

Eve, Prosper, *Le 20 décembre à la Réunion et sa célébration: du déni à la réhabilitation (1848–1980)* [20 December in Réunion and its Celebration: From Denial to Rehabilitation (1848–1980)]. Paris: L'Harmattan, 2000.

Fall, Babacar, *Le travail force en Afrique occidentale française (1900–1946)* [Forced Labor in French West Africa (1900–1946)]. Paris: Éditions Karthala, 1993.

Fallope, Josette, *Esclaves et citoyens: Les Noirs à la Guadeloupe au XIXe siècle dans les processus de résistance et d'intégration (1802–1910)* [Slaves and Citizens: Blacks in Nineteenth-Century Guadeloupe in the Processes of Resistance and Integration (1802–1910)]. Basse-Terre, Guadeloupe: Société d'Histoire de la Guadeloupe, 1992, pp. 48–50.

Federnini, Fabien, *L'Abolition de l'esclavage en 1848: Une Lecture de Victor Schœlcher* [The Abolition of Slavery in 1848: A Lecture of Victor Schoelcher]. Paris: L'Harmattan, 1998.

Feenstra Kuiper, Jan, "Some Notes on the Foreign Relations of Japan in the Early Napoleonic Period (1798–1805)", *Transactions of the Asiatic Society of Japan* 2, 1 (1923): 55–82.

Feeny, David, "The Demise of Corvee and Slavery in Thailand, 1782–1913", in *Breaking the Chains: Slavery, Bondage, and Emancipation in Modern Africa and Asia*, ed. Martin A. Klein. Madison, WI: University of Wisconsin Press, 1993.

Ferrer, Ada, "Speaking of Haiti: Slavery, Revolution, and Freedom in Cuban Slave Testimony", in *The World of the Haitian Revolution*, ed. David Patrick Geggus and Norman Fiering. Bloomington, IN: Indiana University Press, 2009, pp. 223–47.

————, "Haiti, Free Soil, and Antislavery in the Revolutionary Atlantic", *The American Historical Review* 117, 1 (2012): 40–66.

Fick, Carolyn E., *The Making of Haiti: The Saint Domingue Revolution from Below*. Knoxville, TN: University of Tennessee Press, 1990.

————, "Emancipation in Haiti: From Plantation Labour to Peasant Proprietorship", in *After Slavery: Emancipation and its Discontents*, ed. Howard Temperley. London: Frank Cass, 2000, pp. 11–40.

Field, Daniel, *The End of Serfdom: Nobility and Bureaucracy in Russia, 1855–1861*. Cambridge, MA: Harvard University Press, 1976).

Finley, Moses, "Slavery", *International Encyclopedia of the Social Sciences*. New York: Macmillan, 1968, pp. 307–13.

Fischer-Blanchet, M.A.I, "Les travaux de la commission de l'indemnité coloniale en 1848" [The Efforts of the Commission of Colonial Compensation in 1848], *Espaces caraïbes* (1983): 37–56.

Fog Olwig, Karen, "Caribbean Place Identity: From Family Land to Region and Beyond", *Identities: Global Studies in Culture and Power* 5, 4 (1999): 435–67.

Fogel, Robert, *Without Consent or Contract: the Rise and Fall of American Slavery*. New York: Norton 1989.

Forbes, Frederic E., *Dahomey and the Dahomans: Being the Journals of Two Missions to the King of Dahomey, and Residence at His Capital, in the Years 1849 and 1850*, 2 vols. London: Longman, 1851; rpt. London: Frank Cass, 1966, vol. 2, pp. 206–9.

Fox, James J., "'For Good and Sufficient Reasons': An Examination of Early Dutch East India Company Ordinances on Slaves and Slavery", in *Slavery, Bondage and Dependency in Southeast Asia*, ed. Anthony Reid. St Lucia: University of Queensland Press, 1983, pp. 246–62.

Freeze, Gregory, "The Soslovie (Estate) Paradigm In Russian Social History", *American Historical Review* 91, 1 (1986): 11–36.

Frey, Silvia R., *Water from the Rock: Black Resistance in a Revolutionary Age*. Princeton, NJ: Princeton University Press, 1991, pp. 55–6.

Fujita, Midori, *Afurika Hakken: Nihon ni okeru Afurika-zō no Hensen* [The Discovery of Africa: Changes in the Japanese Perception of Africa]. Tokyo: Iwanami Shoten, 2005.

Fuma, Sudel, *L'abolition de l'esclavage à La Réunion: Histoire d'un insertion des 62,000 affranchis de 1848 dans la société réunionnaise* [The Abolition of Slavery in Réunion: History of an Insertion of 62,000 Freedmen into Réunionais Society]. Saint-André, La Réunion: G.R.A.H.TER and Ocean Éditions, 1998.

Gaastra, Femme S., *The Dutch East India Company: Expansion and Decline*. Zutphen: Walburg Press, 2003.

Garraway, Doris Lorraine, *Tree of Liberty: Culture Legacies of the Haitian Revolution in the Atlantic World*. Charlottesville, VA: University Press of Virginia, 2008.

Gaspar, David Barry and Darlene Clark Hine, ed., *More Than Chattel: Black Women and Slavery in the Americas*. Bloomington and Indianapolis: Indiana University Press, 1996.

Gatrell, Peter, *The Tsarist Economy, 1850–1917*. New York: St Martin's Press, 1986.

Gerbeau, Hubert, *Les Esclaves Noirs: Pour une Histoire du Silence* [The Black Slaves: Toward a History of Silence]. Paris: André Balland, 1970.

Geggus, David Patrick, *Slavery, War, and Revolution: The British Occupation of Saint Domingue, 1793–1798*. Oxford: Clarendon Press, 1982.

———, *Haitian Revolutionary Studies*. Bloomington, IN: Indiana University Press, 2002.

Gelman Taylor, Jean, *The Social World of Batavia: European and Eurasian in Dutch Asia*. Madison, WI: University of Wisconsin Press, 1983.

Genovese, Eugene, *From Rebellion to Revolution: Afro-American Slave Revolts in the Making of the Modern World*. Baton Rouge, LA: Louisiana State University Press, 1979, pp. 95–6.

Gerschenkron, Alexander, *Economic Backwardness in Historical Perspective: A Book of Essays*. Cambridge, MA: Harvard University Press, 1962.

Getz, Trevor, *Slavery and Reform in West Africa: Toward Emancipation in Nineteenth-Century Senegal and the Gold Coast*. Athens, OH: Ohio University Press, 2004.

Ghachem, Malick W., *The Old Regime and the Haitian Revolution*. Cambridge: Cambridge University Press, 2012.

Gilbert, Erik, *Dhows and the Colonial Economy in Zanzibar, 1860–1970*. Oxford: James Currey, 2004.

Girollet, Anne, *Victor Schœlcher abolitionniste et républicain* [Victor Schoelcher, Abolitionist and Republican]. Paris: Éditions Karthala, 1999.

Goodwin, Barry K. and Thomas J. Grennes, "Tsarist Russia and the World Wheat Market", *Explorations in Economic History* 35, 4 (1998): 405–30.

Gooszen, Hans, "Population Census in VOC-Batavia 1673–1792", unpublished manuscript. 2008. Deposited at Data Archiving and Networked Services, DANS, www.dans.knaw.nl, accessed 4 Mar. 2015.

Gottlieb, Karla, *The Mother of Us All: A History of Queen Nanny, Leader of the Windward Jamaican Maroons*. Trenton, NJ: Africa World Press, 1998.

Gregory, Paul, *Russian National Income (1885–1913)*. Cambridge: Cambridge University Press, 1982.

Grinberg, Keila Grinberg and Sue Peabody, ed., *Slavery, Freedom and the Law in the Atlantic World*. New York: Bedford/St Martin's, 2007.

Groot, Hans, *Van Batavia naar Weltevreden: Het Bataviaasch Genootschap van Kunsten en Wetenschappen, 1778–1867* [From Batavia to Weltevreden: The Batavian Society of Arts and Sciences, 1778–1867]. Leiden: KITLV Press, 2009.

Guardian, "Slavery Compensation: Caribbean Nations Propose Mau Mau Model", 26 July 2013, www.theguardian.com/world/2013/jul/26/caribbean-countries-slavery-compensation-claim, accessed 5 Jan. 2014.

Gueye, Mbaye, "La fin de l'esclavage à St. Louis et Gorée en 1848" [The End of Slavery in St. Louis and Gorée in 1848], *Bulletin de l'Institut Français d'Afrique Noire* 28 (1966): 637–67.

Haagensen, Richard, *Beskrivelse over Eylandet St. Croix i America i Vestindien* (Description of the Island of St. Croix in America in the West Indies]. København, 1758.

Hahonou, Eric Komlavi, "Slavery and Politics: Stigma, Decentralisation and Political Representation in Niger and Benin", *Reconfiguring Slavery: West African Trajectories*, ed. Benedetta Rossi. Liverpool: Liverpool University Press, 2009, pp. 152–81.

———, "The Struggle for Political Emancipation of Slave Descendants in Contemporary Borgou, Northern Benin", in *Bitter Legacy: African Slavery Past and Present*, ed. Alice Bellagamba, Sandra Greene and Martin A. Klein. Princeton NJ: Markus Wiener, 2013, pp. 29–56.

Hahonou, Eric Komlavi and Lotte Pelckmans, "West African Anti-Slavery Movements: Citizenship Struggles and the Legacies of Slavery", *Vienna Journal of African Studies, Stichprobe* 20 (2011): 141–62.

Hahonou, Eric Komlavi and Camilla Stranbjerg, *Yesterday's Slaves: Democracy and Ethnicity in Benin*, doc. film (2011).

Hall, Neville A.T., "Maritime Maroons: Grand Marronage from the Danish West Indies", *William and Mary Quarterly* 42, 4 (1985): 453–75.

———, "Review of *Cultural Adaptation and Resistance on St John* by Karen Olwig", *Hispanic American Historical Review* 67, 1 (1987): 147–8.

Hall, Neville A.T. and B.W. Higman, eds., *Slave Society in the Danish West Indies: St. Thomas, St. John, and St. Croix*. Aarhus: Aarhus Universitetsforlag, 1992.

Hama, Tadao, *Haichi Kakumei to Furansu Kakumei* [Haiti Revolution and French Revolution]. Sapporo: Hokkaidō daigaku shuppankai, 1999.

Hamilton, Douglas, "Representing Slavery in British Museums: The Challenges of 2007", in *Imagining Transatlantic Slavery*, ed. Cora Kaplan and John Oldfield. Houndmills: Palgrave Macmillan, 2010, pp. 127–44.

Hamilton, Keith and Patrick Salmon, eds., *Slavery, Diplomacy and Empire: Britain and the Suppression of the Slave Trade, 1807–1975*. Brighton: Sussex Academic Press, 2009.

Haneda, Masashi, *Atarashii Sekaishi he: Chikyu shimin no tameno kousou* [Towards a New World History: A Conception of Global Citizenship]. Tokyo: Iwanami Shoten, 2012.

Harrison, J.V., "Coastal Makran", *The Geographical Journal* 97, 1 (Jan. 1941): 1.

Heath, Anthony and Jane Roberts, *British Identity: Its Sources and Possible Implications for Civic Attitude and Behaviour*. Oxford: Oxford University Press, 2006.

Hellie, Richard, *Enserfment and Military Change in Muscovy*. Chicago, IL: University of Chicago Press, 1971.

Helsloot, John I.A., "*Zwarte Piet* and Cultural Aphasia in the Netherlands", *Quotidian: Journal for the Study of Everyday Life* 3 (2012): 1–20.

Hemmy, Gysbert, *Oratio Latina, De Promontorio Bonae Spei, 1767* [A Latin Oration Delivered in the Hamburg Academy, 10 April 1767], tr. and ed. K.D. White. Cape Town: South African Public Library, 1959.

————, *De Testimoniis: The Testimony of the Chinese, Aethiopians and other Pagans, as well as of the Hottentots inhabiting the Cape of Good Hope, likewise about the Complaints of East Indian Slaves*, tr. and annot. Margaret L. Hewett. Cape Town: University of Cape Town, 1998.

Hesselink, Reinier, "People on Deshima around 1700", in *Bridging the Divide: 400 Years The Netherlands–Japan*, ed. Leonard Blussé, Willem Remmelink and Ivo Smits. Leiden: Hotei Publishing, 2000, p. 48.

Hilton, John, "'The Roman-Dutch Law of Evidence at the Cape'" (Book Review on M.L. Hewett (trans. and ed.), De Testimoniis: A Thesis by Gysbert Hemmy on the Testimony of the Chinese, Aetheiopians, and Other Pagans", *Scholia: Studies in Classical Antiquity* 10 (2001): 120–5.

Hirokawa, Kai, *Nagasaki Kenbunroku* [A Record of Personal Observations of Nagasaki]. Nagasaki: Nagasaki Bunkensha, 1973, 1st ed., 1797.

Hoch, Steven, "Serfs in Imperial Russia: Demographic Insights", *The Journal of Interdisciplinary History* 13, 2 (1982): 221–46.

————, *Serfdom and Social Control: Petrovskoe, a Village in Tambov*. Chicago, IL: University of Chicago Press, 1986.

_____, "The Banking Crisis, Peasant Reforms, and Economic Development in Russia, 1857–1861", *American Historical Review* 96, 3 (1991): 795–820.

_____, "On Good Numbers and Bad: Malthus, Population Trend and Peasant Standard of Living in Late Imperial Russia", *Slavic Review* 53, 1 (1994): 41–75.

_____, "Famine, Disease, and Mortality Patterns in the Parish of Borshevka, 1830–1912", *Population Studies* 52, 3 (1998): 357–68.

Hoch, Steven and Wilson Augustine, "The Tax Census and the Decline of the Serf Population in Imperial Russia, 1833–1858", *Slavic Review* 38, 3 (1979): 403–25.

Hondius, Dienke, "Access to the Netherlands of Enslaved and Free Black Africans: Exploring Legal and Social Historical Practices in the Sixteenth-Nineteenth Centuries", *Slavery and Abolition* 32, 3 (2011): 377–95.

Hopkins, Anthony G., ed., *Global History: Interactions between the Universal and the Local*. Basingstoke and New York: Palgrave Macmillan, 2006.

Hopkins, Daniel, Philip Morgan and Justin Roberts, "The Application of GIS to the Reconstruction of the Slave-plantation Economy of St Croix, Danish West Indies", *Historical Geography* 39 (2011): 85–104.

Hopper, Matthew Scott, "The African Presence in Arabia: Slavery, the World Economy, and the African Diaspora in Eastern Arabia, 1840–1940", unpublished PhD dissertation. Los Angeles, CA: University of California, 2006.

Horton James O. and Johanna C. Kardux, "Slavery and the Contest for National Heritage in the United States and the Netherlands", *American Studies International* 42, 2–3 (2004): 51–74.

Hulsebosch, Daniel J., "Nothing but Liberty: Somerset's Case and the British Empire", *Law & History Review* 24 (2006): 647–57.

Hunt, Alfred N., *Haiti's Influence on Antebellum America: Slumbering Volcano in the Caribbean*. Baton Rouge, LA: Louisiana State University Press, 1988.

Huttenback, Robert A., *The British Imperial Experience*. New York: Harper & Row, 1966.

Huussen, Arend H., Jr, "The Dutch Constitution of 1798 and the Problem of Slavery", *Tijdschrift voor Rechtsgeschiedenis* 67, 1 (1999): 99–114.

Huzzey, Richard, *Freedom Burning: Anti-Slavery and Empire in Victorian Britain*. New York: Cornell University Press, 2012.

Iadarola, Antoinette, "Ethiopia's Admission into the League of Nations: An Assessment of Motives", *The International Journal of African Historical Studies* 8, 4 (1975): 601–22.

Inose, Kumie, "Jo-ou ha 'Teikoku no Haha' dattanoka?" [Was the Queen "A Mother of the Empire"?], in *Queen Victoria: Gender, Monarchy, and Representation*, ed. Shizuko Kawamoto and Masaie Matsumura. Kyoto: Minerva-shobo, 2006, pp. 281–332.

————, "Dorei wo Kaihou suru Teikoku" [The Empire Emancipating Slaves], in *Daiei-Teikoku toiu Keiken* [Experiences of the British Empire]. Tokyo: Kodansha, 2007, pp. 131–48.

Irick, Robert L., *Ch'ing Policy Toward the Coolie Trade, 1847–1878*. Taipei: Chinese Materials Center, 1982.

Jacob, Margaret C. and Wijnand W. Mijnhardt, *The Dutch Republic in the Eighteenth Century: Decline, Enlightenment, and Revolution*. Ithaca, NY: Cornell University Press, 1992.

Jacobs, Els M., *Merchant in Asia: The Trade of the Dutch East India Company during the Eighteenth Century*. Leiden: CNWS Publications, 2006.

Janse, Maartje, "Réveilvrouwen en de strijd voor afschaffing van de slavernij (1840–1863)" [Women of the *Réveil* Movement and their Fight for the Abolition of Slavery (1840–1863)], *Documentatieblad van de Nederlandse Kerkgeschiedenis na 1800* 59 (2003): 11–21.

————, "Representing Distant Victims: The Emergence of an Ethical Movement in Dutch Colonial Politics 1840–1880", *Bijdragen en Mededelingen betreffende de Geschiedenis der Nederlanden* 126, 1 (2003b): 53–80.

————, *De Afschaffers: publieke opinie, organisatie en politiek in Nederland 1840–1880* [The Abolishers: Public Opinion, Organization and Politics in the Netherlands 1840–1880]. Amsterdam: Wereldbibliotheek, 2007.

James, C.L.R., *The Black Jacobins*. New York: Dial Press, 1938.

Jennings, Lawrence C., *French Reaction to British Slave Emancipation*. Baton Rouge, LA: Louisiana State University Press, 1988.

————, "Cyrille Bisette: Radical Black French Abolitionist", *French History* 9, 1 (1995): 48–66.

————, *French Anti-slavery: The Movement for the Abolition of Slavery in France, 1802–1848*. Cambridge and New York: Cambridge University Press, 2000.

Jones, Eric, *Wives, Slaves and Concubines: A History of the Female Underclass in Dutch Asia*. DeKalb, IL: Northern Illinois University Press, 2010.

Jones, Robert E., *The Emancipation of the Russian Nobility, 1762–1785*. Princeton, NJ: Princeton University Press 1973.

Joucla, E., "L'esclavage au Sénégal et au Soudan, état de la question en 1905" [Slavery in Senegal and the Soudan, State of the Question in 1905], *Bulletin de la Société des anciens élèves de l'école colonial* 19 (1905): 1–13.

Kabuzan, Vladimir M., *Izmeneniia v razmeshchenii naseleniia Rossii v XVIII–pervoi polovine XIX v* [Changes in the Rate of Growth of the Russian Population during the Eighteenth and the First Half of the Nineteenth Centuries]. Moscow: Nauka, 1971.

Kalff, S., *De slavernij in Oost-Indië* [Slavery in the East Indies]. Baarn: Hollandia-drukkerij, 1920.

Kaminsky, Arnold P., *The India Office, 1880–1910*. Westport: Greenwood Press, 1986.

Kani, Hiroaki, *Kindai Chūgoku no Kūrī to "Choka"* [Coolies and "Slave Girls" of Modern China]. Tokyo: Iwanami Shoten, 1979.

———, "Kanpō Kyūnen Shanhai niokeru Gaikokujin shugekijiken nitsuite" ["On the Anti-foreign Incident in Shanghai in 1859"], *Tōyōshi Kenkyū* 43, 3 (1984).

Kanya-Forstner, A.S., *The Conquest of the Western Sudan: A Study in French Military Imperialism*. Cambridge: Cambridge University Press, 1969.

Kaplan, Cora and John Oldfield, eds., *Imagining Transatlantic Slavery*. Houndmills: Palgrave Macmillan, 2010.

Kaye, Mike, "The Development of the Anti-Slavery Movement after 1807", *Parliamentary History* 26 (2007): 238–57.

Keaton, Tricia Danielle, T. Denean Sharpley-Whiting and Tyler Edward Stovall, eds., *Black France/France Noire: The History and Politics of Blackness*. Durham, NC: Duke University Press, 2012.

Kelly, J.B., *British and Persian Gulf 1795–1880*. Oxford: Clarendon Press, 1968.

Keppen, Petr, *Deviataia reviziia: issledovanie o chisle zhitelei v Rossii v 1851 goda* [The Ninth Census: Study of the Number of Inhabitants in Russia in 1851]. St Petersburg: Tip. Imp. Akademii nauk, 1857.

Kingston-Mann, Esther, "Marxism and Russian Rural Development: Problems of Evidence, Experience and Culture", *American Historical Review* 86, 4 (1981): 731–52.

———, *In Search of the True West*. Princeton, NJ: Princeton University Press, 1999.

———, "Peasant Communes and Economic Innovation: A Preliminary Inquiry", in *Peasant Economy, Culture, and Politics of European Russia, 1800–1921*, ed. Esther Kingston-Mann and Timothy Mixter. Princeton, NJ: Princeton University Press, 1991, pp. 23–51.

Klein, Martin A., "Introduction: Modern European Expansion and Traditional Servitude in Africa and Asia", in *Breaking the Chains: Slavery, Bondage, and Emancipation in Modern Africa and Asia*, ed. Martin A. Klein. Madison, WI: University of Wisconsin Press, 1993, pp. 3–36.

———, *Slavery and Colonial Rule in French West* Africa. New York: Cambridge University Press, 1998.

———, "Slavery and French Rule in the Sahara", in *Slavery and Colonial Rule in Africa*, ed. Suzanne Miers and Martin A. Klein. London: Frank Cass, 1999.

———, "The Emancipation of Slaves in the Indian Ocean", in *Abolition and its Aftermath in the Indian Ocean Africa and Asia*, ed. Gwyn Campbell. London and New York: Routledge, 2005.

———, "The Concept of Honour and the Persistence of Servitude in the Western Soudan", *Cahiers d'Études Africaines* 45 (2005): 831–52.

————, "La traite transatlantique des esclaves et le développement de l'esclavage en Afrique occidentale" [The Transatlantic Slave Trade and the Development of Slavery in West Africa], in *Esclavage et Dépendances Serviles: Histoire comparé* [Slavery and Servile Dependency: A Comparative History], ed. Myriam Cottias, Alessandro Stella and Bernard Vincent. Paris: Harmattan, 2006, pp. 35–54.

————, "Sex, Power and Family Life in the Harem", in *Women and Slavery*, vol. 1, *Africa, the Indian Ocean World and the Medieval North Atlantic*, ed. Gwyn Campbell, Suzanne Miers and Joseph C. Miller. Athens, OH: Ohio University Press, 2007, pp. 63–82.

————, "Slaves, Gum, and Peanuts: Adaptation to the End of the Slave Trade in Senegal, 1817–1848", *William and Mary Quarterly* 66 (2009): 894–913.

————, "Slaves and Soldiers in the Western Soudan and French West Africa", *Canadian Journal of African Studies* 45 (2011): 565–87.

————, "'He Who is Without Family will be the Subject of Many Exactions': A Case from Senegal", in *African Voices on Slavery and the Slave Trade*, ed. Alice Bellagamba, Sandra Greene and Martin A. Klein. Cambridge and New York: Cambridge University Press, 2013, pp. 65–70.

————, "Slavery in the Cities of the Slave Trade", in *Looking for the Tracks*, ed. Alice Bellagamba, Sandra Greene and Martin A. Klein. Trenton, NJ: African World Press, forthcoming.

Klein, Martin A. and Paul Lovejoy, "Slavery in West Africa", in *The Uncommon Market: Essays in the Atlantic History of the Slave Trade*, ed. Jan Hogendorn and Henry Gemery. New York: Academic Press, 1980.

Klein, Martin A. and Richard Roberts, "The Banamba Exodus of 1905 and the Decline of Slavery in the Western Sudan", *Journal of African History* 21 (1980): 375–94.

Kloek, Joost and Wijnand Mijnhardt, *1800: Blauwdrukken voor een Samenleving* [1800: Blueprints of a Society]. Den Haag: Sdu Uitgevers, 2001.

Klooster, Wim, ed., *Migration, Trade and Slavery in an Expanding World: Essays in Honour of Pieter Emmer*. Leiden: Brill, 2009.

Knaap, Gerrit J., "Slavery and the Dutch in Southeast Asia", in *Fifty Years Later: Antislavery, Capitalism and Modernity in the Dutch Orbit*, ed. Gert Oostindie. Leiden: KITLV Press, 1995, pp. 193–206.

Kolchin, Peter, *Unfree Labor: American Slavery and Russian Serfdom*. Cambridge, MA: Harvard University Press, 1987.

Kondō, Michiko, "18 Seiki ikō Dejima ni okeru Marēkei Jūjin no Katsudō: Gakki Ensō ni yoru Nihonjin Hinkyaku e no Motenashi o Jirei to shite" [The Activities of the Malay Inhabitants of Dejima from the 18th Century Onwards: The Example of Entertaining Japanese Guests with Music], *Bunka Ronshū* 17 (2010): 75–111.

Kopytoff, Igor and Suzanne Miers, "African 'Slavery' as an Institution of Marginality", in *Slavery in Africa: Historical and Anthropological Perspectives*, ed. Suzanne Miers and Igor Kopytoff. Madison, WI: University of Wisconsin Press, 1977, pp. 3–81.

Koval'chenko, Ivan D., *Russkoe krepostnoe krest'ianstvo v pervoi polovine XIX v.* [Russian Serfdom during the First Half of the 19th Century]. Moscow: Nauka, 1967.

Koval'chenko, Ivan D. and L. Milov, *Vserossiiskii agrarnyi rynok, XVIII– nachalo XX v.* [The All-Russian Agrarian Market, 18th–Early 20th Centuries]. Moscow: Nauka, 1974.

Kowaleski Wallace, Elizabeth, *The British Slave Trade and Public Memory.* New York: Columbia University Press, 2006.

Kuitenbrouwer, Maarten, "De Nederlandse Afschaffing van de Slavernij in Vergelijkend Perspectief" [The Dutch Abolition of Slavery in a Comparative Context], *Bijdragen en Mededelingen betreffende de Geschiedenis der Nederlanden* 93 (1978): 69–100.

———, "The Dutch Case of Antislavery: Late and Élitist Abolitionism", in *Fifty Years Later: Antislavery, Capitalism and Modernity in the Dutch Orbit*, ed. Gert Oostindie. Leiden: KITLV Press, 1995, pp. 67–88.

Kumar, Ann, "Literary Approaches to Slavery and the Indies Enlightenment: Van Hogendorp's Kraspoekol", *Indonesia* 43 (1987): 43–65.

Kumar, Dharma, "Colonialism, Bondage, and Caste in British India", in *Breaking the Chains: Slavery, Bondage, and Emancipation in Modern Africa and Asia*, ed. Martin A. Klein. Madison, WI: University of Wisconsin Press, 1993, pp. 112–30.

Lambton, Ann, *Qajar Persia*. London: I.B. Tauris, 1987.

Lara, Oruno D., *De l'oubli à l'histoire: Espace et identité caraïbes* [From the Forgotten to History: Caribbean Area and Identity]. Paris: Éditions Maisonneuve et Larose, 1998.

———, *La liberté assassinée. Guadeloupe, Guyane, Martinique, La Réunion, 1848–1856* [Freedom Murdered: Guadeloupe, Guiana, Martinique, Réunion, 1848–1856]. Paris: L'Harmattan, 2005.

Law, Robin, *Ouidah: The Social History of a West African Slaving Port, 1727– 1892*. Athens, OH: Ohio University Press, 2005.

Lecky, W.E.H., *A History of European Morals from Augustus to Charlemagne*, vol. 2, 6th ed. London: Longmans Green, 1884.

Ledovskaia, Irina V., "Biudzhet russkogo pomeshchika v 40–60kh godakh XIX v" [Estate Owners' Budgets in the 1840s–60s], in Akademiia Nauk SSSR, *Materialy po istorii sel'skogo khoziaistva i krest'ianstva SSSR*, vol. 8. Moscow: Nauka 1974, pp. 240–5.

Leonard, Carol, *Agrarian Reform in Russia*. Cambridge: Cambridge University Press, 2011.

Lequin, Frank, ed., *De Particuliere Correspondentie van Isaac Titsingh (1783–1812)*: *Text, Brieven* [The Private Correspondence of Isaac Titsingh (1783–1812)]. Alphen aan den Rijn: Canaletto, 2009.

Lesan al-Mulk Sepehr, Muhammad Taqi, *Nasekh al-tawarikh tarikh-i-Qajariya* [Effacement of the Chronicles of the History of Qajar], 3 vols. Tehran: Asatir, 1377.

Leupp, Gary P., "Images of Black People in late Mediaeval and Early Modern Japan, 1543–1900", *Japan Forum* 7, 1 (1995): 1–13.

Levecq, Christine, "Het Denken over de Oost-Indische Slavernij" [East Indian Slavery Thought], *Indische Letteren* 12 (1997): 147–62.

Lewis, Bernard, *Race and Slavery in the Middle East*. New York: Oxford University Press, 1990.

Lieven, David, *The Aristocracy in Europe, 1815–1914*. New York: Columbia University Press, 1994.

Lincoln, William Bruce, *In the Vanguard of Reforms: Russian Enlightened Bureaucrats, 1825–1861*. DeKalb, IL: Northern Illinois University Press, 1982.

———, *The Great Reforms: Autocracy, Bureaucracy and the Politics of Change in Imperial Russia*. DeKalb, IL: Northern Illinois University Press, 1990.

Litvak, Boris, *Russkaia derevniia v reforme 1861 goda: Chernozemnyi tsentr 1861–1895 gg* [The Russian Countryside in the Reform of 1861: The Central Black-earth, 1861–1895]. Moskva: Nauka, 1972.

Lorimer, John Gordon, *Gazetteer of the Persian Gulf, Oman, and Central Arabia*, vol. 1, part 2. Calcutta: Superintendent Government Printing, 1908–15.

Louis, Abel A., *Les libres de couleur en Martinique. tome 2, Quand révolution et retour à l'ancien régime riment avec ségrégation, 1789–1802* [The Free People of Color in Martinique, vol. 2, When the Revolution and the Return to the Old Regime Coincided with Segregation, 1789–1802]. Paris: Harmattan, 2012.

Lovejoy, Paul, *Transformations in Slavery: A History of Slavery in Africa*, 1st ed. Cambridge: Cambridge University Press, 1983.

———, *Transformations in Slavery: A History of Slavery in Africa*, 2nd ed. Cambridge: Cambridge University Press, 2000.

———, *Transformations in Slavery: A History of Slavery in Africa*, 3rd ed. Cambridge: Cambridge University Press, 2011.

Lovejoy, Paul and Jan Hogendorn, *Slow Death for Slavery: The Course of Abolition in Northern Nigeria 1897–1936*. Cambridge: Cambridge University Press, 1993.

Lucassen, Jan, "A Multinational and its Labor Force: The Dutch East India Company, 1595–1795", *International Labor and Working-Class History* 66 (2006): 12–39.

Lyashchenko, Peter, *History of the National Economy of Russia to the 1917 Revolution.* New York: Macmillan, 1949.

Maestri, Edmond, *Esclavage Et Abolitions Dans L'Océan Indien: 1723–1860* [Slavery and Abolitions in the Indian Ocean: 1723–1860]. Paris: L'Harmattan, 2002.

Mahmmud, Mahmmud, *Tarikh-i Ravabet-i Siasi-yi Iran va Englis* [The History of Political Relations of Iran and Britain], 8 vols. Tehran: Eqbal.

Maki, Hidemasa, *Kinsei Nihon no Jinshin Baibai no Keifu* [A Chronology of Human Trafficking in Early Modern Japan]. Tokyo: Sōbunsha, 1970.

Manchuelle, François, "Emancipation and Labor Migration in West Africa: The Case of the Soninke", *Journal of Africa History* 30 (1989): 89–106.

———, *Willing Migrants.* Athens, OH: Ohio University Press, 1997.

Mann, Gregory, *Native Sons: West African Veterans and France in the 20th Century.* Durham, NC: Duke University Press, 2006.

Mann, Kristin, *Slavery and the Birth of an African City: Lagos, 1760–1900.* Bloomington, IN: Indiana University Press, 2007.

Manning, Patrick, *Slavery and African Life: Occidental, Oriental and African Slave Trades.* Cambridge: Cambridge University Press, 1990.

Marcson, Michael, "European–African Interaction in the Precolonial Period: Saint Louis, Senegal, 1758–1854", unpublished PhD dissertation. Princeton, NJ: Princeton University, 1976.

Martin, Virginia, *Law and Custom in the Steppe: The Kazakhs of the Middle Horde and Russian Colonialism in the Nineteenth Century.* Richmond, Surrey: RoutledgeCurzon, 2001.

Martinez, Jenny S., *The Slave Trade and the Origin of International Human Rights Law.* Oxford: Oxford University Press, 2012.

Matsuda, Kiyoshi, *Yōgaku Soshikiteki Kenkyū.* Kyoto: Rinsen Shoten, 1998.

Matsui, Yōko, "The Debt-servitude of Prostitutes in Japan during the Edo Period, 1600–1868", in *Bonded Labour and Debt in the Indian Ocean World*, ed. Gwyn Campbell and Alessandro Stanziani. Brookfield: Pickering & Chatto, 2013, pp. 173–85.

Matthews, Gelien, *Caribbean Slave Revolts and the British Abolitionist Movement.* Baton Rouge, IL: Louisiana University Press, 2004.

Mayer, Arno, *The Persistence of the Old Regime.* London: Pantheon, 1981.

Maynard, Douglas H., "The World's Anti-Slavery Convention of 1840", *The Mississippi Valley Historical Review* 47, 3 (1960): 452–71.

Mbodj, Mohammed, "The Abolition of Slavery in Senegal, 1820–1890: Crisis or the Rise of a New Entrepreneurial Class?" in *Breaking the Chains: Slavery, Bondage and Emancipation in Modern Africa and Asia*, ed. Martin A. Klein. Madison, WI: University of Wisconsin Press, 1993, pp. 197–214.

McCloskey, Donald, "The Open Fields of England: Rent, Risk, and the Rate of Interest, 1300–1815", in *Markets in History: Economic Studies of the*

Past, ed. David Galenson. Cambridge: Cambridge University Press 1989, pp. 5–51.

McNeill, J.R. and W.H. McNeill, *The Human Web: A Bird's-Eye View of World History*. New York and London: W.W. Norton, 2003.

Meilink-Roelofsz, Marie A.P., *Van Geheim tot Openbaar: Een Historische Verkenning* [From Secrecy to Publicity: A Historical Investigation]. Leiden: Universitaire Pers, 1970.

Melton, Edgar, "Proto-industrialization, Serf Agriculture, and Agrarian Social Structure: Two Estates in Nineteenth-century Russia", *Past and Present* 115 (1987): 73–81.

Midgley, Clare, *Women Against Slavery: The British Campaigns, 1780–1870*. London: Routledge, 1992.

Miers, Suzanne, "Slavery to Freedom in Sub-Saharan Africa: Expectations and Realities", *Slavery and Abolition: A Journal of Slave and Post-Slave Studies* 21, 2 (2000): 237–64.

———, *Slavery in the Twentieth Century: The Evolution of a Global Problem*. Walnut Creek, CA: AltaMira Press, 2003.

Miguel Sierra, Maria, "The World Conference against Racism and the Role of the European NGOs", *European Journal of Migration and Law* 4, 2 (2002): 249–60.

Mironov, Boris, *Vnytrennii rynok Rossii vo vtoroi polovine XVIII–pervoi polovine XIX v.* [The Domestic Market in Russia during the Second Half of the Eighteenth–First Half of the Nineteenth Century]. Leningrad: Nauka, 1981.

———, *The Social History of the Russian Empire*, 2 vols. Boulder, CO: Westview, 1999.

Mironov, Boris and Carol S. Leonard, "In Search of Hidden Information: Some Issues in the Socio-Economic History of Russia in the Eighteenth and Nineteenth Centuries", *Social Science History* 9 (Autumn 1985): 339–59.

Mirzai, Behnaz A., "Slavery, the Abolition of the Slave Trade, and the Emancipation of Slaves in Iran (1828–1928)", unpublished PhD dissertation. Toronto: York University, 2004.

———, "The 1848 Abolitionist *Farmān*: A Step towards Ending the Slave Trade in Iran", in *Abolition and its Aftermath in Indian Ocean Africa and Asia*, ed. Gwyn Campbell, pp. 94–102. London and New York: Routledge, 2005.

Miura, Toshiaki, *Kinsei Jisha Myōmokukin no Shitekikenkyū* [A Historical Study of Nominal Loans by High-ranking Temples and Shrines]. Tokyo: Yoshikawa Kōbunkan, 1993.

Moïse, Claude, ed., *Dictionnaire historique de la Révolution haïtienne (1789–1804)* [Historical Dictionary of the Haitian Revolution (1789–1804)]. Montréal: Éditions Images/Cidihca, 2003.

Moon, David, *The Russian Peasantry, 1600–1930*. London: Longman, 1996.

———, *The Abolition of Serfdom in Russia, 1762–1907*. London: Pearson, 2001.

Morinaga, Taneo, ed., *Hankachō: Nagasaki Bugyō Hanketsu Kiroku (1660–1867)* [The *Hankachō*: Criminal Records of the Governor of Nagasaki (1660–1867)], 11 vols. Nagasaki: Hankachō Kankōkai, 1958–61.

Morita, Tomoko, *Kaikoku to Chigai Hōken* [The Opening of Japan and Extraterritorial Rights]. Tokyo: Yoshikawa Kōbunkan, 2004.

Motylewski, Patricia, *La Société française pour l'abolition de l'esclavage, 1834–1850* [The French Society for the Abolition of Slavery, 1834–1850]. Paris: L'Harmattan, 1998.

Mulligan, William, "Introduction: The Global Reach of Abolitionism in the Nineteenth Century", in *A Global History of Anti-Slavery Politics in the Nineteenth Century*, ed. William Mulligan and Maurice Bric. Basingstoke: Palgrave, 2013, pp. 1–16.

Murakami, Ei, *Umi no Kindai Chūgoku: Fukkenjin no Katsudō to Igirisu/ Shinchō* [Maritime History of Modern China: Local Fujian Actors and the British and Chinese Empires]. Nagoya: Nagoya Daigaku Shuppankai, 2013.

Myers, Walter Dean, *At Her Majesty's Request: An African Princess in Victorian England*. New York: Scholastic Press, 1999.

Nafziger, Stephen, "Communal Institutions, Resource Allocation, and Russian Economic Development", unpublished PhD dissertation. New Haven, CT: Yale University, 2006.

Nagasaki-shi Deshima Shiseki Seibi Shingikai, ed., *Deshima-zu: Sono Keikan to Hensen* [Illustrations of Deshima: Its Appearance and Transformation]. Tokyo: Chūō Kōron Bijutsu Shuppan, 1987.

Nash, Gary B. and Jean R. Soderlund. *Freedom by Degrees: Emancipation in Pennsylvania and its Aftermath*. New York and Oxford: Oxford University Press, 1991.

Nelson, Thomas, "Slavery in Medieval Japan", *Monumenta Nipponica* 59, 4 (2004): 463–92.

Nesbitt, Nick, *Universal Emancipation: The Haitian Revolution and the Radical Enlightenment*. Charlottesville, VA: University of Virginia Press, 2008.

New York Times, "Caribbean Nations to Seek Reparations, Putting Price on Damage of Slavery", 20 Oct. 2013. www.nytimes.com/2013/10/21/world/americas/caribbean-nations-to-seek-reparations-putting-price-on-damage-of-slavery.html, accessed 5 Jan. 2014.

Ng Chin-keong, "The Amoy Riots of 1852: Coolie Emigration and Sino-British Relations", in *Mariners, Merchants and Oceans: Studies in Maritime History*, ed. K.S. Mathew. New Delhi: Manohar, 1995.

Ngaidé, Abderrahmane, *L'esclave, le colon et le marabout. Le royaume peul du Fuladu de 1867 à 1936* [The Slave, the Colonizer and the Marabout: The Kingdom of the Peul Fuladu, 1867–1936]. Paris: Harmattan, 2012.

Niemeijer, Hendrik E., *Batavia: Een Koloniale Samenleving in de 17e Eeuw* [Batavia: A Colonial Society in the 17th Century]. Amsterdam: Uitgeverij Balans, 2005.

Nimako, Kwame and Glenn Willemsen, *The Dutch Atlantic: Slavery, Abolition and Emancipation*. London: Pluto Press, 2011.

Nishisato, Yoshiyuki, *Shinmatsu Chūryūnichi Kankēshi no Kenkyū* [The Relationship between China, Ryūkyū and Japan during the Late Qing Period]. Kyoto: Kyōto Daigaku Gakujyutsu Shuppankai, 2005.

Nishiyama, Matsunosuke, "Kuruwa", in *Nishiyama Matsunosuke chosakushū 5: Kinsei Fūzoku to shakai* [A Selection from Nishiyama Matsunosuke's Works, vol. 5, Manners and Society in Early Modern Japan]. Tokyo: Yoshikawa Kōbunkan, 1985.

Northrup, David, *Indentured Labor in the Age of Imperialism 1834–1922*. Cambridge: Cambridge University Press, 1995.

Norton, Holly A., "The Challenge in Locating Maroon Refuge Sites at Maroon Ridge, St. Croix", *Journal of Caribbean Archaeology* 7 (2007): 1–17.

Obinata, Sumio, *Nihon Kindai Kokka no Seiritsu to Keisatsu* [Birth of Modern State of Japan and Police]. Tokyo: Azekura Shobō, 1992.

O'Brien, Patrick, "Historiographical Traditions and Modern Imperatives for the Restoration of Global History", *Journal of Global History* 1, 1 (2006): 3–39.

Okamoto, Takashi, *Kindai Chūgoku to Kaikan* [China and the Maritime Customs System in Modern Times]. Nagoya: Nagoya Daigaku Shuppankai, 1999, pp. 179–203.

Oldendorp, Christian Georg Andreas and Johann Jakob Bossart, *Geschichte der Mission der evangelischen Brüder auf den caraibischen Inseln S. Thomas, S. Croix und S. Jan:…enthaltend die Geschichte der Mission von 1732 bis 1768* [A History of the Mission of the Evangelical Brothers on the Caribbean Islands of St. Thomas, St. Croix, and St. John, including a History of the Mission from 1732 to 1768], vol. 2. Laux, 1777.

Oldfield, John R., *Popular Politics and British Anti-Slavery: The Mobilisation of Public Opinion against the Slave Trade, 1787–1807*. Manchester: Manchester University Press, 1995.

Oostindie, Gert, ed., *Fifty Years Later: Antislavery, Capitalism and Modernity in the Dutch Orbit*. Leiden: KITLV Press, 1995.

———, *Facing up to the Past: Perspectives on the Commemoration of Slavery from Africa, the Americas and Europe*. Kingston: Randle Publishers, 2001.

———, "Squaring the Circle: Commemorating the VOC after 400 Years", *Bijdragen tot de Taal-, Land- en Volkenkunde* 159, 1 (2003): 135–61.

————, "The Slippery Paths of Commemoration and Heritage Tourism: the Netherlands, Ghana, and the Rediscovery of Atlantic Slavery", *New West Indian Guide* 79 (2005): 55–77.

————, ed., *Dutch Colonialism, Migration and Cultural Heritage*. Leiden: KITLV Press, 2008.

————, "Slavernij, Canon en Trauma: Debatten en Dilemma's" [Slavery, Canon and Traumas: Debates and Dilemmas], *Tijdschrift voor Geschiedenis* 121, 1 (2008): 4–21.

————, "History brought Home: Post-colonial Migrations and the Dutch Rediscovery of Slavery", in *Migration, Trade and Slavery in an Expanding World: Essays in Honour of Pieter Emmer*, ed. Wim Klooster. Leiden: Brill, 2009, pp. 305–27. Also in *Post-Colonial Immigrants and Identity Formations in the Netherlands*, ed. Ulbe Bosma. Amsterdam: Amsterdam University Press, 2012, pp. 155–73.

————, *Postcolonial Netherlands: Sixty-five Years of Forgetting, Commemorating, Silencing*. Amsterdam: Amsterdam University Press, 2010.

Oostindie, Gert and Jessica Vance Roitman, "Repositioning the Dutch in the Atlantic, 1680–1800", *Itinerario* 36, 2 (2012): 129–60.

"Oranda Shumi: Sakoku-shita no Ekizochishizumu" [The Craze for Holland: Exoticism during the Period of Isolation], catalogue. Tokyo: Tobacco & Salt Museum, 1996.

Otō, Osamu, *Kinseinōmin to Ie, Mura, Kokka; Seikatsushi/Shakaishi no Shiten kara* [Early Modern Peasantry and Family System, Village and State: From the Perspective of Life History and Social History]. Tokyo: Yohikawa Kōbunkan, 1996.

Otsuki, Gentaku, "Ransetsu Benwaku" [A Clarification of Misunderstandings in Theories about the Dutch] (1799) in Chūryū Morishima, *Kōmō Zatsuwa/Ransetsu Benwaku* [A Miscellany about the Red-hairs], ed. Tsutomu Sugimoto. Tokyo: Yasaka Shobō, 1972.

Ozawa, Junko, "1852 nen Amoi Bōdō nitsuite" [The Amoy Riot of 1852], *Shiron (Tōkyō Joshi Daigaku)* 38 (1985).

Paasman, Albertus N., "Reinhart: Nederlandse Literatuur en Slavernij ten tijde van de Verlichting" [Reinhart: Dutch Literature and Slavery During the Period of Enlightenment], unpublished PhD dissertation. Amsterdam: Universiteit Amsterdam, 1984.

Pago, Gilbert, *Les Femmes et la liquidation du système esclavagiste à la Martinique 1848–1852* [Women and the Liquidation of the Slave System]. Paris: Ibis Rouge, 1998.

Pallot, Judith, *Land Reform in Russia 1906–1917: Peasant Responses to Stolypin's Project of Rural Transformation*. Oxford: Clarendon Press, 1999.

Pâme, Stella, *Cyrille Bissette: Un martyr de la liberté* [Cyrille Bissette: A Martyr for Freedom]. Fort de France: Désormeaux, 1999.

Pasquier, Roger, "A Propos de l'émancipation des esclaves au Sénégal en 1848" [Concerning the Emancipation of Slaves in Senegal in 1848], *Revue française d'histoire d'outre-mer* 54 (1967): 188–208.

Peabody, Sue, "The French Free Soil Principle in the Atlantic World", *Africana Studia* 14, 1 (2010): 17–27.

———, "An Alternative Genealogy of the Origins of French Free Soil: Medieval Toulouse", *Slavery & Abolition* 32, 3 (2011): 341–62.

———, "Free Soil: The Generation and Circulation of an Atlantic Legal Principle", *Slavery and Abolition: A Journal of Slave and Post-Slave Studies* 32, 3 (2011): 331–9.

Pelckmans, Lotte, *Travelling Hierarchies: Moving In and Out of Slave Status in a Central Malian Fulbe Network.* Leiden: African Studies Center, 2011.

———, "To Cut the Rope from One's Neck? Manumission Documents of Slave Descendants from Central Malian Fulbe Society", in *Bitter Legacy: African Slavery Past and Present,* ed. Alice Bellagamba, Sandra Greene and Martin A. Klein. Princeton, NJ: Markus Wiener, 2013, pp. 67–86.

Peterson, Derek R., ed., *Abolitionism and Imperialism in Britain, Africa, and the Atlantic.* Athens, OH: Ohio University Press, 2010.

Peterson, J.E., "Britain and the Gulf: At the Periphery of Empire", in *The Persian Gulf in History,* ed. Lawrence G. Potter. New York: Palgrave Macmillan, 2009.

Pétré-Grenouilleau, Olivier, *Les Traites négrières: Essai d'histoire globale* [The African Slave Trades: Essay in Global History]. Paris: NRF-Gallimard, 2004, pp. 271–3.

———, "Introduction" and "Abolitionnisme et nationalisme: le douloureux positionnement des abolitionnistes français" [Abolitionism and Nationalism: The Distressing Positioning of the French Abolitionists] in *Abolitionnisme et société (France, Suisse, Portugal, XVIIIᵉ–XIXᵉ siècles, Actes d'un colloque tenu à Lorient en 2004* [Abolitionism and Society (France, Switzerland, Portugal, 18th–19th Centuries, Proceedings of a Colloquium Held in Lorient in 2004], ed. Olivier Pétré-Grenouilleau. Paris: Éditions Karthala, 2005.

Phillips, Mike and Trevor Phillips, *Windrush: The Irresistible Rise of Multi-Racial Britain.* London: Harper Collins, 1998.

Pitou, Françoise and Claude Wanquet, *Les affranchis et les engagés à la Réunion (1848–1870)* [Freedmen and the Indentured in Réunion (1848–1870)]. N.p., 1989.

Pintner, Walter M., *Russian Economic Policy under Nicholas I.* Ithaca, NY: Cornell University Press, 1967.

Popenoe, Paul, "The Distribution of the Date Palm", *Geographical Review* 16, 1 (Jan. 1926): 117–21.

Popkin, Jeremy D., *You Are All Free: The Haitian Revolution and the Abolition of Slavery.* Cambridge: Cambridge University Press, 2010.

Postma, Johannes M., *The Dutch in the Atlantic Slave Trade, 1600–1815*. Cambridge: Cambridge University Press, 1990.

Pravilova, Ekaterina A., *Zakonnost' i prava lichnosti: administrativnaia iustitsiia v Rossii, vtoraia polovina XIX v.–oktiabr' 1917* [Legality and the Rights of the Person: Administrative Justice in Russia in the Second Half of the Nineteenth Century to October 1917]. St Petersburg: Izd-vo SZAGS2000.

Pretty, David, "Neither Peasant nor Proletarian: The Workers of the Ivanovo-Voznesensk Region", unpublished PhD dissertation. Providence, RI: Brown University, 1997.

Price Richard, ed., *Maroon Societies: Rebel Slave Communities in the Americas*. Baltimore, MD: Johns Hopkins University Press, 1996.

Quarles, Benjamin, *The Negro in the American Revolution*. Chapel Hill, NC: University of North Carolina Press, 1961.

Quirk, Joel and David Richardson, "Religion, Urbanisation and Anti-Slavery Mobilisation in Britain, 1878–1833", *European Journal of English Studies* 14, 3 (2010): 263–79.

Raben, Remco, "Batavia and Colombo: The Ethnic and Spatial Order of Two Colonial Cities 1600–1800", unpublished PhD dissertation. Leiden: Universiteit Leiden, 1996.

———, "Cities and the Slave Trade in Early-Modern Southeast Asia", in *Linking Destinies: Trade, Towns and Kin in Asian History*, ed. Peter Boomgaard, Dick Kooiman and Henk Schulte Nordholt. Leiden: KITLV Press, 2008, pp. 119–40.

Ra'in, Esma'il, *Daryanavardi-yi Iranian* [Iranian Navigation]. Tehran: Sekka, 1350.

Ranjeva-Rabetafika, Yvette, René Baesjou and Natalie Everts, "Of Paper and Men: A Note on the Archives of the VOC as a Source for the History of Madagascar", *Itinerario* 24, 1 (2000): 45–67.

Raynal, G. Th., *Histoire Philosophique et Politique des Etablissements et du Commerce des Européens dans les Deux Indes* [A Philosophical and Political History of the Settlements and Trade of the Europeans in the East and West Indies]. La Haye, 1770 and later editions.

Reid, Anthony, ed., *Slavery, Bondage and Dependency in Southeast Asia*. St Lucia: University of Queensland Press, 1983.

Reinhardt, Catherine A., *Claims to Memory: Beyond Slavery and Emancipation in the French Caribbean*. New York: Berghahn Books, 2006.

Reinsma, Reimer, *Een merkwaardige episode uit de geschiedenis van de slavenemancipatie* [A Remarkable Episode in the History of Slave Emancipation]. 's Gravenhage: Van Goor & Zonen, 1963.

Reis, João José and Flávio dos Santos Gomes, "Repercussions of the Haitian Revolution in Brazil, 1791–1850", in *The World of the Haitian Revolution*, ed. David Patrick Geggus and Norman Fiering. Bloomington, IN: Indiana University Press, 2009, pp. 284–313.

Régent, Frédéric, *Esclavage, métissage, liberté: la révolution française en Guadeloupe, 1789–1802* [Slavery, Hybridity, Freedom: The French Revolution in Guadeloupe, 1789–1802]. Paris: B. Grasset, 2004.

Renault, François, "L'Abolition de l'esclavage au Sénégal: L'Attitude de l'Administration française (1848–1905)" [The Abolition of Slavery in Senegal: The Attitude of the French Administration (1848–1905)], *Revue française d'histoire d'outre-mer* 58 (1971): 5–81.

———, *L'abolition de l'esclavage au Sénégal: l'atitude de l'administration française* [Abolition of Slavery in Senegal: The Attitude of the French Administration]. Paris: Société Française de l'Histoire d'Outre-Mer, 1972, pp. 83–7.

Rieber, Alfred, "Alexander II: A Revisionist View", *The Journal of Modern History* 43, 1 (1971): 42–58.

Riesman, Paul, *First Find Your Child a Good Mother: The Construction of Self in Two African Communities*. New Brunswick, NJ: Rutgers University Press, 1992.

Rigoulet-Roze, David, "A propos d'une commémoration: L'Abolition de l'esclavage en 1848" [Concerning a Commemoration: The Abolition of Slavery in 1848], *L'Homme: Revue française d'anthropologie* 145 (1998): 127–36.

Roberts, Richard, "The Case of Faama Mademba Sy and the Ambiguities of Legal Jurisdiction in Early Colonial French Soudan", in *Law in Colonial Africa*, ed. Kristin Mann and Richard Roberts. Portsmouth, NH: Heinemann, 1991, pp. 185–201.

———, *Litigants and Households: African Disputes and Colonial Courts in the French Soudan, 1895–1912*. Portsmouth, NH: Heinemann, 2005.

Robertson, Claire and Martin A. Klein, eds., *Women and Slavery in Africa*. Madison, WI: University of Wisconsin Press, 1883.

Rodet, Marie, *Les migrantes ignorées du Haut-Sénégal (1900–1946)* [Forgotten Migrants of Upper Senegal (1900–1946)]. Paris: Éditions Karthala, 2009.

Rossi, Benedetta, "Slavery and Migration: Social and Physical Mobility in Ader", in *Reconfiguring Slavery: West African Trajectories*, ed. Benedetta Rossi. Liverpool: Liverpool University Press, 2009.

———, "Without History? Interrogating Slave Memories in Ader (Niger)", in *African Voices on Slavery and the Slave Trade*, ed. Alice Bellagamba, Sandra Greene and Martin A. Klein. Cambridge and New York: Cambridge University Press, 2013, pp. 536–54.

Roopnarine, Lomarsh, "Maroon Resistance and Settlement on Danish St. Croix", *Journal of Third World Studies* 27, 2 (2010): 89–108.

Russell, John G., "Excluded Presence: Shoguns, Minstrels, Bodyguards, and Japan's Encounters with the Black Other", *Zinbun* 40 (2007): 15–51.

Ryndziunskii, Pavel G., *Gorodskoe grazhdanstvo doreformennoi Rossii* [Urban Citizenship in Russia before the Reforms]. Moscow: Nauka, 1958.

Sackur, Amanda, "The Development of Creole Society and Culture in Saint Louis and Gorée", unpublished PhD dissertation. London: University of London, 1999.

Saga, Ashita and Nobuyuki Yoshida, ed., *Shirīzu Yūkaku Shakai 1: Santo to Chihōtoshi* [The World of the Pleasure Quarters 1: Three Cities and Local Towns]. Tokyo: Yoshikawa Kōbunkan, 2013.

Saint-Ruf, Germain, *L'épopée Delgrès: la Guadeloupe sous la Révolution française (1789–1802)* [The Delgrès Epic: Guadeloupe during the French Revolution (1789–1802)]. Paris: Éditions Librairie de l'Étoile, 1965. 2nd ed., Paris: Editions L'Harmattan, 1977.

Sakamoto, Tadahisa, *Tenpō Kaikaku no Hō to Seisaku* [Law and Society in Tempo Reform]. Tokyo: Sōbunsha, 1997.

Sanneh, Lamine, "Slavery, Islam and the Jakhanke People of West Africa", *Africa* 46 (1976): 80–97.

———, "The Origins of Clericalism in West African Islam", *Journal of African History* 17 (1976): 17–49.

Saunders, Daniel, *Russia in the Age of Reaction and Reform, 1801–1881*. London and New York: Longman 1992.

Savage, Elizabeth, ed., *The Human Commodity: Perspectives on the Trans-Saharan Slave Trade*. London: Frank Cass, 1992.

Schmidt, Nelly, *Victor Schoelcher et l'abolition de l'esclavage* [Victor Schoelcher and the Abolition of Slavery]. Paris: Fayard, 1994.

———, *Abolitionnistes de l'esclavage et réformateurs des colonies, 1820–1851: Analyse et documents* [Abolitionists of Slavery and Reformers of the Colonies, 1820–1851: Analysis and Documents]. Paris: Éditions Karthala, 2000.

———, *La France a-t-elle aboli l'esclavage? Guadeloupe, Martinique, Guyane, 1830–1935* [Did France Abolish Slavery? Guadeloupe, Martinique, Guyana, 1830–1935]. Paris: Perrin, 2009.

Schœlcher, Victor, *La correspondance de Victor Schœlcher* [The Correspondence of Victor Schœlcher], ed. Nelly Schmidt. Paris: Maisonneuve et Larose, 1995.

Schrikker, Alicia, *Dutch and British Colonial Intervention in Sri Lanka, 1780–1815: Expansion and Reform*. Leiden: Brill, 2007.

Schutte, Gerrit G., *De Nederlandse Patriotten en de Koloniën: Een Onderzoek naar hun Denkbeelden en Optreden 1770–1800* [The Dutch Patriots and the Colonies: An Investigation of their Opinions and Actions 1770–1800]. Groningen: Tjeenk Willink, 1974.

Scott, Rebecca J., *Slave Emancipation in Cuba: The Transition to Free Labor, 1860–1899*. Princeton, NJ: Princeton University Press, 1985. 2nd ed., Pittsburgh, PA: University of Pittsburgh Press, 2000.

Scott, Rebecca J. and Jean M. Hébrard, *Freedom Papers: An Atlantic Odyssey in the Age of Emancipation*. Cambridge, MA: Harvard University Press, 2012.

Searing, James, *West African Slavery and Atlantic Commerce: The Senegal River Valley, 1700–1860*. Cambridge: Cambridge University Press, 1998.

Sehou, Amadou, "Some Facets of Slavery in the *Lamidats* of Adamawa in North Cameroon in the Nineteenth and Twentieth Centuries", in *Bitter Legacy: African Slavery Past and Present*, ed. Alice Bellagamba, Sandra Greene and Martin A. Klein. Princeton, NJ: Markus Wiener, 2013, pp. 182–90.

Selassie, Haile, *My Life and Ethiopia's Progress*, vol. 2, ed. Harold Marcus et al. East Lansing, MI: Michigan State University, 1994.

Sens, Angelie, "Dutch Antislavery Attitudes in a Decline-Ridden Society, 1750–1815", in *Fifty Years Later: Antislavery, Capitalism and Modernity in the Dutch Orbit*, ed. Gert Oostindie. Leiden: KITLV Press, 1995, pp. 89–104.

———, *'Mensaap, Heiden, Slaaf': Nederlandse Visies op de Wereld rond 1800* [Ape, Pagan, Slave: Dutch Conceptions of the World around 1800]. Den Haag: Sdu Uitgevers, 2001.

Sepinwall, Alyssa Goldstein, "The Spector of Saint-Domingue: American and French Reactions to the Haitian Revolution", in *The World of the Haitian Revolution*, ed. David Patrick Geggus and Norman Fiering. Bloomington, IN: Indiana University Press, 2009, pp. 317–38.

———, *Haitian History: New Perspectives*. New York: Routledge, 2013.

Shaikh, Farida, "Judicial Diplomacy: British Officials and the Mixed Commission Courts", in *Slavery, Diplomacy and Empire: Britain and the Suppression of the Slave Trade, 1807–1975*, ed. Keith Hamilton and Patrick Salmon. Brighton: Sussex Academic Press, 2009, pp. 42–64.

Sheil, Lady Mary, *Glimpses of Life and Manner in Persia*. New York: Arno Press, 1973.

Sheller, Mimi, "Sword-Bearing Citizens: Militarism and Manhood in Nineteenth-Century Haiti", *Plantation Society in the Americas* 4, 2–3 (1997): 233–78.

———, *Democracy After Slavery: Black Publics and Peasant Radicalism in Haiti and Jamaica*. Gainesville, FL: University Press of Florida, 2000.

Shepherd, William Ashton, *From Bombay to Bushire, and Bussora*. London: Richard Bentley, 1857.

Sheriff, Abdul, *Slaves, Spices and Ivory in Zanzibar: Integration of an East African Commercial Empire into the World Economy, 1770–1873*. Athens, OH: Ohio University Press, 1987.

Shiba, Kōkan, *Kōkan Saiyū Nikki* [Kōkan's Diary of a Ship to the West], in *Shiba Kōkan Zenshū* [The Complete Works of Kōkan Shiba], vol. 1. Tokyo: Yasaka Shobō, 1992.

Shimada, Ryuto, "Jūhasseiki-matsu Nagasaki Dejima ni okeru Ajiajin Dorei: Oranda Higashi Indogaisha no Nihon Bōeki ni kansuru Hitotsu no Shakaishiteki Bunseki" [Asian Slaves on Nagasaki Dejima at the End of the 18th Century: A Social-Historical Analysis of the Japan Trade of the Dutch East India Company], in *Chi'ikikan no Rekishi-sekai: Idō, Shōtotsu, Yūgō* [The World of Inter-Regional History: Migration, Collusion, Fusion], ed. Takeo Suzuki. Tokyo: Waseda Daigaku Shuppanbu, 2008, pp. 339–63.

Shimojū, Kiyoshi, *Miuri no Nihonshi: Jinshin Baibai kara Nenkiboko e* [Japanese History of Human Trade: From Human Trafficking to *Nenki-boko*]. Tokyo: Yoshikawa Kōbunkan, 2012.

Simms, Jr, James Y., "The Crisis in Russian Agriculture at the End of the Nineteenth Century: A Different View", *Slavic Review* 36, 3 (1977): 377–98.

———, "The Crop Failure of 1891: Soil Exhaustion, Technological Backwardness, and Russia's Agrarian Crisis", *Slavic Review* 41, 2 (1982): 236–50.

Siwpersad, Jozef R., *De Nederlandse regering en de afschaffing van de Surinaamsche slavernij (1833–1863)* [The Dutch Government and the Abolition of Surinamese Slavery (1833–1863)]. Groningen: Bouma's Boekhuis, 1979.

Sklar, Kathryn Kish, "'Women Who Speak for an Entire Nation': American and British Women Compared at the World Anti-Slavery Convention, London, 1840", *Pacific History Review* 59, 4 (1990): 453–99.

Sklar, Kathryn Kish and James Brewer Stewart, *Women's Rights and Transatlantic Antislavery in the Era of Emancipation*. New Haven, CT: Yale University Press, 2007.

"Slavernij" Encyclopaedie van Nederlandsch-Indië ["Slavery" Encyclopaedia of the Netherlands East Indies], vol. 3. 's Gravenhage: Martinus Nijhoff, 1919, 2nd ed., pp. 800–8.

Sōgōjoseishi Kenkyūkai, ed., *Jidai wo Ikita Joseitachi: Shin-nihon Josei Tūshi* [Women Lived the Times: New Overview of History of Women]. Tokyo: Asahi Shimbun Publications, 2010, pp. 228–325.

Solomon, Peter, ed., *Reforming Justice in Russia, 1864–1994: Power, Culture, and the Limits of Legal Order*. New York: Armonk, 1997.

Solow, Barbara Lewis and Stanley L. Engerman, eds., *British Capitalism and Caribbean Slavery: The Legacy of Eric Williams*. Cambridge: Cambridge University Press, 1987.

Sonoda, Setsuko, *Nanboku Amerika Kamin to Kindai Chūgoku: Jyūkyūsēki Transnashonarumaigrēshon* [Overseas Chinese in the Americas and Modern China: Transnational Migration in the Nineteenth Century]. Tokyo: Tokyo Daigaku Shuppankai, 2009.

Stanley, Amy, *Selling Women: Prostitution, Markets, and the Household in Early Modern Japan*. Berkeley, CA: University of California Press, 2012.

Stanziani, Alessandro, "Les statistiques des récoltes en Russie, 1905–1928", *Histoire et mesure*, vol. VII, nr. 1/2 (1992): 73–98.

_____, *L'économie en révolution. Le cas russe, 1870–1930*. Paris: Albin Michel 1998.

_____, "Les enquêtes orales en Russie, 1861–1914", *Annales ESC*, 55, 1 (2000): 219–41.

_____, "Free Labor-Forced Labor: an Uncertain Boundary? The Circulation of Economic Ideas between Russia and Europe from the Eighteenth to the Mid-nineteenth Century", *Kritika: Explorations in Russian and Eurasian History* 9, 1 (2008): 1–27.

_____, *Bondage, Labor and Rights in Eurasia, 17th–20th Centuries*. New York and Oxford: Berghahn Press, 2014.

_____, *After Oriental Despotism: Warfare, Labour and Growth in Eurasia, 17th–20th Centuries*. London: Bloomsbury, 2014.

Stein, Robert, "The Abolition of Slavery in the North, West, and South of Saint Domingue", *The Americas* 41, 3 (Jan. 1985): 47–55.

Stewart, Watt, *Chinese Bondage in Peru: A History of the Chinese Coolie in Peru, 1849–1874*. Westport, CT: Greenwood Press, 1970.

Stoler, Ann, *Along the Archival Grain: Epistemic Anxieties and Colonial Common Sense*. Princeton, NJ: Princeton University Press, 2009.

Storch, Heinrich, *Cours d'économie politique ou exposition des principes qui déterminent la prospérité des nations*, 5 vols. St Petersburg: A. Pliushar, 1815, booklet 5.

Struve, Petr, *Krepostnoe khoziaistvo. Issledovaniia po ekonomicheskoi istorii Rossii v XVIII i XIX vv.* [The Serf Economy: Studies on the Economic History of Russia, 18th to 19th Century]. St Petersburg, 1913.

Suzuki, Hideaki, "Indo-you nishi-kaiiki ni okeru 'doreisen' gari: 19 seiki dorei koueki haizetsu katsudou no ichidanmen" ["Slaver" Hunting in the Western Indian Ocean: An Aspect of the 19th-century British Campaign against Slave Trade], *Afurika Kenkyū* 79 (2011): 13–25.

_____, "Baluchi Experiences under Slavery and the Slave Trade of the Gulf of Oman and the Persian Gulf, 1921–1950", *The Journal of the Middle East and Africa* 4, 2 (2013): 205–23.

Tanaka-van Daalen, Isabel, "Het Graf van Gijsbert Hemmij bij de Tennenji Tempel in Kakegawa" [The Grave of Gijsbert Hemmij at the Tennenji Temple in Kakegawa], unpublished report for the occasion of the restoration of Hemmij's grave. 2004.

Tang, Dirk J., *Slavernij: Een Geschiedenis* [Slavery: A History]. Zutphen: Walburg Press, 2013.

Tanquary Robinson, Geroid, *Rural Russia under the Old Regime*. Berkeley, CA: University of California Press, 1970.

Temperley, Howard, "Capitalism, Slavery and Ideology", *Past and Present* 75 (1977): 94–118.

———, ed. *After Slavery: Emancipation and its Discontents*. London and Portland: Frank Cass, 2000.

———, "The Delegalisation of Slavery in British India", *Slavery and Abolition: A Journal of Slave and Post-Slave Studies* 21, 2 (2000): 169–87.

Termorshuizen, Thio, "Indentured Labour in the Dutch Colonial Empire 1800–1940", in *Dutch Colonialism, Migration and Cultural Heritage*, ed. Gert Oostindie. Leiden: KITLV Press, 2008, pp. 261–314.

The Deshima Dagregisters: Their Original Tables of Contents, 13 vols. Leiden: Institute for the History of European Expansion, 1986–2010.

The Deshima Diaries: Marginalia, 1700–1800, 2 vols. Tokyo: Japan–Netherlands Institute, 1992, 2004.

Thélier, Gérard and Pierre Aliber, *Le grand livre de l'esclavage: des résistances et de l'abolition* [The Big Book of Slavery: Of Resistances and Abolition]. Réunion: Orphie, 2000.

Thomas, Dominic, *Africa and France: Postcolonial Cultures, Migration, and Racism*. Bloomington, IN: Indiana University Press, 2013.

Thornton, John K., "'I Am the Subject of the King of Congo': African Political Ideology and the Haitian Revolution", *Journal of World History* 4, 2 (Fall 1993): 181–214.

Tinker, Hugh, *A New System of Slavery: The Export of Indian Labour Overseas, 1830–1920*. Oxford: Oxford University Press, 1974.

Tobin, Jacqueline L., *From Midnight to Dawn: The Last Tracks of the Underground Railroad*. New York: Knopf Doubleday, 2007.

Toledano, Ehud R., *The Ottoman Slave Trade and its Suppression: 1840–1890*. Princeton, NJ: Princeton University Press, 1982.

Tomich, Dale W., *Through the Prism of Slavery: Labor, Capital, and World Economy*. Lanham: Rowman and Littlefield, 2004.

Troinitskii, Aleksandr', *Krepostnoe naselenie v Rossii po 10 narodnoi perepisi* [The Russian Serf Population according to the Tenth Census]. St Petersburg: Wulf, 1861.

Trouillot, Michel-Rolph, *Silencing the Past: Power and the Production of History*. Boston, MA: Beacon Press, 1995.

Tsukada, Takashi, *Mibunsei Shakai to Shimin Shakai: Kinsei Nihon no Shakai to Hō* [Status-based Society and Civil Society: Society and Law in Early Modern Japan]. Tokyo: Kashiwa Shobō, 1992.

———, *Kinsei Mibunsei to Shūen Shakai* [Early Modern Class System and Marginal Society]. Tokyo: University of Tokyo Press, 1997.

Upham, Mansell, "'This Corner of the World Smiles for Me above all Others': Gysbert Hemmy from Africa—A Reappraisal", *Quarterly Bulletin of the National Library of South Africa* 63, 1 (2009): 17–30.

Usami, Misako, *Shukuba to meshimori-onna* [Post Station and Meshimori Onna]. Tokyo: Dousei-sha, 2000.

Van Dam, Pieter, *Beschrijvinge van de Oost-Indische Compagnie 1639–1701* [A Description of the East India Company, 1639–1701], 7 vols, ed. F.W. Stapel et al. 's Gravenhage: Martinus Nijhoff, 1927–54.

Van der Chijs, Jacobus A., ed., *Nederlandsch-Indisch Plakaatboek, 1602–1811* [Book of Dutch East India Proclamations, 1602–1811], 17 vols. Batavia: Landsdrukkerij, 1885–1900.

Van der Wal, Anne Marieke, "Waarom wordt slechts de helft van ons slaven-verleden herdacht?" [Why is only Half of Our Slave Past Commemorated?], *Volkskrant*, 1 July 2013.

Van Gulik, Willem, *The Dutch in Nagasaki: 19th-century Japanese Prints*. Amsterdam: Uitgeverij Stichting Terra Incognita, 1998.

Van Haeften, Barend, *Oost-Indië Gespiegeld: Nicolaas de Graaff, een Schrijvend Chirurgijn in Dienst van de VOC* [East India Mirrored: Nicolaas de Graaff, a Writer-Surgeon in the Service of the Dutch East India Company (VOC)]. Zutphen: WalburgPers, 1992.

Van Hoëvell, Wolter R., *De Emancipatie der Slaven in Neêrlands-Indië: Eene Verhandeling* [The Slave Emancipation in the Dutch East Indies: A Treatise]. Groningen: C.M. van Bolhuis Hoitsema, 1848.

———, "Eene slaven-vendutie" [A Slave Auction], *Tijdschrift voor Nederlandsch-Indië* 15 (1853): 184–91.

Van Hogendorp, Dirk, *Kraspoekol, of De Slaavernij: Een Tafereel der Zeden van Neerlands-Indië* [Kraspoekol, or Slavery: A Tableau of Morals in the Dutch East Indies]. Delft: Roelofswaert, 1800.

Van Meerkerk, Edwin, *De Gebroeders Van Hogendorp: Botsende Idealen in de Kraamkamer van het Koninkrijk* [The Brothers Van Hogendorp: Clashing Ideals in the Delivery Room of the Kingdom]. Amsterdam: Atlas Contact, 2013.

Van Rossum, Matthias. *Kleurrijke Tragiek: De Geschiedenis van Slavernij in Azië onder de VOC* [Colourful Tragedy: The History of Slavery in Asia under the VOC]. Hilversum: Verloren, 2015.

Van 't Veer, Paul, *Geen blad voor de mond: Vijf radikalen uit de 19de eeuw* [Speaking Out: Five Radicals in the 19th Century] Amsterdam: Arbeiderspers, 1958.

Van Welie, Rik, "Patterns of Slave Trading and Slavery in the Dutch Colonial World, 1596–1863", in *Dutch Colonialism, Migration and Cultural Heritage*, ed. Gert Oostindie. Leiden: KITLV Press, 2008, pp. 155–259.

———, "Slave Trading and Slavery in the Dutch Colonial Empire: A Global Comparison", *Nieuwe West Indische Gids* 82, 1–2 (2008): 47–96.

Van Winter, Johanna M., "Public Opinion in the Netherlands on the Abolition of Slavery", in *Dutch Authors on West Indian History: A Historiographical Selection*, ed. Marie A.P. Meilink-Roelofsz. The Hague: Nijhoff, 1982, pp. 100–28.

Vaughan, James H., "Mafakur: A Limbic Institution of the Margi (Nigeria)", in *Slavery in Africa: Historical and Anthropological Perspectives*, ed. Suzanne Miers and Igor Kopytoff. Madison, WI: University of Wisconsin Press, 1977, pp. 85–102.

Vidal, Cécile, ed., *Être et se revendiquer Français dans le monde atlantique: Nation, empire et race (XVIe-mi-XIXe siècle)* [French? The Nation and Debate between the Colonies and the Metropole (16th–19th Centuries)]. Paris: EHESS, 2014.

Vink, Markus P.M., "'The World's Oldest Trade': Dutch Slavery and Slave Trade in the Indian Ocean in the Seventeenth Century", *Journal of World History* 14, 2 (2003): 131–77.

———, "Freedom and Slavery: The Dutch Republic, the VOC World, and the Debate over the 'World's Oldest Trade'", *South African Historical Journal* 59 (2007): 19–46.

Vosmaer, Arnout, *Beschrijving van de Aap-soort, gen. Orang-Outang, van het eiland Borneo, leevendig overgebragt in de Diergaarde van den Prinse van Oranje* [A Description of the Ape Species, Named Orang-Outang, from the Island Borneo, brought Alive to the Zoological Garden of the Princess of Orange]. Amsterdam, 1778.

Vucinich, Alexander, *Social Thought in Tsarist Russia*. Chicago, IL: University of Chicago Press, 1976.

Waaben, Knud, "*A.S. Ørsted og negerslaverne i København*" [A.S. Ørsted and Negro Slaves in Copenhagen], *Juristen* 12 (1964): 321–43.

Wagner, William, *Marriage, Property and Law in Late Imperial Russia*. Oxford: Oxford University Press 1994.

Walkowitz, Judith R., *Prostitution and Victorian Society: Women, Class, and the State*. Cambridge: Cambridge University Press, 1980. Japanese tr. Tomomi Nagatomi, *Baishun to Bikutoria Cho Shakai*. Tokyo: Sophia University Press, 2009.

Wang Sing-wu, *The Organization of Chinese Emigration 1848–1888: With Special Reference to Chinese Emigration to Australia*. San Francisco, CA: Chinese Materials Center, 1978.

Wanquet, Claude, *La France et la première abolition de l'esclavage, 1794–1802: le cas des colonies orientales, Ile de France (Maurice) et la Réunion* [France and the First Abolition of Slavery, 1794–1802: The Case of the Eastern Colonies, Île de France (Mauritius) and Réunion]. Paris: Editions Karthala, 1998.

Wanquet, Claude and Benoît Julien, *Révolution française et océan Indien: Prémisse, paroxysmes, héritages et déviances, Association historique de l'océan indien* [French Revolution and the Indian Ocean: Premise, Climaxes, Legacies and Deviations]. St Denis/Paris: Université de la Réunion/L'Harmattan, 1996.

Ward, Kerry, *Networks of Empire, Forced Migration in the Dutch India Company*. Cambridge: Cambridge University Press, 2009.

Westergaard, Waldemaar, *The Danish West Indies under Company Rule (1671–1754): With a Supplementary Chapter, 1755–1917*. New York: Macmillan, 1917.

Wheatcroft, Stephen, "Crisis and Condition of the Peasantry in Late Imperial Russia", in *Peasant Economy, Culture and Politics of European Russia, 1800–1921*, ed. Esther Kingston-Mann and Timothy Mixter. Princeton, NJ: Princeton University Press, 1991, pp. 101–27.

Whigham, H.J., *The Persian Problem*. New York: Charles Scribner's Sons, 1903.

White, Ashli, *Encountering Revolution: Haiti and the Making of the Early Republic*. Baltimore, MD: Johns Hopkins University Press, 2010.

Wilbur, Elvira M., "Was Russian Peasant Agriculture Really that Impoverished? New Evidence from a Case Study from the 'Impoverished Center' at the End of the Nineteenth Century", *Journal of Economic History* 43, 1 (1983): 137–44.

Williams, Eric, *Capitalism and Slavery*. Chapel Hill, NC: University of North Carolina Press, 1944.

Wilson, Arnold T., *The Persian Gulf*. London: George Allen & Unwin, 1959.

Wilson, D., "Memorandum Respecting the Pearl Fisheries in the Persian Gulf", *Journal of the Royal Geographical Society of London* 3 (1833): 283–6.

Winn, Phillip, "Slavery and Cultural Creativity in the Banda Islands", *Journal of Southeast Asian Studies* 41, 3 (2010): 365–89.

Wirtschafter, Elise Kimerling, *Structures of Society: Imperial Russia's "People of Various Ranks"*. DeKalb, IL: Northern Illinois University Press, 1994.

———, *Social Identity in Imperial Russia*. DeKalb, IL: Northern Illinois University Press, 1997.

Wood, Marcus, "Significant Silence: Where was Slave Agency in the Popular Imagery of 2007?" in *Imagining Transatlantic Slavery*, ed. Cora Kaplan and John Oldfield. Houndmills: Palgrave Macmillan, 2010, pp. 162–90.

Worden, Nigel, *Slavery in Dutch South Africa*. Cambridge: Cambridge University Press, 1985.

———, "Indian Ocean Slavery and its Demise in the Cape Colony", in *Abolition and its Aftermath in Indian Ocean Africa and Asia*, ed. Gwyn Campbell. London and New York: Routledge, 2005, pp. 29–38.

———, "The Changing Politics of Slave Heritage in the Western Cape, South Africa", *Journal of African History* 50 (2009): 23–40.

Wortman, Richard, *Development of a Russian Legal Consciousness*. Chicago, IL: University of Chicago Press, 1976.

Wright, Denis, *The English among the Persians during the Qajar Period 1787–1921*. London: Heinemann, 1977.

Yen, Ching-hwang, *Coolies and Mandarins: China's Protection of Overseas Chinese During the Late Ch'ing Period (1851–1911)*. Singapore: Singapore University Press, 1985.

Yokoyama, Yuriko, *Meiji Ishin to Kinnsei Mibunsei no Kaitai* [The Meiji Restoration and Abolishment of Status System]. Tokyo: Yamakawa Shuppansha, 2005.

————, "19 Seiki Toshi Shakai ni Okeru Chiiki Hegemony no Saihen: Onna-kamiyui, Yūjo no Seizon to 'Kaiho' o Megutte" [Reorganization of the Local Hegemony in the Urban Society in the 19th Century: Focusing on Subsistence and Release of Female Hairdressers and Prostitutes], *Rekishigaku Kenkyu* 885 (2011): 12–21.

————, "Geishougi Kaihourei to Yūjo: Shin-yoshiwara Kashiku Ikkenn no Shoukai wo Kanete" [The Release Act and Yūjo: Introducing the Kashiku Documents], *Tokyo Daigaku Nihonshigaku Kenkyu Kiyo* [Studies in the Social History of Early Modern Japan, Bulletin of the Department of Japanese History, Faculty of Letters, University of Tokyo (Supplement)] (2013): 159–71.

Yoshida, Nobuyuki, "*Yaku* to *Chou*: Edo Minamitenma *Chou* 2-*choume* hoka Three *Chou* wo Rei toshite" [Class Marginality and Sociocultural Structure], in *Kinsei Kyodai Toshi no Shakai Kōzō* [Social Structure of Early Modern Megalopolis]. Tokyo: University of Tokyo Press, 1991.

————, *Kinsei Toshi Shakai no Mibun Kōzō* [The Structure of Status in the Urban Society in Early Modern Japan]. Tokyo: University of Tokyo Press, 1998, pp. 292–7.

————, *Mibunteki Shūen to Shakaibunka Kōzō* [Class Marginality and Socio-cultural Structure]. Kyoto: Burakumondai Kenkyūsho, 2003.

————, "Yūkaku shakai" [Society around the Yūkaku], in *Mibunteki Shūhen to Kinsei Shakai 4: Toshi no Shūhen ni Ikiru* [Class Marginality and Early Modern Society 4: Living on Urban Periphery], ed. Takashi Tsukada. Tokyo: Yoshikawa Kobunkan, 2006, pp. 49–51.

Young, Lola, "The Truth in Chains: Two Centuries after Britain Began to Dismantle the Slave Trade, the Whole Issue is Still Beset by Myths, Half-truths and Ignorance", *Guardian*, 15 Mar. 2007, G2 Section, pp. 17–8.

Zaionchkovskii, Pavel Andreevich, *Otmena krepostnogo prava v Rossii* [The Abolition of Serfdom in Russia], 3rd ed. Moscow: Izd-vo Kniga, 1968. Ed. and trans. Susan Wobst, Gulf Breeze, FL: Academic International Press, 1978.

Zakharova, Lidia, ed., *Velikie reformy v Rossii, 1856–1874* [The Great Reforms in Russia]. Moscow: Nauka, 1992.

Zakharova, Lidya, *Samoderzhavie i otmena krepostnogo prava v Rossii, 1856–1861* [Autocracy and the Abolition of Serfdom in Russia, 1856–1861].

Moscow: Izdatel'stvo Moskovskogo Gosudarstvennogo Universiteta, 1984.

Zanco, Jean-Philippe, *Dictionnaire des Ministres de la Marine, 1689–1958* [Dictionary of the Ministers of the Navy, 1689–1958], Kronos 58. Paris: SPM, 2011, pp. 263–6.

Zdanowski, Jerzy, *Slavery and Manumission*. Reading: Ithaca Press, 2013.

Zhuang Guotu, *Zhongguo Fengjian Zhengfu de Huaqiao Zhengce* [The Chinese Feudal Government's Policies towards Overseas Chinese]. Xiamen: Xiamen Daxue Chubanshe, 1989.

Zuiderweg, Adrienne, "Nieuwsgaring in Batavia tijdens de VOC" [News Gathering in Batavia under the VOC], *Tijdschrift voor Tijdschriftstudies* 28 (2010): 108–26.

Zyrianov, Pavel' N., *Krest'ianskaia obshchina Evropeiskoi Rossii 1907–1914 gg.* [The Peasant Commune in the European Russia, 1907–1914]. Moscow: Nauka, 1992.

Index